The Squandered Computer

Evaluating the Business Alignment
of Information Technologies

Paul A. Strassmann

The Information Economics Press
NEW CANAAN, CONNECTICUT
1997

Published by
THE INFORMATION ECONOMICS PRESS
PO Box 264
New Canaan, Connecticut 06840-0264
Order Directly from Publisher:
800-800-0448 or fax: 203-966-5506

Printed in the United States of America
1 2 3 4 5 6 7 8 9 10

Strassmann, Paul A.
The Squandered Computer
1. Strategic Planning. 2. Information Technology
3. Business Management I. Title
1997   658.4
Library of Congress Catalog Card Number 96-095315

ISBN 0-9620413-1-9

Parts of the text and some graphics have previously appeared in Mr. Strassmann's articles in
Computerworld magazine, Copyright by IDG Communications, Inc., 500 Old Connecticut Path,
Framingham, MA 01701. Reprinted with permission of *Computerworld.*

TABLE OF CONTENTS

Illustrations

INTRODUCTION

"In the near future somebody will write a book about how executives in the 1990s spent too much money on information technology because they were afraid to manage it properly. They put their trust in technological experts to deliver business value from IT investments."[1]

Here it is. The message is timely. It is the first of three volumes that will show why and how management fails to apply the same rigorous examination to computers that it applies to other expenditures. My purpose is to explain how to manage information technologies to deliver improved profitability in business, and improved results in the public sector. My objective is to show how to align computer expenditures with the objectives of an organization.

Despite much talk about the cyber economy, information age, or knowledge-based enterprise, as yet there are no generally accepted economic or financial principles to guide executives in spending money on computers. Decision makers find it difficult to reconcile the claims of computer advocates with their staff's ability to prove that IT investments are profitable. These books will offer a new perspective from which to interpret the economics of computerization. They will explain the difference between promises and facts. They will show how misperceptions and negligence diminish the worth of perhaps the most potent tool, since the invention of fire, ever placed in the service of humanity.

Until about a decade ago, information systems managers did not have to work very hard to demonstrate how IT contributed to the economic viability of their firms. The assumption was that the miraculous power of information technologies could cure every conceivable business malfunction. This uncritical embrace yielded fifteen to thirty percent annual growth rates for computer systems budgets in the 1970-85 period. The rigorous scrutiny normally given to manufacturing investments was then mostly absent. Computer applications concentrated on administrative processes which required little justification because they were essential for coordination and control of every enterprise.[2]

---

1   Battles, B.E., and Mark, D., "Companies That Just Don't Get IT," *The Wall Street Journal*, December 9, 1996. Because of frequent use throughout this book, the abbreviation "IT" stands for information technology henceforth.

The sparseness of demonstrable financial results delivered from the computer investments has its roots in the executives' inability to understand how to measure investment returns on intangible services. The efficiency of clerks and administrative personnel, such the number of invoices they processed per hour, or how many insurance claims they would file, could be calculated using the same techniques as applied to factory machine tools.

Improving the effectiveness of executives, managers, and professionals escaped analysis. What management delivered was not quantifiable since talking, reading, and meeting made up more than eighty percent of their time. In due course, computerization enabled the automation of routine paper-pushing. It then started affecting how enterprises organized their affairs. At that point the basis for comparing the promises of the computer proponents with their actual accomplishments disappeared.

After 1985 the annual expenses for information technologies began exceeding the total economic value delivered by major corporations. Computer department budgets at that point were equal to one fifth of payroll costs. Capital investments in computers were making up more than a third of purchases for tooling expenses in the us economy.[3] Executives consider computers both a necessity as well as an extravagance, except no one seems to know with any certainty when it's one or another.

It is the central theme of this series that the era of exuberant business spending for computers will end in the next decade. This trend will begin in the us and then spread worldwide. Reasserting the importance of economics over electronics does not suggest elimination of computers. It augurs a discernible shift in expectations. Such a change in priorities does not mean that the intoxicating computer-guzzling party is over. It only anticipates a sobering up of organizations inebriated with unjustified helpings of IT. Organizations will insist on realizing the benefits from the dramatically lower costs of computing and software. That attitude will replace the current tendency to keep increasing budgets in the hope of reaping the benefits from systems alleged to cost less.

2   Twenty years later the situation may not be much different. According to a recent survey by the accounting and consulting firm of Grant Thornton, only fifteen percent of companies bothered to measure the Return on Investment from their information technologies. Meanwhile they were boosting IT spending on the average by twenty-three percent between 1994 and 1995. See "ROI Who?," *Computerworld*, June 24, 1996.
3   For an elaboration of this point see Chapter 8 on *Investments in Computers*. The us government defines tooling investments as producer durable investments.

This book series will then show why and how the emphasis on demonstrable value from computerization will displace the age of open wallets for everything connected with IT.

OUTLINE OF THIS BOOK

The Squandered Computer is the first installment in the series. It offers critical insights as well as constructive guidelines for how executives should examine proposed computerization budgets.

Part 1, Alignment, outlines the context within which to understand the meaning of "alignment." I take the position that only financial measures of gains in long term economic value-added can measure the economic contribution of computers in the for-profit sector of the economy.

Part 2, Facts, concentrates on debunking the prevailing myths concerning how to judge computer expenditures. It shows how some of the existing methods have a bias favoring spending without demonstrable economic value. It warns about misleading practices so that executives can spot unfounded claims advocating spending without economic benefit.

Part 3, Explanations, gives plausible explanations for bogus measures that find widespread acceptance among computer proponents. It reveals that it is not fraudulent intent, but short-sighted incompetence, that explains must of the inflated claims.

Part 4, Justifications, explains the flight from quantifiable measures to unverifiable promises. It highlights the uncritical role of the computer press in promoting computer sales.

Part 5, Outsourcing, discusses how the prospects of outsourcing computer services brings the evaluation of computer expenditures under the closest examination ever.

Part 6, Causes and Consequences, offers insights as to why expenditures for computers do not tend to become long-lived assets. It discusses why the build-and-junk solutions erode the potential value that is inherent in computer technologies.

Part 7, Residual Value, prescribes what executives should expect from investment proposals. It offers prescriptions for what a chief information officer must do to enhance the contributions of computers.

Part 8, Evaluation Methods, demonstrates analytic methods for appraising the worth of computer equipment, software and training. It shows how to determine the expected amount of computer spending.

Part 9, New Agendas, suggests that information security and the preservation of knowledge capital will require the adoption of new methods for evaluating how much money to spend on safeguarding a firm's information assets.

FOLLOW-ON WORK

My objective is to complete this *Alignment* series through follow-on volumes that will address the evaluation of *Information Productivity*® and how to assess a firm's *Knowledge Capital*®.[4]

The exploration of information productivity is necessary because even a favorable evaluation of computer expenditures offers no guarantee of competitive viability. The examination of information productivity covers much more than just the costs of computers. It concerns primarily the effectiveness with which information workers take advantage of the benefits of automation. *Information Productivity* is the topic of the next volume that will deal with these questions.

The discovery of the importance and vulnerability of knowledge assets is the principal reason why my work on alignment expanded beyond its initial scope. The need to analyze *Knowledge Capital* arose from studies of outsourcing contracts. In each case, the oursourcers showed reductions in computer expenditures as well as improvements in information productivity. In each case there were massive layoffs of personnel and extensive scrapping of software. I was concerned about the possibility that what appeared as gain was actually a form of anorexia; desirable appearances are not always conducive to long term physical or mental health. To measure the tradeoffs between expenditures and asset I succeeded in quantifying the financial value of *Knowledge Capital*. This led to the discovery that the *Knowledge Capital* assets of us corporations now exceed their financial assets.

My lecture notes from courses at the School of Information Warfare at the National Defense University also expanded beyond initial expectations. With the assets of organizations residing on computer networks, questions about vulnerability, theft and denial of service rise in importance as alignment issues. Therefore, my discussions about the acquisition and nurturing of *Knowledge Capital* will also elaborate on the need to pre-

---

4   Information Productivity ® and Knowledge Capital ® are registered us trademarks of Strassmann, Inc.

serve and safeguard the information assets of an organization. The final volume in this series, on *Knowledge Capital*, will discuss the methods for increasing the value of information assets.

ACKNOWLEDGMENTS

I am most grateful to Erik Brynjolfsson, Walter Carlson, Dan Doernberg, Peter Keen, Ron Knecht, Tom Lodahl, Rick Smith, Andrew Strassmann, and Steven Strassmann for their critical comments and observations. Some of the statistical studies are based on survey data obtained in connection with the *Computerworld Premier 100* studies, supported with enthusiasm by Paul Gillin, Editor of *Computerworld.*

Special thanks belong to David Shaw of Belm Design, who encouraged me to follow him in setting new standards for typographical excellence. Mona Strassmann, the publisher of The Information Economics Press, endorsed David's prompting to strive for a higher level of quality than one finds in self-publishing ventures.

The initial draft of this book lacked cohesion because it was originally conceived as a series of essays. It was Allan Alter who discovered how to string diverse ideas into a more coherent sequence. I am convinced that his thoughtful editing made a great contribution to improving the legibility of this work.

WHAT TO EXPECT

The readers will not find step-by-step prescriptions showing how information technologies will deliver economic value in their specific circumstances. The purpose of this book is to offer lessons on what to favor and what to avoid. It lends itself to the construction of a checklist of questions that proponents of spending should be able to answer. The text offers advice how to evaluate computer spending before committing to yet another cycle of IT investments.

This is not a textbook, but a collection of essays that examine computer spending from a variety of perspectives. Computers are now so pervasive that no single point of view will deliver a full scrutiny. Perhaps the best way to read this work is to seek out topics of personal interest instead of following the pages in a sequence as if it was a work of fiction. Computers have relevance only in the context of a particular organization.

xix

Readers may find it more useful to explore what is useful to themselves instead of seeking a tutorial that fits all conditions.

This book discusses only expenditures for computers. It answers the question of how to determine the appropriate levels of IT spending. That is necessary, but certainly not sufficient. Managing expenses is important but not the sole ingredient for success. The reader should have the patience to wait until the final volume in this series before collecting a full set of prescriptions for what to do about aligning information technologies with business objectives.

I trust that the reader will find my way of looking at computers helpful. It should aid in dispelling apprehensions of whether spending additional money on computers will deliver demonstrable business benefits.

New Canaan, Connecticut
March 1997

Part I
Alignment

- The meaning of alignment
- Significance of evaluation
- Computerization and business plans
- Valuation of computer investments
- Planning for alignment

1 The Context of Alignment

Alignment is the delivery of the required results.

To LINE up IT with business plans requires the adoption of the language used in dealing with financial matters. Alignment is the capacity to demonstrate a positive relationship between information technologies and accepted measures of performance. Computer investments must show as enhancements to a business plan. Executives should measure what, how and when it supports improvements in the delivery of operating results.

What is Alignment?

Aligning information systems to corporate goals has emerged as the number one concern over the last five years in surveys of information systems executives.[5]

What does it mean that information technologies line up with the business plans? How does one make alignment verifiable? How does one judge the credibility of project proposals that compete for scarce funds?

To line up IT with business plans require the adoption of the language used in dealing with financial matters. While project managers may praise customer satisfaction, quality, and workflow simplification, CEOs and shareholders evaluate projects primarily on the basis of contributions to net cash flow. Therefore, alignment is the capacity to demonstrate a positive relationship between information technologies and the accepted measures of performance.

Market share, customer satisfaction, taking care of employees, acting as good citizens, innovation, and innumerable other virtues are also essential. They are desirable, but only as the means for reaching the objective of creating value which is ultimately measurable only as a favorable financial

---

5 Aligning systems and corporate goals is the perennial No. 1 priority. It was on top of the list again in 1996, according to survey of 346 North American companies with revenues over $250 million by the Computer Sciences Corporation. See Savoia, R., "Custom Tailoring," CIO *Magazine*, June 15, 1996.

outcome for a commercial enterprise. For the public sector that means support in the delivery of superior services to the public.

WHY EVALUATION COMES FIRST

Information technologies will shape our society, our business organizations, and our governmental institutions in the information era. Investment justification methods that follow the traditional approaches of the industrial era are like using X-rays for something that calls for a blood test. It is my purpose to show that the search for cause-and-effect relationships associated with computerization calls for much more careful analysis than industrial engineers and financial analysts apply customarily.

In these books I address the aspects of computerization that apply to commercial firms and to government organizations. How the proliferation of computers influences consumer behavior is left for others to contemplate. In this context, the discussion of computers is limited to the effects they have on relationships among employees, their employers, customers, or the public and suppliers.

Before an organization can begin to align information technologies, management needs to know what evaluation methods are already in place for alignment to be feasible. That requires passing a simple test: Are the consequences of individual computer projects clearly linked with a firm's planning and budgeting commitments? If the answer is yes, then computer investments have a chance of becoming catalysts of organizational change instead of discrete expenses. Buying a computer is not like purchasing a machine tool, a truck, or a factory building, all of which have clear and workable financial treatments because they can be analyzed in isolation.

Computers are simultaneously financial and social catalysts because they also effect relationships among people. Computer networks are not merely commonplace fixed assets, but an influence that will alter an established organizational and social ecology. Computers are not merely like some sort of strap-on prosthetic contraption to enhance the calculating powers of individuals. They are primarily an irrepressible intrusion and disruption of the economic and power relationships that exist in the culture of advanced post-industrial organizations.

The effectiveness of a computer is largely dependent on its capacity to enhance the health or worsen the malaise of organizational units. The

4

technical merits of computer equipment is of secondary importance. This is why many of the methods, and certainly the statistical techniques, described in these pages carry a close resemblance to the practice of diagnostic medicine or the analysis of socio-economic phenomena.

Before one tries to prescribe solutions to problems, one must necessarily understand and interpret the problems correctly.

How to Realize the Alignment of IT and Business Plans

There are several requirements a firm must meet to ensure a successful alignment. These must survive changes in organization, will have to shift with re-directions in business goals, and adapt to changes in top leadership personalities.

Alignment Must Show Enhancements to a Business Plan

Every computer project proposal should demonstrate the discounted cash flow of its proposed business improvement. It should show the high and low expected financial returns. A display of the ranges in risks will enhance the credibility of the proposed venture. Experienced executives must realize that computer-based changes in business processes are perilous. They should not trust a forecast that specifies a single target payoff number.

The business case should deliver its summaries as add-ons to the previously approved financial budget. In this way the proponents can be accountable for their documented promises. Actual results would then be comparable to the revised budgets and performance plans at stated intervals, such as monthly, quarterly, and certainly not more than annually.

Alignment Must Remain Updated as the Business Evolves

All project plans are subject to change. Approval of a proposed investment is only the starting point for a continually widening gap between the stated objectives and the capacity to deliver results. There are no plans that can remain unaltered while an innovative project is underway. Customers will discover unanticipated improvements. They will change what they had originally requested. The completion schedule and the spending forecasts will also require modification. Failed promises, human errors, and unforeseen happenings can show up even in the best laid plans.

To keep up with reality, best laid plans need continuous adjustments to avoid misleading management or creating self-delusions. Most importantly, there must be a steady exchange of information between the systems organization and everyone else. Without continuous feedback the technologists will drift away from the business and misalignment will prevail.

Alignment Must Overcome Obstacles to its Purposes

There are no resource commitments that can remain fixed as the scope of a project changes and as new implementation problems surface. All cost estimates and schedules for technology investments are tentative targets. Nobody can predict the extent of customer or employee resistance to business process innovations.

Resistance to change may come from hundreds of sources. Management may not be able to change operating procedures, despite best intentions. Implementation may run into difficulties in training the operators to the desired standards of performance. A previously disguised opposition from entrenched stake holders will scuttle even the best laid plans. Whenever that happens, it will certainly not appear in the newspapers. It will remain covered up just as some family episodes remain unseen and untold.

The recriminations, misunderstandings, and confusion that take place in most periodic project reviews are destructive to morale and to careers. Budgets are summarily cut. Projects come to an abrupt termination when management finally acknowledges that the effort is out of control. There are too many examples of that happening. Perhaps the largest and most notorious of such calamities is the chronic failure of the Internal Revenue Service to acquire a functioning information system. The estimated cost to the government from this disaster is fifty billion annually.[6]

Why to such disasters happen? The fault lies in the increasing divergence between the assumptions at the conception of a project and the reality that becomes visible only during execution. Initial project plans must

6 Anthes, G.H., "IRS Project Failures Cost Taxpayers $50B Annually," *Computerworld*, October 14, 1996. The IRS computerization efforts over the last thirty years offer the most comprehensive catalogue of everything that can possibly go wrong. Reports from the General Accounting Office concerning this effort should be required reading for anyone who wishes to gain a better comprehension of what forms one can find as enemies of alignment.

necessarily appear in terms that cannot be too specific. The budget is a blanket to cover what is unknown. Not everything that requires altering the information flows in a firm is knowable in advance. When implementation starts, the tracking of actual project events always occurs in great detail. The expense statements reflect every minute expense item.

The problem is that technical personnel find it easier to deal with the minutiae because the larger economic and political issues are mostly beyond the scope of their responsibilities. Planning by telescope while implementing under microscope will assure that the disparity between promises and results will always diverge as a project progresses.

The evidence about the widespread incidence of problems in executing computer projects comes from a recent survey.[7] They showed that thirty-one percent of all IT projects suffered cancellation before completion, at an estimated cost of $81 billion. Fifty-three percent of projects would suffer ninety percent over-runs above original estimates, at a penalty of $59 billion.[8] Only sixteen percent of projects would show successful completion on time and on budget.

This deplorable situation is worse in the case of large corporations. Here only nine percent of their projects came in on time and on budget. Even those projects that met these criteria of success delivered only about forty-two percent of the original features and functions. Frequent restarts were the single largest cause of these failures. For one hundred projects there were ninety-four restarts, which includes multiple efforts pursuing the identical objective.[9] Poor planning, flimsy technology, and ill-conceived designs explain almost all of such futility.

Alignment Must be Planned

The original project plan requires documented agreements of any changes to keep it current. It should not gather dust in files, until recovered by auditors after a project is ready for autopsy. As conditions change, the initial assumptions and dependencies call for re-examination and re-adjustment to reflect what has been learned. The project plan then becomes the

---

7 The Standish Group, *Chaos: Charting The Seas of Information Technology*, 1994. The survey covered 365 respondents and 8,400 applications.
8 This average does not reveal that thirteen percent of projects suffered from overruns in excess of 200%.
9 One of the signs of fundamental incompetence is continued persistence regardless of uninterrupted failure.

record of approved changes to the baseline budget and to any subsequent revisions. I call this continual updating of plans an evergreen alignment, since keeping IT projects related to business goals is not a one-time happening, but an ongoing struggle.

Perhaps the most important benefit of focusing on alignment in this way is its use as a managerial process. It offers an opportunity to display a perspective that keeps connecting goals, programs, measures of performance, projections, expectations, and actual results by means of a consistent approach. Alignment is also a perpetually current executive reporting system that insures that the linkage of IT project plans to standard corporate metrics of performance remains intact.

The best planning method for alignment is to make IT invisible. It is not IT that aligns with business, but computerization that lines up with those who get customers, serve customers, and keep customers. IT should not ask business for alignment; instead, business should demand what, how, and when IT must deliver results.

IT must not stand as an isolated cost center seeking to align itself with what generates revenues. Instead, the firm's engines of value creation should include IT as the profit-generation tool that offers the highest yield for money spent. Alignment requires reliable feedback of results to contain all automation on the path of stated objectives. Alignment must not take place through IT push, but through operational pull.

ALIGNMENT AND THIS BOOK

In my 1995 book, *The Politics of Information Management,* I promised to address the linking of business and IT planning in a forthcoming volume with the title *The Business Alignment of Information Technologies.* As work progressed, I ended up with more than nine hundred pages of text. Bearing in mind the most frequent complaints about my two prior books was the exhausting coverage, I decided to release the *Alignment* title in three installments. This partitioning keeps a very complex subject down to manageable size. It also reflects the decision to assist in publishing much of what I said about business alignment as the *BizCase*™ software package.[10] With assistance from the *BizCase* decision aid the reader should be able to practice business alignment every time they link projects to business plans.

Getting operationally useful software into the hands of the readers is a welcome departure from the monologues that typify all texts. Nowadays, IT managers are looking for workable solutions and not for lectures or reams of print. *BizCase* extracted logic from chapters nine and ten of my 1990 book *The Business Value of Computers.* How to apply it for the enhancement of information productivity and knowledge assets will be one of the topics in the sequel to this book.

The trilogy that commences with this volume asserts that a verifiable evaluation phase must always precede the resolution of questions concerning organizational design, especially one which specifies the rules of governance and organization. Only after completion of these preliminaries is it safe to plan specific IT investments. What presently occupies most of the time of IT executives, namely questions about process improvement, resource management, and operating excellence, follows after the organizational phase is done.

For IT alignment to result in information superiority the *Alignment Evaluation* processes are the prerequisite for all that follows.

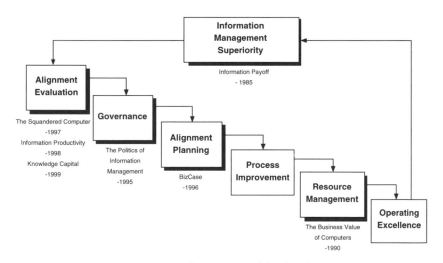

Figure 1   The context of this book

---

10 The *BizCase*™ software is now available from its developers, the Systems Research and Applications Corporation, 2000, 15th Street North, Arlington, Virginia 22201 as well as from Strassmann, Inc. A demonstration version of *BizCase* is available from <http://www.sra.com>.

What to Do

- Show the discounted cash flow of a proposed business improvement that depends on information technologies.
- Reveal the high and low expected financial returns for all computer proposals.
- Display the business case for a computer investment as an add-on to a financial plan and as a gain in approved performance metrics.
- Keep all investment proposals updated to reflect changing conditions as computer projects progress.

2 Technology that Delivers Profits

Expectations must precede the choice of technology.

How much to spend on computers comes only after one answers what are the benefits. It is the organizational structure, the size of the corporate overhead, the opinions about the benefits of computerization, the proliferation of personal computers, and the number of staff people that dictate the demand for computing. The IT budget, as an expense item, contains no meaningful insights by which someone can judge either its utility or its appropriate size. It is more important to manage the justification for the demand before examining whether the supply is efficient. The effects of IT investments are observable only by comparing how a particular organization performs differently with or without added computer investments. What distinguishes high information productivity firms is that they do not spend much money on functions that do not address customer needs.

To achieve alignment, one must first identify the sources of misalignment. If profitability or performance does not meet expectations, there must be enumerable reasons why this is so. There is no point in picking the latest technologies as a remedy if the problem is curable by changing management practices. Such action may not require computers at all. It may call for investing in people rather than in technology. How much to spend comes only after one answers what are the benefits.

It is not prudent to set the corporate IT budget by some arbitrary rationale. Computer spending need not keep to a constant ratio of sales or increase along with inflation. Such rationing will result in a steady leakage of costs from where they are visible to where they are hard to trace. Expenses for computing will be camouflaged as consulting fees, service contracts, office supplies. or wasted time of administrative personnel. The expenses for information management are now sufficiently pervasive that it is easy to hide them into unrelated accounts.

Outputs, such as profits or revenue, do not determine the demand for information technologies. It is the organizational structure, the size of the corporate overhead, the opinions about the benefits of computerization, the proliferation of personal computers, and the number of staff people that dictate the demand for computing. All of these are input. Output is a consequence. In the absence of trustworthy metrics, the current corporate and public sector practice is not to budget computers according to specified results, but according to the perceived needs of its proponents.[11] Consultants and government bureaucrats reinforce this bias by offering advice on best practices for managing inputs in the hope that this will somehow yield superior outputs.[12]

Budget analysts usually find it more rewarding to examine IT costs rather than examining what a computer funding request will deliver. The IT budget, as an expense item, contains no meaningful insights by which someone can judge either its utility or its appropriate size.

The primary focus for any reviews of IT spending should be the scrutiny of computing that is unrelated to revenue from external customers. There is no point in checking the utility of computers for unnecessary staffs. If a company decides to employ additional accountants or financial analysts, then the budget must provide for their computing sustenance, just as one arranges for their secretarial support, personnel services, furniture, or telephones. If there is a demand for computing services, there should be a sufficient supply to satisfy it. It is more important to manage the justification for the demand before examining whether the supply is efficient.

It is not realistic to expect that during the annual budget reviews the chief computer executive can prove what are the profit gains from the proposed computer spending. Only operating executives who have harmonized their organizations to compete effectively can extract value from information technologies. In that arena, computers certainly do have a role, often a leading one, but certainly not one that is decisive. What matters is superb management and people who have the motivation to deliver superior results. A computer without such commitments is worth only its resale or scrap price, which is not much.

---

11 It follows the bureaucrat's first principle of keeping a job: Do not commit to what you will deliver, but insist on getting what you ask for.
12 From cybernetic and servomechanism theory we have learned that overspecifying inputs without controlling for outputs will lead to an inherent instability and to a likely failure of such design.

Benefits of Computers

Are the enormous commitments of resources to information technologies paying off? Almost every economist states that there is no conclusive proof that they are. Nobody is able to show the benefits of computers using national productivity statistics. Our society lacks the standards by which to judge how well we are taking advantage of our most important tools.

Computers are like drugs: they can either kill you or cure you, depending on informed choices. It is not the drug that should get the exclusive credit for bringing anyone back to health. It is the doctor who has prescribed the right drug with the appropriate dosage that matters more than any other influence. It is also the care a patient takes in administering the drug that makes the difference whether the prescribed therapeutic regime will be successful. Most importantly, good health is the consequence of inheritance, nutritious food, simple sanitation, and reasonable precautions in avoiding accidents. The absence of sickness is perhaps the best measure of health. The degree of wellness differs by individual, country, age, civilization, and economic conditions. What is admirable in Zaire is unacceptable in Connecticut.

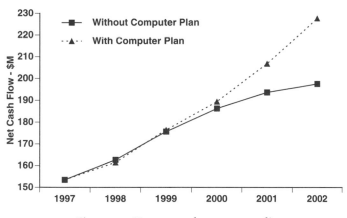

Figure 2   How to evaluate IT spending

The effects of IT investments are observable only by comparing how a particular organization performs differently with or without added computer investments.

After project completion, actual results will tell whether the reality resembles the plans. This process is similar to testing the effects of pharmaceuticals. Clinical observers will measure and evaluate how behavior changes under the influence of a dose that is either a drug or a placebo.

Any quantification of the benefits of computerization must be sufficiently rigorous to show not only sustained improvement but also the absence of deterioration. To constitute a proof that it was the computers that improved profitability requires first removing all savings that could have accrued anyway, without computer intervention. Getting rid of unnecessary paperwork is not a computer savings, but management process improvement.

Computer projects frequently involve the making of innovative and long overdue improvements in the way an organization operates. Only after setting aside gains that would accrue from an introduction of better management practices is it legitimate to attribute additional savings to computerization. For improvements that must use computers, their value is the cost advantage in accomplishing the identical task by other means.[13]

IT proponents often credit all gains from management actions to computerization, whereas most of the savings could come from judicious elimination of organizational obstacles. Without meticulously prepared plans, these after-the-fact evaluations tend to uncover added benefits whenever projects run over budget. The ensuing disputes diminish everybody's credibility.

How can one experiment with IT applications as if they were a questionable pharmaceutical? That is only possible if management authorizes pilot tests and small scale experiments that demonstrate how an organization performs with or without computer-enhanced assistance. For this reason incremental and evolutionary approaches to computer investments improve chances of delivering measurable results. Dramatic systems overhauls or drastic reorganizations in information management practices may not score as a success if nobody can tell what they accomplished.

MAKING COMPARISONS

To link promised gains from computerization to profitability requires a financial planning and budgeting system that incorporates computer pro-

---

13 In business data processing I do not know of a task that cannot be accomplished by pencil, paper, and telephone.

ject commitments into measurable yearly, quarterly, and even monthly targets. In the absence of such a discipline, insisting on a direct tie-in between increased funding for computers and operating profits encourages contrived projections. Fabricated estimates of huge payoffs discredit both those who produce them and those who accept them. The value of an oil furnace is not in reducing hypothetical medical bills, but the price of delivering reliable heat.

Management must have the necessary assurances that operating executives have committed to verifiable performance improvement. Also, there must be a demonstrable link that such plans hinge on support from computer services. If such is the case, then examining the efficiency of delivering computer services becomes much easier. It is not the absolute amount of money spent on the IT budget that matters, but what it delivers.

The most useful insights for judging the proposed levels of computer budgets come from competitive comparisons of the full costs of delivering computer services. If the expected levels of spending, as calculated by multifactor methods, seriously deviate from the actual spending, then a more thorough examination is in order.[14] Figure 3 shows an example of such an evaluation.

For the purpose of budget reviews, Figure 3 can also appear as a tabulation to show how much the actual spending differs from what calculations show, in comparison with look-alike firms (Figure 4).

If the comparisons show that the actual spending is below expectations, then management can authorize a further review of the effectiveness of the computer budget. Well-understood value-engineering techniques are available to do that. To address the broader question of whether the computer spending is efficient requires productivity-based metrics.[15]

14 For a detailed discussion of this technique see Chapter 37. The expected spending is calculated from the constants and coefficients of a regression equation that fits look-alike firms with a very high level of probability.
15 How to do that will be the topic of Volume II in this series of books.

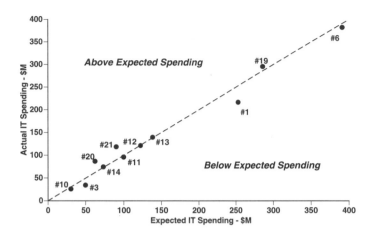

Figure 3   Above and below expected IT spending for look-alike firms

	Actual IT Spend - $M	Expected IT Spend - $M	Difference - $M	Difference - %
1	217	253	(36)	(17%)
3	35	50	(15)	(44%)
6	383	391	(9)	(2%)
10	26	31	(5)	(17%)
11	96	100	(4)	(4%)
12	121	122	(1)	(1%)
13	140	139	1	1%
14	75	73	1	2%
19	296	286	10	3%
20	87	62	25	28%
21	119	90	29	24%

Figure 4   Firm #1 is proposing a budget that is lower than expectations

Intra-corporate Comparisons

One of the problems with benchmarking is the question of its relevance to a particular firm, especially if the findings are unexpected or unfavorable. It is easy to complain about the accuracy of the benchmarking data, since good competitive information is hard to get and even harder to verify. Even if the data is reasonably accurate, there will always be someone who will debate its applicability.[16] The management of every corporation believes that it is different. Ratios that may work for others may not be acceptable for guiding its own budgeting decisions.

A practical solution is not to start with external benchmarking at all, but to compare the corporation's (or government department's) operating divisions against each other. This involves collecting exhaustive information about internal operations. That has the advantage of assured consistency and unblemished acceptability.

There are global, multi-divisional firms that have more than fifty separate profit centers. Usually, they have common ways for identifying spending for information technologies. Their accounting practices are generally consistent. Under such circumstances a multifactor cost model for determining the expected spending levels is not only more reliable, but is also more likely to receive management endorsement.

After completing the intra-corporate comparisons one should also test these findings against external competitive data, to check against potential misjudgments about the validity of the internal data.[17]

WHAT IS THE RIGHT IT BUDGET?

Companies with low information productivity tend to spend the bulk of IT in servicing the demands originating from overhead staffs. They do not concentrate their applications in support of personnel involved in the production or delivery of whatever generates revenues. Excellent firms allocate most of their IT in catering to the needs of those who are adding to whatever a customer will perceive as value-added. A paying customer does not care how much IT the firm spends on administration and coordination. Paying customers do not care about the architecture of the head-

---

16 In a recent case I ranked a firm as the lowest in information productivity, lowest in profits, and the highest in IT spending among forty-seven peers. Their R&D expenses were much higher than anybody else's. The evaluation was not accepted. The firm did not trust their suppliers to offer sufficiently modern equipment and kept a huge R&D department to duplicate what competitors were able to buy for much less. The engineers and researchers were profligate spenders on computers.

17 In 1976 I discovered that the IT budget for Fuji-Xerox, marketing identical products against identical competitors as Xerox in the US, was remarkably lower than that for Xerox, USA. The Japanese placed labor-intensive customer care functions within small marketing branch offices. The US practice was to find how to eliminate labor through centralized automation. The combined total of computer spending plus administrative expenses was identical and therefore the difference in IT expenses did not matter.

quarters building, the sophistication of the systems architecture, or the magazine recognition awards earned by the systems staffs.

The US Marine Corps uses a term they call the tooth-to-tail ratio. Combat troops are the teeth for doing what the Marines can accomplish on the battlefield. Everybody else, especially in the Pentagon, is the tail just hanging there to hold up the teeth. If the tail gets too big, and you put too much of your energy into it, you will go the way of the dinosaur.[18]

I have examined the profitability and information productivity of over four hundred firms. What distinguishes high information productivity firms is that they do not spend much money on functions that do not address customer needs. They do not have an excessive number of planners, expediters, checkers, auditors, controllers, facilitators, and advisors who are always big consumers of IT. The information resources aim primarily to support the needs of operating and marketing people. Excellent companies deploy more of their information resources to satisfy the needs of paying customers than to provide for intra-corporate coordination.

When I walk into a corporation and I want to find out whether they are a good user of IT, I never inspect the data center at first. That is the last place to find out whether IT is productive. In rare instances I had someone count the windows on floors dedicated exclusively to administration.[19] I also look up the annual financial statements and try to estimate the ratio of overhead to operating costs. It also helps to know some of the key ratios, such as the company's value-added divided by revenue. Then I calculate the firm's information management costs as related to its profitability. Ratios like that, as compared with similar ones for leading competitors, are indicators of whether the firm makes better uses of information technologies than competitors.

The appropriate level of spending for IT has little to do with computer budgets but everything to do with how an enterprise deploys its computer resources. If an organization can manage with fewer information workers because they receive good support from effective computing, then that organization can show results that one associates with superior enterprises. They can take savings in information expenses and distribute

18 US defense spending has fallen nearly forty percent since 1985. With these reductions the warfighting to support function ratio has declined from 50/50, it is now 30/70 and falling. See McInerney, T.G., and Weiss, S.A., "Re-engineering the Pentagon," *The Washington Times*, December 24, 1996.
19 There are 1.5 windows per official, manager, and professional in a typical office building.

them as dividends to the shareholders. Managers, administrators, and support staffs missing from the payroll do not need computer services.

The principal purpose of investing in IT is not overhead cost reduction but value-creation. Cutting costs can contribute to profitability, but in the long run one does not prosper through shrinkage. The objective of all investments is to improve overall organizational performance. Firms may be spending exactly what the benchmark comparisons state as the expected level, yet they may still be failing. Thus one should perform benchmarking of computer budgets only after one has the assurance that the firm's overall information productivity is superior to its competitors'.

What to Do

- Identify the sources of all misalignment.
- Begin reviews of IT spending by an examination of all computing that is unrelated to revenue from external customers.
- Remove from benefit estimates all savings that could have accrued anyway, without computer intervention.
- Authorize pilot tests and small scale experiments that demonstrate how an organization performs with or without computer-enhanced assistance.
- Institute competitive comparisons of the full costs of delivering computer services.

Part II
Facts

- Supposed links between IT and effectiveness of firms
  - Absence of a relationship between profits and IT
- Absence of a relationship between revenues and IT
    - Correlation with overhead expenses
  - Differences in consumption of computer services
  - Importance of capital investments in computers

3 Spending and Profitability

Computer spending and performance are unrelated.

MANAGEMENT is insisting on verifiable proofs that the large increases in IT expenditures have resulted in improved financial results. No agreement exists on how to assess the profit contributions of information technologies. The "computer paradox" reflects the observation: "We see computers everywhere but not in the productivity statistics." The plea that computers are still in infancy does not hold up. There is no evidence that computer investments are exhibiting the economies of scale that conform to the economists' assumption about the increasing returns realized from investments in capital goods. There is no correlation between spending on computers and profitability. Operations in most large corporations would rapidly come to a halt if their computers ceased to function. The lifeline of all advanced post-industrial societies now rests on the proper functioning of computers that control the electric power, telecommunications, and financial services.

Information-age gurus, IT managers, computer vendors, and systems researchers insist that computers deliver competitive gains, speed up business transactions, increase customer satisfaction, deliver superior quality, and lead to improved profitability. This has become generally accepted wisdom. How could US corporations otherwise keep spending more money on computers than on any other tooling investment? [20]

There are, however, a few skeptics who keep searching for solid evidence that computers are indeed profitable. Management is also starting to insist on verifiable proofs that the large increases in IT expenditures have resulted in improved financial results.

---

20 Baatz, E.B., "Digesting the ROI Paradox," *CIO Magazine*, October 1, 1996, reports about a typical situation: "We asked, is it feasible? We defined costs, risks, manpower requirements. We knew we were going to do the project because the CEO said so. When the moving target is the transformation of the business through technology, the ROI exercise seems at best a questionable use of precious time, and at worst, stupid."

EARLY DOUBTERS

The first widely publicized challenge that computers may not be delivering economic value was William Bowen's article in 1986.[21] Subsequently Gary Loveman reported that investment in computers would offer the least attractive returns as compared with other investment options.[22] After that, the voice of the skeptics became louder. Steven Roach, a Morgan Stanley economist, provided the econometric underpinning for those who were uncertain about the validity of utopian advertisements by computer manufacturers. Roach showed that information worker productivity had not increased in more than twenty years while organizations were installing increased amounts of computer capital equipment.

The reaction from the computer industry, academia, consultants, and the technical press to the growing acceptance of Roach's thesis was one of puzzlement. Business publications filled the gap by generating a large number of anecdotal cases that claimed, but did not substantiate, economic gains. This may have sold magazines, but certainly was not hard evidence. To demonstrate that rising economic benefits were directly attributable to increased computerization would necessitate the adoption of a generally accepted method for relating the contributions of computers to profits. No such method was available. No agreement existed on how to approach such an assessment.[23] The proponents of information capital expenditures did not have anything comparable to the pioneering work of George Terborgh in the early 1920s who defined a way to justify investments in manufacturing automation.[24]

All of this confusion gave rise to the widely quoted "computer paradox" phrase, originally attributed to the Nobel Prize economist Robert Solow who said, "We see computers everywhere but not in the productivity statistics."

21 Bowen, W., "The Puny Payoff from Office Computers," *Fortune*, May 1986. He received my documentation of research showing that the relationship between computer spending and any measure of corporate profitability was random.
22 Sloan School of Management, *Management in the 1990s,* Massachusetts Institute of Technology.
23 Absence of a generally accepted methodology did not deter prominent magazines from making annual awards to firms that claimed the largest Return on Investment numbers. For further discussion of this phenomenon see Chapter 20, Computer Profitability Claims, announcing the award for a computer project that generated a fourteen-thousand percent Return on Investment.
24 Terborgh, G.W., *Dynamic Equipment Policy,* McGraw-Hill, 1949.

The purpose of my 1990 book about the value of computers was to contribute to the then emerging debate on evaluation of IT investments. It showed that there was no correlation whatsoever between expenditures for information technologies and any known measure of profitability. Subsequent studies by Eric Brynjolffson from MIT confirmed that there was no such relationship.[25] In the 1995 book by Tom Landaucr one can find another cogent critique of the questionable economic benefits from computerization.[26]

The Gartner Group has now joined the rank of skeptics by announcing that the net average return on IT investments for the period from 1985 through 1995 was only one percent.[27] Since the Gartner analyst estimated the minimum return for computer projects to be eighteen percent annualized, the estimated average return fell far short of expectations.

AMOUNT OF SPENDING

Figure 5 shows the 1996 estimated world-wide corporate and governmental spending on information technologies.[28]

To place the total estimated spending of $1,076 billion into a proper perspective one must consider that the total 1995 profits for the 13,409 global largest corporations were only $750 billion.[29] Whenever the cost of any technology for a firm exceeds profits, the highest executive levels must pay attention. A sense of urgency to understand the benefits of computer spending ought to apply now to all organizations.

25 Brynjolfsson, E., "The Productivity Paradox of Information Technology," *Communications of the ACM*, 35 (December): 66-77, (1993). This paper includes the widely quoted finding that the marginal profitability of computer investments is extremely high.
26 Landauer, T. K., *The Trouble with Computers*, The MIT Press, 1995.
27 Stewart, B., "Enterprise Performance Through IT: Linking Financial Management to Contribution," *Gartner Group, Symposium/ITxpo '96*, Lake Buena Vista, Florida.
28 Hill, C.G., "The Battle for Control," *The Wall Street Journal*, November 18, 1996. Listing includes only purchases for information technologies, which account for about forty percent of the total IT spending. The remaining sixty percent are estimates of internal corporate expenditures for staff and operations based on Strassmann, Inc.'s sample of 220 major corporations. The Director of Technology Research for Montgomery Research announced on December 19, 1996 at the 14th Annual *Technology Week* Investment Conference that the estimated worldwide spending for IT will exceed $1,400 billion in year 2000, up from approximately $950 billion in 1996.
29 There were 10,986 profitable corporations, with a sum total of $894 billion of profits, and 2,423 corporations with losses adding up to $144 billion. See Disclosure Incorporated, *Corporate Information on the World's Leading Companies*, November 1996.

	$ Billions	% of Total
Servers and Mainframes	59	6%
PCs and Workstations	101	9%
Data Communications Equipment	20	2%
Packaged Software	85	8%
Services	165	15%
TOTAL - PURCHASES	430	40%
Data Communications Services	43	4%
Application Expenses	269	25%
Training	22	2%
Operating Expenses	172	16%
Overhead and supplies	97	9%
Expenses not in IT budget	43	4%
TOTAL - INTERNAL COSTS	646	60%
TOTAL CORPORATE SPENDING	1,076	100%

Figure 5   World-wide corporate and government spending
on information technologies

There are two ways of coming up with the US share of global spending. For the last few years the US operated about half of the world's installed computer capacity.[30] That suggests US expenditures of $500 billion. Another way of forming an estimate is to consider that the US generates 22% of the world's GDP and that its ratio of IT costs to GDP is about double the rest of the world.[31] That suggests IT spending of $473 billion.

A third estimate would use the Morgan-Stanley 2.8% ratio of 1995 IT purchases to US GDP. That would set the US budgets for IT at approximately $505 billion.[32]

---

30 "The Growth of Computing Power," *Fortune*, December 13, 1993.
31 Roach, S.S., *The Economics of Competitive Advantage*, Morgan Stanley International Investment Research, November 14, 1996.
32 The 1996 third quarter US spending for IT was $251 billion, or 3.6 percent of the nation's total output of goods and services. With IT purchases equal to about forty percent of the total IT budget, this sets the 1996 year-end US budgets for information technologies at about $627 billion. See Zuckerman, L., "Do Computers Lift Productivity?" *The New York Times*, January 2, 1997.

Anyway you look at it, these are large sums. US IT spending exceeds the sum of 1995 profits of 2,971 US corporations by $175 billion.

THE INTERNATIONAL DIMENSION

The US, with 4.6 percent of the world's population and 21.3 percent of the sum of all gross national products, has installed about fifty percent of the total global computing power: [33]

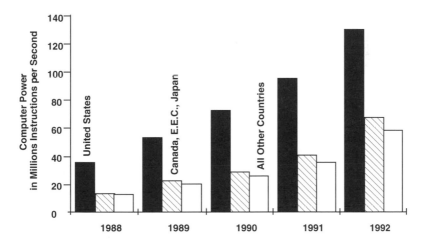

Figure 6   The importance of US computing power

The key technologies of the information age are microprocessors, operating systems, computer languages, and office application software. They all derive their leadership from US corporations. No other nation has seen fit to make as heavy investments in computerization, no matter what measure one utilizes to make these comparisons.[34] The following tabulation shows the relative importance of IT spending in selected country groups: [35]

33 US Bureau of the Census, *Statistical Abstract of the United States*, 1995, Table 1373, "Gross National Product by Country."
34 "The Growth of Computing Power," *Fortune*, December 13, 1993, p. 68.
35 Roach, S.S., *The Economics of Competitive Advantage*, Morgan Stanley International Investment Research, November 14, 1996, Table 4.

	Growth Rate, 1987-94	Share of GDP
United States	8.1%	2.8%
Canada, Australia, New Zealand	7.0%	2.0%
Europe	7.2%	1.7%
Japan	7.8%	1.4%
Other Asia	14.9%	0.5%
Latin America	19.0%	0.8%

Figure 7   IT spending growth rates and share of GDP

The United States devotes a higher percentage of the Gross Domestic Product (GDP) to IT spending than any other country. Only New Zealand (with 2.6 percent of GDP), Sweden (with 2.4 percent), and Switzerland (with 2.4 percent) come close to US spending. It is also noteworthy that Japan, with its historically high rates of productivity growth, spends only 1.4 percent of its GDP on IT.

The high growth rates in IT spending for other Asian and Latin American countries reflect catch-up efforts, but they have relatively low levels of GDP. Though Japan together with Europe exceed the US total GDP, it does not appear likely that they will surpass US spending. The high growth rate in US spending is likely to continue. Therefore, the concentration of global IT spending within the US will remain close to the present fifty percent share in the immediate future.

Singapore offers a puzzling case of exceptional economic growth while keeping IT spending unusually low. In the last six years Singapore has emerged as the country ranking consistently as number two in global competitiveness.[36] Despite widely publicized aspirations to become the world's first information island, they allocate only half of a percent of GDP to information technologies.[37] It is conceivable that Singapore's exceptionally low levels of the government's share of the GDP may account for the sparseness of computer-gobbling demands by bureaucrats.[38]

36 Ratings by the International Institute for Management Development (IMD) and the World Economic Forum.
37 National Computer Board, "IT 2000, A Vision of an Intelligent Island," National Information Infrastructure Division, Singapore, 1993.
38 My reviewers offered a number of theories to explain this phenomenon. In the absence of reliable data I would like to suggest that this matter is worthy of a thorough research study.

28

The American Electronics Association's 1993 report on capital purchases also highlights the relative importance of information technologies.[39] Electronics amounted to seventy-three percent of a total of $646 billion global investments.[40] The us accounted for thirty-six percent of that. What I find interesting is the importance of information technologies as compared to all other electronic equipment. Consumer sector purchases for electronics accounted for only eleven percent of the total. This suggests that speculations about entertainment products becoming the leaders of the next growth wave of electronic industry may be premature.

One measure of the value of information technologies to the us economy concerns its standing relative to international competition. We need evidence that the us has either gained or lost its relative economic standing in the world because of its extraordinary emphasis on IT investments. Such findings would place the discussion about the productivity paradox not only in its domestic, but also in its international context.

In fact, the high rate of us expenditures for information technologies did not diminish the us standing as the country ranking number one in global competitiveness. Meanwhile, our principal competitors keep paying higher hourly wages.[41] What may appear as a computer paradox may in fact be a socio-economic paradox.

GATHERING OF EVIDENCE

The Xerox Experience

While I was CIO at Xerox I was able to get reliable data about computer budgets, business indicators, and financial results for more than fifty operating divisions. These units competed with identical products, against identical competitors, at worldwide locations. Yet, the financial results delivered by each operating unit varied enormously, even though their computer budgets as well as computer applications were comparable. My 1974 analysis showed that there was absolutely no correlation between

---

39 AEA 1993 study, as quoted in *Forbes*, April 11, 1994, p. 41.
40 Defined as computers, peripherals, office equipment, software, and telecommunication equipment.
41 Roach, S.S., *The Economics of Competitive Advantage*, Morgan Stanley International Investment Research, November 14, 1996, Table 3. The hourly compensation in manufacturing in the highly computerized us is $17.20 per hour. The less computerized Europe pays $21.25 and the even least computerized Japan pays $23.66.

computer budgets and profits for Xerox operating units. Information systems were important, but certainly not a key to profitability, as was claimed by computer vendors, automation consultants, and academics in departments of computer science.

Examination of Industrial Firms

Subsequently, I spent seven years gathering data from a collection of other firms to see if they showed a similar diversity as Xerox operating units. By 1985 I was able to show a scatter diagram that displayed profit performance for eighty-four companies, as related to their computer expenses.[42] It showed no connection between computer spending and financial results, regardless of the measures of profitability or indicators of computer usage.

By 1990 I assembled data from 292 enterprises while engaged in consulting work. These findings showed up as a diagram that portrayed a random scatter pattern between computer budgets and returns on investment.[43] Most computer people and quite a few academics did not know what to make of such randomness. It did not conform to what was expected by those who wished to see a strong positive correlation.

One of the objections to these findings was that the data originated as by-product of my consulting practice. Only troubled firms would be seeking diagnostic help about their computer spending. This argument does not hold up, because the sample included a large number of businesses with little computer spending and high profitability, as well as many firms with enormous computer spending and dismal financial results.

The Infancy Plea

Others maintained that it would take decades before convincing evidence about the benefits of computers would appear. There is a widely held belief that all new technologies require an extended gestation period before they can become profitable. *The Economist* explained the apparent lack of returns on IT investments by pointing out that it took from 1900 until 1920

---

42 Digital Equipment Corporation, "Measuring Management Productivity," *The Consultant*, Merrimack, N.H., No. 1, 1986.
43 Strassmann, P.A., *The Business Value of Computers*, The Information Economics Press, 1990.

for electrical motors to show substantive returns.[44] Accordingly, computerization was, at this point of time, still in its introductory stage and therefore expectations of demonstrated profitability were premature.[45] The lack of correlation between computer spending and profitability at present still reflects transient conditions that would disappear in due course.

More than forty years have passed. *Fortune* magazine dates the advent of the computer age to the introduction of the UNIVAC computer in 1952.[46] Soon thereafter sophisticated business applications became feasible. I suggest that the forty-five years of the computer age no longer qualify IT for an infancy exemption from economic accountability. The frequently used argument that there is an as yet unrevealed economic potential for computerization has little merit.

Another hypothesis is that computer profitability is still in the transition phase and will soon produce demonstrable results, because of the lag between investments and profits. Unfortunately, I cannot find support for this either. The scatter diagram pattern between corporate results and computer spending has retained the same shape for over twenty years. In fact, the pattern of the results is trending away from the positive. As the sample of companies keeps increasing, the correlation is acquiring a slightly negative bias. Greater spending on computers relative to employment levels is now associated with greater losses than before.

Grosch's Law as a Guide to Profits

For a long time the reigning theory about the economics of computerization was Grosch's Law. It asserted that there are huge economies of scale available because of the rapidly declining costs of computers with the size of a computer.[47] Accordingly, the profitability of computerization would show up when firms bought large-scale equipment and centralized the workload in data centers for more efficient processing.

44 *The Economist*, January 22, 1994.
45 *Fortune*, June 27, 1994, p. 81. For instance, in 1954-55 I used an IBM CPC (Card Programmed Stored Program Calculator) computer to develop a complex business application, published as a MIT dissertation on *Forecasting Traffic and Scheduling of Toll Collection Personnel on the New Jersey Turnpike*. There were applications as early as in 1952 that offered excellent examples of what computers can accomplish.
46 *Fortune*, June 27, 1994, p.81.
47 Named after Herbert Grosch, a one time IBM researcher and subsequently the Director of the Center for Computer Technologies, National Bureau of Standards, US Department of Commerce.

Grosch said that computing power increases with the square of its costs, thus producing enormous economies of scale. However, it was never clear whether Grosch's law was a reflection how IBM priced its computers or whether the prices related to costs. Given IBM's dominance of the mainframe computer business, enormous gross margins which made costs meaningless, and IBM's price umbrella over the entire computer industry, I suspect that what was supposed to be a "law" was nothing but a reflection of IBM's marketing strategy.

Though Grosch never published his work, his theories became the accepted truth for computer capacity planning for more than twenty years.[48] It provided the rationale that a bigger computer is always better. The IBM sales force used Grosch's rationale to persuade organizations to acquire more computing capacity than they needed. Grosch's Law also became the justification for offering time-sharing services from big data centers as a substitute for distributed computing.

As yet, there is no evidence that computer investments are exhibiting the economies of scale that confirm to the economists' favorite assumption about the increasing returns realized from investments in capital goods. Though now thoroughly disproved, Grosch's Law should serve as a reminder that the history of the economics of computing has an abundance of unsupported misperceptions.

Ideas of how to invest in new technologies acquire temporary popularity until conveniently abandoned for yet another rationalization about how to spend money. For example, the once popular idea that desktop computers were an easy way of obtaining inexpensive corporate computing qualifies for the title of an expensive fallacy. The most likely next candidate for delusions that only wait for their demise will be over-featured software office suites.

Insufficient Opportunities

One explanation of the lagging computer payoffs proposes that information technologies are just too difficult to use. Accordingly, learning and using software costs US firms five million hours a year, or $100 billion, thus reducing the observed productivity gains. Computer users may take more

---

48 *Encyclopedia of Computer Science and Engineering*, 2nd edition, Van Nostrand Reinhold Company, 1983, p. 668.

time to complete their work as the tasks they perform become less tedious and more enjoyable.[49]

The Gartner Group priced the end-user labor for operating a personal computer at close to $4,000 per employee per annum, or approximately ten percent of their working hours.[50] If one considers that the average cost of ownership of networked client computers to be at least $9,500, which amounts to about twenty percent of average payroll costs, a firm must then demand at least that much in productivity gains. However, the estimated cost of $9,500 per client may be low. When Microsoft outsourced the support of their client/server network, the contract numbers revealed the magnitude of their expense, which was $16,000 per client per year.[51] With service sector productivity gains recorded as less than one percent per year, twenty percent productivity gains would be difficult to find easily.

Historic productivity increases over the last century averaged about 2.5 percent per annum. It may be unreasonable to expect computerization to achieve much more than that in the future. Meanwhile, computer proponents such as the Gartner Group publish results of surveys where the operators of networked personal computers claimed per person value-added of $50,000 per year. This adds up to approximately one hundred percent productivity gains. In the absence of independently verifiable financial results, the claims made on the basis of surveys are not believable.

The US employs 1,750,000 software engineers, 437,500 software personnel, and 273,438 software managers generating new applications for a business population of about sixty million information workers. The $100 billion per year estimate of costs for learning how to design applications and how to use them is not far-fetched. It could account for increased costs that are eating up many of the productivity gains realized elsewhere in the organization.[52]

---

49 Krohe, J. Jr., "The Productivity Pit ," *Across the Board*, October 1993. What may influence productivity more are the effects of widespread access to distributed networked computers from a workforce that plays games and seeks entertainment.
50 Dec, K., "Client/Server Payoff," CIO *Magazine*, April 15, 1996, p. 72.
51 Manes, S., "A Bogus but Useful Measure," *InformationWeek*, January 15, 1996.
52 The estimate of the total software population comes from Capers Jones of the Software Productivity Research Corporation. Using Jones' numbers I come up with a $150 billion per annum cost estimate for software plus an additional $70 billion for computer operations labor.

THE TALE OF THE SCATTER DIAGRAM

The following diagram reflects financial results and computer spending for 468 corporations.[53] The financial results are for 1994, which by all standards was a prosperous year. Included are US, European, and Canadian firms. The points represent a random sample of diverse businesses that include manufacturing, retailing, banking, and utility firms.[54]

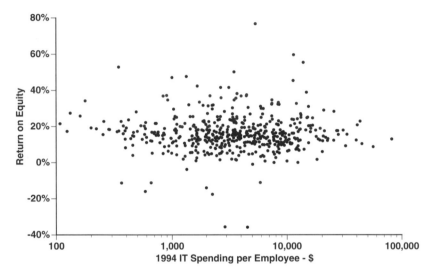

Figure 8   No correlation in spending on computers and profitability

The random pattern does not contradict the facts that computers frequently make decisive contributions to efficiency, competitive viability, and value creation. However, high or low spending levels for computers can be associated with both inferior or superior results. High-performing firms do not allocate more money to IS than low-performing firms.[55]

---

53 At the time of final editing of this book the sample size grew to 539.
54 Although these findings are for large corporations, the absence of a correlation between IT spending and profitability was also found for 131 small businesses with sales under $5 million and less than 50 employees (see Palvia, P., Means, D.B., Jackson, W.M., "Determinants of Computing in Very Small Businesses," *Information & Management*, 27 1994).
55 In a study of 200 largest companies in Finland the researchers found no evidence that a high level of IS investment relates to high profit performance (see Kivijarvi, H., and Saarinen, T., "Investment in Information Systems and the Financial performance of the Firm," *Information & Management*, 28 1985).

This randomness did not change with other measures of profitability, such as Return on Assets, Return on Net Investment, or Economic Value-Added divided by Equity. Similarly, no measure of technology intensity, such as IT spending per revenue dollar or IT spending per asset value, made any difference. I have even tried to correlate profitability with preferences for mainframe computing or distributed computing: none of that was conclusive.

It is safe to say that so far nobody has produced any evidence to support the popular myth that spending more on information technologies will boost economic performance. The presumption that more IT spending is better remains one of the most cherished beliefs of computerdom.[56] It took experimental science to dispel the dogmas of the ancients. It may take better research and better metrics before executives will come to recognize that IT is a subtle influence and that an overdose of what works can also disable.

AN EXAMINATION OF FOOD FIRMS

Differences between industrial segments could perhaps explain why there is no relationship between information technologies spending and Return on Equity. To test this conjecture I segmented the entire database of over five-hundred firms into fifty-four industrial groupings. The following illustrates the results for US food firms.

This figure shows that the Quaker Oats Company, with an exceptionally high Return on Equity is spending less than one fourth of the per-capita IT spending of H.J. Heinz and Archer Daniels. Yet CPC International, Sara Lee, and Dean Foods show only one third of the profitability, even though their IT spending levels are comparable to that of Quaker Oats. Close competitors, such as Pepsico and Coca-Cola, show enormous differences both in IT spending and in profitability. Therefore, one cannot associate computerization either with favorable or unfavorable corporate performance.

56 Violino, B., "The Billion $ Club," *InformationWeek*, November 25, 1996. The article quotes MIT's Brynjolfsson that "... firms that spend more on IT tend to do better."

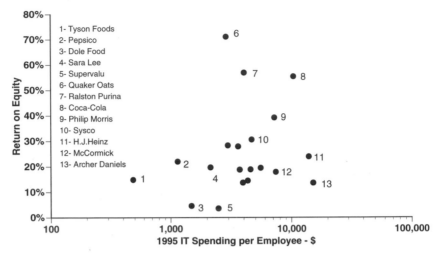

Figure 9   No correlation in spending on computers and profitability
in food industry

Other Food Industry Studies

One of the most detailed recent studies of the relationship between expenditures for computers and revenue-related determinants comes from Akram Yosri.[57] He collected one hundred and two variables for each of thirty-one major food firms covering the period from 1987 through 1990. He categorized IT costs as strategic, tactical, or operational. Yosri studied the allocation of these costs to key activities, such as support of order entry, sales and marketing activities, and back office operations. As measures of performance he tracked sales growth, market share, new market penetration, measures of quality improvement, and productivity. Yosri collected data on training, organizational stability, extent of centralization, and the state of technologies. Clearly, this was a very ambitious study.

At the enterprise level of analysis, there were no significant correlation between IT spending and sales growth, market share gain, effectiveness, quality, or productivity. Profits and economic value-added are missing from these analyses, but it is unlikely that these would have shown a relationship with IT anyway.

57 Yosri, A., *The Relationship Between Information Technology Expenditures and Revenue Contributing Factors in Large Corporations*, Ph.D. dissertation, Walden University, 1992.

At the functional level of analysis, the only noteworthy effects were the contributions of IT spending in order entry and back office operations to sales growth and productivity.[58] These functions are unglamorous, but essential, applications of computers.

This thorough study suggests that the competency in managing fundamentally important administrative processes remains the key to the management of IT investments. In my 1990 book, *The Business Value of Computers*, I arrived at an identical conclusion.

AN EXAMINATION OF BANKING FIRMS

The great diversity in the food industry could conceal a fundamental connection between computers and profitability. Factory operatives and laborers account for as much as thirty percent of the workforce in food companies. If computers relate to productivity that will surely reveal itself in a sector where information handling is the sole occupation. Banking and insurance companies buy over one third of the corporate computer processing capacity. They should reveal such an association if there is one at all. Figure 10 shows the relationship between Return on Equity and IT expenditures per capita for thirty banking firms.[59]

Identical computer spending for Wells Fargo and BankAmerica, two competing banks, does not result in identical profitability. Wells Fargo performs two times better than BankAmerica. NationsBank Services spend fifteen times more than Regions Financial Corporation, but shows almost identical profitability. Similarly, Chase-Manhattan spends almost twice as much as Citicorp, yet Chase is materially less profitable.

All this proves is that it is not computers, but how a firm manages them, along with everything else, that makes the difference. The philosopher William James, one of the founders of the school of pragmatism, has put that perhaps more simply: "A difference that makes no difference is no difference." [60]

Elevating computerization to the level of a magic fetish of this civilization is a mistake that will find correction in due course. It leads to the diminishing of what matters the most in any enterprise: educated, com-

---

58 The measure of productivity reflected only labor costs. It did not consider capital as an input.
59 The dots without names stand for banks whose names did not fit into the graphic.
60 William James (1842-1910).

mitted, and imaginative individuals working for organizations that place greater emphasis on people than on technologies.

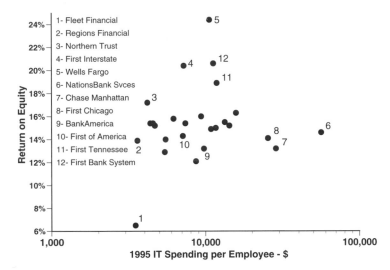

Figure 10   No correlation in spending on computers and profitability in banking

Value of Computers

Operations in most large corporations would rapidly come to a halt if their computers ceased to function. The lifeline of all advanced post-industrial societies now rests on the proper functioning of computers that control the electric power, telecommunications, and financial services. The increased vulnerability of our society to a deliberate attack on computers that operate our information infrastructure is now subject to a new military discipline, information warfare.[61]

Computers are only a tool. Computers are not an unqualified blessing. An identical machine with identical software that performs admirably in one company will make things worse in an enterprise that has inferior management. They enhance sound business practices. They also aggravate inefficiencies whenever the people who use them are disorganized and unresponsive to customer needs. The best computer technologies will

---

61 For the past three years the author has been teaching this subject at the National Defense University, Ft. McNair, Washington, DC.

always add unnecessary costs to a poorly managed firm. The problem seems to rest not with the inherent capabilities of the technologies, which are awesome, but with the managerial inability to use them effectively. For instance, Gartner Group researchers allege "Seventy percent of IT projects have not delivered their expected benefits because they have failed to integrate the results into work processes."[62] How these researchers have found what may be some of the most closely held corporate secrets is a mystery. Nevertheless, this view appears often in press interviews with top corporate executives.

Business productivity has its roots in well organized, well motivated, and knowledgeable people who understand what to do with all of the information that shows up on their computer screens. It would be too much to hope for such excellence to prevail in all businesses. If computer expenditures and corporate profitability show no correlation, it is a reflection of the human condition that excellence is an uneven occurrence. It is unrealistic to expect that computerization could ever change that.

NOT A SIMPLE RELATIONSHIP

Business executives as well as computer experts must recognize that the fortunes of an enterprise originate with the people who administer, coordinate and manage employees, suppliers, and customers. The cost of computerization equals, on the average, less than one fiftieth of revenues. Therefore, it is absurd for a CEO, COO, or CFO to demand that the Chief Information Executive prove how computer budgets relate directly to profits. The best that computerization can deliver is to make information-handling people more effective.

The lack of a direct causal relationship between corporate profitability and computer spending has not changed in more than twenty years. It is unlikely that any direct relationship between computerization and profitability will appear in the future.[63] Computers are only a catalyst. Identically trained people in different organizations can come to opposite conclusions from an examination of data obtained by identical means.

---

62 Stewart, B., "The Second Age of IT: Increasing the Return on Technology", *InSide Gartner Group*, October 1995
63 After an exhaustive study the Stanford Research Institute came to the identical conclusion (see McAteer, J.F., "Measuring the Return on Information Technology," SRI International Business Intelligence Program, Report D95-1964, November/December 1995).

What matters is not just what people see on their computer screens, but what informed actions they take with what they learn.

Unless robots end up running completely automated businesses, the relationship between computerization and profitability will remain a random scatter diagram for many years to come.

What to Do

- Avoid quoting isolated anecdotal cases to substantiate economic gains.
- Obtain reliable estimates of IT spending, including expenses that do not show up as the IT budget.
- Track IT expenditures as a ratio of profits, economic value-added, and operating costs.
- Collect consistent sets of data and performance indicators if organization consists of multiple operating units.
- Benchmark total IT spending as compared with look-alike firms or government organizations.
- Insist that only operating personnel are asked to justify their IT spending.

4 Profits and Value

Investing without verifiable benefits is gambling, not managing.

ECONOMIC Value-Added is the best measure for judging the output of a firm. Companies that have unfavorable economic performance relative to their computer spending outnumber those that show positive results. A significant number of firms should find it attractive to reduce their IT expenditures unless they can prove contributions to corporate profitability.

How do the expenditures for computers relate to profits? This question is asked with increasing frequency by top executives. So far as I can tell, nobody has as yet proved a direct relationship between the levels of computer expenditures, regardless how defined, and business performance, regardless how measured.

In 1983-84, I directed a research study conducted by the Strategic Planning Institute of Cambridge, Massachusetts. This was the MPIT Project (Management Productivity and Information Technology). We examined operating results, costs, and IT expenditures for 292 manufacturing cases. Seventy-two percent came from the US and Canada, the balance from England, Holland, and France.

The amounts of IT spending, as measured by the IT Expense-to-Revenue ratio, did not correlate with Return on Investment. Comparisons against Return on Assets, Return on Equity, Return on Sales, Return on Shareholder Value, Information Technology per Capita, per Value-Added, per Employee Costs were also inconclusive.

Although the percentage of IT spending varied over a wide range, its relation to Return on Investment was slightly negative. This raised the question about claims that a steady increase in computer budgets was a sign of increased technological maturity in firms. A closer examination of the spending habits of firms with superior financial results revealed that they spent less money on IT than firms that showed below-average financial results.

Computers and Economic Value-Added

To understand the relative significance of IT spending, which is one of the input costs, one has to understand Economic Value-Added, which is the best measure for judging output.

The Economic Value-Added of an enterprise is approximately profits minus an amount equal to shareholder equity multiplied by the cost of capital. The average cost of US shareholder equity capital for 1994 was 10.5 percent, though for particular firms it could range anywhere from 6.5 percent to 17.5 percent. This method is a conservative approximation. It excludes minority interest, surplus capital, and other related entries on the balance sheet. My estimates represent this indicator in the most favorable way.[64]

The technique I use is comparable to and is an approximation of the EVA values compiled by the firm Stern-Stewart.[65] Their valuations have origins in elaborate analyses of the financial structure of US industrial firms, using proprietary software. For purposes of this book our approximation is adequate, although I check it against the published Stern-Stewart database whenever the data is available.[66] In instances requiring greater accuracy one can apply more precise measures.[67]

The best way of demonstrating the importance of computer budgets is by examining the relationship between the Economic Value-Added and IT budgets. The following diagram shows the distribution of the 1994 differences in which the Economic Value-Added is either greater or less than the firm's corresponding IT budgets:

64 When analyzing operating units of multi-divisional global corporations, I determine the shareholder value by subtracting Total Liabilities from Total Assets. In the case of some companies that place large reserves on their balance sheet as a way of improving their reported Return-on-Equity, this estimating method is preferable.

65 EVA™ is a trademark of Stern-Stewart & Co. A comprehensive description of this concept is in Stewart, G.B. III, "The Quest for Value," *Harper Business*, 1991. A good discussion is also in Stewart, G.B. III, "EVA Works, But Not If You Make These Common Mistakes," *Fortune*, May 1, 1995.

66 Economic Value Added, in its various forms, is becoming the most widely used metric in the corporate world. It is implemented in setting long-range financial targets by eighty-four percent of US major corporations. Sixty-five percent of US corporations use it for identifying strategic opportunities and executive compensation. See Christinat, D., "All about EVA," CFO *Magazine*, November 1996.

67 A correlation between the published Stern-Stewart values of EVA and the approximations used in my illustrative cases is eighty-six percent.

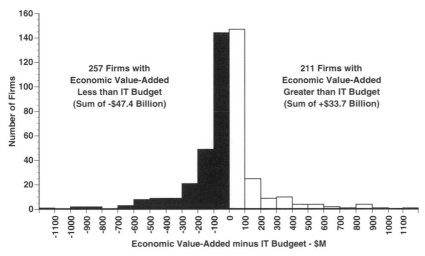

Figure 11   IT budget exceeds the Economic Value-Added for most firms

Companies that have unfavorable economic performance relative to their computer spending outnumber those that show positive results. This outcome repeats itself in all of my studies. In 1994, an otherwise prosperous year, losers outnumbered winners.

If IT budgets are comparable to the Economic Value-Added of firms, then any reductions in IT expenses could have a favorable effect on profits. Although the expense for information technologies as compared to revenues is a relatively small number, when matched against the economic surplus that number is significant. Minimizing the IT budget, just as minimizing expenses, is therefore always good practice if it does not impair the conduct of business. Spending money on IT without proof as to profitability is gambling and not science or engineering.

COMPUTERS AND PROFITS

Many executives do not use the concept of Economic Value-Added and prefer making comparisons with profits. For 138 largest US firms the ratio of profit-after-taxes to IT budgets averages from one to three:

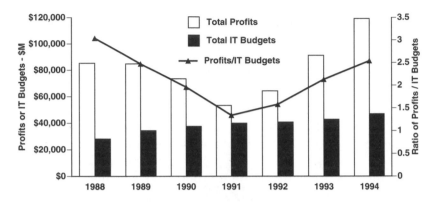

Figure 12   Ratio of profits divided by IT budgets

In 1994 the IT budget exceeded or was comparable to profits for more that a quarter of 468 large US firms. As inconclusive as profit-after-taxes ratios may be as a measure of the importance costs, IT expenditures surely warrant attention. A significant number of firms should find it attractive to examine whether these expenditures contribute to corporate profitability in ways that are demonstrably positive.

What to Do

- **Adopt Economic Value-Added metrics for assessing the contributions of information technologies.**
- **Collect data about the Economic Value-Added of competitors for making comparisons of all spending.**

5 Spending and Revenues

Customers do not care how much a firm spends on computers.

INFORMATION technology as percentage of revenue is the favorite measure for evaluating computer spending. A higher ratio of IT to revenue does not prove higher effectiveness in the use of computers. More spending is not a sign of technological progress. Spending money for IT is not dependent on gross revenues. The preferred way of making judgment about IT spending is to examine key business processes, such as customer care, goods production, post-sale support, and product innovation. Revenue and expense ratios for information technologies are not only inaccurate and irrelevant, but also deceptive when applied in the public sector.

Revenue-related Ratios

The IT expense/revenue ratio is the most frequently used measure of computer usage. Corporate and government budget analysts use it as the key indicator for making judgments about IT spending.[68] This ratio is popular because it is easy to calculate. It does not require probing deeper into the reasons why organizations spend money on computers. It makes computer spending something ordained by external forces or a prerequisite for doing business. It transforms acts that call for deliberate planning and alignment with business needs into something that is more like membership dues a firm must pay to do business.

The computer magazine with the largest circulation in the world selected every year the "100 US companies investing most effectively in information systems" on the basis of revenue ratios.[69] The greatest weight to the annual effectiveness score rating came from IT expenses as related to sales. Accordingly, a higher ratio of IT to revenue suggested higher effec-

---

68 The CIO of Hughes Aircraft said that his company was on track to meet the business objective of cutting IS expenses by 30 percent by reducing expenditures from 4-5 percent of sales to 3-4 percent. See Slater, D., "Rocket Science," *CIO Magazine*, September 1, 1996, p. 88.
69 Appearing as a special insert in *Computerworld* magazine from 1987 through 1993.

tiveness on the presumption that companies would not spend more money on computerization if it would be ineffective.

Stages-of-Growth Theory

For more than two decades, the most widely accepted theory of the contributions of information technologies in business was the stages-of-growth hypothesis.[70] Its purpose was to explain why some firms reported higher IT spending ratios than others. The stages-of-growth conjecture related rising IT expense/revenue ratios to the estimated levels of technological advancement as well as to corresponding managerial methods. Although it would have been easy to do, this rationale was untested against profitability. Nevertheless, the stages-of-growth theory supported numerous requests to increase IT budgets. Accordingly, more spending would be a sign of increased technical progress.

My own research supports the stages-of-growth theory, but not as intended. Firms that pursue state of the art IT technologies always spend more than calculated by an equation that tells what one can expect to spend. Unfortunately, the economic value-added of such firms is rarely superior as compared with firms that avoid being the technological avant-garde.

Even unproved theories reflect some aspects of reality. An interesting correlation exists between the length of time a small business has been in existence and IT spending. These firms had less than fifty employees and median sales below one million.[71] When very small businesses start up, they are always short of cash. In due course the survivors can spend more money on computerization. However, this is not technological sophistication, but affordability.

IT as percentage of revenue is perhaps the favorite measure in dozens of system consultant surveys that try to evaluate the relevance of computer spending. Without fail they include tabulations, segmented by industry, of the ratios of IT budgets to revenue. Such surveys serve a good purpose at budget time, when a below-average ratio becomes an indicator of competitive backwardness that calls for increased spending. The identical sur-

---

70 Nolan, R.L., "Managing the Computer Resource: A Stage Hypothesis," *Communications of ACM*, 16, No. 7 (July 1973).
71 Palvia, P., Means, D.B., Jackson, W.M., "Determinants of Computing in Very Small Businesses," *Information & Management*, 27 (1994), p. 161.

vey results find good use also at performance appraisal time, when a below average ratio becomes an indicator of superior efficiency that calls for a bonus. Whichever of these mutually contradictory positions are beneficial offers no proof to a top business executive, who must make a decision on how much money to spend. Revenue-related ratios cannot demonstrate what spending makes sense. They cannot validate that the executives in charge of the information systems function are indeed productive.

TRADE PRESS ESTIMATES

The most elaborate scheme for estimating spending on information technologies is the annual issue of the magazine *InformationWeek*, the "500 Biggest and the Best Users of IT."[72] Consultants refer to it as the authoritative source for the benchmarking IT spending. There are numerous academic studies that use this data to arrive at their conclusions about IT costs. Because of the widespread uses of the *InformationWeek* data, it is desirable to validate these numbers. This is important because over two thirds of the quoted spending figures are estimates based on average ratios and not known expenses.

It is not necessary to analyze every one of the approximately 350 estimated budgets. For illustrative purposes I concentrate on the 1996 *InformationWeek* food industry table. A check of the other industry sectors revealed similar characteristics.

Only thirteen of the thirty-three food industry budgets were actual amounts. As it turned out, a statistical test of the *InformationWeek* estimates explained them with a great accuracy. The graph displaying estimated as well as actual IT budgets revealed the following:

---

72 *InformationWeek*, September 9, 1996. The winners were rated according to a CII Index, whose exact make-up remains a mystery, being a valuation of a company's IT activities by the Computer Intelligence Corporation. It is based on telephone conversations with LAN, PC, and data center administrators. Values are assigned to size and technologies. A site with 500 LAN users would get a higher score than one with 100 users. A Pentium PC receives a higher score than a 386. EDI and client/server rate better than mainframes. Reengineering scores particularly favorably. It is not at all clear that this has anything to do with productivity, as claimed by the *InformationWeek*, except that it signals the raters' point of view of what earns meritorious endorsement.

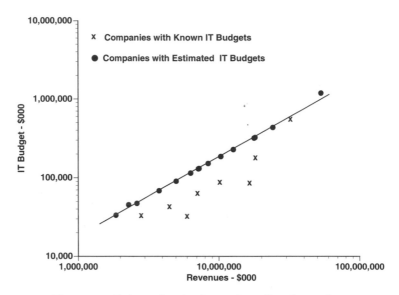

Figure 13   Estimated IT budgets relate directly to sales,
actual IT budgets do not.

Statistical analysis showed, with 99% reliability, that the *Information-Week* analysts calculated just about every estimated budget by multiplying revenues by 1.80%. It was a simplistic way of coming up with an answer that assumes that in the food industry it is revenue that generates the demand for computers. That just is not so. However, the straight-line relationship between IT spending and revenues did not apply to firms reporting actual spending. The differences between the actual and the revenue-estimated numbers were as large as fifty percent.

Just to make sure an error did not creep in, I supplemented the actual *InformationWeek* data with known budgets of four food companies. These are cases where the IT expense numbers are verifiable. The food companies with actual IT budgets did not fit the linear revenue-based estimating formula at all.

This example again confirms that spending money for IT is not revenue-dependent. There are many other factors that influence the spending levels, such as the proportion of information workers in the workforce, extent of automation of the workforce and affordability.

Despite repeated demonstrations of the futility of resorting to simple revenue-based ratios, magazines and consultants persist in using this method for producing estimates though they are likely to mislead. It appears that nobody objects. Perhaps this is because in almost every case the estimates suggest firms ought to be spending more than they actually do.

FINDINGS ABOUT REVENUE RATIOS

My analyses of IT budgets is based on data available from public and private sources for 508 corporations.[73] This data reflects a bias that favors larger organizations with median annual IT spending of $100 to $120 million dollars:

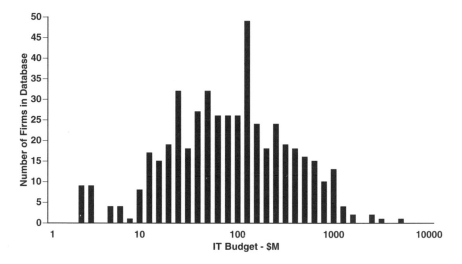

Figure 14   Distribution of annual budgets for IT

In financial institutions, such as banking and insurance companies, IT is generally the single largest cost center. In commercial banking, IT costs equal up to twenty-five percent of the non-interest expenses. I estimate the total IT spending by US commercial banks for the last ten years to be more than $200 billion. This is greater than the sum of their total present equity capital.

---

73 The budgets could be understated by as much as twenty percent, because in most cases they do not include the full costs of distributed computing. The sum total of all the 1994 budgets for the 508 corporations is $83 billion.

FINDINGS ABOUT PER CAPITA RATIOS

Per employee expenditures in banking range from $3,760 to $49,000 per annum. In selected instances there are high-risk and high-payoff operations, such as in currency trading, arbitrage and hedging, where the per capita expenses are higher. In such cases one can encounter IT expenditures as high as $60,000 to $80,000 per analyst.[74]

Another way of understanding the relative importance of IT budgets is to examine per employee spending:

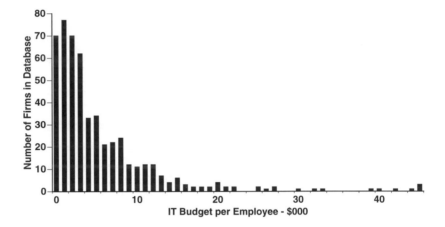

Figure 15   Distribution of annual IT spending per employee

Although most of the annual spending is under $5,000 per employee, there are firms that show allocations of IT spending as high as $66,000 per employee. There is an enormous diversity in spending patterns not only as a function of industry sector, but also as a characteristic of the workforce it employs, compensation levels, and dependence on automation. The following tabulation for selected sectors illustrates this point:

---

74 None of these ratios apply to computer services companies where most IT expenses are in the cost of sales, just as if they were factory expenses. There are a few specialized on-line information services companies that average IT spending in excess of $200,000 per person.

	Median	Minimum	Maximum
Discount & Fashion Retail	$1,086	$584	$3,200
Railroads	$3,400	$2,002	$4,298
Chemicals	$3,441	$923	$11,493
Drugs & Research	$4,000	$2,140	$12,104
Coal, Oil, & Gas	$5,310	$1,746	$16,901
Utilities	$6,366	$1,967	$21,296
Banks	$7,869	$3,757	$49,036
Computers & Peripherals	$9,113	$6,186	$13,569
Insurance	$10,737	$3,518	$33,287

Figure 16   Diversity in spending of IT per employee

Despite the enormous diversity in ratios, controllers and financial analysts find it convenient to evaluate IT budgets in terms of revenue-related ratios. Consultants and computer magazines publish tabulations of IT as a percentage of revenue. The federal government and a number of states publish IT expenses as a percentage of each agency's total appropriations. Corporate and public sector managers then use these numbers to conclude whether a firm is overspending or underspending on IT. None of this makes much sense, because all average ratios are misleading.

RELATING FUNCTIONAL SPENDING TO REVENUES

The attention given to the IT-to-revenue average ratios does not appear to match the scrutiny given to other corporate functions. After an exhaustive search, I have been able to obtain representative revenue-related ratios only for the personnel function. It was eight tenths of one percent of total operating costs. The staffing of the personnel function accounted for one percent of total corporate employment.

Despite a decade of trying, I have never been able to find the total functional costs for finance and accounting for any corporation or government agency. I suspect that these numbers are much larger than for any other overhead expense functional category. If it were to become public, it would certainly attract a great deal of attention, especially in the public sector. A glimpse of such potential embarrassment comes from the

Defense National Performance Review which found that it took \$2.4 billion of processing costs to reimburse \$2 billion of travel expenses.[75]

To calculate the full costs of finance and accounting, I would include in the total everyone's time to prepare, negotiate, report, and explain all finance and accounting demands received by others. Such a review should certainly include the costs of all computing efforts prompted by requests from finance and accounting. It should also account for the time the operating staffs consume in defending themselves in matters related to all budgetary inquiries. Making public such full costs would open a remarkable challenge to financial controllers and congressional appropriation committees.

It is very hard to identify what share of total IT spending is used in activities due to the requirements imposed by the Chief Financial Officer. Accounting and financial tasks take place everywhere in an organization, since they occupy much of the time of all management. The last time that I had any data, this spending was well over fifty percent of the total IT cost. It is dysfunctional to concentrate on computer spending if the costs of the financial bureaucracy get no attention. Much of this argument applies also to the marketing function.

Before one relates the costs of computers to revenues, one must first understand how computer-consuming functions such as finance, marketing, research, personnel, and legal services contribute to the value-added of the firm.

Even the analysis of functional costs will fall far short of explaining how the processing of information contributes to the delivery of superior value to the customer. The preferred way of making that judgment is to examine key business processes, such as customer care, goods production, post-sale support, and product innovation. Only through a scrutiny of the work that makes up a business process can one understand where and how information becomes productive.

REVENUE DOES NOT EQUAL VALUE-ADDED

The use of information technologies is unrelated to the gross revenue or to the funds appropriated to run a public sector organization. A firm that adds value to most of what it sells has a high level of vertical integration. It will require more computing than a firm that has a low level of vertical

---

75 *Federal Computer Week*, April 11, 1994, p. 42.

integration. Firms that purchase from others most of what they resell are an unintegrated (or hollow) enterprise. They add little value because they acquire most their raw materials, components, and services from outside suppliers.[76] Firms in the same industry, offering identical products, operate with different levels of vertical integration and therefore would be consuming varying amounts of computing in support of their activities. A hollow enterprise requires little computing because the suppliers already include in their prices the expenses for information processing.

A diagram that shows the distribution of IT spending as a percentage of sales will show a wide range of values:

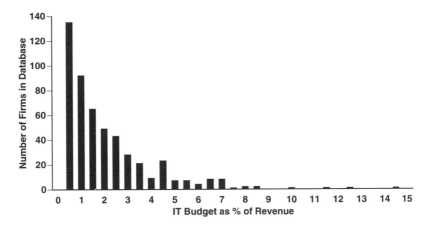

Figure 17   IT as % of revenue shows wide range of ratios

The dispersion in the percentage of IT to revenue ratio is also attributable to the need for different employee skills in conducting business. For instance, banks employ a much larger proportion of people in information-handling positions than do coal, oil, and gas firms.

The effects of vertical integration and employee occupation yield big differences in the ratio of IT as a percentage of revenue. Without data about of the structure of a firm, all comparisons based on simple ratios are meaningless.

76 Value-Added is defined here as revenues minus purchases. In public sector the Value-Added would be the department's appropriations minus transfer payments minus purchases.

Setting Targets for IT Spending

The demonstrable irrelevancy of using the percentage of revenue has not deterred a number of consulting schemes that claim that they can set targets for the IT budget. These schemes persist because the collection of percentage of revenue information is easy. They are welcome by CIOs in search of effortless explanations. One of the most elaborate models for calculating desirable IT spending comes from the Gartner Group.[77] It prescribes the following sequence:
- Step 1: Establish the need for enterprise benefits from competitive analysis. Competitors define the percentage of revenue that any firm needs in order to excel.

Given the wide ranging dissimilarities in the structure of businesses, it is hard to understand how a firm could know whether that percentage of revenue would meet this objective. In the Gartner case, that number was taken to be five percent of revenue.
- Step 2: Define the baseline cost for IT as the percentage of revenue that is essential to support ongoing operations. It is the IT budget without which the firm could not function.

In the Gartner case, that number is a consensus estimate of 2.43 percent of revenue.
- Step 3: Estimate how much an enterprise gains in profitability through information technologies. This defines what share of the total enterprise profits derive from IT deployments.

Such a number is unverifiable unless a firm has in place an audit process for continually monitoring benefits from all past investments. To the best of my knowledge there is no enterprise that has ever been able to accumulate such information. In the illustrative example, the estimate of the share of total profits from computerization was forty percent. In other words, computerization accounted for two fifths of all of the benefits that the firm derived from all sources. It states that top management would be willing to attribute to computers two thirds of whatever the workers, salesforce, management, capital, and research contributed to the enterprise.

---

77 Gartner Group, "Asking the Right Questions about IT Spending," *The Gartner Group Monthly Research Review*, July 10, 1996 and Report TV-190-112 (6/27/96).

This makes computers more valuable than all employees, including management – an unlikely conclusion.

- Step 4: Set the expected average Return on Investment
  for all new projects.

In the Gartner case the expected average Return on Investment was fifteen percent. That is only a small premium over the average cost of capital of US firms. Whether that recognizes the risks of IT projects, the cost of capital, or current levels of profitability is not clear. The cost of capital for some firms is a multiple of risk-free interest rates, and could be as high as thirty percent. The risks of some state-of-the-art computer projects are sufficiently high that they must earn a multiple of the cost of equity, which could mean setting the required Return on Investment rates in excess of thirty percent. Firms are also realizing high returns on investments that are unrelated to computerization. Consequently, the expected return for computer investments cannot be an average, but a rate that exceeds the returns for all other opportunities that carry lower risks.

- Step 5: Estimate what are the IT expenditures to achieve
  the target Return on Investment for all IT projects.

Somehow the CIO must come up with the costs of all IT proposals that expect to deliver ROIs above the average rate for the firm. That sum is expressed again as a percentage of revenue. In the illustrative case, the expected sum was 1.7 percent of revenues.

- Step 6: Calculate the proposed IT spending. It is the
  sum of the expenditures to achieve the desired Return
  on Investment returns plus the current baseline costs.

In the illustrative example, the projected IT budget is 4.13 percent of revenues, or 0.87 percent below competitive needs.

The entire six-step process for determining the "right" levels of IT spending, according to the Gartner Group, is as shown in Figure 18.

I have displayed this tortuous thinking in full detail to illustrate the problems with many similar techniques based on simple revenue ratios. They employ elaborate logic. They calculate results with an accuracy of at least two decimal points. The complicated reasoning is then assumed to produce a result that has the appearance of rigorous legitimacy.

The problem is both in the flimsiness of the data and in the questionable assumptions. There is no way that IT, as a percentage of revenue, can be the benchmark for competitiveness. There is no way that one can validate what share of the enterprise total profits are directly attributable

55

to past or present IT expenditures. Setting the expected average Return on Investment for all corporate activities as the hurdle rate for approving new IT projects will always be a figure that is too low.

	Estimates
Need for Enterprise Benefits Based on Competitive Analysis	5% of Revenue
Share of Enterprise Benefits Achieved by IT Deployments	40% of Benefits
Expected Average ROI for All Activities	15% on Capital Invested
Expenditures Required to Achieve Average ROI Returns	1.7% of Revenue
Current Baseline Support Costs	2.43% of Revenue
Projected Level of Total IT Spending	4.13% of Revenue

Figure 18   Percentage of revenue calculations of required IT spending

Determining the IT development budget by calculating how much to spend to reach the expected Return on Investment is backwards. Coming up with an IT budget as a percentage of revenue on the basis of an unverifiable sequence is sleight-of-hand juggling. It does not offer credible planning advice. The cardinal rules of managing IT should be to look for benefits first, and only then to check if one can afford IT spending to obtain them.

Relating IT to Revenues of Baldrige Award Firms

In search of simple ratios that would tell what IT spending should be, one client requested information about IT expenditures in terms of percentages of revenues of firms distinguished for their excellence. The client defined excellence as the attributes possessed by the winners of the Baldrige Award for Quality awarded annually by the US Department of Commerce.[78]

A study of IT budgets showed the following pattern: [79]

---

78 The corporate winners with known IT budgets were: AT&T, Corning, Federal Express, General Motors, GTE, IBM, Motorola, Solectron, Texas Instruments, Westinghouse, and Xerox.

79 The Mean value = 0.034, Median = 0.0359, Minimum = 0.012, Maximum = 0.064.

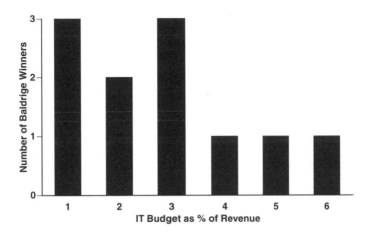

Figure 19   Distribution of IT as percent of revenue for Baldrige winners

Recognized excellence by the US government certainly does not seem to be associated with any particular percentage ratio of IT costs to sales. Other attempts to pick peer groups based on geography, Standard Industrial Code, or an estimate of technological maturity of the firm are equally inconclusive.

STATE GOVERNMENT RATIOS

The business processes one finds in use by state administrators are largely comparable. Therefore, one could expect that the ratios of IT expenditures to a state's total expenses would be similar and within a closer range than for commercial firms. However, that is not the case (Figure 20).[80]

The spread between the highest and lowest percentage ratios is greater than a factor of six, even though state government enterprises should be reasonably alike. This just proves that expense-based ratios, even for the public sector, are not useful for making comparisons. Revenue and expense ratios for information technologies are not only inaccurate and irrelevant, but also deceptive when used to explain public spending to the electorate.

80 Fiscal Year 1996 Estimated Information Resources, *Federal Computer Week*, September 2, 1996.

	Total IT Budget - $ millions	% of Total State Budget
Virginia	$528	3.30%
Texas	$974	2.74%
California	$1,600	1.68%
Florida	$298	1.34%
New Jersey	$204	1.34%
Georgia	$126	1.33%
Michigan	$350	1.23%
North Carolina	$180	1.02%
Pennsylvania	$304	0.91%
Ohio	$297	0.52%

Figure 20   IT as percentage of total state spending

What to Do

- Do not compare IT spending levels using percentage of revenue ratios.
- Trust only IT budget estimates from reliable sources, not from magazine surveys.
- Collect indicators of IT spending that relate to the sources of demand for computing services, such as demographics of the workforce, customer transactions, or business characteristics.
- Relate IT spending to activity-driven events and key business processes, especially in support of customer care, goods production, post-sale support, and product innovation.

6 Spending and Overhead Costs

Computers are the bureaucrats' factories.

Information technology budgets tend to relate to Sales, General, & Administrative expenses. Overhead personnel generates most of the demand for information services. Firms, as well as government agencies, have different information needs because they differ in how they deploy their administrative overhead. The spending on it is more a reflection of organization than of what business is conducted.

After much experimentation I found that information technology budgets showed a simple correlation with a line item on all financial statements, the Sales, General, & Administrative expense (sg&a).

SG&A as an Indicator

A closer examination showed that sg&a shown in published financial reports undervalued the total costs of information. In my consulting I obtained full accounting of all information expenses, including those allocated to the cost of sales but not counted as sg&a, such as the costs of supervisory and administrative personnel in a factory. The sg&a from audited financial statements understated the verifiable costs of information management by about fifteen percent, on the average.[81] What I define as the cost of information management is equal to what most executives designate as "overhead." That is equivalent to what some economists call the information coordination costs.

This correlation is as good as anything one is likely to find to indicate how much firms spend on computers. Neither revenues, profits, nor competitive advantage, such as market share, correlate as well with the computer budget as an examination of a firm's overhead expenses. The advantage of this rule is that it is repeatable and independent of subjective

---

81 Whenever a firm delivers information as a product or service, information-handling costs are excluded from our definition of information management since they are already included in the costs of goods sold.

judgments.[82] It is overhead, defined approximately as SG&A, that corresponds to IT spending.

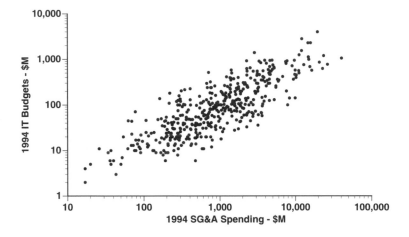

Figure 21   Overhead expenses and IT spending for a wide range of firms [83]

Although the IT/SG&A ratio shows a greater consistency than any other ratio, there are extremes that reflect unusual accounting treatment. This happens when, for example, accountants reclassify overhead as a cost of goods sold for inter-company pricing or whenever the government regulates prices on the basis of costs. Therefore, caution is in order before using any SG&A ratios to predict the IT expenses.

US corporations spend about eight cents of IT for every dollar of overhead, but this is not a fixed number. To come up with a rough estimate of IT spending on the basis IT/SG&A ratios is likely to give an inaccurate

82 There is a consulting firm that claims research findings having ninety percent or better accuracy in predicting the effectiveness of IT. They achieve that feat by collecting a small number of opinions from corporate executives. That is like asking parents and grandparents to evaluate the intelligence of their descendants. You may come up with consistent opinions, but not with verifiable metrics.

83 From the 1994 Information Productivity data base. The coefficient of determination is seventy-three percent, for a sample of 468 companies in a wide range of industries. Aerospace and a small number of transportation companies were excluded because they included avionics and reservations computers in their IT budgets. An almost identical correlation was obtained when R&D was added to SG&A costs, except that R&D is usually not reported on all financial statements and our sample for this expense was too small to be significant.

estimate. For a fair approximation, one needs to verify how the accountants reported this expense. Different firms show different levels of overhead depending on the extent of outsourcing. The overhead ratio also depends on the skills of the local accountants in tucking away overhead into the costs of sales, where any excesses are likely to be less conspicuous. In the public sector the masking of overhead costs is an art form to avoid taxpayer and legislative inquiries.

Overhead Costs

Firms, as well as government agencies, differ in how they structure their management and in how they deploy their administrative overhead. The collection of consistent overhead cost ratios across similar enterprises is rare because firms, and particularly government agencies, are reluctant to disclose information that might be embarrassing. This is especially true of tax-exempt charitable organizations that may deliver less than one third of their collections to the nominal beneficiaries.[84]

Perhaps the largest consistent sample of administrative cost ratios has its origins in the 1990 reports from 6,400 hospitals to the Medicare health insurance program administered by the us federal government. Nationwide administrative costs averaged 24.8 percent of total hospital spending, but ranged from 20.5 percent in Minnesota to 30.6 percent in Hawaii. These values compare unfavorably with the much lower – nine to eleven percent – administrative cost ratios in Canadian hospitals.[85]

Some of these differences could be explained by the way that hospitals organize or account for their work. Increasingly, medical services providers depend on contractors to deliver goods and services, which the hospitals then show as their own spending. Depending on the accounting treatment of such costs, the overhead ratios will differ.

Similar ratios are useful in any examination of the us Department of Defense. Over 640,000 military and civilian personnel engaged in commercial-like support functions for 1.5 million uniformed personnel. That yields an approximate overhead payroll ratio of over fifty percent, since the personnel in the support functions draw higher pay than those in combat-related roles.

84 Obtaining a credible statement about the uses of charitable funds is an exercise that should be attempted at least once as a sobering experience.
85 Woolhandler, S., Himmelstein, D.U., Lewontin, J.P., "Administrative Costs in us Hospitals," *The New England Journal of Medicine*, August 5, 1993.

Hospital Case

It is unreasonable to expect that one can evaluate the consumption of IT by means of any one simple ratio. The spending on IT is more a reflection of organization than of how one differs from others.

In 1968, US hospitals employed 435,000 managers and clerks to assist in the care of 1,378,000 patients. That is an administrative ratio of 31.6 percent. With increased government intervention, presumably intended to reduce costs, the number of managers and clerks increased to 1,221,600 by 1992.[86] Meanwhile, the average number of patients staying in hospitals came down to 853,000. This shift came about largely as result of shortening the length of hospital stay. This yielded an administrative ratio of 143.2 percent.

The consequence is that the relative costs of IT would rise regardless of the amount of medical services provided to patients. An opportunistic hospital administrator will surely claim that the increased patient turnover is possible because of computer-expedited admission and dismissal of hospital occupants.

This data reinforces the importance of good data collection and of careful benchmarking to understand the relationship between information technology and the activity of organizations.

What to Do

- Separate the costs of the organization between information-generating and goods-producing segments for the purpose of analysis of IT costs.
- Segregate external purchases for goods and services from all other expenses in order to obtain an index of demand for intra-organizational information services.
- Collect administrative cost ratios for separate segments of the organization for the purpose of assessing the extent of computerization for each business function.

---

86 Much of this increase comes from paperwork dictated by the increased vulnerability to litigation. This calls for elaborate documentation of every step taken in providing medical care.

7 Spending and Personnel

The need to contain chaos generates the demand for computers.

IT SPENDING corresponds to the number of information workers. Decreased costs for computer services must recognize that lower IT costs could be the result of a lower demand for IT services. Trends in per capita IT spending, rather than volume-driven IT cost ratios, are a useful indicator of efficient information management. Even close competitors will employ a different mix of resources to differentiate their products or services. Such diversity will result in the expenditures for different amounts of information resources. IT expenditures are concentrated in a small group of people, primarily in programming, finance, personnel, and market research. The size of the information staff and the IT budgets relate closely, except where outsourcing takes place.

My database encompasses information about the composition of the workforce of many firms. This includes the count of executive, managerial, professional, technical, sales, administrative, clerical, craft, operator, and service labor. People not counted for in the cost of goods or services are more likely to be in information-related occupations, and these make up most of the overhead costs.[87] In most cases IT spending corresponds to the number of information workers (Figure 22).[88]

The close relationship between information workers and IT costs suggests that when corporate cost-cutting is necessary, one should begin with the elimination of personnel performing unnecessary tasks, or shifting personnel into value-creating assignments. Any claims of the decreased

---

87 Business services firms, such as software, data services, engineering design, consulting, financial services, and banking include much of their information workforce in the direct cost of goods, whenever cost-accounting practices make that possible. I exclude such personnel from calculations since conventional industrial engineering methods apply to analyzing direct labor expenses. My research focuses on the costs of intra- and inter-organizational coordination that consumes most of the IT budget in almost every case.

88 From the information worker database. The coefficient of determination equals 78.4 percent for sixty-nine cases in this relationship.

costs for computer services must recognize that lower IT costs could be the result of a lower demand for services. It may not be a consequence of improved cost-effectiveness of the IT function.

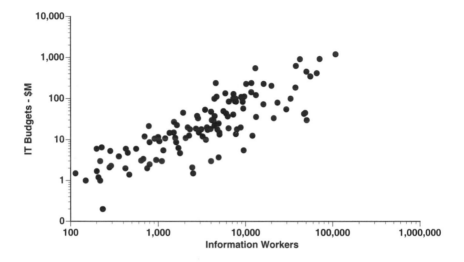

Figure 22   Information workers are a predictor of IT expenses

Information workers who are not on payroll cannot ask for computer support. Reducing IT expenses while the number of information workers declines should be a budgetary requirement, not be a noteworthy accomplishment. For a particular firm, trends in per capita IT expenditures for information workers, rather than total IT cost ratios, are a useful indicator of efficient information management.

For instance, the current claim of the US Department of Defense of holding the IT budget without any increases for four years at about $9.4 billion per annum is not impressive. One must consider that, since 1993, the Air Force, Army, and Navy have reduced airplanes, combat divisions, and warships, by approximately forty percent.[89] If the defense bureaucracy would have experienced similar cuts, one might have expected a similar reduction in IT costs.

89 The number of Army divisions was reduced from 18 to 10, or forty-four percent; fighter wings from 24 to 13, or forty-six percent; missile submarines from 34 to 14, or fifty-nine percent; while keeping most of the 640,000 non-warfighting positions without corresponding cuts. See McInerney, T.G., and Weiss, S.A., "Re-engineering the Pentagon," *The Washington Times*, December 24, 1996.

The amount of money spent per information worker varies and depends on the mix of occupational skills. Professional workers, such as computer programmers, financial analysts, and market researchers can spend as much as their salary on IT services. Clerical personnel, and particularly technicians, will consume only a fraction of their compensation for computer services per annum. The ranges in the amounts of per capita spending are as follows: [90]

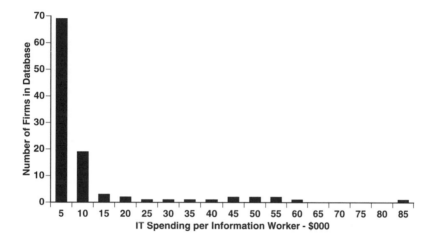

Figure 23   IT spending per information worker

It is the information workers who are the major participants in all information management processes and who consume just about all of the computer services.[91] In our sample, information workers averaged fifty percent of the total workforce and consumed $9,200 of IT services per person per year. Of that amount, the professional and clerical workers took up over eighty percent of the total IT budget. Yet, the average costs of IT for the entire firm was only $4,200 per person. This leads to the possible conclusion that for all practical purposes non-information workers consumed hardly any IT.

---

90 The median expenditures for a sample of seventy-nine manufacturing firms is $8,500 per annum, equaling approximately twelve percent of salaries.
91 Information workers are defined by the Bureau of Labor Statistics as officials & managers; professionals; technicians; sales workers; office and clerical workers.

It is the information workers, not revenue, that generate most of the SG&A costs. In turn, it is information work that breeds the spending for information technologies: [92]

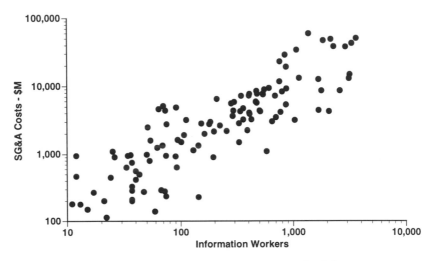

Figure 24   The information workforce generates much of the SG&A expense

There is no good reason for proposing that any business sector, such as food packaging, appliance manufacturing, or life insurance needs a fixed percentage of revenue to be allocated to the SG&A expenses. Even close competitors will employ a different mix of resources to differentiate their products or services. Such diversity will result in the expenditures of different amounts of information resources. How much will depend on whether management decides to purchase more of their resources from others rather than keeping people on their payroll. Two corporations, competing in the same industry, reporting identical revenues, may show a completely different overhead cost structure. The amount of computing power they will absorb in supporting their production, purchasing, administrative and selling activities will therefore vary a great deal.

SPENDING AND PERSONNEL

If revenue ratios are useless, then maybe some other ratio would be useful as a metric for making comparisons. Let us take a look at another fre-

92 An information worker, on the average, costs $126,000 of SG&A.

66

quently used measure: headcount ratios. The IT per capita expenditures show an even greater variance than IT per revenue ratios.

Just consider the case of two manufacturing companies in the same industry. One purchases seventy percent of materials and parts, the other purchases only thirty-five percent. The revenue/employee ratio is much higher for the company that has the lower Value-Added because it is the suppliers who employ most of the labor. Since it is employees who consume IT, the company with more people can justify buying more computers than the company with fewer people. In my manufacturing database I found that purchased materials and parts range from fifteen percent to eighty percent of revenue. No wonder that the IT/personnel ratios will vary, because employment levels will differ even for companies reporting identical revenues.

Materials and part purchases are not the only cause of distortion of the per capita ratios. In the last ten years there has been a massive substitution of purchased services for employees performing information management tasks, such as lawyers, engineers, auditors, and researchers as well as on-line computer services. As the ratio of purchased services to total employment cost increases there may be a corresponding rise or even decline in the IT/personnel ratios. It all depends on whether the outsourcing is for manufactured parts or for information services.

One would expect that knowledgeable analysts would understand the incongruity of making comparisons among firms based on personnel ratios. Unfortunately, that is not the case. I stumble into personnel-related statistics every time someone asks me to check requests for increased corporate spending plans. The most widely used formal method for justifying computer expenditures commences its analysis precisely with such evaluations.[93]

At one company, increases in per capita revenues as well as rising per capita IT expenses, as compared with a competitor, were used as the rationale for justifying a massive expansion in the IT budget. The entire rationale was faulty. The firm in question retained a large factory workforce, whereas the competitor contracted out most of its production to Malaysia. The competitor's employment consisted mostly of computer-guzzling staffs. It was a mistake to escalate the per capita IT spending to match the IT-to-revenue ratio. The firm ended up with excessive IT costs, unnecessary overheads, and falling profits.

93 A proprietary product of one of the largest consulting firms in the world.

Executives find it surprising when they see the results of my studies. I show that IT expenditures are concentrated on a small group of people, primarily in programming, finance, personnel, and market research. Highly automated administrative departments spend more than fifty percent of their total costs on IT. To fully understand the effectiveness of computer automation one must therefore study individual business functions, not the entire firm.

Operating personnel may average as little as three to five percent of their wages in computer expense. Staff management salaries are usually three times larger than the average wages in operations. Thus per capita expenditure ratios are of little value when the occupational composition of the workforce changes. During the current era of corporate restructuring this is certainly the case.

It just happens that during the last decade every unsuccessful manufacturing firm has followed the pattern of reducing operations labor and increasing the ratio of information workers to total employment. As the business Value-Added declined, management saw escalating demands for computing. What was a prescriptive model was nothing more than the reflection of a shift in labor composition.

IT AND INFORMATION STAFF

The size of the information staff and the IT budgets relate closely. I did not expect such a high correspondence between headcount and IT expenses. It suggests that what is shown as the IT budget may reflect the bias of those who do the reporting. The official IT budget data would include only what central staffs consider to be under their control.

The close relationship between the size of IT staffs and IT costs suggests a strong correlation.[94] In the case of outsourcing, the staffing would fall materially below the trend line.

---

94 From the information worker database. The coefficient of determination equals 87.2 percent for 150 cases.

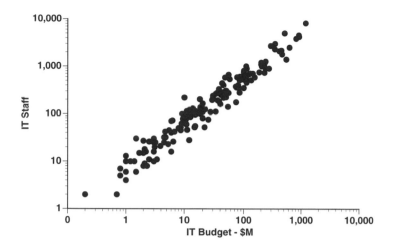

Figure 25   IT staff and IT budgets are linked

As shown in Figure 26, IT staffs could make up a significant share of total employment.

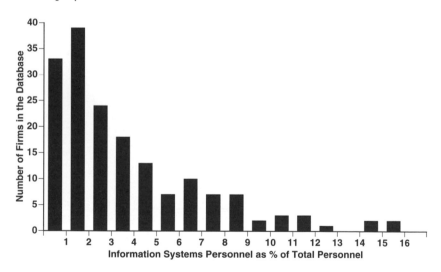

Figure 26   IT staffs as a % of total employment [95]

95 Based on a sample of 152 firms. The median value for the percent of information systems employment of total employment is 2.2 percent.

69

If a banking firm with a large IT staff outsources its IT, it will show gains in the revenue per capita even though it may be actually worse off. It is misleading to make judgments about productivity from gains shown in revenue per employee. Regrettably, such claims about productivity gains are welcomed even by sophisticated financial analysts. Whenever massive outsourcing takes place the only ratios that will reveal productivity gains will be those based on Economic Value-Added calculations and not on headcount-related indicators.

PER CAPITA SPENDING IN STATE GOVERNMENT

The functions of state governments should be comparable to each other. If the ratios based on spending are not consistent, perhaps the per capita expenditures for information technologies would be closer to each other. Unfortunately, that is not the case: [96]

	Employment (000s)	Per Capita Spending
California	323	$4,954
Virginia	116	$4,552
Texas	240	$4,058
Michigan	138	$2,536
Pennsylvania	143	$2,126
Ohio	140	$2,121
Florida	164	$1,817
New Jersey	116	$1,759
North Carolina	109	$1,651
Georgia	114	$1,105

Figure 27   Per capita IT spending for states

[96] The state information resources budgets are for 1996, the employment for 1992, from the US Bureau of the Census, *Statistical Abstracts of the United States: 1995*. Since employment levels in state government are stable, the differences in the calendar years should not cause a significant error.

Although the business functions performed by the states should be comparable, the way that they structure their workforce is not. The per capita spending covers a range of four-hundred fifty percent. One should not, however, venture an opinion about the relative merits of computer spending when comparing Georgia with California.

What to Do

- Examine opportunities for budgeting and charging for IT services based on per capita assessments.
- Keep track of per capita spending for IT, by employee function, as one of the indicators of lowered unit costs and IT efficiency.
- Develop indexes of IT expense concentration ratios to identify unusually high usage patterns without corresponding value-added contributions.
- Use the correlation between IS staffs and IT budgets as a measure of outsourcing intensity.

8 INVESTMENTS IN COMPUTERS

Tools mold the civilization.

INFORMATION technologies have become the preferred business tooling investment for US corporations. The bias that views profits primarily as the consequence of good capital investments is the fundamental flaw in current methods for justifying IT spending. Capital investment comparisons are particularly unreliable when comparisons are made on an inflation-adjusted basis. Computer vendors and employees accept payment denominated only in current currency. Computer tooling cycles offer a marked departure from similar investment cycles in manufacturing or in transportation. Computer investments have their origins within internal administrative organizations or captive monopolies, and are not as yet subject to price competition. In due course price competition for information services will resemble that which has happened in the global markets for materials and goods.

IT AND CAPITAL INVESTMENTS

How do executives come to suspect that the firm's IT expenses do not contribute to profitability? Why pick on information technologies as a possible cause of unfavorable performance?

The source of all of such apprehensions is a bias to view profits primarily as the result of good capital investments. That is why Return on Investment remains the primary measure of performance. If spending money on equipment does not deliver profits and results, such equipment cannot be effective. The proof of the utility of computers remains hidden in returns on their value as a capital asset. In the past, the relative amount of tooling investments always favored production workers. Office workers were always at a disadvantage, but that has changed. There are now more information workers than production workers and the costs for computers now exceed the costs for basic industrial equipment.

Information technologies have become the preferred business tooling investment for US corporations. Economists define business tooling as producer-durable equipment. It is one of the most telling indicators of business priorities. The number of executives who say they will increase spending on computer hardware and software has more than doubled in the past five years. This now exceeds the amounts spent on new product development, sales promotions, and facility expansion: [97]

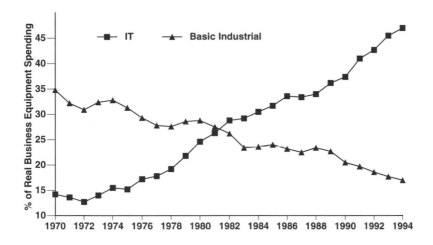

Figure 28   Trends in US capital equipment spending

The expenditures in the above graph are not strictly equivalent, because they display gross, not net, investment.[98] The gross IT put in place in the last decade had an extraordinarily short life whereas modern basic industrial equipment has now greater longevity because of its greater reliability. Computer equipment heads for the scrap heap at an accelerating rate, whereas basic industrial equipment benefits from design that extends its life. Therefore, on a net asset basis, I doubt if the current value of computing equipment now exceeds that of all other tooling. The productivity of the US capital assets may be actually declining as short-lived investments receive a higher priority than long-term possessions.

97 "Computers Capture Capital Spending," *Business Week*, June 3, 1996, p. 8.
98 *Morgan Stanley US Investment Research Newsletter*, July 15, 1994, p. 13.

Problems with Inflation-Adjusted Statistics

The capital spending trends in Figure 28 are in constant 1987 dollars. This means that the importance of computer capital is actually greater as computer prices drop faster than the government inflation adjustment indexes may indicate. The standard government index for adjusting the prices of computing capital does not adequately reflect the gains in the capacity of computing in terms of 1994 purchasing power for computing. As result of such manipulation the government ends up overstating US productivity growth.

The most vocal critic of the government's statistical contortions is the economist David A. Wyss.[99] It is a fallacy to make a 1994 lap-top computer equivalent to a 1964 mainframe machine even though both have equivalent technical ratings. The lap-top rests in someone's briefcase most of the time and handles only a few applications. The data-center machines of yesteryear worked around the clock, attended by dozens of operators to maximize useful output. In the 1960s the big computers had an economic life of at least eight years. Nowadays, laptops end up as disposable equipment in less than three years. The government's number grinders have used technical specifications such as processor speeds to come up with an estimate of the value of work delivered by the new computers. They estimated the value of the work by accepting the assumption that the engineering characteristics of computers reflect their capacity to deliver results. No wonder they came up with productivity gains higher than they are in reality.[100]

The opposite bias in government reporting applies to the way the federal government accounts for the IT budgets. When I assumed responsibility for the largest of such expenditures, the Department of Defense, I was surprised to see how much growth showed up in the budget plans, even though the expenditures remained level in terms of current dollars. The total IT budget numbers reported to the Office of Management and Budget were in constant 1987 dollars, which understated past spending and overstated future projections.

---

99 Koretz, G., "The Revolution in US Productivity May be Overstated," *Business Week*, August 29, 1994.
100 It is the purpose of government statistical offices to make the administration look as good and competent as possible. To this end one does not need to invent numbers. Interpreting statistics in the best possible light usually does the job.

In 1992 I met with the statistical staff from the Department of Commerce to gain an understanding of how they translated current IT budgets into comparable 1987 dollars. The analysts relied primarily on the mainframe manufacturers' published claims about the declining costs of dollars per Million Instructions per Second (MIPS) for their adjustment calculations. The statisticians did not make adequate allowance for the eighty percent of IT budgets that were for salaries which had inflated steadily. The government projections about the growth of computer budgets in the Federal government understated historical costs. Such abstract calculations made possible claims about past cost containment. They made it possible to claim future expense reductions against fictitious costs that would never happen.

The discussion about the use of inflation-adjusted comparisons should serve as a warning against attempts to use such numbers for making any comparisons about IT spending. Computer vendors accept payment denominated only in current currency. The payroll checks are in real currency and not in inflation-adjusted cash. Despite frequent attempts by government and vendors to change the scale with which IT is measured, only current cash flow is appropriate for any evaluations. The argument that if a Rolls-Royce would be a computer, it would now cost only twenty cents is irrelevant when asking for repeated budget increases that exceed revenue, profit and inflation growth.

SIGNIFICANCE OF IT INVESTMENTS

IT is now the single largest line item expense in corporate America's capital spending budgets. After a period of stagnation in 1986-1988, when preoccupation with the introduction of microcomputers affected the capacity of corporations to absorb technological change, IT is again leading a new investment wave.

The new upsurge began in 1991 with the proliferation of decentralized computing and local area networks. Often these investments carry the label of client/server computing, even though there have always been clients and servers. This misnomer is a good example of the tendency of computer vendors to attach catchy labels to any phenomenon that triggers yet another wave of spending. The client/server surge is nothing but the continuation of a much older trend toward dismemberment of the centralized data processing organizations in favor of distribution of computing towards greater local controls. In terms of investment economics, the client/server happening is a testimonial that the worshippers of Moore's Law have displaced the adherents to Grosch's Law.[101]

If one interpretation of Grosch's Law was "IBM gives and IBM takes away," Moore's Law is "Intel gives and Microsoft takes away." In each case, these abstractions became the rationale for a new trend in capital spending and for enormous gains in the wealth of the primary beneficiaries derived from each development. As I write this there are already early signs that even Moore's megatrend is waning in much the same way as Grosch's did, thus devaluing most of the recently invested computer capital.

It is the success of Moore's Law that diminished the importance of equipment expenses as the decisive element in the costs of computing. As microprocessor life cycles shrink from years to months, they become a disposable supply item. For instance, the first commercial microprocessor, the Intel 4004, had a life of seven years (from 1971 until 1978). Its successors were the Intel 8086 (1978-1982), Intel 80286 (1982-1985), Intel 386 (1985-1989), Intel 486 (1989-1993), and the Intel Pentium (1993-1995), with a technology cycle of less than two years.[102] With shorter life and enormous expansion in the processing power, the microprocessor will be easier and cheaper to replace than keyboards, display screens or power supplies. Software and employee training, not electronics, will end up as the major lasting benefit from IT investments.

Though IT accounts for only about two percent of the revenues of firms, it is its relative importance as a capital investment that gives it its historic significance. Man is a tool-making creature. What historians write about early civilizations comes from an examination of the tools people use. Therefore, one may rightfully designate the US as having entered into the computer age, in the same way as historians describe evolutionary progressions in terms of the stone, bronze and iron ages.

The Outcome of Investment Cycles

Each of the prior IT investment cycles has ended up by expanding the scope, capacity, and pervasiveness of information technologies in the life-

---

101 For a discussion of Grosch's Law see Chapter 3. Moore's Law states that the number of microprocessor circuits will double every eighteen months without an increase in costs. It is the rationale for moving supercomputer power to the desktops and laptops to make it easier to sell increasingly complex software to customers.

102 Maibach, M.C., "Government Must Get Up to Speed," *Upside*, October 1996.

blood of businesses and ultimately in consumer habits. Most importantly, at each stage of development, the investment cycle expanded the knowledge capital by increasing the number of people involved in the computerization processes.[103]

The cost reductions claimed at every turn of the investment cycle rarely, if ever, could be proven because organizations did not have in place the metrics by which to compare results with expectations. In this respect the investment cycles in computer tooling are a marked departure from similar investment cycles in manufacturing or in transportation. In those instances, lower labor costs were not only measurable, but reflected in lower prices and improved quality of goods and services.

The difference between the manufacturing and computer investment cycles is that the manufacturing tooling investments were subject to the discipline of a global competitive market place. In the case of computer investment cycles, they have their origins within internal administrative organizations or captive monopolies, and therefore they are not subject to price contention.

This condition is changing, but only very slowly. The Internet has introduced elements of price competition for global offerings that make on-line purchases practical, such as for airline reservation systems, financial markets, luxury goods, and entertainment. It may take another ten to twenty years, however, before the price for information services resembles that which has happened to global markets for materials and goods.

In the case of the public sector, which consumes perhaps as much as twenty percent of the computer expenses, there is little evidence that cost reductions were ever the reason for computerization. In the absence of competitive constraints, the public sector bureaucracies keep justifying increased computer investments to cope with steadily increasing administrative complexity, much of which is self-generated or imposed by the legislatures.

The build-and-tear down practices associated with each of the computerization investment cycles are the primary reason that we have not seen effective cost reductions in overall information processing costs in our society. Top management has become accustomed to short life expectancies of their systems investments and have paid little attention to the need to preserve IT capital by expecting a longer useful life from it.[104]

103 For a detailed discussion of computer cycles see Chapter 25.
104 For an elaboration of this theme see Chapter 38.

Not much has carried over from one IT investment cycle to the next without enormous maintenance and conversion costs at each turn.

Executives will recognize soon that discarding the accumulation of past systems investments is not the only way to manage IT expenses. The pressure for lowering the costs of ownership of computers will surely bring forth better investment policies. Their primary criteria will be the preservation of knowledge, both in the machines and in the newly acquired capabilities of the employees. Such a change will surely favor technology options that segregate the rapid obsolescence of the electronics from the relative constancy of the elementary tasks found in business processes.

The great excitement stimulated by the Java language from Sun Microsystems reflects the dawning recognition that businesses must find new ways to preserve their information assets. The Java language offers the possibility of making application logic independent of investments in computer equipment. It is the breaking of the chains that tied short-lived investments, microprocessors, operating systems and language compilers, to the long-term assets that will be the scene for staging the scenarios for gaining new economic advantages.

Economic Significance of IT Spending

The share of capital investments in computers is not the only measure of their importance. Some forty percent of American households had computers in 1996, with the prospect of saturation levels reaching that of color television within a decade. Sales of computers accounted for one-third of the economic growth during the 1992-1996 economic expansion. The 1996 spending on computers accounted for close to three percent of the GDP, compared to three-and-half percent for automobiles and light trucks, which have dominated consumer durable goods spending for the last seventy years.[105] The six-fold increase in computer spending in the last decade has taken place even though the relative price per unit of computing power kept dropping at a rate of at least twenty percent per year.

The US economy is placing an overwhelming bet on computerization as one of the primary solutions to its declining productivity. Therefore, the capacity to extract discernible productivity gains from information tech-

---

105 "Computers Put the Zip in the GDP," *Business Week*, November 4, 1996, p. 206.

nologies becomes one of the most important challenges faced by managers.

What to Do

- Avoid using Return on Investment (ROI) methods for justifying computer projects.
- Use only current cash values for making IT investment comparisons. Inflation-adjusted comparisons are unreliable and misleading.
- Do not apply technical performance ratios, such as dollars per MIPS or costs for functions point, for predicting the performance of IT investments.
- Prepare for dramatic cost reductions as outsourcing companies start competing for market share on a massive scale.

Part III
Explanations

9 COMPUTER PARADOX REVISITED

Actions without verifiable consequences are paradoxical.

POST-INDUSTRIAL economies show a decline in productivity as they shift from industrial to information-based occupations. The causes for this decline remain an unsolved puzzle, though ineffective computerization surely must explain some of the shortfalls in productivity. The concentration on the marginal productivity of installed computer capital assets has influenced most academic research. It lead to studies of computers as a capital investment, as if they were machine tools, which is misleading because computers are primarily artifacts that influence the costs and behavior of people. Micro-economic studies are more useful than macro-economic analyses that occupy economists. The dramatic disparity between low growth in employment and high growth in revenues, profits, and overhead for major US corporations raises questions about the effectiveness of computer investments.

Everyone attributes the term "computer paradox" to the Nobel Prize winner in economics, MIT professor Robert Solow, though I could not find a formal paper where he defines exactly what this means. It appears that Solow searched, in the early 1980s, for evidence of computer-induced gains and mentioned the paradox phrase in a talk. He must have reflected on the fact that US labor productivity in the business sector had declined to an annual growth rate of only 0.8 percent while computer technology purchases were rising at an annual growth rate of eleven percent. *The Economist* reported the widespread deceleration in productivity gains as shown in Figure 29.[106]

All post-industrial economies show a decline in productivity as they shift from industrial to information-based occupations. However, one should not attribute such weakening entirely to computerization though the choice of computers as the primary investment in the last decade must account for some of this slow-down. Not having convincing evidence of the reasons for the decline, economists keep arguing about the causes of

---

106 "The Hitchhiker's Guide to Cybernomics," *The Economist*, September 28, 1996.

the productivity lags. It remains an unsolved puzzle, though ineffective computerization surely must explain some of the productivity shortfalls.

	1960-1973	1973-1995
France	5.3%	2.5%
Japan	8.4%	2.4%
Italy	6.3%	2.1%
Britain	3.9%	1.9%
Germany	4.5%	1.6%
Canada	2.9%	1.2%
United States	2.6%	0.8%

Figure 29   Annual average % increases in business sector labor productivity

I believe that the substance for the idea of a computer paradox originally came from a paper by Gary Loveman, also from MIT. In the late 1980s his work about poor returns from investments in computers became the source of most academic references on this subject. My book about the absence of a relationship between computer spending and productivity dates from the same period.[107] Whereas Loveman emphasized returns on capital, I concentrated on the inconclusive ratios of value-added to spending for information.

Loveman's findings appeared in the MIT program *Management in the 1990s*.[108] He concluded that "… expenditures on information technology capital were less effective in improving productivity than any other type of expenditures considered." The Strategic Planning Institute of Cambridge, MA, was the source of the data on which Loveman based his conclusions.[109] The faculty at the Graduate School of Industrial Management at Carnegie-Mellon University used identical MPIT data. Their researchers

107   Strassmann, P.A., *Information Payoff – The Transformation of Work in the Electronic Age,* The Free Press, 1985.
108   Loveman, G.W., "An Assessment of the Productivity Impact of Information Technologies," in *Information Technology and the Corporation of the 1990s: Research Studies,* Allen, T.J. and Scott-Morton, M.S., (ed.), MIT Press, Cambridge, MA, 1994.
109   The data gathering for the Strategic Planning Institute's research on Management Productivity and Information Technology (MPIT) was under the direction of Paul A. Strassmann and guided by Sidney Schoeffler.

confirmed that IT spending did not correlate with business perfor-mance.[110]

Loveman chose to concentrate on the profitability of computers as capital assets. It just happened that the value of computer assets was one of the smallest line items collected through elaborate MPIT data forms. My examination of this data found that the valuation of computer assets was perhaps the least reliable of the many survey items. Companies reported their installed asset valuations of computers with little consistency. For example, many reported their leased equipment as an expense and not as depreciable property. This was often because in the early 1980s a large share of computer budgets paid for expensive mainframe equipment, and approximately one third of that was not purchased but came from leasing firms.[111]

In my research I avoid using computer asset valuations as an indica-tor of IT spending because these data are unreliable. Because economists and econometricians favor analyses of capital costs over an examination of operating expenses, Loveman concentrated his attention on the reported capital assets. He showed that any marginal capital investments in com-puters, on the average, would be the worst investment choice for firms in the research sample. He missed the point that it is not the average perfor-mance, but the differences in the profit performance between superior and inferior firms that matters. It is the understanding of differences, not the analysis of averages, that offers the best insights into the effectiveness of computers.[112]

Nevertheless, Loveman's discovery received widespread attention and provided the basis to those who claimed that a paradox was present.[113] His concentration on the marginal productivity of installed computer capital

---

110   Barua, A., Kriebel, C., and Mukhopadhyay, T., "Information Technology and Business Value: An Analytic and Empirical Investigation," University of Texas at Austin Working Paper (May 1991).

111   Leasing companies took care of remarketing used equipment whenever capacity or software needs dictated replacing existing equipment. Corporate customers did not have the expertise to do that.

112   It is this neglect that gave rise to the story about the statistical economist who drowned in a river that was, on the average, two feet deep.

113   A more accurate description would have been a conundrum, which is any question of a perplexing nature. A paradox is a statement that is contrary to common belief, or a statement that is self-contradictory, absurd. The economic returns from computers are indeed perplexing. They are not self-contradictory or absurd, unless one approaches the matter with the presumption that computers are indeed always profitable.

assets influenced the follow-on academic research at MIT. It lead to studies of computers as a capital investment, as if they were machine tools. It applied theories that were useful in studying investments in industrial capital, instead of analyzing computerization as an organic element of information management. What Loveman began continued to channel researchers into inquiries that were not only difficult but contradictory.

EXAMINATION OF THE PARADOX

I prefer repeatable measurements, especially if the data collection follows a standard routine for securing procedurally consistent data. Instead of analyzing macro-economic data from government statisticians, I favor micro-economic corporate financial results as certified by auditors for examination by stock market analysts.

The US Bureau of Labor Statistics publishes tables used in most productivity analyses. This data is unreliable or incomplete for fifty-eight percent of the total US output that originates from service industries. Its reliability is suspect for many other sectors, such as education, health care, and the government. Without a market that sets competitive prices, the government defines the productivity of these sectors as one hundred percent. The characterizations of the output value of government, education, and health care as being equal to the costs of its inputs results in a meaningless ratio which almost certainly overstates real effectiveness. Consequently, the productivity paradox derived from government data must be surely worse than even the most vocal critics of computerization can claim.

Annual reports of corporations contain data about revenues, employment, profits, and assets. This information is timely, comes from a sufficiently large number of sources, and is subject to scrutiny by accountants, shareholders, stock market analysts, and financial institutions. These checks and the quarterly publication of results reduce the likelihood of misleading reporting. The Securities Exchange Commission, the Financial and Accounting Standards Board, the tax authorities, and elaborate auditor practice manuals guide the procedures for gathering and reporting operating results. They follow prescribed rules for certification as being suitable for investment advice.

A number of commercial firms collect and edit the data from corporate annual reports and publish the results with reasonable uniformity and reliability. This makes such data comparable over a period of years, consistent across industrial sectors and independent of geographic location. Consequently, it is possible to understand the elements that drive the creation of economic value by major corporations. The engines of growth, productivity, employment, and national wealth are the corporations that report about their performance in this manner.

Obtaining information about computer expenditures over an extended time is much harder. The best we have are numbers from articles and tabulations found in computer magazines. I managed to collect from public sources the annual IT budgets for one hundred thirty eight giant US corporations for the period from 1988 through 1994. Because of large overhead costs concentrated in these firms, this sample accounts for about a third of total corporate IT spending in the US.

However, my most reliable data come from clients who wish to benchmark their spending against their look-alike peers. Paying clients do not have much of an incentive to distort their data, because they would be only misleading themselves when accepting any comparisons.

Knowing IT spending and the corresponding financial performance makes it possible to test whether there is a computer paradox. If the growth in profitability (i.e., a measure of economic output) of corporations is greater than the growth in spending for IT (i.e., input) then the computer paradox would vanish. This would signal that expenditures for computers could yield improved economic performance. On the other hand, if the gains in profitability are less than the growth in IT, the computer paradox would remain unresolved. Such a condition would suggest that the links between computers, productivity, and economic performance are inconclusive.

FINDINGS FOR 1988-1994

During this period, with a 67.4 percent gain, IT budgets increased much faster than the growth in revenues (29.6 percent) or the rise in profits (39.7 percent). Only employment lagged, gaining 2.3 percent, as shown in the following: [114]

---

114   Data obtained from clients of Strassmann, Inc. are included in the averages.

The growth rates for revenues, profits, and overhead and those for IT budgets do not reflect favorably on the contributions of computers. Particularly discouraging is the discovery that the Sales, General, and Administrative (SG&A) overhead has grown faster than revenues or profits. Yet, it is these information overheads that everyone assumed would be most amenable to computerization.

	1988	1990	1992	1994	Growth
Total Revenues ($M)	1,587,64	1,813,27	1,882,90	2,057,34	29.6%
Total Profits ($M)	85,321	73,500	64,290	119,213	39.7%
Total SG&A ($M)	256,366	308,246	346,722	363,706	41.9%
Total IT Budgets ($M)	28,061	37,544	40,723	46,973	67.4%
Total Employees	9,235,00	9,507,67	9,442,40	9,450,43	2.3%

Figure 30   Growth rates in key indicators and IT spending

Information workers also contribute most to the SG&A expenditures. It is these workers who have received the largest share of computer capital as compared with all other workers: [115]

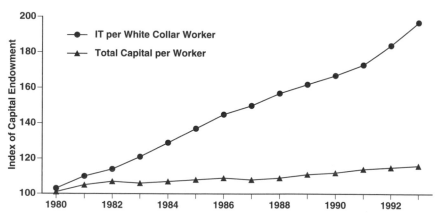

Figure 31   Capital investments concentrated on computerization of information workers

115   Morgan Stanley, *US Investment Research Newsletter*, July 15, 1994.

If high levels of computerization of office workers had delivered the expected productivity gains, then SG&A should be slowing down in comparison with revenues, profits, and employment. That would give a strong indication that the much desired computer payoff was taking place. It has not happened.

The dramatic disparity between low growth in employment and high growth in revenues, profits, and overhead created a passionate debate when I first passed around these findings. Computer advocates claimed that keeping corporate personnel growth below revenue and profit gains proved that computers were productive.

The most plausible explanation for slow growth in employment in the major corporations was that computerization may have contributed to reducing direct labor costs through factory and goods-handling automation.[116] However, most reductions in personnel did not originate in productivity gains but from outsourcing labor-intensive functions in manufacturing.

One would expect that the costs of corporate overhead would decrease with the relatively small gains in overall employment and heavy computerization. The opposite happened. The costs of information handling, management, and coordination (concentrated in SG&A) rose faster than all other measures of performance. Despite widely heralded announcements that corporations were slimming down their overhead bureaucracies through computerization, the data clearly show that the US information costs for management and coordination grew despite increasingly hefty computer budgets.[117]

116 This conclusion is supported by recent findings from a DRI/McGraw Hill study for 1994-95. While the manufacturing sector showed annual productivity gains of four percent, the total non-farm business productivity increased only 0.5 percent. That suggests that the service-sector productivity, which accounts for most of the non-farm businesses productivity, has been either declining or is negative. Even after making an allowance for the alleged under-reporting of overall productivity numbers, the performance of the computer-gobbling service sector does not look good. See Koretz, G., "How to Raise us Productivity," *Business Week*, December 9, 1996.

117 The peculiarities of this phenomenon will be the principal subject in the forthcoming information productivity book.

What to Do

- Avoid using computer asset valuations as an indicator of IT spending because this information is irrelevant.
- Rely primarily on verifiable corporate information instead of highly unreliable government data about information technologies and productivity.
- Keep track of long-term growth rates of employment, overhead, purchases, economic value-added, and workforce composition to collect useful indexes of demand for information services.

10 Importance of IT Spending

Cash on the table is the best measure of business priorities.

IT BUDGETS have grown faster than any other indicator of corporate performance. The inexorable rise in IT costs is finally attracting the top executives' attention to the actions of CIOs, but not in the way they always hoped to get. Exhaustive hearings about IT budgets are taking place. It is not how much one spends on computers, but how well management spends it for realization of gains.

IT spending is now comparable to about half of the profits of major corporations, as shown in the following tabulation: [118]

	1988	1989	1990	1991	1992	1993	1994
Total Revenues	1.8%	2.0%	2.1%	2.2%	2.2%	2.2%	2.3%
Total Profits	32.9%	40.5%	51.1%	74.9%	63.3%	47.0%	39.4%
Total SG&A	11.0%	12.5%	12.2%	11.9%	11.8%	12.2%	12.9%

Figure 32   IT spending as % ratio of selected indicators

The decline in the IT spending as a ratio of profits for 1993 and 1994 arises from the cyclical gains in corporate profits. There is every reason to believe that during the next economic downturn IT spending will revert to its long-term average. In that case it would continue to exceed fifty percent of corporate profits.

Steven Roach, the chief economist of the Morgan Stanley investment firm, seems to support this outlook. He announced in 1991 that productivity may have finally turned around because of downsizing and streamlining of corporate staffs. He changed his mind in 1996 when he announced that "... the productivity gains of the 1990s are more a by-

---

118   The share of the US gross domestic product is also a good indicator of IT growth. The 1980 purchases of information technologies were $47 billion, or one percent of the nation's total output of goods and services. This grew to $251 billion by end of 1996, amounting to 3.6 percent of GDP. This shows a compound annual growth rate of eleven percent, or faster than any other economic index. See Zuckerman, L., "Do Computers Lift Productivity?" *The New York Times*, January 2, 1997.

product of downsizing than a reflection of the upgrading in the quality of worker contributions. ... Increasingly hollowed companies are the end game of an approach that is dominated by downsizing ... this is a path that ultimately is not sustainable either from the standpoint of productivity or improved competitiveness."[119]

Independent of any cycles in profits, revenues, and productivity, the most noteworthy indicator of the rising importance of IT spending is the steady rise in its expenditure per employee. With IT per capita spending in 1994 averaging $4,970 per employee, this cost is the second largest indirect expense, after health, pension and other personnel benefits:[120]

	1988	1989	1990	1991	1992	1993	1994	Growth
$ IT per capita	3,039	3,628	3,949	4,258	4,313	4,668	4,970	63.6%

Figure 33   Per capita IT spending

The inexorable rise in IT costs is finally attracting the top executives' attention to the actions of CIOs, but not in the way they always hoped to get. Exhaustive hearings about IT budgets are taking place, but not for the reasons they had hoped. It is always easier to examine requests for computers than to understand why an organization has an insatiable appetite for data. It is very difficult for CIOs to explain why demand for computing keeps growing faster than revenues, profits, and employment. Without a good explanation the frustrations of top corporate executives will keep rising. They will find it difficult to reconcile increasing expenditures for computers in the absence of demonstrable profit contributions. The most predictable outcome of such dissatisfaction will be the immolation of yet another computer executive.

On the other hand, the relative importance of IT in the cost structure of firms may be much higher than indicated in reports. As the IT expenditures attract high level scrutiny, there is a growing inclination by local operators to acquire hardware, software, and consulting services that do not show up in the IT budget. That makes an explanation of the business value of computer investments even more confusing and makes computer budget reviews unhappy episodes for those who are supposed to be accountable for total spending levels.

119   Morgan Stanley, *US Investment Research Newsletter*, May 17, 1996.
120   There are firms that spend in excess of forty percent of payroll expense on IT.

Computer Spending as a Necessity

When statistics about the growth of IT being faster than SG&A and profits first appeared in the press, I received many letters suggesting that my conclusions were unwarranted.[121] Many of the writers wondered if competitive pressures were hiding the positive productivity contributions of computers. They cited the example of a bank that had to install new computer applications because competitors were taking similar actions. Accordingly, the bank had to do it because otherwise their market share and gross revenue would erode.

The "must do" argument is typical of the most widespread reasoning to rationalize the mounting IT expenditures. It implies an inevitability without having to examine causality. The problem with "the competitor made me do it" answers to spending money is that one would have to prove that profits would have decreased without increased computer spending.[122] That may work by attributing all incremental profits to a favorite computer project. It does not prove that a firm could have improved profitability by other means at a lesser cost.

The plain fact is there is no correlation whatsoever between IT spending and profitability in banking or any other industry. Therefore, the hypothetical arguments are hard to sustain when subjected to thorough financial examination. It is not possible to prove losses that could have possibly happened, in the same way as it is impossible to conjecture savings lost without additional computers. All we can do is abstain from speculation and record the reality as it is. Companies spend money on computers primarily because they incur the costs of coordination. Such costs are comparable for look-alike firms, even though their profits are not. The only conclusion is that it is not how much one spends on computers, but how well management spends it that delivers gain.

The best thing a corporate chief executive can do is make sure that the rise of computer spending does not get ahead of gains in profitability and productivity. But, this will require a different approach to the measurement, planning, and execution of IT projects than is currently the case.

---

121 Strassmann, P.A., "Spending Without Results?" *Computerworld*, April 15, 1996.
122 That may be the case when competition introduces a computer-based innovation that benefits customers. For every successful banking ATM (Automatic Teller Machine) there are many failed attempts to bring electronic services to the consumer. It took a long time before ATMs became profitable.

THE PERSISTENT DOUBTS

It may be too early to banish the computer paradox into oblivion, despite contrary claims and headlines by leading magazines about its demise.[123] For instance an editorial in one of the most prestigious information systems journals announced that "... in the past year, studies have shined some powerful light into the dark corners of the alleged paradox. These studies permit the kinds of high-visibility charges we have seen in the past to be intelligently confronted. Much of this new evidence has come from the work of Eric Brynjolfsson and Lorin Hitt. ... Based on their data ... the productivity paradox has disappeared by 1991."[124]

What to Do

- Prepare for an era where corporate management will start applying tough financial criteria to all its spending proposals, including an examination of ongoing operating and maintenance expenses.
- Install comprehensive metrics that not only concentrate on technological efficiency but also convey convincing evidence of managerial effectiveness.

123 *The Economist* of January 22, 1994 said that the reported eighty-one per cent average gross annual returns on IT investments shows there is "... reason for IT to finally pay off." Also see, Brynjolfsson, E. "Technology's True Payoff," *InformationWeek*, October 10, 1994 asserted that "... the pendulum has now swung with full force in the opposite direction ..." as a reaction to the press discussions of the computer paradox which was "... out of proportion to the more carefully worded academic papers on the subject."
124 *Management Information Systems Quarterly*, Vol. 18, Number 2, June 1992.

11 Exorcising the Computer Paradox

Absolution is more comfortable than understanding.

TRADITIONAL macroeconomic data do not capture the benefits that accrue to firms from deployment of information technologies. The financial impact of information technologies has not always been positive and the "information paradox" has not disappeared, contrary to claims. The reasoning that computer inputs increased business productivity by boosting outputs, as measured by revenue gains, is also not credible. What academics declared as productivity gains largely reflects structural shifts in the goods producing sector of the economy. Expecting unreasonably high returns on computer investments inhibits taking advantage of sound but unspectacular opportunities.

The lack of any evidence that computers have improved the competitive position of the US economy has continued to haunt the purveyors of information technologies. The very small number of studies which document claims that computers do indeed deliver great economic wealth receive repeated citations. Therefore, they deserve special attention here.

NATIONAL RESEARCH COUNCIL REPORT

In the spring of 1991 the Computer Science and Telecommunications Board of the National Research Council convened a committee to study the impact of IT on the performance of service activities. Its purpose was to settle once and for all the debates about the relationship between computerization and productivity in the US.

Focusing on the service industries' uses of computers is appropriate for any examination of the computer paradox. Service enterprises bought eighty percent of the information processing equipment sold in the US during the 1980s. According to NRC estimates, that computer equipment was worth $750 billion, not counting software. Most of this investment was in the air transport, distribution, telecommunications, health, banking, and insurance sectors. Although this investment was substantial, productivity in the service sector increased only by an average of about 0.7 percent per year over the productivity of the prior two decades. This was materially less than the historical gains in US productivity, which had averaged over 2.5 percent for over a century. The actual productivity gains could be less, since the macroeconomic indicators for measuring productivity in the services sectors tend to overstate output.[125]

After prolonged debates and extensive hearings the NRC report was issued in 1994. The process of coming up with conclusions took two and a half years. The long lead-time in publishing the findings suggests that answers were not easy to come by.[126]

The findings of this prestigious Board are ambivalent. They conclude that "... traditional macroeconomic data collected to date do not capture many important benefits or costs that accrue to firms from deployment of information technologies." The Board thus sidestepped dealing with the utility of the productivity statistics from the US government even though it was this data that originally was the reason for questioning the productivity of computers.

The Board neither proved nor disproved whether there was such a thing as a computer paradox. It reported that: "... The use of information technologies has had a direct and positive operational impact on the performance of services by many individual firms, but the financial impact has not always been as positive."

The Board thus conformed to the long Washington tradition of making inconclusive pronouncements about a controversial topic. To arrive at its findings, it sent out a questionnaire and conducted interviews with executives of forty-six companies that had a public reputation as IT innovators. It should not have been surprising that the Board received glowing reports. The acknowledged technology proponents reported the computers' great contributions in achieving competitive gains and realizing improvements in customer service. Since no data or economic analysis was necessary to support any of the claims, the Board was thus free to report all findings as encouraging anecdotes.

The selective reporting of accolades to computerization did little to exorcise the paradox, since no hard data supported any of the claims. Evidence obtained from a sample of advocates of computerization may be

125 *Banquet Paribas,* "The Economic Consequences of Information Technologies," 1995.
126 National Research Council, "Information Technology in the Service Society," *National Academy Press,* Washington, DC, 1994.

helpful for illustrative purposes, but this is not acceptable as a research methodology. The Board just did not deliver any verifiable conclusions on the productivity gains.

The NRC report concluded: "... the rapid growth of services and changes in the nature of service activities ... underscore the need for a better understanding. Better statistical data is not the only need. Specific research and continuous monitoring are also needed to better understand ... impacts of information technologies."

What we received is a research report calling for further research, which is usual whenever researchers do not have the facts to support their conclusions. The work of the Board began as an auspicious effort to offer scientifically valid insights about the effects of information technologies on the service economy. Unfortunately, no evidence appears anywhere in this 270 page report.[127] The computer paradox thus received another reprieve from judgment.

Making the Paradox Disappear

It was with a sense of jubilation that both *Fortune*[128] and *Business Week*[129] announced that Erik Brynjolfsson and Lorin Hitt of MIT disproved the existence of the computer paradox. These researchers found that the average gross return from 1987-1991 on IT investments was eighty-one percent for 367 large manufacturing and service companies. The press concluded that "... the productivity paradox disappeared in 1991." *The Economist* joined in the celebration of these results.[130]

---

127 The service economy accounts for about 74 percent of the value added to the US GDP and about 76 percent of national employment.
128 Magnet, M., "The Productivity Payoff Arrives," *Fortune*, June 27, 1994, p. 79, on the basis of Brynjolfsson's studies concluded "... for years, info tech didn't seem worth the investment. But at last, some smart companies are figuring out how to make computers pay."
129 The cover of the June 14, 1993 special report by *Business Week* announced: "The Technology Payoff – Now Productivity is Finally Bursting out ..." The feature story gave credit to Brynjolfsson and Hitt for discovering that "... the return on investment information systems averaged a stunning fifty-four percent for manufacturing and sixty-eight percent for all businesses surveyed."
130 "What Computers are For," *The Economist*, January 22, 1994.

The Revelation

In a widely quoted article, Brynjolfsson extended his original claims by asserting that "... computers improved productivity significantly more than any other type of investment ... the gross ROI (Return-on-Investment) averaged over fifty percent per year for computers, compared with less than ten percent for other types of capital."[131]

News that one could reap enormous returns on computer investments must have been welcome to corporate controllers. Financial executives are aware that the ten year average shareholder returns for the top *Fortune 1000* corporations was only 14.9 percent while the cost of capital was 12.8 percent.[132] After allowing for business risks, the 2.1 percent spread to create wealth and increase the living standards of the US population was a very small number as compared with what computers claimed to offer. Announcing that a large chunk of the capital invested by corporations could be earning eighty-one percent returns would certainly merit everybody's exhilaration.[133]

The postulated good news was that computer investments should be realizing investment returns sixty-eight percent above the average costs of corporate capital. The conspicuous bad news was that the actual results from corporate financial reports did not match expectations. If the largest share of investments can earn extraordinary profits, why were the average shareholder returns only 2.1 percent above the cost of capital? Where were the leaks?

It's All in the Calculations

The reason that Brynjolfsson and Hitt came up with eighty-one percent investment returns depends on their assumptions and the way they calcu-

131 Brynjolfsson, E., "Paradox Lost?" *CIO Magazine*, May 1, 1994, p. 26.
132 Stern Stewart Management Services, *The Stern Stewart Performance 1000 Database*, New York, NY, 1994
133 While reviewing this text Brynjolfsson noted that comparing the 12.8% cost of corporate capital with the claimed 81% returns was misleading because the cost of IT capital is much higher than the average cost of corporate capital. Enticing financial executives with expectations of an average 81% return for investments in computer capital is unrealistic and unverifiable. It is largely irrelevant because computer capital makes up less than 10% of the life cycle cost of computer projects.

lated productivity improvements.[134] In their original paper they asserted that increases in revenue for 1987-1991 reflected gains in output. They argued that the increases in revenues were caused by a one percent increase in computer capital "... when all the other inputs were held constant."[135]

This approach is a reflection of the bias of the Cobb-Douglas production function equations. This is a favorite tool of econometric academics and the basis of the productivity calculations by Brynjolfsson and Hitt. These equations consider capital and labor inputs as the determinants of all outputs. It is this adherence to industrial age thinking that assumes that only a small number of input factors, particularly capital, explain the generation of productivity gains.

Even if Brynjolfsson's and Hitt's data and measures were reliable and accurate, their dependence on the Cobb-Douglas framework makes their findings questionable. Nowadays information and knowledge are a significant component in the costs of goods and services, but they do not fit Cobb-Douglas. By relying on a limited production function equation, the startling conclusion was: computer capital generates an average ROI of eighty-one percent. This was welcome to every academic, computer guru, vendor and systems manager who was having a hard time demonstrating a link between rising IT spending and corporate profitability.

The magazine articles announcing the new claim did not qualify it by identifying it as a gross number. They did not attribute to the cost of capital significant operating costs, such as network management, software expenses, and telecommunications. This is contrary to corporate ways of computing a Return-on-Investment ratio. In corporate practice one computes ROIS after subtracting all costs, or a net ROI. To calculate the payoffs from computer investments requires subtracting life-cycle cost of ownership from life-cycle cash flow of benefits. The depreciation of computer capital in such evaluations is negligible and may be less than five percent

134   In a revised paper, Brynjolfsson, E., and Hitt, L., "Paradox Lost? Firm-level Evidence on the Returns to Information Systems Spending," MIT, Center for Coordination Science, October 1993, the gross returns previously reported as averaging eighty-one percent now become a gross marginal contribution of eighty-one percent. There is a difference between a gross average and a gross marginal ROI. The marginal product is how much the last dollar of input would add to output. The average return suggests the profitability of all invested dollars.

135   Brynjolfsson, E., Hitt, L., "Information Technology as a Factor of Production: The Role of Differences Among Firms," Working Paper #3715, Sloan School of Management, MIT, August 1994.

of the total cash flow. Life cycle cash flows from computer projects are almost entirely labor cost and not the expense for depreciation of IT capital.

THE EFFECTS OF A CHANGING ECONOMIC STRUCTURE

The reasoning that computer inputs increased business productivity by boosting outputs, as measured by revenue gains, is not credible. In the last decade *Fortune 1000* firms have been boosting revenues without corresponding additions to labor. They have done this by increasing external purchases for capital, materials, parts, and services. For instance, the automobile manufacturers, the largest employers in the US, have been steadily increasing the percentage of parts outsourced domestically or internationally. The percentage of the value of outsourced parts is fifty-five percent for General Motors, sixty percent for Ford, and sixty-four percent for Chrysler.[136]

Wages and salaries as a percent of corporate revenues have declined from seventy-three percent in 1983 to sixty-seven percent in 1994.[137] Consequently it took fewer and fewer workers to generate rising revenues. Figure 34 illustrates the decline in the number of employees in major corporations. As revenues kept increasing, employment kept shrinking, largely as result of subcontracting and outsourcing.[138]

For high-technology firms such as computers, computer peripherals, telephone equipment, and business machines the percentage of manufactured parts and components outsourced to Asia is now well over fifty percent.[139] Outsourcing of capital inputs also took place through an enormous expansion of capital leasing, instead of ownership.[140] In that process

136 *The Wall Street Journal,* April 26, 1996, p. A2.
137 "Getting Stingier," *Fortune,* November 14, 1994, p. 28.
138 From analysis of histories of 138 major US corporations in the Strassmann, Inc. database, with total employment of 9.5 million in 1994 and predominantly in the manufacturing sector.
139 The incentives for outsourcing the manufacture of labor-intensive components are overwhelming. The average 1995 hourly labor cost in US manufacturing was $17.20. The corresponding cost in Brazil was $4.28, Hungary $1.70, Malaysia $1.59, Mexico $1.51, the Philippines $0.71, and China $0.25, as reported by *The Economist,* November 2, 1996.
140 By excluding financial service industries from their analysis, Brynjolfsson and Hitt missed a significant shift in the ownership of capital.

the large US corporations reduced their economic value-added, as shown in Figure 35.[141]

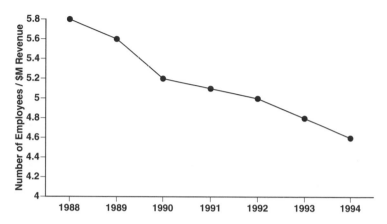

Figure 34   Decline in the number of employees per million dollars of revenue

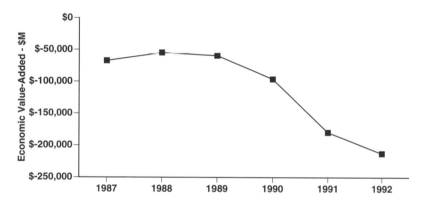

Figure 35   Decline in Economic Value-Added of the largest US industrial firms

Perhaps the most dramatic evidence of the structural changes in the US economy for the period under examination by Brynjolfsson and Hitt comes from national economic and national employment statistics. Their

141 *Stern Stewart Performance 1000 Database*, May 1996, which excludes banking and financial services, and matches the *Fortune 500* industrials. Brynjolfsson's findings are based on comparable 367 large firms also representing large *Fortune 500* firms, but excluding telecommunications and financial services.

THE SQUANDERED COMPUTER

widely publicized findings about the productivity of computers reflects data from 802 corporations in the goods producing sector and 319 corporations in the service sector. The goods producers constitute seventy-two percent of their total sample of firms.[142]

In the period from 1980 through 1994 the GDP from the goods sector declined from forty-nine percent to forty-two percent of the total. In the same period the employment in the goods sector declined from thirty-three percent to twenty-six percent of the total, as follows: [143]

	1980	1985	1990	1994
Gross Domestic Product ($B) - Goods	$1,176	$1,652	$2,185	$2,584
Employment (000's)- Goods	32,500	31,984	32,796	31,728
Gross Domestic Product ($B)-Services	$1,215	$1,939	$2,849	$3,576
Employment (000's)-Services	66,803	75,166	85,118	91,332
Share of Goods- Based on GDP	49%	46%	43%	42%
Share of Goods-Based on Employment	33%	30%	28%	26%

Figure 36   Decline in GDP and employment in the goods producing sector

Consequently, what Brynjolfsson and Hitt declared as productivity gains largely reflects structural shifts in the goods producing sector. The increase in revenue per employee was not entirely a gain in the ratio of output over input, but a change in the composition of resources. This phenomenon is often labeled as "the of hollowing out of America."[144] Many of the gains in this measure of productivity would not be attributable to computers. They are the consequence of changes in the ways how corporations created their products and services.

142 Brynjolfsson, E. and Hitt, L., "New Evidence on the Return of Information Systems," MIT, Sloan School of Management, CCS WP #162, January 1994, Figure 4.
143 US Bureau of Census, *Statistical Abstract of the United States*, 1995. Employment data from Table 653. GDP data from Table 701.
144 In the 1980s the Xerox Corporation used Return-on-Assets and Revenue per Employee as the key measures for granting executive bonuses. An astute divisional manager managed to get large bonuses for several years by gradually dismantling his manufacturing capacity. After the manager took early retirement, the division was sold for a fraction of its original acquisition cost.

Problems with the Data

Brynjolfsson and Hitt attribute to computers most of the productivity gains calculated from increases in revenue. Unfortunately, IT operating costs, defined as information systems labor, account for only 0.7 percent of the revenue of companies in their database. Their 1991 statistics show output as $1,834 billion, and information systems labor as $12.3 billion, or 0.67 percent of output. The computer capital stock of $64.7 billion was only 3.3 percent of total capital stock of $1,964.7 billion.[145] That makes IT a sufficiently small influence that it should not receive credit as the cause of all the gains, even if Cobb-Douglas equations show it with a great confidence level attached.

With such small effects, and so few variables, one would expect high precision in the sources of data. Yet, approximations in the analysis keep compounding. The researchers used controversial deflation adjustments to obtain comparable measures of output, capital investment, and expenses in current dollar terms. Their information systems spending numbers were self-reported by corporate IT staffs responding to survey questionnaires. Such information is questionable as the IT budgets have been losing visibility to central corporate oversight.

Data gathered by means of mail-in questionnaires or telephone surveys are incomplete and may come from interpretations that deal more with the views of the respondent than the facts. I had an opportunity to compare two identical survey findings from *Computerworld* and *InformationWeek* magazines. There was little consistency in replies to identical and unambiguous questions. In twenty percent of the instances, there were significant differences in the reported amounts. It is an administrator, usually at the non-supervisory level, who answers the questionnaires that keep coming from magazines, university professors, consultants, research centers, and graduate students. A typical CIO may be receiving a new research questionnaire at least once a week. The person filling out the questionnaire forms would reflect what a headquarters administrator knows, which may be a steadily diminishing quantity, as computerization proliferates beyond anybody's control.

---

145 Brynjolfsson, E., and Hitt, L., "New Evidence on the Return of Information Systems," MIT, Sloan School of Management, CCS WP #162, March 15, 1993.

The estimated value of terminals and personal computers came from estimated averages.[146] The budget calculations for determining the costs of information systems staffs used an average percentage for all firms. Such approximations do not recognize that revenue-related average percentages vary enormously.[147]

Such imprecision has a tendency to accumulate and to make conclusions untrustworthy. A closer examination shows the following ROIs: one hundred fifty percent (in 1987); one hundred fifty-five percent (in 1988); one hundred forty percent (in 1989); forty-one percent (in 1990); and thirty percent (for 1991). There is no reason given for the five-fold decrease, in five years, in the financial returns from computers. I find the assertion that "... the productivity paradox disappeared by 1991 ..." inconsistent with their rapidly decreasing ROIs.

REVISIONS AND IMPROVEMENTS

In due course Brynjolfsson and Hitt came to appreciate that the measure of output should not be revenue, but value-added.[148] They revised the Cobb-Douglas model to includes this new definition.[149] It is an improvement, but it still falls short of calculating the economic value-added as measure of output, because it did not subtract many other significant cost elements.

Finally, the researchers fixed some of their computational problems by introducing a further modification to Cobb-Douglas. It meant introducing a general variable that would adjust for a factor that neither the capital nor labor data could explain. The researchers called this the firm effects factor.[150] With recalculations, the claimed marginal productivity of IT capital investments came down from the original eighty-one percent to forty-six percent, as the unspecified firm effects changed the results.

146 There is no such thing as an average value of personal computers or terminals. That number ranges anywhere from $2,000 per year to $22,000 per year, as shown earlier.
147 However, Brynjolfsson and Hitt are using such data, as suggested in their article, "The Customer Counts," *InformationWeek*, September 9, 1996.
148 Brynjolfsson, E., and Hitt, L., "Information Technology as a Factor of Production: The Role of Differences Among Firms," Working Paper #3715, Sloan School of Management, MIT, August 1994.
149 Value added was defined as total sales converted to constant 1990 dollars, minus labor expense, partially estimated from the average wages for the sector, multiplied by number of employees. Converted to constant 1990 dollars.
150 In sharpshooting and artillery this is called windage.

These evolving discoveries show how changes in modeling assumptions can alter research findings, though none of decreases in the expected computer payoffs were of interest to the press. This also demonstrates that beneficiaries of favorable publicity find it difficult to modify their original pronouncements.

The Disclaimers

As a follow-up to the questions about the large marginal returns of computers continued, Brynjolfsson and Hitt extended their research. They confronted the incontrovertible data that there was no correlation between corporate profitability and IT expenditures. To deal with a contradiction concerning high marginal returns for computers and no correlation with profits, they produced a study stating that there were three logically separate and unrelated ways of looking at the economic impacts.

Accordingly "... computers have led to higher productivity and created substantial value for consumers, but these benefits have not resulted in measurable improvements in business performance."[151] They continued their assertion that computers have increased productivity by using 1988-1992 data. They also used these data to calculate the Return-on-Assets and Return-on-Equity, which led to the conclusion "... firms with one percent higher computer capital spending are associated with a reduction of about 0.03 percent shareholder return" and that "... there is little evidence that IT is correlated with ... firm performance, if anything, there is a negative effect."[152]

Clearly, these are startling conclusions. If computer investments depress shareholder returns and if there is no evidence that IT spending correlates with profitability, one must wonder where to find the highly publicized marginal returns on computer investments. Moreover, in ex-

---

151 Brynjolfsson, E., and Hitt, L., "Creating Value and Destroying Profits? Three Measures of Information Technology's Contributions," *Proceedings of the Fifteenth International Conference on Information Systems*, 1994.

152 When Brynjolfsson and Hitt repeated this analysis on a year by year basis, a significant effect was found only for total shareholder returns in 1990, and for Return-on-Assets in 1988 and 1990, with the effects for each varying over time. They also noted that the predictive ability of their analyses was relatively low and the overall effect of IT could be simply lost in statistical noise. In a subsequent communication Brynjolfsson wrote that the statistical noise did not apply to the production function, but to the capacity to correlate with shareholder returns or return on asssets. I agree with the "statistical noise" hypothesis as it concerns the effects of computer capital.

ploring the relationship between IT and profitability Brynjolfsson and Hitt concluded that "... the effect of IT on performance is consistently negative ... although the results were not statistically significant because they may have reflected weaknesses in their economic model."[153] This brings us back a full circle. Indeed, the paradox persists.

A POINT OF VIEW

After following a long trail of publicity, claims, and analyses, we still end up with inconsistencies that do not make the computer paradox disappear. On the one hand, the MIT researchers continue adhering to their original position that in using the production function the gross rate of return from computer capital is nearly eighty-seven percent. On the other hand, using identical data, they find no evidence of a positive effect of computer capital on business performance and "... even some evidence of a small negative impact."

Corporate executives focus on improving generally accepted indicators of business performance. So do the stock market analysts. One can easily calculate, audit and report ratios such as ROA, ROE and ROI in quarterly and even monthly statements. Unfortunately, corporate executives do not yet have positive proof from any public source that there is a positive correlation between conventional performance measures and IT spending. They certainly do not know how to make Cobb-Douglas calculations guide their investment decisions. That inability should make the decision-makers reluctant to commit a major share of their discretionary capital to computers.

Corporate operating executives and stock market analysts have no way of determining, auditing, or reporting the marginal returns on computer capital. They do not have a clue how to do that in their companies, especially if this requires using Cobb-Douglas production function mathematics. Therefore, all claims of potentially earning a large multiplier of the costs of capital should be seen as hollow and unverifiable promises.

The *Fortune 500* corporations experienced wrenching re-alignments in management practices in the period from 1987-1992. They made changes in their capital ratios through junk bonds, leverage buy-outs and

153   This is in accord with my own findings, except I use the full IT budget for making the comparisons, whereas Brynjolfsson and Hitt used the value of computer capital, which is only a small fraction of the annual costs.

acquisitions. They engaged in campaigns to achieve significant overhead cost reductions. They placed increased reliance on quality methods and on consolidation of excess capacity. They outsourced, contracted out, transferred to off-shore production and converted to global procurement.

To propose IT as a primary driver for realizing any productivity gain overstates its potency, assuming that there was any productivity gain at all. There is no reason for resort to hard-to-reproduce calculations to come up with the conclusion that computers are exorbitantly profitable. To let advocates to claim an average eighty-one percent or marginal eighty-seven percent return on computer investments is not useful in deciding whether to fund new computer projects. Financial executives will receive such claims as an inducement to impose excessive hurdle rates on computerization projects if they view them with disfavor.

Expecting unreasonably high returns on computer investments will also inhibit a company from taking advantage of less munificent opportunities. Any investment yielding more than the risk-adjusted cost of capital is a good investment. Unfortunately, the computer paradox will continue as an unresolved puzzle so as long as economists persist in treating computers as a capital asset instead of evaluating what effective management can accomplish with the cooperation of computer-empowered information workers.

What to Do

- Do not rely on government or economic reports for setting standards for what to expect from IT investments.
- Set the threshold for investments in IT projects on the basis of risk-adjusted net cash flows, not on academic studies.
- View with skepticism all survey data about IT spending gathered by means of mail-in questionnaires or telephone surveys.
- Rely on prescribed financial methods for justifying investments, not on econometric equations that are accepted for academic purposes only.

12 No Links with Spending

There is no formula for excellence.

THERE IS no consistent picture that shows why and how companies with a record of superior information productivity use computers. Excellence arises from the way management harmonizes its available resources and these are different in each organization. Every firm is different, every organization has different needs and therefore every information system implementation must fit the unique characteristic of the people employed in a particular enterprise and not vice versa. There is no "best" way to spend an IT budget. There are many equally effective methods a company can use to achieve superior performance. IT budget reviews are incomplete because they exclude distributed costs such as copying, facsimile, voice communications, voice mail, videoconferencing, and microfilm.

The principal finding from analyzing the characteristics of the *Computerworld Premier 100* companies is that they are different in just about every conceivable measure. No pattern of best practices emerged.[154] Their CIOs report at varying levels of the organization, not necessarily to the top. Some of them distribute personal computers widely, others do not. Some companies have large IT expenditures per capita and others are miserly in their spending habits. Some devote over half of their budget to new systems development while others are mostly coasting along on program maintenance. Those who have large training and education budgets are not the most profitable.

There is no consistent picture that shows why the two hundred *Computerworld* excellent companies achieve their high levels of productivity. This conclusion is the reflection of twenty-nine performance indicators for companies whose financial and productivity for 1992-1994 was indisputably superior to nine hundred other US corporations.

---

154   *Computerworld* in September 19, 1994 and October 9, 1995 featured, as special 54 page inserts, *The Premier 100 Companies*. The Information Productivity index was used to rank these firms.

Excellence arises from the way management harmonizes its available resources and these are different in each organization. The future belongs to those who can cultivate adaptability to conditions of the marketplace, rather than follow preconceived theories. For this reason I believe the current fashion of telling companies about generic best practices is mostly a promotional tactic of vendors to make their practices more attractive. It also gives legitimacy to the consultants' claims that they can deliver low cost, quick turn-around solutions that do not require much effort. It gives hope to unhappy top executives that a shrink-wrapped solution will alleviate their frustrations with their own system managers.

Unfortunately, the indiscriminate followers of whatever happens to be the latest fad that carries the label of the best practice are likely to face many disappointments.[155] Every firm is different, every organization has different needs, and therefore every information system implementation must fit the unique characteristic of the people employed in a particular enterprise, and not vice versa. The history of computerization over the last forty years carries a consistent thread of ever increasing diversity and enhanced local autonomy of the customers. This trend is a reflection of the inexorable forces that keep increasing the variety of available practices instead of limiting them to a look-alike set.

THERE IS NO MAGIC POTION

Some of the prominent consultants and magazines publish survey results about IT spending patterns. It is a way of offering advice on how and

155 Here is a partial list of the most recent management improvement schemes, each with its jargon, tools, and methodologies. These become buzzwords upon publication of an article in a prominent business journal or as a widely promoted book: Customer Intimacy, Just-in-Time Management, Concurrent Engineering, Total Quality Management, Time Compression Management, Electronic Data Interchange, Employee Empowerment, Gainsharing, Activity-Based Management, Process-Based Management, Competitive Benchmarking, Activity-Based Costing, Target Costing, Activity-Based Budgeting, Time to Market Production, Industrial Dynamics, Self-Directed Work Organization, Learning Organization, Knowledge-Based Management, Corporate Information Management, Business Process Reengineering, Balance Scorecard Management, Cosourcing, Best Practices Management, and Business Process Redesign. The possibilities for coming up with new ideas involving better ways to manage are limitless. The opportunities for lashing together English words into a catchphrase are infinite. The combination of these two generates a flood of new books and articles, in which anyone can claim innovation even though it may be nothing more than repackaging.

where to allocate budgets for information technologies. The problem with such data is that the readers do not know what they get. The surveys do not make it clear what the ranges are in the reported average percentages in spending for mainframes, servers, or desktops. The surveys do not reveal whether they report spending practices of losers or of winners. They do not disclose whether the very small proportion of survey results reflect only a sample of firms that employ people who have the luxury of spending time on public relations.[156]

Is there a best way of spending a firm's IT budget? Unfortunately, there is no such way. My data show that there are many ways that an otherwise excellent company can achieve superior performance without falling into a pattern with its IT expenditures. I have based these conclusions on analyzing the budgets of the *Computerworld Premier 100* companies over a two year period. These organizations enjoyed information productivity performance that was superior to all other US corporations.[157]

The *Premier 100* allocations of their IT expenditures do not exhibit any consistency or commonality. Only one variable clearly stands out: the *Premier 100* do not show any tendency favoring massive outsourcing of their IT operations.

SPENDING PATTERNS SHOW A WIDE RANGE

A display of the full distribution of *Premier 100* IT spending would be a useful addition to the published survey findings that almost always show only a single average number for each class of expenditures. The box plots that follow represent the characteristics of excellent organizations with known financial, organizational, and technological capabilities. They summarize over two thousand data elements supplied by companies after they qualified as being the best. For any spending category these firms show no uniformity.

Figure 37 displays selected *Premier 100* ratios. It shows the median, twenty-five percent, and seventy-five percent spending percentages of the total information technology budget:

---

156 A highly publicized and widely quoted survey by a leading consulting firm shows less than a fifteen percent response rate.
157 Volume II will cover the definition and discussion of information productivity. Those who wish to peek ahead may look it up on the web at <http://www.strassmann.com>.

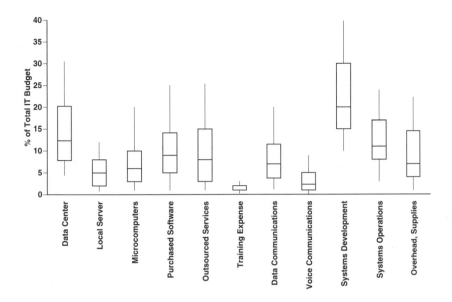

Figure 37 – Distribution of IT spending for excellent firms

Excellent corporations deploy computer equipment in widely differ-ent ways. Many of them rely on older mainframe machines. Some spend a great deal of money on server hardware or desktop machines, others do not. Some devote up to a quarter of the budget on systems development and systems engineering, while others coast along on program mainte-nance and spend everything on the best and latest equipment.

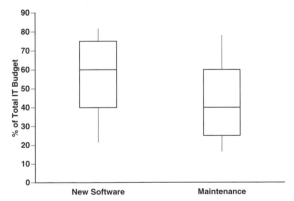

Figure 38 – Distribution of development spending for excellent companies

111

No consistent pattern emerges from the budget allocations of highly productive companies. Companies are excellent because they have found distinctive ways of differentiating themselves from their competitors. The last thing an excellent company would wish to do is to imitate an organization that is average.

TELECOMMUNICATIONS OMISSIONS

What information technologists report as the IT budget generally understates actual spending. There are a number of factors that keep escaping all IT budget reviews and surveys, including copying, which is migrating from optical to computer-like processing. IT budgets also omit the costs of facsimile, which is becoming an appendage of network printing.[158] Most significantly, IT budget reviews tend to overlook the costs of telecommunications which disappear into office overhead allocations.

The reasons for such understatements are largely organizational. It is a condition that has its origin in the distinctively separate evolutionary paths of the computer and telecommunications industries.[159] Computer people rarely possess the expertise needed to deal with the complexities of switched networking, especially if it involves voice transmission and negotiations with phone companies. Likewise, telecommunications people do not fit into conversations whenever CIOs gather to discuss their concerns.

Such differences become institutionalized. When the Office of Management and Budget, Executive Office of the President, reports about information resources costs, it does not include telecommunications, voicemail, videoconferencing, courier services, mail, printing, copying, microfilm, typing, dictation, or facsimile. In my data gathering it is very rare to find a CIO who can fully account for the wide range in form of communication expenses.

158 There is no reason why network-connected printers equipped with low-cost scanners should not substitute for facsimile equipment and much of convenience copying. Different administrative organizations and separate budgets inhibit such cost-saving consolidations.

159 Despite the frequent rhetoric about the convergence of computer and telecommunications, there is very little evidence it is taking place organizationally. IBM failed in its voice switching venture. AT&T failed at least three times in its attempts to enter the computer business. There are many lesser examples of intrinsic incompatibilities between these two tribal cultures not only in the US but also internationally. Much of that has its roots in the competitive origins of the computing industry in contrast with the heavy hand of governmental regulation of communications.

For some time I suspected that the survey results did not fully account for communications expenses. Better insight into the relationship between the IT budget and communications became available when *Computerworld* cooperated with *NetworkWorld* to name the top twenty-five outstanding users of networking technologies.[160] In this case it was the telecommunications managers who reported their spending:

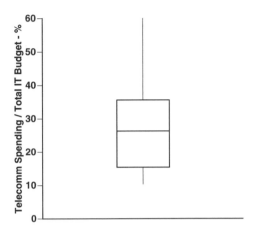

Figure 39 – Distribution of telecommunications spending relative to IT budgets

The median spending for telecommunications as twenty-six percent of the IT budget does not surprise me. It is at least four times greater than what one finds in reports from CIOs. It is also comparable to the ratio I found in Xerox after more than four years of searching for all of the administrative accounts carrying copying, courier service, telephony, telex, voice-messaging, and facsimile expenses.[161]

160 "The Twenty-Five Network Users," *A Computerworld Supplement*, September 6, 1996.
161 I received the best education about communications costs from the late Bernard Overeynder, my communications deputy and one of the foremost experts in this field. Bernard also served as the president of the International Communications Association. The Xerox ratio of telecomm expense to the IT budget was thirty-four percent in the mid 1970s.

COMPARISON OF CHARACTERISTICS

Running statistical correlations between IT and other indicators is one way to study which attributes link with superior information productivity.[162] Another way of learning about patterns of success is to divide the data into two groupings:

- Characteristics of the top ranking firms, whose information productivity is positive.
- Characteristics of the bottom ranking firms, whose information productivity is negative.

From such comparisons of traits, one may infer which factors are favorable and which are not. However, a word of caution is in order. Isolating a high ranking attribute is not conclusive; as in credit investigations or in military intelligence work, one should pay attention only if most clues point to the same finding.

Financial Differences

Corporations with large IT budgets are almost twice as likely to be among the bottom ranking firms.[163] Corporations with smaller IT budgets are more than twice as likely to be among the top ranking firms. This finding demonstrates that the amount of spending on computers does not relate to information productivity.

Corporate management appears to recognize contributions from computerization. Top ranking firms budgeted fourteen percent increases in IT spending in 1993-1994, whereas bottom ranking ones realized only six percent increases. This may be more a matter of affordability than of deliberate financial planning. If IT departments in top ranking firms request a large budget increase, they may get a less careful examination of whether the funds are being invested in support of business objectives. In contrast, the bottom ranking firms can afford less and tend to conserve their resources for less risky investments than IT.

Bottom ranking firms spent thirty percent of their budget on outsourcing, whereas the top ones spent only fifteen percent. This distinction may hold the answer to the question: who is the most likely prospect for

---

162 The study covered 183 widely diversified firms, including manufacturing and service organizations.

163 Large IT budgets averaged $253 million. Small IT budgets averaged $147 million.

outsourcing? A firm that experiences lower information productivity will have every incentive to ask others to supply what they cannot provide for themselves. Another possible conclusion is that top ranking firms view IT as an essential managerial function. It would hold on to all systems functions unless it could demonstrate that competitively acquired outside services could perform some functions better or less expensively.

Bottom ranking firms spent eighteen percent of their IT budget on reengineering, whereas top ranking firms spent five percent. Apparently, reengineering receives more attention from firms that have poorer performance. All productive firms are already addressing their needs as a matter of everyday business, while bottom ranking firms are more likely to adopt one-time business process reengineering programs that promise delivery of rapid solutions. A corporation that has positive management productivity does not need a formal reengineering program because that is already locked into the ways they follow in continually improving their operations.

Top ranking firms spend 4.1% of their staff costs on training, whereas bottom ranking firms devote only 2.7% to it. This is exactly what one could expect. Top ranking firms can afford to spend the money on training and enhance the capabilities of their people, which makes them more attractive as employers.

Among enterprises that added to their overall employment, the top ranking firms created four times more new jobs in a two year period than the bottom ranking firms that averaged only 2.2% gains in total employment. However, for enterprises that reduced their overall employment, the bottom ranking firms suffered more severe layoffs, averaging forty percent. Even some top ranking firms had to reduce employment, but only by twelve percent in the 1993-1994 period.

Organizational Differences

Among top ranking firms only six percent of the CIOs report directly to the CEO. For bottom ranking firms this number is nineteen percent. I had to rerun this analysis a few times to make sure that there was no mistake. This indicator is counter to much that appears in the press about this topic.[164] There are magazines that cater to the ego of the CIOs that consistently promote the idea that for maximum effectiveness the CIO should report at the same level as the Chief Financial Officer.

Even more revealing were statistics about the relative number of companies with centralized MIS departments, as compared with delegation of systems functions to operating divisions or departments. Fifty-nine percent of the top ranking firms continued to operate as centralized functions. Bottom ranking firms were largely decentralized, retaining only twenty-two percent of their operations in a centralized form.

The dominant view in magazines today is that firms must banish centralized management of information systems as well as mainframe computers. In place of that, the distributed client/server is posed as the most economical solution. This may happen someday, but 1994-95 numbers do not support the view that productivity and decentralization are synonymous. Thirty-eight percent of the total IT staff of bottom ranking units worked in decentralized business units. That number was only twenty-six percent for top ranking units. That finding is consistent with the observation that the top ranking firms are more likely to retain strong corporate direction over systems activities.

IT Differences

Nothing stimulates the passion of systems professionals and systems researchers like debates about the merits of various technology options. The collection of indicators in this class was meager. None of the top ranking firms admitted to being technology-driven. Their votes went either to applications or strategy driven directions. However, I found it curious that eight percent of the bottom ranking respondents insisted on being driven entirely by technology.

The ratio of laptops to desktops for the top ranking firms was sixty percent, for the bottom ranking firms only thirty-two percent. Here is a clue that the differences between top and bottom ranking firms may be

---

164 CEOs and CIOs view problems differently. They may not work together well. 631 CEOs were asked to rank their perceptions about information technologies. Their rankings were correlated with their CIO's assessments. There was a very low correspondence between their views. See Goren, S., Siong, N., and Yin, W., "IT Payoff in Singapore," *Proceedings of the 27th International Conference,* IEEE, 1994.

where they deploy their technologies. Possibly those who work on laptops are closer to customers.

According to a popular view, in a sophisticated company everyone has a personal computer. That may not be so. For the top ranking firms in productivity the PC coverage was only forty-five percent, as compared with sixty-four percent for the bottom ranking firms. We would need to know much more about the composition of the workforce before we could understand the reasons for such differences. One can only speculate that the top ranking firms have more people in operations than in overhead positions. Since it is the overhead people who get most of the PCs, it is plausible that the top ranking firms may not need as many.

What to Do

- Adopt best practices of others only after verifying that this would solve, in a demonstrable way, existing problems.
- Do not pay attention to average cost ratios for an industry or a set of applications. What matters is competitive performance and superior profitability, and that should be gained by applying unique solutions.
- Obtain reliable data about information handling expenditures outside of the usual scope of a computer department, such as voice telecommunications, facsimile, copying, printing, micro-film, videoconferencing, and courier services.

13 STEALTH SPENDING

The shell game and computing budgeting have much in common.

USER costs of personal computers greatly exceed the costs of equipment depreciation. Nobody knows for sure what is the magnitude of stealth spending which covers the unaccounted costs of computer ownership. IT spending must also include costs, even though they do not show up under the control of the computer executives, such as the time spent in overcoming the confusion when computers stop all work. The most damaging consequences of computer-generated failures will never show up as increased costs but as danger to security, health, or life.

Lately there has been a shift in the debates over the relative merits of personal computers (PCS) as compared with network computers (NCS). Originally, the claims of the NC proponents concentrated on the lower costs of the equipment. Accordingly, a five-hundred dollar device would save much money to everyone who now spends up to three thousand dollars for a PC. The squabbles over hardware costs disappeared when the prices of desktop PCS dipped to close to one thousand dollars.

PEOPLE COST $85, PCS ONLY 35¢ PER HOUR

Over ten years ago I demonstrated that the user costs of personal computers exceed the costs of equipment depreciation. With deflation in the costs of electronics and the steady inflation of labor wages, it would be only a matter of time before user costs will dominate all cost analyses. This why the user cost of ownership of a PC is now on everybody's agenda. To support a new wave of investment to replace costly PCS vendors must demonstrate new savings. The differences in hardware costs between PCS and NCS are insufficient to deliver another $100 billion worth of benefits that are necessary to kick off a new investment cycle.

Suddenly, everyone wishes to save money that does not show up anywhere – the stealth spending. That includes funds that purchase computer equipment and ready-made software for support of innumerable hobby-shop computer ventures that invariably spring up in each organization. That includes the time PC users spend maintaining their equipment and software. If one needs a brand new explanation for increasing the IT budget, the best way to achieve that is to demonstrate virtual savings through elimination of stealth cost. The unfathomable would chase the unseen just as in a mystery play.

The problem is that nobody knows for sure what is the magnitude of stealth spending. I have a limited sample of what that may be. Depending on the mix of mainframe computing and PC use, the expenses can vary a great deal. An analysis of data from one hundred forty-two firms reveals the following:

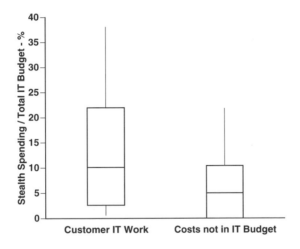

Figure 40 Distribution of stealth spending to perform IT related work

If the responses from my clients are reasonably reliable, one must wonder about the cost impacts of stealth costs. The median value of fifteen percent of the total IT budget for the two categories of stealth expense is not overwhelming. It is the high range adding up to over thirty percent of the IT budget that is worrisome.

The lesson is figures executives see at budget time as IT costs are not necessarily the whole story. Before anybody can count on savings from a reduction of stealth expenses, it would be advisable to understand where, how, and why they take place.

THE EFFECTS OF STEALTH SPENDING

The costs, as well as the benefits, of ownership of personal computers primarily reflect the roles of those who make use of them. In the absence of customer involvement, the equipment will remain sitting on desks gathering dust. A great number of computers do exactly this; they are a person's assertion of office privileges. An expensive personal computer that is only rarely used for email messages adds little value to the effectiveness of business.

Ultimately, what is needed is the intelligence, understanding, and commitment of the customer in making any automation project deliver what the original proposal promised. The end-customer must dedicate a significant amount of time in learning and applying what is potentially useful.

It is not easy to quantify the amount of stealth spending on personal computers, since it is hard to observe and nobody wants to account for it. CIOs are glad that these costs do not encumber their budgets. Employees delight in any opportunity to improve their marketable skills at the company's expense, without having to ask permission. When the support of personal computers is outsourced to a contractor, end-user operations will show up as a cost that the contractor need not incur.

It is therefore mandatory that any report about actual IT spending also include estimates of the stealth expenditures, even though they do not show up under the control of computer executives. There are a number of techniques for making such estimates, statistical sampling of a random population offering the most practical solution. My data collection efforts included such costs. The answers to our survey questions range from total denial that there any costs apart from the approved channels, to detailed estimates that include responses to some of the following:

- An estimate of the number of individuals, apart from the formal organizational channels, who perform computing assistance tasks, such as troubleshooting, consulting, software acquisition, waiting for technical assistance, and performing low-grade programming or operational computing tasks.
- An estimate of the hours per month that people who are not classified as computing professionals expend on computer-related work.

• An estimate of the number of hours per month during which people are unable to perform their work because computer services are not available. Such estimates can be verified by means of network control monitoring.

In spite of the estimating problems, the most widely quoted Gartner Group number quoted above for end-user operations is about $5,000 dollars per year, consisting of the following ingredients:

• Six percent for formal learning, such as attending courses.

• Ten percent for casual learning, where the user spends time with vendor help desks, reading manuals, or soliciting assistance from the firm support staffs.

• Fifteen percent for application development using rudimentary programming tools such as spreadsheets, report generators or data-base query languages.

• Ten percent for data management, involving tasks such as backups, rearranging files, purging records, and transferring data into electronic archives.

• Seven percent for supplies, since the purchase of paper, toner for printers, cartridges of all sorts, and magnetic storage media is usually left to the user organization.

• Twenty-two percent for peer support. Academic research has consistently reaffirmed that the capacity to converse with one's peers, and particularly with the omni-present local guru/hacker, is a requirement for all successful computer uses in organizations.[165] Learning is a social phenomenon. It happens in groups and it requires favorable conditions to make it possible. The idea that people will master the intricacies of computers by merely attending classes or reading technical manuals is not realistic.[166]

---

165 Winter, S.J., Chudoba, K.M., Gutek, B.A., "Misplaced Resources? Factors Associated with Computer Literacy Among End-Users," *Proceedings of the International Conference on Information Systems*, 1992.

166 Stewart, T.A., "The Invisible Key to Success," *Fortune*, August 5, 1996, p. 173.

- Thirty percent for the "futz factor."[167] This accounts for the time users spend in a befuddled state while clearing up unexplainable happenings that pop up on the screens of their computers. Such time-consuming behavior can receive a stimulus from anything, such as a software virus, a failed circuit board, a disk crash, or a forgotten password. Computer magazines delight their readers by providing an inexhaustible list of new foul-up experiences. Futzing is the time spent in overcoming the confusion and panic when computers produce enigmatic messages that stop work.[168]

FUTZ STORIES

The Minnesota Mining & Manufacturing Co. determined the time people spend recovering lost data.[169] It found that, in business applications, almost thirty percent of the users of personal computers lose data annually and that they spend an average of one week to reconstruct or recover it. A week's lost time of a person unable to perform productive work would be worth more than the purchase price of a personal computer.

SBT Accounting Systems Inc., a software concern, asked customers to estimate how much time they spent futzing with their PC. Based on this survey, David Harris, SBT's vice president, says people spent five hours a week fiddling with their computers. SBT says that about nineteen percent of the futz time is waiting for computers to run programs or to print reports. This includes the time wasted waiting for help with a problem. Seventeen percent of wasteful effort is in checking or formatting printed documents. People consume another seventeen percent loading and learn-

---

167 Futzing is a frequently used computer term. Its precise meaning is not established, since the word does not appear in any dictionaries. However, the *Oxford English Dictionary*, Volume IV, offers the following descriptive clues: "fuzz," a fuddled or muddled state; "to fuzz," dealing twice with the same deck of cards; "fuzz," the notion of blurring or confusing. Unfortunately, there is also a slang meaning to futz, which is an indecent connotation. Searching the Internet produces numerous examples that cater to both meanings of this word. In this book the term speaks to its technological context.

168 Some of my clients have started estimating the annual costs per personal computer for futzing. The median cost estimate is $737, peaking at $5,206, per personal computer.

169 From Bulkeley, W.M., "Data Trap: How Using Your PC Can Be a Waste of Time, Money," *The Wall Street Journal*, January 4, 1993.

ing new programs. Office workers average sixteen percent of their time discussing computer matters with co-workers. Fourteen percent organizing and erasing old files. The rest is for unspecified activities.[170]

Gary Loveman, an assistant professor at the Harvard Business School, said that the power of the personal computer makes it fairly easy but rather time-consuming to make an endless number of refinements in whatever people do. Loveman says researchers found that when Internal Revenue Service examiners used laptop computers they did examinations faster, but did not increase the number they performed. They spent the time writing more aesthetically pleasing reports and playing games.

The Disappearing Personal Computer

The ability to estimate the number of personal computers from the population of information workers offers a good check of whether the actual inventory of devices approaches the estimated numbers. Such a test is important, since accounting for the number of personal computers is difficult. Consider the following problems with instituting asset control over PCs: [171]

- A major manufacturer hires summer interns to inventory hardware and software configuration on 50,000 desktops. By the end of the summer the inventory is obsolete because the number of units and who possessed them changed.
- A *Fortune 100* company handed out 250 laptops to its sales force. After a year it can account for only half of them.

The relaxed attitude that many corporations have adopted in the pursuit of personal computing becomes apparent when one asks if there is a reconciliation between the installed base and purchase orders.

Unhinging

The most damaging consequences of computer-generated confusion will never show up as increased costs but as a failure that endangers security, health, or life. That is why this phenomenon deserves a different label from

---

170   *SBT Accounting Systems,* "The PC Futz Factor," October 1992.
171   *Infoworld,* August 16, 1993, p. 1.

futzing, which is wasteful but non-malignant. I call this variant of computer misdeeds "unhinging," although some of my associates call it "the Pearl Harbor effect." It occurs when an interaction between operator and computer results in the disruption of a trusted link on which someone depends for protection and safety.

A telling example of how unhinging happens is the case of the bombing that took place during the 1996 Olympic Games. A warning call to an emergency number gave the place and time when the bomb would go off. It took ten minutes, half of the available warning time, for the operator to log the threat into a computer. The delay occurred because the program prohibited entries without a street address.[172] The operator did not know how to handle such a situation because the new Olympic park did not have a street address in the master files.[173]

LEARNING AS A USEFUL FUTZING EXPERIENCE

People prefer to learn using computers through trial and error, which is sure to dismay the professional trainers, educators, and authors of pre-programmed training sequences.[174] Research studies show that non-traditional methods of learning, such as experimenting, asking co-workers and friends for help, and relying on menu prompts, are superior. Traditional learning methods, such as formal seminars, computer-based tutorials, video lectures, and particularly videotaped presentations, score low in effectiveness. Perhaps the most surprising result is the poor showing of classroom lectures and seminars, which to most educators are synonymous with training.

Spending money on training, help desks, and advanced technologies is beneficial, but this is not what makes office workers computer literate. Training classes, on-line tutoring, and computer-aided routines are the preferred means by which central authorities try to influence behavior and performance of computer users. That view is a modern adaptation of

---

172 In a subsequent inquiry the officials claimed that such an entry was possible by invoking a special bypass command. However, the confused operator did not know how to do that.

173 An investigation discovered that the operator did not attend a training class covering such contingencies. I have used this story in talks about information security to support Niccolo Machiavelli's observation that one need not look for conspiracy if incompetence can explain most mishaps.

174 Harp, C., "Winging It," *Computerworld*, October 21, 1996.

industrial engineering methods to make workers more efficient. Credible research findings show that greater computer literacy springs forth from the distribution of knowledge among the users, by informal means, and through cooperative arrangements. A peer group finds informal exchanges with local computer experts much more rewarding than the structured question and answer interviews with remote assistants, each having only narrow expertise. Infiltrating each work group with an enthusiastic computer expert may be the most effective way of increasing the capacity of local groups to master the intricacies of computer systems.

BUSINESS PROSPECTS

Futzing is likely to grow as new business services make it easy for computer operators to purchase consulting assistance without the intervention of the corporate systems organization. The most prominent vendor of such capabilities is Microsoft through their *AnswerPoint* service.[175] It provides a range of on-line advisory services via the Microsoft Network. Built-in options, from within Microsoft software applications, will trigger consulting requests by means of a simple click of the mouse. For instance, the *AnswerPoint* priority service will charge $35 per incident involving usability issues and collect money through credit cards or billing to a 900 number. For more sophisticated inquiries, including assistance for office workers experimenting with advanced development features, the cost for handling each incident rise from $55 to $195. Advance purchase plans are also available. They charge $9,995 per year for purchasing support that covers up to seventy-five incidents.

There is also an *AnswerPoint* line to schedule consultations on how to use Microsoft products. It provides telephone access to technical personnel and is charged by the hour. The minimum one hour charge is $195, billed by credit card. It covers assistance with activities such as design, coding and debugging. The next version of the ubiquitous Microsoft Office Suite will occupy one hundred fifty megabytes, or about ten million lines of code. The demand for personal assistance is likely to grow to cope with such complexity. On-line support offers an easy way for individuals to obtain computer education without having to petition corporate bureaucracies to request tuition and time off for professional development.

---

175 Microsoft Corporation, *AnswerPoint* Service Price List, September 1996.

From the standpoint of Microsoft the promotion of *AnswerPoint* services is an attractive business proposition. The revenue and profit potentials are enormous if eighty percent of the world's desktop computers come under the control of a Microsoft operating system. If each of the fifty million networked personal computers in the near future generate only one inquiry per month, at the lowest price of thirty-five dollars, that amounts to twenty-one billion dollars. At a gross margin of well over eighty-five percent, the support of individual futzing becomes the single most profitable opportunity in the computer business for years to come. The attractiveness of this business will surely pull in new competitors.[176]

With economics favoring the selling of services, a likely scenario is that present vendors of software will give it away. Knowledge capital will then reside not in the program code but in the relationship between the user and the software publisher. Free software will also eliminate software piracy, which is presently unavoidable.

Firms such as Microsoft may even find it expedient to give away equipment if network-managed computing devices become sufficiently inexpensive, provided that the customer signs up for a long term support contract. Customers may also find it beneficial to let the software supplier manage not only their hardware and software configurations but also other services, such as banking, entertainment, and education. After all there were times when banks gave away toasters, radios, and even personal computers just to attract long-term deposits.[177] The installers of direct broadcasting satellites now offer huge rebates as long as customers sign up for a multi-year contract to buy movies.

As the customer base for computing shifts from a half million systems specialists to more than a billion consumers in the next two decades, the structure of the entire industry will change. A relatively small number of developers will still keep up the traditional relationships. However, most of the revenues and just about all profits will originate from new forms of symbiotic relationships between the vendors and consumers.

---

176 The latest entry is the GE Information Services unit and the GE Capital Information Technology Solutions organization. They will offer consolidated desktop and network administration services. See Caldwell, B., "GE Businesses Offer IT Services," *InformationWeek*, November 11, 1996

177 In 1986 the Connecticut National Bank offered free Macintosh Classic computers in return for a five thousand dollar, seven year certificate of deposit, bearing an otherwise competitive rate of interest. Families with retirement accounts acquired computing capacity for children, cousins, and friends.

What to Do

- Do not depend on virtual savings that reduce invisible (stealth) costs. Real costs warrant real savings.
- Use statistical sampling of a random group of customers to identify the probable stealth costs associated with computing.
- Institute full configuration controls over computer equipment and software, which should include the tracking of the location and use of all information technology assets.
- Encourage the spread of computer literacy through local computer experts.

14 Workload without Payoff

Just shifting work is not a gain.

ONE OF the explanations of the computer paradox is spending that generates no value for customers but responds to government requirements. The tax-paying corporations spent $98 billion in federal government paperwork so that Washington could collect $175 billion in taxes. One hundred and eleven companies not paying taxes because of losses could report pre-tax income instead of pre-tax losses. The costs of compliance with government regulations, mostly in the form of information-intensive paperwork, exceeds taxes as well as profits. Approximately $30 billion of computer processing is necessary just for reporting to the federal government. This amounts to about ten percent of all IT budgets.

In the past, when I had to explain why I needed yet another large increase in the IT budget, I found it convenient to show a schedule of new mandatory reports to the government. Every year I reinforced my requests for more money with a long list of required reporting requirements from accounting, personnel, environmental safety, equal opportunity administrators, warehousing, and health care. That list always grew. The number of my customers threatened with fines for non-compliance never shrank. There were years when I could explain up to twenty percent of my requests for new funds as offering no other payoffs than the avoidance of penalties or even jail sentences.

THE COMPUTER PARADOX AND GOVERNMENT PAPERWORK

All along I suspected that one of the likely explanations of the computer paradox was in spending that generated no value for customers: responding to government mandated requirements creates no value, but costs plenty.

Meanwhile, a long procession of Paperwork Reduction Commissions, Reinventing Government programs, and National Performance Review initiatives have made claims that they were cutting the burdens of business reporting. They cited elimination of reports, without ever mentioning that new workloads appeared as a result of more than 200,000 added pages of laws, regulations, and administrative instructions. This regulatory flood emanates not only from Washington, but also from state capitals, counties, and municipalities.[177]

A few months ago I discovered the widely quoted work of economics professor Dr. Thomas D. Hopkins.[178] His reports show annual federal paperwork compliance costs ranging from $2,267 to $6,726 per employee, depending on the size and industry classification of a firm. This data allowed me to compare his data with statistics that would be relevant to a corporate CIO.

Paperwork, the Hidden Tax

To visualize the relevance of the costs of government paperwork I compared them with taxes paid and with corporate overhead expenses. I extracted, from the Disclosure Incorporated database, information on the 2,808 largest tax-paying US corporations, which had 29.4 million employees. I also collected data on 667 major US corporation who did not pay any taxes in 1994, which had two million employees.

The tax-paying corporations spent $98 billion in federal government paperwork so that Washington could collect $175 billion in taxes. Without such paperwork, corporate pre-tax profits could have been twenty percent higher. As shown in Figure 41, there were firms that incurred as much as ten dollars of compliance paperwork for every dollar of taxes actually paid. The high ratios of the costs of government compliance as compared with the taxes paid are the consequence of a disproportional burden of paperwork on smaller companies. In most cases, small businesses must fill out the same forms as giant corporations.

The companies that did not pay any taxes incurred an estimated total compliance cost of $6.3 billion. Without such paperwork, their total pre-tax losses would have decreased by twenty percent. One hundred and eleven companies not paying taxes because of losses would be now able to

---

177 The 1995 Code of Federal Regulations was 138,186 pages, up from 122, 090 pages in 1989. See Forbes, S., "Fact and Comment," *Forbes*, November 4, 1996.
178 Hopkins, T.D., "Profiles of Regulatory Costs," Report to the US Small Business Administration, November 1995.

report pre-tax income instead of pre-tax losses if they could have dispensed with government paperwork.

National economics statistics offers another way of looking at the enormous costs of complying with government regulations: [179]

	1988	1989	1990	1991	1992	1993	1994
Corporate Profits before Tax ($B)	348	343	366	365	396	462	525
Corporate Tax Liability ($B)	137	141	139	131	140	173	203
Compliance Costs - ($B)	549	561	595	624	643	644	652
Cost Ratios:							
Compliance Costs/Corporate Taxes	401%	397%	429%	476%	460%	372%	322%
Compliance Costs/Profits before Tax	158%	164%	163%	171%	162%	139%	124%

Figure 41   Ratio of government compliance costs, taxes paid, and profits

The cost of compliance with government regulations, mostly in the form of information-intensive paperwork, exceeds taxes as well as profits. Instead of resorting to unpopular taxation to pay for a growing bureaucracy, the government is using the clever tactics of distributing its workload to individual firms.

To what extent did the federal paperwork compliance costs explain corporate overhead expenses? One measure of these costs is the number reported as Sales, General, & Administrative (sg&a) expense. For the tax-paying corporations, the federal regulatory compliance costs accounted for less than ten percent of their sg&a. This exceeded the total expenses for research and development in almost every instance.

My database includes information about more than six hundred corporate it budgets and how they relate to corporate overhead. A dollar's worth of corporate administrative costs consumes anywhere from fifteen to twenty-five cents of computer expenses. That suggests that approximately $30 billion of computer processing is necessary just for reporting to the federal government. This amounts to about ten percent of all it budgets, which is computer expense for work that creates no economic-value added.

179   *Statistical Abstracts of the United States,* us Bureau of Census, 1995. See Table 707 for Corporate Profits before Tax, Corporate Tax Liability.

I have no data on comparable expenses for the rapidly increasing paperwork required by state and local governments. That processing would represent a noticeable addition on top of the already sizable federal requirements.

IMPLICATIONS FOR CIOs

- These findings illuminate some of the causes of the computer paradox.[180] Corporate overhead costs escalated forty-two percent from 1988 through 1994. They grew faster than revenues or profits despite a sixty-seven percent rise in expenditures for computers. Government-dictated paperwork diminishes productivity gains realized in the delivery of improved performance to paying customers.
- If work for the government increases the number of inspectors, clerks, administrators, and auditors disproportionately, one should not expect to produce increased profits from computerization.
- Information management chiefs should highlight the costs of the impacts of government paperwork burdens. Despite frequent pronouncements from Washington about paperwork reductions, the only place where such claims have any substance is when one can show what would be the taxpayers' reduced expenses for handling the government's paperwork burden.
- Grumbling about government bureaucracy is futile. CIOs should reveal what government paperwork requirements do to their firms' profits. They should leave it to the accountants to report the actual taxes, while themselves taking on the responsibility for informing management what the hidden taxes are.
- Fifty-five percent of 3,477 major US firms spent more on paperwork to comply with federal regulations than they paid in taxes in 1994. This total paperwork burden amounts to a tax surcharge of fifty-nine percent!

180 A new way of defining the computer paradox: you spend money and do not know why.

they paid in taxes in 1994. This total paperwork burden amounts to a tax surcharge of fifty-nine percent! Whenever questions come up about inadequate corporate information productivity CIOS would be well advised to show how much of their work is for activities that have no value.

A large share of new systems development and maintenance expenses have their origins in changes in government regulations, or from added government reporting requirements. If the work for the government adds to the size of overhead staffs, then one should not expect to show information productivity gains from computerization for those individuals. The best one can do is to minimize the costs of the added paperwork.

What to Do

- Do not expect to produce increased profits from computerization if work for the government increases the number of inspectors, clerks, administrators, and auditors disproportionately.
- Highlight the costs of the impacts of government paperwork burdens during budget reviews of IT spending.

Part IV
Justifications

- Best practices myths
- Questionable merits of government ratings
- Vendor-inspired claims of profitability
- The metaphysics of computer benefits
- Extraordinary claims from computer magazines
- The perils of excellence ratings

15 In Search of Best Practices

What is food to one is to others bitter poison.[180]

AN IDEALIZED list of what is best in somebody's opinion is irrelevant when dealing with the long list of problems that are always specific to a particular firm. There are too many best practices to adopt as models of what to do. Organizations, like individuals, with an excessive number of objectives will end up executing none of them well. A high "balanced scorecard" rating does not necessarily insure success.

Making recommendations on the basis of opinions is easier than coming up with advice based on factual evidence. Some of the most prominent us IT consultants present their clients with comprehensive check lists that include, in their opinion, the best practices in managing information systems. A recent series of full page advertisements from one of the largest consulting firms declares that "... our professionals will start by sharing ... what works best for others."

How consultants come up with their lists, and how these fit a particular client, does not include any explanation other than occasional references to surveys by experts. The assertions are dogmatic, as if they were articles in a catechism of theological beliefs. The originators of these lists do not explain how or whether they validated their prescriptions by independent measures of performance, such as profitability, stock market valuation, or competitive gains, as signaled by gains in market share.

I keep a collection of best practices from consultants, academics, and computer magazines. Each of these lists contains different prescriptions for excellence, in varying order of importance. Where such an enumeration of desired virtues keeps showing up for several years, the relative importance of the items keeps changing. For instance, the initiation of re-engineering projects topped most of the consultants' lists in 1991. By 1996 it was near the bottom of the recommendations. The phased program management approach popularized by IBM and Andersen Consultants in

---

180 Lucretius, *On the Nature of Things,* ca. 70 BC.

the 1970s has now disappeared altogether, to be substituted by rapid pro-
totyping or spiral systems development processes.

There was a time when owning IBM stock, smoking Lucky Strikes,
driving a Cadillac, depositing your retirement money in a Savings & Loan
Association, and taking megadoses of vitamin C would make somebody's
list of desirable habits. If you suspect that you have acne or malaria, none
of these will do you much good; you had better find someone with sufficient knowledge to correctly prescribe the remedy to cure your specific
affliction.

An idealized list of what is best in somebody's opinion is irrelevant
when dealing with the long list of problems that are always specific and
mostly unique in a particular firm. Experimenting with some guru's full
list of best practices without an understanding of the culture, personalities, priorities, or costs, is a sure way of losing money, and probably your
job. The only advantage is having a buzzword-compliant resume while
searching for a new position.

I find such preconceived prescriptions of how to manage information
systems of questionable value. All remedial efforts by information managers should start with a thorough and uncompromising diagnosis of the
current situation, as it is in reality. Outsourcing contractors who come to
assist troubled companies would do well to follow this advice before committing to measurable results. One should start searching for proven and
workable answers only after a thorough understanding of the harsh reality of prevailing conditions. There are too many and too changeable best
practices lists to adopt as models of what to do. Organizations, like individuals, with an excessive number of objectives will end up by executing
none of them well.

ADVANTAGES OF BEST PRACTICE CHECKLISTS

The best practice approaches allow a consultant to write a comprehensive
report based on his firm's established practices and preferred methods. If
a firm possesses proprietary solutions, they invariably show up on that list.
Best practice templates are particularly useful if a consultant lacks prior
operating experience, as happens when freshly minted MBAS do most of
the work. Making recommendations is easy because the conclusions do
not require painstaking fact-finding.

A consultant who relies on analysis and diagnosis will spend much time examining why an organization malfunctions and what characteristics are contributing to the existing difficulties. This is hard, it requires patience and calls for a great deal of substantive knowledge about the conditions in the workplace and the particular marketplace. That's why consultants with ready-made check-lists can always offer their services at a lower cost than those who dig to uncover the real causes.

Therefore, beware of consultants who invoke uniformly applicable best practices as the source of their authority. When it comes to information management, nobody has yet demonstrated that they are in the possession of universal insights that ensure systems superiority. The presumption that a consulting firm can compile a generic list of the means for achieving superior information management overstates what anybody knows about the causes of superior organizational performance. The current fad of awarding recognition for excellence, based on juries assigning points to a limited set of desirable attributes, is insupportable. This approach is more suitable for selecting beauty contest candidates than for arriving at substantive business judgments.

I have checked the names of the declared winners from a number of computer magazine contests and find that they show a dismal post-award record of economic performance. As will be shown later, a surprising large number of these winners are losing economic value. Over half of the nominees of popular magazine excellence awards are likely to become losers in economic value within three years after scoring well on somebody's check-list of best practices.[181]

Balanced Scorecard

A highly imaginative variation on the theme of best practices is the idea that each firm should produce a custom-made balanced scorecard.[182] Accordingly, management will choose a limited set of performance indicators, such as market share, employee turnover, customer satisfaction, manufacturing, scrap, or delivery delays to characterize their business. One technique suggests arranging these indicators into a hierarchical

---

181 Over half of the CIOs nominated for the CIO of the Year by *InformationWeek* recognition will leave their job within three years, according to my tracking over the past four years.

182 Kaplan, R.S., and Norton, D.P., "The Balanced Scorecard," *Harvard Business School Press*, 1996.

structure, so that operating personnel can relate their actions to higher level corporate strategies. This approach is superior in that it will highlight which key influences need attention to improve performance. A well constructed balanced scorecard will also show how changes in operations could deliver better results.

My primary concern with the balanced scorecard schema is similar to the difficulties I have described in evaluating compliance with best practices. Evidence that one achieves a high balanced scorecard rating does not necessarily insure success. This approach requires the firm to assign weights to the indicators. Unfortunately, the possibilities of misdirection then arise from the way the weights are distributed. Achieving ninety-five percent performance on customer service criteria (weighted heavily) may not necessarily show up as improved profits if factory productivity (weighted lightly) is only tagging along at sixty-two percent.

A company that has clearly defined vision displays its six statements of values on every wall, states its seven business goals on every budget document, arrays its projects according to eight strategic priorities, and distributes plastic pocket cards to everyone with nine balanced scorecard indicators does not necessarily deliver superior profits. Without a clear correlation of visions, values, goals, strategic priorities, and items on the balanced scorecard, the plethora of signals from top management is a sure recipe for confusion.[183]

What to Do

- **Begin all remedial efforts by a thorough and uncompromising diagnosis of the current situation as it is, not what fits a preconceived idea of what the solution is.**
- **Search for proven and workable best practices answers only after a thorough understanding of the prevailing conditions.**

---

183 There are situations, especially in the public sector, where overemphasis on delivering against a scorecard target may lead to results that are opposite of what management expects. When that happens, that approach turns into malicious compliance. Such incidents have been immortalized in Hasek, K., *The Good Soldier Svejk*, Penguin Books, 1953.

138

16 THE GOVERNMENT'S WAYS

Government is incapable of prescribing virtue.

COMPLIANCE with someone's best practices does not necessarily guarantee success as measured by the ultimate yardstick: rewards earned in the competitive marketplace. One of the Baldrige Prize winners in 1990 filed two years later for bankruptcy. Elaborate criteria for picking excellent companies have consistently turned out to be misleading. The information resources management practices of most large organizations are over-defined, over-specified, and over-supplied with rules covering the minutiae of systems work. Yet, systems projects continue to fail at an alarming rate because technologists concentrate on the means instead of the desired and measurable accomplishments.

THE INCONSISTENCIES OF THE BALDRIGE AWARD

By far the most comprehensive catalogue of what recognized experts believe to be best practices is the checklist that allows a firm to qualify for the Malcolm Baldrige National Quality Award. The US Congress authorized this prize in 1987 and directed the Department of Commerce to administer it.[184] Applying for the Baldrige calls for an elaborate process. Specially appointed examiners assign prescribed ratings to hundreds of acts before they can designate an organization as having earned the nomination. The criteria for earning the point ratings cluster in the following categories: leadership, information and analysis, strategic planning, human resource development and management, process management, business results, and customer focus and satisfaction.

My review of the record of Baldrige winners came up with startling facts:

- From 1988 through 1995 there were twenty-three Baldrige Award recipients. Ten organizations are pri-

---

184 The cost for administering the coveted Malcolm Baldrige National Quality Award is $3.4 million per year according to *Business Week*, May 29, 1995

vate firms or merged with others so that financial data are not available. One of these firms, Wallace Co., won the Baldrige in 1990, only to file two years later for bankruptcy protection as the costs of its best practices soared.[185]

- Of the remaining thirteen, results are available only for the parent company that entered one of its major divisions into the contest. Nevertheless, in each case the parent company as well as the Department of Commerce have spread the fame to the entire firm.[186] Therefore, an examination of the economic value-added of Baldrige winners from 1988 to 1994 should be useful. My purpose was to discover if economic performance showed a relationship with the Baldrige criteria.
- Only two of the thirteen firms show a positive Economic Value-Added for the seven year period. The Solectron Corporation and Corning, Inc. added $134 million to the US economy.
- Eleven of the winning firms, such as Armstrong World Industries, Motorola, Eastman Chemical, Xerox, Federal Express, Texas Instruments, Westinghouse, General Motors, and IBM, showed a negative Economic Value-Added. They subtracted a total of $100.7 billion from the US economy.[187]

Compliance with someone's best practices does not necessarily guarantee success as measured by the ultimate yardstick: rewards earned in the competitive marketplace. The most convincing proof of that comes from one of the best selling business books of all time.[188] The authors were

185 Greising, D., "Quality, How to Make it Pay," *Business Week*, August 8, 1994.
186 US *Department of Commerce News*, "Quality Management Proves to be a Sound Investment," National Institute of Standards and Technology, NIST 95-05, February 3, 1995.
187 General Motors entered their Cadillac Division and IBM the Rochester Division. The Baldrige juries judged only those operating units. The award to the Cadillac Division is particularly interesting. It has been losing market share steadily. Its position as the most prestigious automobile brand name in the US has steadily declined and continues diminishing to the present time.
188 Peters, T.J., and Waterman, R., *In Search of Excellence: Lessons from America's Best-Run Companies*, Harper & Row, 1982.

principals in perhaps the most prominent management consulting firm in the world and had access to the best inside information available. Their book described elaborate criteria they used to pick forty-three companies that possessed distinct characteristics of excellence for each of the selected attributes. Unhappily, within ten years, thirty-one of the excellent companies, or seventy-one percent, no longer met the authors' criteria.[189] In retrospect, one can now make a case that the widely heralded selections by the authors were not realistic when they were made. Most of the firms were already on their way towards mediocrity by the time their excellence became a cause for celebration of the prowess of American business knowhow.

Another example of praiseworthy conduct followed by dismal results is the case of the Mutual Benefit Life insurance company.[190] Following principles of re-engineering, this firm cut the time to issue an insurance policy from about three weeks to a day. Mutual Benefit then came close to bankruptcy and had to be taken over by state regulators. The shortening of the policy cycle had a negative payoff.

PERVERSE RATINGS

Rating organizations conduct their work on the assumption that the subject will try to attain the highest score possible. An interesting twist on the incentive to be rated as low as possible comes from the Software Engineering Institute (SEI) Compatibility Maturity Model (CMM) for Software.[191] It appears that technical executives wish to show, at least initially, the lowest CMM levels possible so that they can subsequently claim remarkable gains.[192] Consultants hired to assess the CMM ratings also have a vested interest in a low initial rating, because it will be easier to persuade top management to hire them to guide further improvements. Without

---

189 Wind, J., "Creating a 21st Century Enterprise," 2nd International Workshop on Economics and Management, Santiago, Chile, October, 1996.
190 Keen, P.G.W., "Putting the Payoff Before Process," *Computerworld*, November 18, 1996. Keen notes that Michael Hammer used the Mutual Benefit Life firm as one of the two main exemplars of good reengineering in his widely quoted article in the *Harvard Business Review*.
191 Baker, R., "The Corporate Politics of CMM Ratings," *Communications of the ACM*, September 1996.
192 For a detailed review of the Baldrige award criteria, as well as comparisons with the SEI (CMM) and ISO 9000 evaluations, see Tingey, M.O., *Comparing ISO 9000, Malcolm Baldrige and SEI CMM for Software*, Prentice Hall, 1997.

independently verifiable and repeatable methods for confirming any of the rating schema, nobody can tell the difference between fact and bias.

FUTILITY OF BEST PRACTICES – THE FEDERAL CASE

A noteworthy example of how elaborate prescriptions of conduct may be counterproductive comes from the General Accounting Office (GAO), the auditing and investigation arm of the US Congress.[193] The essence of the GAO's prescription for success are the following eleven best practices:

- Recognize the need to improve information management.
- Create line management ownership.
- Take action and maintain momentum.
- Anchor strategic planning in customer needs and mission goals.
- Measure key mission delivery process performance.
- Focus IT on process improvement in the context of an architecture.
- Manage IT projects as investments.
- Integrate planning, budgeting, & evaluation processes.
- Establish customer-supplier relationships between IT and line professionals.
- Position a chief information officer as a senior management partner.
- Upgrade knowledge and skill in information management.

It is hard to object to any of the above recommendations, except when one understands the context in which they find their application. The GAO plans to use the above principles as a compliance check-list. The Federal Government already prescribes an enormous number of practices in the form of elaborate regulations, manuals, directives, and review processes. If anything, the information resources management practices of the federal government are over-defined, over-specified and over-supplied with rules covering the minutiae of systems work.

Yet, despite the enormous accumulation of how-to-do-it practices, government's files bulge with thousands of GAO reports that contain the

193 Robinson, B., "GAO Study May Set Benchmark for IT Management," *Federal Computer Week*, March 21, 1994.

world's largest collection of stories about negligence and incompetence in information management.[194] Each of these audit reports traces the source of malfeasance to failures in following the multitude of rules that are already on the record. Each of these audit reports concludes with well thought out recommendations on how to correct the situation by reasserting the need to follow approved practices. Presumably, if the officials would only adhere to all of the enumerated best practices, there would be no failures. What ails IT management in the federal government, these reports conclude, is insufficient compliance with what somebody, at some time, under different circumstances, has ordained.

What the GAO misses is exactly what has been the fault with the government's information management practices. The increasing volumes of congressional dictates, legislative directives, Inspector General guidelines, General Services Administration rules, and departmental standards manuals have not improved performance as systems complexity keeps increasing. GAO has worked the problem from the wrong end. They have tried to induce excellence by adding to an already unmanageable volume of requirements that define practices and methods, instead of insisting on better methods for specifying results and performance measures. The more the prescriptive checklists of desired practices grow, the less manageable the practices and methods will become. A project manager who complies with every single one of the thousands of required rules, directives, standards, and regulations will never be able to complete the work because he or she will run out of time and money.

Successful users of information technologies always specify economic and service outcomes first. Only afterwards can they choose from a menu of good practices which are the best fit for a specific situation. For instance, there are security reasons that affect line management ownership (GAO Best Practice 2) that may call for severe restrictions on how to design and administer computer applications. There are times when taking action and maintaining momentum (GAO Best Practice 3) depends entirely on who controls the budget and whether funding is short-term or long-term. Anchoring strategic planning in customer needs and mission goals (GAO Best Practice 4) is desirable, but would not be feasible if there were a

194 One of the principal authors of the GAO best practices list is C. Hoenig, Assistant Director of GAO's Information Management and Technology Division. He is quoted (in Robinson, op. cit.) as stating that the federal government invested about $200 billion in IT during the last ten years and got very little for it.

rapid turnover of political appointees who control top management expectations.

Focusing IT on process improvement in the context of an architecture (GAO Best practice 6) is certainly desirable. Unfortunately, the evidence is overwhelming that the government's piecemeal procurement practices do not make that practicable. Also, when the government confronts emergencies, such as the prospects of many systems malfunctioning in at the start of year 2000, adherence to an architecture may seem relatively unimportant.[195]

The GAO spent over two years coming up with the list of generic best practices, which is admirable. Because auditors have a natural propensity for audit checklists, their approach to the government's chronic mismanagement of computerization is perfectly predictable. However, this undertaking could have been of much greater service if it had concentrated first on how to correct the fundamental flaws of all federal information management: the persistent separation between IT budgeting, performance metrics, productivity indicators, and overall spending levels for an agency or a department.

The present federal government information management processes are inherently defective. They over-define methods (inputs) instead of allowing agencies to commit to performance objectives that deliver measurable end-results (outputs). Instead of formulating how information management should conduct itself, GAO should have worked on changing how government operating executives can be encouraged to commit to delivering improved results, sometimes aided by information technologies.[196]

195 Upgrading the sails and improving the rudder is desirable, but not while the ship is sinking.
196 If you do not know where and when you must arrive, even the best means of transportation will not be of much use.

What to Do

- Rely on consistent and superior profit performance in a competitive marketplace as the ultimate measure of corporate performance.
- Encourage excellence, but not by adding to an unmanageable volume of practices and methods.
- Insist on better ways of specifying the desired results and how to measure and track accomplishments.

17 Economics over Technology

Opinions are insufficient for sustaining success.

THE CURRENT methods of investment analysis do not evaluate full life cycle costs. Physically, software does not wear out. Economic utility and independent measures of customer satisfaction must be the ultimate arbiters of all judgment about the utility of software. The merits attributed to computer technologies can be misleading, especially if the metrics used to prove value do not reflect economics. What matters is the accumulation of knowledge capital in the tools and the experiences, as they exist in the heads of customers, programmers, systems analysts, and software industry developers.

The current approach to calculating payoffs from IT investments is defective. It disregards what is perhaps its most valuable contributions to building up the software-based assets of a firm. The current methods of investment analysis focus only on the up front costs of acquiring software. They do not evaluate full life cycle costs. They neglect impacts beyond the typical short-term, three to four year, corporate planning horizon.

Physically, software does not wear out. Indeed, it is potentially immortal. Given this fact, disregard of the effects of software's residual value is specially damaging. It will tend to increase maintenance, conversion, and overhead expenses. It will continue to destroy the incentive to build up software as a major capital asset of any firm.

For the last eighty-five years, children have grown up with various versions of the story of the three little pigs. Most persons know the moral of that story. The time has come for the managers of information systems to apply this lesson to software management. Ventures that build shanty-like constructs out of scraps of code, glued-together shrink-wrap applications, and consultants' packages are not likely to find that the system can hold up over an extended time. I am convinced that, in due course, systems managers who can demonstrate that their software constructs make it possible to accumulate enduring knowledge are more likely to achieve more lasting careers.

SUBSTITUTE MEASURES OF EFFECTIVENESS

Without an explicit process for linking productivity of organizations to software investments, technology proponents will always pick measures that they can influence. This reminds me of the story about the person who was looking for keys under a street light: although it was not where they were lost, it was where the illumination made it possible to see.

There is nothing wrong with getting a certificate for being compliant with the standards promulgated by the International Organization for Standardization, the ISO 9000 qualifications.[197] I find no fault in complying with a check list for Level Three accomplishment according to the Software Engineering Institute (SEI). They attest to passing a specified level of testing. However, it does not follow that superior software will always result from compliance with checklists that experts believe to be the guarantors of excellence in the software process.[198]

For instance, programmers who programmed calendar routines over the last thirty years believed that they were applying the best software practices. Many of them passed not only ISO 9000 but also SEI examinations. This just shows that even good metrics could be irrelevant if organizations end up with costs now estimated in the hundreds of billions just to fix a two digit omission in dates for the year 2000.

The proper measurement of the success of software investments requires more than compliance with models of technical perfection. Technical excellence of programming code is highly desirable, but clearly insufficient. Nowadays, the most profitable and popular software in the world is notorious for its bugs and glitches. Economic utility and independent measures of customer satisfaction must be the ultimate arbiters of all judgment about the utility of software.

TECHNICAL SUPERIORITY WITHOUT SUCCESSES

Another example of inappropriate presumptions about productivity is the case of the Ada programming language and its compiler. Its proponents

197 The costs of ISO 9000 certification averages $220,000, yet there is no conclusive evidence that complying with elaborate quality standards has improved quality, from the customers' standpoint (see Karon, P., "Confronting ISO 9000," *Infoworld*, July 29, 1996, p. 61). About 100,000 businesses worldwide have received such certification, roughly half in the United Kingdom.
198 One can build bad cars on the most modern production line.

have generated elaborate comparisons, such as the number of instructions from the use of Ada versus those when using C compilers. This comparison was taken as positive proof of the superiority of the Ada language in improving the capacity to design reliable defense systems at the lowest cost.

As a result of the Ada investments, the Department of Defense now possesses code that is expensive to maintain, particularly because contractors are losing staff to more rewarding career opportunities. Ada has not found a widespread adoption in commercial applications. Meanwhile, the defense business is declining. Consequently, computer professionals may not wish to invest time in achieving Ada competency as a foundation for their advancement. Ada will ultimately atrophy in the same way as other limited-use languages, such as Jovial and Pascal, the latter having been advocated and taught for years by academics as a sure way of improving software productivity.[199]

The merits attributed to computer technologies can be misleading, especially if the metrics used to prove value do not reflect economics. Market power and organizational effectiveness dictate which computer technologies will become useful. There are many examples that show why marketing strategy and power can overcome superior technologies.

Even though UNIVAC computers were often technically superior to IBMs, this did not matter. The same issue applies to lessons from the lost battles of the technically superior Macintosh over the clearly backward early Windows designs. Digital Equipment Corporation's Alpha microprocessor offered twice the speed of Intel Corporation's best Pentium, yet the Intel product line outsold DEC's in a ratio of four hundred to one. Xerox's misbegotten Star computer is perhaps the best example that superior technology will not win unless it has the benefit of a concerted effort to gain the customers' mindshare.

Proponents of the technical metrics for assessing the value of computers should cease paying most of their attention to compilers, clever code, or impressive benchmark tests of electronic components. That mat-

---

199 Belatedly this recognition shows up in the report by the National Research Council, *Ada and Beyond: Software Policies for the Department of Defense*, 1996. The report recommends abolishing the long standing mandate for universal use of Ada for all defense applications and suggests that it be reserved primarily for weapon systems. The NRC report gives insufficient attention to the economics of life cycle maintenance costs for weapons software that relies on a language which is understood by only a handful of defense contractors.

ters, because poor performance can preclude all other options. However, what matters more is the accumulation of knowledge capital in the tools and the experiences, as they exist in the heads of customers, programmers, systems analysts, and software industry developers. Most of the cost of making computers come alive is not in the circuitry or algorithms, but in the minds of the people who make the computer an economically useful artifact. Neglecting to include the value of the mindshare of customers may yield methodologically defensible indicators of technological performance, but such measures will remain sterile and misleading.

What to Do

- Evaluate full life cycle costs of IT projects.
- Include impacts beyond the short-term, three to four year, corporate planning horizon.
- Measure the economic utility of software in terms of life cycle discounted cash flows which include maintenance, upgrading, and migration expenses as well as retraining costs for the developers, maintainers, operators, and users.

18 Unverifiable Spending

The wrapping paper does not make a gift more useful.

THE DISCOUNTED Net Present Worth of a project should exceed the contingency reserves that a firm must set aside to take care of cost over-runs and benefit shortfalls. The negotiation, manipulation, and reconciliation of opposing views are integral to the budget process when allocating cash for IT. It is the unspoken and undocumented assumptions at the time of project authorization that are likely to produce most of the subsequent undesirable outcomes. The basic flaw in the current state of computer science is its attachment to the study of the omissions in implementation instead of mistakes during origination. The faulty point-rating and value-weighing schemata for evaluating the merits of IT projects remain the mainstay of the prevailing budgeting practice for making computer investments.

Rational executives should continue investing in computers if the expected returns, adjusted for risk, exceed their cost of capital over the life of the investment. For risk-free computer projects, the cash flow over the life of an investment should yield about ten percent returns, the cost of corporate bonds in 1994. Applying formal methods of financial analysis, the discounted Net Present Worth of a project should equal at least the contingency reserves that an investor must set aside to take care of cost overruns and benefit shortfalls.[200]

    This problem occurs because computer investment proposals for approval by top management are not required to quantify life expectancy or risks of the proposed system. If any discussion about the risk levels arises, it is rhetoric and not numbers that indicates the advantages and disadvantages of the prospective outcomes. Project payoff calculations hardly ever show how specific risks affect the discounted Net Present Worth of the project.

---

200 Another way of stating this proposition is to define the Net Present Worth as the insurance premium that would have to be paid for obtaining a performance guarantee bond on a risky computer project.

The most popular methods for evaluating computer investments are more like opinion polls than verifiable financial analyses. The techniques used for proposing computer investments focus on getting the money and avoid setting up financial measures that would subsequently allow executives to make comparisons of actual versus promised results.

Different Viewpoints

How organizations propose, justify, and evaluate IT investment depends on the top executives' view of the management of information. The prevailing attitude is that IT is a means by which managers can impose their visions and will on the organization. One could paraphrase Clausewitz by characterizing the debates about computer investments as "… perpetuation of management power by other means." All decisions about computer investments will somehow perturb the precarious balance between privilege and control. Therefore, negotiation, manipulation, and reconciliation of opposing views become a part of the budget process when the time comes to allocate cash for any managerial innovations.[201]

If the negotiations about control over information resources are political in nature, it follows that rigorous financial analysis will interfere with the settlement of differences. Executives who recognize that information is the source of all power will take the position that there are just too many intangibles to consider in making decisions about computer systems. They abhor making investment decisions from the point of view of shareholder merit only.

There is another slant on how to address the justification of expenditures for information technologies. It contends that computerization offers the capacity to generate outputs that exceed inputs by an exceptionally favorable margin. What carries the label of "intangibles" in the corporate parlance and "prerogatives" in the public sector is only the set of differences in the assumptions and ways to choose among alternatives. Accordingly, the purpose of all investment analysis is to apply consistent

201 In LaPlante, A., "Rethinking the Numbers," *Computerworld*, June 24, 1996, one of the CIOS observes astutely, "Figure out what's really at issue when you are asked to justify IS activities, the question can be a symptom of deeper problems."

criteria to all available choices. In this way the consequences of sometimes arbitrary decisions will not be hidden from further examination.²⁰²

If the after effects of alternate choices are not explicit, a project will go on while carrying the burden of the hidden agenda. It is unspoken and undocumented assumptions that are likely to produce unexpected outcomes. This is not unlike the future of a creature that comes into existence with genetic defects.

GENETICS AND PROJECT MANAGEMENT

If the genetic code has missing or erroneous links, there will be an effect that is similar to an incomplete statement of project requirements. Genetic defects and poorly conceived project objectives both have a tendency to get worse as time progresses. Normally, biological organisms compensate for hereditary errors by giving birth to large populations of which only a small fraction are expected to survive. Computer projects are a relatively rare occurrence. Project managers will use every conceivable stratagem to compensate for omissions at conception. Top management will tolerate extravagant expenditures to correct conditions whenever the inherent faults surface for everybody's attention.

Much of medical technology concerns discovery of new methods for fixing defects that have origins in impaired biological functions. The pharmaceutical industry thrives on high-technology compensatory remedies, such as inoculations, vitamins, or insulin. Similarly, the software industry offers a wide assortment of computer-aided engineering diagnostic tools that have many of the characteristics of expensive surgical devices. However, nobody has been able to figure out how to correct for the fundamental defects dating from the act of conception, which take place whenever computer projects receive approval. The basic flaw in the current state of computer science is its attachment to the study of the omissions in implementation instead of mistakes during origination.

In most instances, computer projects disrupt an existing power equilibrium of a firm. Thus, obtaining passage of a project proposal through a steering committee and getting quick approval from an investment review

---

202 The futility of any formal cost justification has been articulated by Michael Hammer, "… social-psychological theory is the only one that can possibly account for the ludicrous lengths to which some firms go in attempting to justify their office automation expenditures." See *Computerworld*, June 13, 1984.

board is often feasible only if the proposal is artfully ambiguous. To cover for this lack of clarity, computer projects must masquerade as financially sound ventures. Computer consultants and computer vendors offer a large repertoire of techniques for coming up with attractive payoff numbers. They deliver precisely what is demanded. They ensure passage through the obstacle course of corporate approvals. These procedures may have been satisfactory for the industrial era, but are not applicable in an information-based economy.

METHODOLOGY EXAMPLES

The most popular technique for justifying investments in computer projects is a collection of methods labeled as the science of information economics.[203] This approach grew out of an IBM research program to assist increasingly anxious salespeople in helping customers justify additional expenditures.[204]

IBM's ISIS

Late in 1987 IBM launched information economics as the ISIS (Information Strategies for Information Systems) solution for overcoming increasing resistance to sales methods that had worked well in the prior decade. ISIS received widespread advertising and promotion. The IBM Advanced Business Institute organized a program to take thousands of salespeople, accompanied by their customers, through three days of training. The objective of ISIS was to reposition IBM salespeople from sellers of equipment to systems planning experts.

The demand for faculty and training facilities was so great that IBM ended up leasing portions of a posh hotel in Greenwich, Connecticut. A double page advertisement in The Wall Street Journal proclaimed "… an IBM team of experts … will work closely with your senior management to plan the information systems…. This doesn't mean selling you a piece of hardware here and a piece of software there. It means sitting down with

---

203 Semich, J.W., "Here's How to Quantify IT Investment Benefits," *Datamation*, January 7, 1994.
204 Parker, M.M., Benson, R.J. with Trainor, H.E., *Information Economics: Linking Business Performance to Information Technology*, Prentice Hall, 1988, and Parker, M.M., Trainor, H.E. and Benson, R.J., *Information Strategy and Economics*, Prentice Hall, 1989.

you and understanding your goals, and demonstrating the financial return of our solutions."[205]

The intrinsic flaws of ISIS have received ample discussions elsewhere.[206] After a comprehensive internal review, IBM abandoned ISIS as an approach that lacked both credibility and customer acceptance. Nevertheless, the ideas planted by IBM have continued to flourish as embattled CIOS seized on information economics for the rationing of scarce resources. One evidence of the continued vitality of information economics is its persistent appearance on meeting agendas when senior IT executives meet. The best practice manuals of some leading systems consulting firms continue to publish reincarnations of ISIS every few years.

Oracle's CB-90

The widespread acceptance of information economics by computer managers is not surprising. Simplistic ideas have enticing attraction when answers to complex problems are not readily forthcoming. When such solutions receive endorsement with sufficient frequency, they can eventually be mistaken for truth.

An influential company, Oracle, adopted information economics as its vehicle for assisting customers in understanding the benefits of Oracle products. They developed a software model, CB-90, which "... takes IS managers step by step through the process of building an IT investment decision matrix.... The firm initially offers this service to potential customers for free to help them in applying the techniques.... Oracle subsequently charges a consulting fee for wider-ranging analysis of the firm's IT plans."[207]

Free offers of something that is highly valuable to CIOS warrants attention. The CB-90 manual declares that "... ROI analysis does not always give a clear signal." Accordingly, "... management questions the value of IT investments because the standard business school techniques for figuring ROI are based on labor cost savings and not on improving business processes, enhancing marketing and boosting competitiveness." To overcome such ambiguities, and to enlarge the scope of analysis for intangible

---

205 *The Wall Street Journal*, January 19, 1988.
206 Strassmann, P.A., *The Business Value of Computers*, The Information Economics Press, 1990, pp. 422-430.
207 Semich, op. cit., p.45. All examples, tables and quotations that follow are from this source.

benefits as well as intangible risks, the following example was shown to prospective CB-90 users:

		PROJECT 1		PROJECT 2		PROJECT 3	
Benefits:	Weight	Rating	Score	Rating	Score	Rating	Score
Headcount Savings	30%	0	0	2.2	66	2.7	81
Other Savings	35%	0	0	2.2	77	2.7	5
Flexible Budgets	6%	1	6	2	12	4	24
Improved Reporting	5%	1	5	2	10	5	25
Improved Analysis	3%	1	3	4	12	5	15
Better Responsiveness	2%	1	2	4	8	5	10
Boost IT Productivity	2%	1	2	4	8	5	10
Risks:							
Slow Response Time	5%	(4)	(20)	(2)	(10)	(1)	(5)
Staff Resistance	5%	0	0	(2)	(10)	(4)	(20)
Avoid Splinter Systems	3%	(5)	(15)	(4)	(12)	(2)	(6)
Poor Systems Integration	2%	(2)	(4)	(2)	4	(3)	(6)
Risk of Losing Best Staff	1%	(4)	(4)	(1)	(1)	(1)	(1)
Incomplete !mplementation	1%	(3)	(3)	(2)	(2)	(2)	(2)
	100%		(28)		152		218

Figure 42   Investment risk analysis using information economics methods

Doing nothing and continuing with existing mainframe solutions (Project 1) gets a rating of minus 28. The build and buy alternative (Project 3) receives the highest rating of 217.5 points, in preference of building the application with internal resources (Project 2)with a rating of 152 points.

How much of an improvement is the CB-90 over conventional methods of financial analysis? To what extent can it be credible with top management in justifying computer investment decisions?

All a CIO has to do is to convince the finance committee of the merits of the relative weights in the tables. For instance, the CIO would have to show why other savings are indeed worth thirty-five percent of the total tangible benefits. One would have to explain why staff resistance is only a five percent risk. Somebody would have to come up with good arguments that show why the strength of systems integration can scale from minus one to minus five points. A CIO may also have to explain where and how he got the numbers that result in a composite numerical score, accurate to decimal points. An inquisitive finance committee may ask why the Project 3 choice is superior by forty-three percent points and how it will contribute to corporate earnings.

I doubt if anyone could answer all the above without stretching credibility or even integrity. Yet, point-rating and value-weighing schemata for evaluating the merits of a portfolio of projects remain the mainstay of the best budgeting practice for computer investments. Their presentation formats and details of rating items keeps growing. They compensate in form for what they lack in substance. Moreover, the academics who write papers about such schemata have a field day in working out new conceptual frameworks in which meaningless numbers can be juggled by means of advanced mathematical techniques.

INFORMATION ECONOMICS METHODS

Information economics has been consistent in advocating a process for utilizing point rating scores for assessing the investment benefits and strategic relevance of information technologies. The following sequence is said to accomplish this objective:
- Form a committee of affected managers.
- Obtain consensus on intangibles.
- Quantify the importance of benefits and risks on a relative scale.
- Estimate the probabilities on a scale of zero to five.
- Multiply each estimate by the weight and probabilities.
- Sum the numbers. Select the best alternative as one that has the largest sum.

The problem with this approach is that it relies entirely on consensus of subjective opinions. The technique lacks independent authentication or after-fact assessment. There is no way that anybody can link the synthesized ratings to business plans or to cash flow projections. Verifiable inputs do not enter into these deliberations in any formal way, except when a participant argues to give a favored option a greater scoring weight.

If disputes ever arise about a failed decision, no two participants will be able to agree on what, if anything, was the meaning of their numerical entries. In the absence of defined criteria, numerical rating schemata have only temporary significance. When the individual scores become averages for decision-making they become completely meaningless.

The overwhelming advantage of this method is that it serves well in building political support for favored programs. It offers legitimacy for dismissing improvements that may severely disturb existing arrangements. It should, however, be noted that if the company experiences a major economic setback, the people who are likely to be the ones who have caused it will sit around the table to decide on the ratings. They may have every inducement to reflect past biases in the way they vote. Verifiable hard numbers such as market share, price erosion, and excessive overhead costs will not constrain their opinions about the source of the firm's troubles. Average consensus ratings, as the information economics practice dictates, blur or eliminate the possibility of accountability.[208] Without accountability there can be no valid investment commitments. Projects aided in birth by means of information economics methods are likely to carry inborn conflicts about what they are trying to accomplish.

Generic definitions used in information economics ratings make it difficult, if not impossible, to manage customer expectations. Systems requirements call for definitions set forth in simple operational terms. The metrics should consist of a limited number of indicators, since nobody knows how to balance more than two or three objectives at the same time. The results should be easy to measure. They must be comprehensible in the context of a particular organization. Companies should not aim at better responsiveness. As an example, they should target shipping 99.9 percent of orders within four hours, but not later than by 23:00 of the same day.

The subjectively weighted point ranking scheme cannot mislead too much as long the tangible benefits of the various alternatives are sufficiently different. Unfortunately, project selections are never that polarized. What matters is the trading of present certain cash outflows for tomorrow's risky cash inflows. Information economics does not evaluate that. It may serve well as the most acceptable means for reaching a consensus at the time of the meeting. During such sessions it can aid in placating managers who participate in the budget allocation exercise whose requests do not receive adequate funds.

---

208 In group decision-making, new and potentially most valuable information is not in the averages, but in the unconventional opinions.

With regard to those managers who receive their funding, whatever their assertions may be at the time of approval of projects, they will surely change when implementation commences. The information economics point scales are not sufficiently specific enough to constrain actions by the people who later take over control over expenditures, specifications, schedules, and tactical tradeoffs.

Indeed, information economics as an investment rationing process has no explicit feedback connection to investment execution. Therefore, it cannot function as a valid tool for making decisions about information technologies. Nevertheless, information economics has received much favor from computer vendors, government commissions, contracting officers, and corporate staffs that are sufficiently remote from operations to require some sort of numerical results for approving funding requests. The method offers a superb means for avoiding embarrassing questions about provable financial merits of investment proposals.

I admire the way that information economics can stimulate discussions about contentious opinions. Nevertheless, one should not confuse the expediency of group dynamics with an analytic discipline; that would be like confusing psychotherapy with brain surgery. Both therapies have a place, but one cannot serve as a replacement for the other. Information economics does have a place in governance through consensus. As a method for committing hard dollars to enhance corporate profits, it fails. It cannot show what needs fixing when the project deliverables do not resemble what the approving participants thought they originally authorized.

Accepting synthetic point ratings in place of tangible numbers assumes that informed peer consensus will always come up with the best choice. If a corporation is already successful, then an experienced information steering committee is likely to come up with the right priorities. A problem occurs if the company is already in difficulties because the people who caused the troubles will have a human tendency to absolve their past misjudgments. When that happens, top management will probably opt for replacement of the systems steering committee instead of changing the investment decision-making methods.

Unfortunately, then, learning from mistakes will not have taken place. The insights that could have come from documented experience will not be available because it is easy to forget subjective ratings. Without factual analysis and measurable commitments it will not be easy to decide which opinions were realistic and which were not. The old dictum "those who cannot learn from the past will suffer to repeat it" will apply every time a new group of decision-makers convenes to apply information economics methods for spending money.

The Options Model

In terms of mathematical sophistication, professor John C. Henderson's Options Model is by far most difficult to understand, and even more difficult to apply. Its origins are in the valuation of complex financial transactions such as stock trading, currency arbitrage, and pricing of currency futures.[209] At the core of this model, one would find the Cox-Rubinstein equation to assess the risks of a bet on the future price of a financial asset. A graduate degree in advanced mathematics or statistics would surely help in understanding how Cox-Rubinstein works.

There is little doubt that the insertion of advanced mathematical modeling methods has greatly improved the capacity of investment analysts to track and evaluate millions of financial transactions involving trillions of dollars. Nowadays computerized trading goes on with a velocity that transports the worth of the world's entire gross product every seven to ten days across the computer screens of the financial marketplace. Multiprocessors with the power of the former largest mainframes of the 1970s now sit on the desks of financial traders, monitoring tens of millions of global currency, commodity, or stock market transactions every hour.

These financial models are heuristic in that they benefit from the enormous volume of transactions. They track, store, and analyze not only what happened, but what could have happened if the model had made a bet on an option. The model can then dynamically adjust its structure and coefficients to improve its chance next time the computer recommends making another bet.

However, there is no true resemblance between trading in financial options and planning computer projects. Investment proposals for information systems are relatively rare events as compared with the frequency of financial transactions. A company with a relatively large IT budget of $200 million would only handle about a dozen major new computer projects per year. The remainder of the budget is either in operations or soft-

209 For an excellent summary see Moad, J., "Time for a Fresh Approach to ROI," *Datamation*, February 15, 1995.

ware maintenance. The poor quality of data, inconsistencies in analytic methods, and the lack of rigor in dealing with non-quantifiable effects make data gathering about computer investment proposals and their results extremely difficult. A consistent after-fact assessment of project failures is only rarely feasible, as the offenders find many ways of disguising what happened or disappear altogether.

The mathematical rigor of the Option Model would be a welcome addition to an otherwise simplistic collection of investment decision-making tools typically used by computer executives. The Option Model deserves every benefit of doubt until proven otherwise. The proponents must first demonstrate the applicability of this technique in managing portfolios of systems investments. They would need to show how to gather and evaluate data that would make the planning and allocation of scarce funds a repeatable and verifiable experiment.

What to Do

- Adopt risk-adjusted discounted cash flow models for analysis of IT projects.
- Apply consistent criteria to all available IT implementation choices. This should include quantification of "intangibles" in cash terms.
- Pay disproportionate attention to the conception, definition, goals, and measures of performance when a project is initiated.
- Beware of vendor IT investment justification methodologies. They will always reflect a bias favoring preferred choices.

19 VIRTUAL JUSTIFICATIONS

Astrology will prevail in the absence of science.

THERE ARE cost justification techniques which reflect opinions instead of verifiable facts. Executives are apprehensive about methods that have removed computerization from an investment-driven discipline, such as methods applied in justifying investments in tooling or production capacity. The times of the easy computer sell disappeared fifteen years ago when shrinking profit margins forced the reexamination of every significant overhead expense. Computerization should be under the purview of strategic planning, where its major potentials stand the best chances of discovery, where the benefits can be measured, and correct assessment of the investments stands a chance of being discovered.

Some organizations find information economics and option modeling methods too elaborate and seek a more direct way of sorting out funding requests.

ANALYTICAL HIERARCHY

The analytical hierarchy method dispenses completely with any attempts to come up with numerical rating scales. It avoids breaking down project attributes into generic rating categories by asking how individuals feel about different investment proposals.[210] These sentiments find their expression as either poor, fair, good, very good, or excellent ratings.[211]

---

210 The dyslexic executive prefers to check off pictograms. There is a version of the analytical hierarchy method that does not call for any words. A beaming smile signifies an excellent rating, an angry wrinkled face a poor rating. I found a surprising number of high level corporate executives who were dyslexic and averse to numerate matters. They could only listen to a presentation, not study a report or analyze spreadsheet tabulations. Most of those I knew rose rapidly through marketing positions where interpersonal relationships are more important than literate skills.

211 Millet, I., "Who's on First," *CIO Magazine*, February 15, 1994, p.27. The rating scale calibrates as follows: Excellent = 1.00, Very Good = 0.60, Good = 0.30, Fair = 0.10, Poor = 0.

	Weight	Project 1	Project 2	Project 3	Project 4	Project 5
Short Term Benefits	16%	Excellent	Good	Very Good	Excellent	Poor
Long Term Benefits	36%	Excellent	Excellent	Very Good	Good	Fair
Market Share	10%	Excellent	Good	Very Good	Excellent	Good
Retain Customers	16%	Excellent	Excellent	Very Good	Good	Very Good
Cost Management	8%	Excellent	Good	Very Good	Excellent	Excellent
Infrastructure Contribution	14%	Excellent	Excellent	Very Good	Good	Good
Overall Score	100%	1.00	0.76	0.60	0.54	0.28

Figure 43   Selections of projects based on analytical hierarchy

Although the analytical hierarchy method carries an impressive label, it is closer to judging swimsuits or beauty contests than to a disciplined assessment. It is certainly not trustworthy for making decisions that could possibly make the difference in a firm's competitive survival. It will not, however, upset information politics, because anybody can read whatever they wish into the results.

CREDIBILITY AND RISKS

The chief executive's attitude towards investment in computerization has been evolving from passive acceptance to skeptical reluctance. This shift stems from the absence of professionally sanctioned and financially supported approaches to evaluating computer investments. Despite enormous spending on information technologies, the discomfort about it still prevails. Executives are apprehensive about methods that have removed computerization from an investment-driven discipline, such as applied in justifying investments in tooling and production capacity, to exercises in bargaining. When this happens, effective lobbying for appropriations becomes more important than economic merits. In this respect, spending on computers has become more like discretionary spending for employee morale, customer relations, and general publicity than a calculation of payoffs from capital investments.[212]

212   Mr. Charles Mortimer, the former CEO of the General Foods Corporation, was reputed to have said that he knew that half of his huge advertising budget was wasted, but he could not tell which half. Many contemporary CEOs are likely to hold a similar view about their computer expenses, with the exception that they would not have even a clue about how much of it should be assessed as a waste.

In the 1960s and 1970s the purchases of computers were not subject to tight scrutiny. Under the watchful eye of the comptroller and with ample money available, computer salespeople found little resistance to the promise that the rapidly growing administrative workload would become manageable through computerization. The excessive risks of installing computers were tolerable as long as there were prospects for realizing large savings. Besides, the financial executive could always rely on the IBM salesforce for assurance that all will end up well. It was the strength of IBM that it had established a reputation for underwriting technology risks.[213]

The times of the easy computer sell disappeared fifteen years ago when shrinking profit margins forced the reexamination of every significant overhead expense. Technology budgets now account for a much larger share of operating expenses than fifteen years ago. If a major computer project fails it could make a large dent in profits. Although the belief still persists that computer applications may give companies a competitive advantage, the executives now recognize that computer investments are large and risky. The risk premium, as thirty percent or higher discount rates on computer projects illustrate, is a reflection of the low credibility attributed to promises from the proponents and suppliers. If a CFO demands twelve to eighteen month payback on projects, the firm is effectively taxing the computer investment at a usurious premium rate over the cost of capital. Thus, the financial methodology can tilt all decision-making towards the expediencies of unreasonably short-term solutions.[214] Because of such acts, the firm will remove computerization from the purview of strategic planning, where its major potentials stand the best chances of discovery, where the benefits can be measured, and correct assessment of the investments stand the best chances of being discovered.

---

213 It was the loss of that reputation that explains, perhaps better than any other influence, IBM's fall from its one-time predominant position. Whenever an organization disregards the customers' costs and concentrates primarily on safeguarding its own revenues, its position is likely to erode. That's the fate of all monopolies, regardless of how powerful.

214 A world seen exclusively through a microscope will reveal only bugs.

RATIONALIZATIONS

Wealth as Justification for Overspending

There is a financial services organization with an IT budget that is so large that it did not fit into my statistical correlation model for estimating IT expenses. Curiosity about such an anomaly led me to ask: What is so unusual about this firm? The answer was simple, the CIO said. They had only 2,400 employees, and their net profits were about $400,000 per employee. Therefore, it would not matter how much they spent on technology. The CIO claimed that spending over $60,000 per person per year on IT was justifiable. The best and the latest technologies provided superb support for marketing the firm's services. User satisfaction with the large color displays and dynamic formats was very high.

All anomalies must have an explanation. It turned out that the high profits per employee came not at all from employee productivity, but from the interest income realized from lending out over $40 billion of funds. The claim of exceptional operating profits was incorrect – in fact the firm barely broke even in their return on the cost of capital.

The Economic Value-Added created by employees of this firm was a small fraction of the net profits per employee. It was not much different from that found in a slightly above-average manufacturing firm. It was much less than earnings by the firm's competitors. The claim that it did not matter how much was spent on computers did not stand up to scrutiny. The IT budget per employee exceeded the Economic Value-Added per employee. I concluded that an examination of ways to cut IT costs would not be a bad idea after all.

Frugality as Justification for Overspending

In this case an external review board was to review an atypically large IT budget. The CIO presented it as a penny-pinching operation. The CIO proudly asserted that his ratio of IT expenditures was the lowest in the food industry, amounting to less than half a percent of revenues. It was an impressive presentation until I checked on the total employee count. It was under five hundred.

The sales reported by this firm reflected brokerage transactions. Only a very small percentage of handling costs contributed to tens of billions of revenue. The firm was enormously profitable. It booked huge revenues while employing practically no equity capital and hardly any work force.

On a per capita basis, this firm was by far the largest spender on computers in the food industry. Its structure was more like that of wholesale banking and financial brokerage than food processing. The relatively simple transactions that typified this business could not possibly justify the expenditures of over $30,000 of computer expense per administrative employee per annum.

However, cutting back on what appeared to be profligate computer spending would make no difference whatsoever in the financial results of this firm. Yet it was not appropriate for the CIO to claim exceptionally low levels of computer spending. It discredited his explanations, even though he maintained a truly luxurious computer setup.[215] Nevertheless, there was no reason to recommend cutting the IT budget. It would not increase profitability in noticeable way, and would only upset the people who truly enjoyed their work and perks.

Forced Spending

Up to fifty percent of IT spending carries the label "mandatory."[216] This includes expenditures on projects with unquantifiable benefits, such as:
- Reprogramming a legacy application to keep it from falling apart from an accumulation of undocumented maintenance fixes.
- Upgrading to improved technologies, such as to COBOL II, which offers additional language features.
- Migration of software to keep up with vendor strategies, such as switching to Windows 95 from a perfectly functional version of Windows.
- Keeping up with vendor software releases, especially when maintenance of older versions ceases, such as adopting the latest release of IBM's IMS database system.

215   The computer setup was consistent with the luxurious corporate headquarters and a fleet of the most expensive airplanes.
216   Jones, C., "Justifying Computer Integrated Manufacturing," *Gartner Group Research Notes*, December 1995

- Modification of dysfunctional code, such as fixing up the year 2000 deficiencies in applications resulting from the use of two digit codes for the calendar year.
- Retraining skilled personnel who are reluctant to continue maintaining applications that use obsolete coding methods or languages, such as RPG (Report-Generation Language).
- Modification of existing application programs, or development of new ones, to comply with mandatory changes in government regulations.

Management often has no choice but to approve this spending, especially if requests for additional funds claim an incipient disruption of operations or legal liability. Nevertheless, management may wish to examine the aggregate sum of expenditures that do not have demonstrable payoffs. How much of what is an urgent expense is fixing previously badly designed and poorly maintained software? To what extent is the spending a reflection of accumulated neglect rather than a sudden catastrophe descending on an unsuspecting computer staff? Most significantly, what share of the ongoing development and maintenance is spent redoing poorly conceived projects that were rushed into completion by the management's own expediency? [217]

Shifting Expenditures

A great deal of spending on information technologies is justified through cost reductions that will appear as IT savings to that organization. In due course many of such savings may vanish because the effort must be taken up as additional work somewhere else, especially where such increases are not easily discernible. This technique is highly effective in shifting costs to customers and suppliers. In the case of government, the displacement of costs to businesses has now become an art form for collecting virtual revenues without increasing the visible burdens of taxation. Here are a few examples:

- Distribute computer paper reports electronically. Customers will incur substantial additional printing

---

217 Project cost overruns are rare. The problem is that the identical project must be redone many times over before it is complete.

costs for hardware, coordination, supplies, and support.

- Promote distributed computing. Remove labor intensive applications from data centers for completion by local operators. This will give rise to point-of-use costs that do not show up as offsets against savings that are claimed at the center.
- Shift data entry to customers. The best examples are automatic teller machines and online banking. Customers get a number of worthy inducements to do the data entry previously performed by bank employees. This displaces the responsibility for errors from the banks to the originators.
- Shift transaction costs to the suppliers by giving them responsibility for reordering and inventory management at points of sale. Wal-Mart stores have perfected this technique, with the result that they have been able to reduce their administrative expenses.
- Submit information electronically. The Internal Revenue Service now requires all companies, except the smallest, to submit tax reports by email. Large firms now insist that all suppliers submit invoices and delivery information in electronic format. Savings accrue to the party that dictates the electronic format. Hardly anyone has any incentives to evaluate the incremental expense imposed on others.

What to Do

- Use only cost justification techniques that translate dollar costs into dollar benefits.
- Discount the expected benefits of computer using explicit risk assessments.
- Include computer investments as an element in the firms' strategic long-range plans.

20 COMPUTER PROFITABILITY CLAIMS

Boasting is a sign of doubt.

ONE SHOULD not claim profitability from overcoming neglect to follow good business practices. Contests that trumpet astronomical ROIS do a great disservice to information systems managers and to the computer industry. ROI computation should not divide the total cost reductions from replacing an incompetent system by the costs of hardware, software, and development. The correct ROI is the cost advantage of performing the identical functions after making all of the feasible improvements by other means.

THE 1995 *CIO MAGAZINE* ENTERPRISE VALUE AWARD

CIO Magazine has the mission of promoting the accomplishments of information technologies. The pinnacle of these efforts is the annual *CIO* Enterprise Value contest. The magazine parades the winners of this competition as paragons of achievement and models for computer managers. The applications that receive citations are case studies of successful uses of computers. Considering the stories from the reporters, the applications are exactly what every reasonable system executive would want to put into effect in order to improve information management in their firms.

The K-Mart Award

Considering the rather unspectacular financial returns realized by US corporations, it was with a sense of excitement that I turned to the 1995 *CIO Magazine* awards. I expected to find there what should be the best that IT could offer. The opportunity to uncover a new record of extraordinary results came from a tabulation that showed Return on Investments of the top three winners. The highest ranking firms reported 578 percent, 5,028 percent and (believe it or not) a 14,659 percent gain. The highest numerical accomplishment came from the K-Mart organization, which installed an innovative computer application for inventory management.

When you confront something that is four-hundred twenty times better than the best, it pays to check the facts. The calculations were impeccable. Dividing the total claimed cumulative benefits of $365 million by an expenditure of only $2.49 million yielded the 14,659 percent figure exactly.[218] There was no question that the technology purchases, systems development, maintenance, and operations numbers yielded the calculated result.

Next I checked the costs. $2.49 million bought a system that allowed headquarters to review sales and inventory positions daily. These reports allowed the corporate staff to maintain listed prices and to replenish fast moving items while lowering prices and inventory for slow moving items. A corporation with 2,350 stores spending only $2.49 million on improved sales and inventory reporting looked like an extraordinary bargain.

This left me with the task of understanding the $365 million of benefits explained as reduced inventory, reduced operating costs, and enhanced revenue. The headquarters controllers certified the savings to CIO Magazine for the award. This implied that the availability of daily sales and inventory reports made the headquarters staff $365 million smarter in applying good management practices to managing inventories. However, that does not mean that it is the computer project that should receive the credit for all of the inventory reductions. Computer reports are only a means to an end. The inventory managers deserve all the accolades, because they could have either used or misused the inventory reports.

The Engineer's Allegory

The reasoning in the K-Mart case reminds me of a story about the engineer who went to Africa, and contracted a case of debilitating amebic dysentery. The engineer had to stay in a hospital for two months, which cost $35,000. The fellow who replaced him bought a $49.95 water filtration device and completed the job in good health. Upon return the second engineer claimed that the water filtration widget was worth a 70,000 percent Return on Investment.

218 To fully appreciate the significance of this number one should consider at that rate one dollar would be worth exactly $466,948,992 at the end of five years, which would almost have covered K-Mart's 1995 reported losses of $496 million.

One cannot claim profitability from overcoming neglect that comes from not following good business judgment. The return on the water filtration widget is the difference between its cost and the next least expensive solution, such as drinking only boiled water, soda, wine, or beer.

The K-Mart Finale

If merchandising people do not pay attention to sales and inventory levels, the return on the computer investment is the difference between the computer investment and the cost of improving management practices by the least costly means. It was not the computer that generated the savings, but a realization that the K-Mart staff could be doing their jobs better.

The cio *Magazine* award to K-Mart, now carrying the proud designation as the ESPRIT Award, was announced on January 15, 1995. The K-Mart cio, David M. Carlson, received recognition as someone who delivered business value as well as a spectacular Return on Investment. These honors coincided with Carlson leaving abruptly, along with 300 of K-Mart's 1,200 is staffers.[219] cio *Magazine* remarked that, "Carlson was shifted from K-Mart's top is spot to other, unspecified duties, reportedly because of dissatisfaction over problems plaguing K-mart's inventory replenishment system."[220] Subsequently, K-Mart management dismissed ten other top is managers.

The Moral of the Story

Contests that trumpet astronomical ROIs can do a great disservice to information systems managers and to the computer industry. They effectively

219   Caldwell, B., and McGee, M.K., "K-Mart's is in Turmoil," *InformationWeek*, March 13, 1995. Carlson's replacement left after two months on the job. There are grounds to question the reliability of the claims for the cio award. According to the article "... store buyers wouldn't even use their pcs.... they had the technological tools but they wouldn't use them."
220   Santosus, M., "A Seasoned Performer," cio *Magazine*, January 15, 1995. The myth of K-Mart's accomplishments persists. For instance, in Brynjolfsson, E., and Hitt, L., "The Productive Keep Producing," *InformationWeek*, September 18, 1995, suggests that the fumbling General Motors management should imitate the example set by K-Mart.

reject rationality and encourage hucksters.[221] They inflate unwarranted expectations. They encourage laughable manipulations of numbers. They diminish credibility. They devalue the merits of solid accomplishments. They demean the distinguished consultants engaged to pick the award winners. They demoralize professionals who assume that the press does not publish laudatory stories even though they have a demonstrably poor record.

THE 1996 *CIO MAGAZINE* ENTERPRISE VALUE AWARD

In 1996 *CIO Magazine* scaled down its profit expectations. This time they awarded the top prize for a 628 percent Return on Investment as the winning case in The *CIO* Enterprise Value Award.[222] The accomplishments by the winner, McDonnell Douglas Helicopter Systems, in streamlining paperwork is indisputable. What is questionable is an attempt to unnecessarily embellish the facts to suggest that they are totally gains from computerization.

McDonnell Douglas did, indeed, shorten its sales cycle from forty-eight days to less than a week. However, little of this time reduction is attributable to computerization. It did not require a week's review by one of the engineering bureaucracies to find out that the standard options put together by a sales person would work. One could avoid such delay merely by simple administrative means, better training and a floppy disk. Another week consumed by the contract department to check terms on an order is just a reflection of bad practice that does not necessarily require computerization for streamlining. The sequential insertion of the finance department into the workflow sequence due to the need to calculate payments is another reflection of poor organizational practices. The typing delay by secretaries and incessant rerouting back to various levels of approval is just faulty process design.

---

221 "The ultimate ROI, if anyone were so enslaved by numbers to take the time and trouble to measure it, is astronomically high. The better the relationship between the CIO and the CEO, the less likely the IS team will be shackled into trying to measure how IT has transformed the business," quoted in Baatz, E.B., "Digesting the ROI Paradox," *CIO Magazine*, October 1, 1996
222 Santosus, M., "Birds on a Wire – The *CIO* Enterprise Value Awards," *CIO Magazine*, February 1, 1996. This issue includes similar stories that distinguish themselves with Return-on-Investment savings well in excess of 300 percent.

The *CIO* article also mentioned some other flaws: price lists were unavailable, sales calls had to wait pending receipt of latest prices, and sales representatives could not find out if equipment options were compatible. All paperwork required redoing three to five times as customers kept changing their minds, because delays in the sales cycle encouraged it.

Clearly, installing an integrated computer system that optimizes the workflow sequence seems to be the right solution and I would certainly consider funding it. However, it does not follow that the ROI computation should merely divide the total cost reductions from replacing an incompetent system by the costs of hardware, software, and development. The correct ROI is the cost advantage of performing the identical functions after making improvements by other means. The benefit of renting a parking space for an automobile in New York City is not the avoidance of police parking fines: it is the difference in the cost from the next least expensive parking alternative.

The average Return on Equity for US industry for the last decade, for profitable firms, has been about fifteen percent. The single most profitable year for the single most profitable industry recorded a Return on Equity of 34.5 percent. If a computer executive boasts to knowledgeable executives about realizing a 628 percent Return on Equity it will only confirm their suspicion that they are dealing with a questionable promoter.

CHECKING FOR PLAUSIBILITY

All claims of savings from computer projects need to be examined for common-sense plausibility. For instance, the Xerox Corporation claims the elimination of $1.5 million of printing expenses by installing a $2 million client/server network for delivery of personnel data to its 10,000 US-based salaried employees. Since computer printing costs per page of text range from 2 to 3 cents, this suggests that Xerox has eliminated approximately 60 million sheets of paper, or 6,000 pages per employee per year. I wonder what Xerox employees could be doing with that much paper.[223] The claim of savings may be nothing but a long overdue executive decision to cut down on paperwork.[224]

---

223 This is a pile thirty to thirty-five inches high, if there are no staples or paper clips. It would fill about two file drawers.
224 Zarrow, C., "People Power," *CIO Magazine*, May 1, 1996, p. 86.

What to Do

- Calculate the returns on computer investments as the difference between the costs of automation and the next least expensive solution.
- Do not attribute to computerization gains that are attainable by other means.

21 OPINION POLLS

Beliefs cannot substitute for reality.

SURVEYS about customer happiness are unreliable unless they correlate with profitability and revenue gain. Opinions of customers who have defected to competition are some of the most reliable sources of useful information. The misuse of satisfaction surveys and the misapplication of statistics are a frequent occurrence. Appearance, publicity, promotion, and reputation take over too often in the absence of measurable productivity gains from the use of computers.

Too often companies use satisfaction surveys to evaluate their effectiveness. However, surveys about customer happiness are unreliable tools unless they correlate with profitability and revenue gain.[225] That is hardly ever the case. The gathering of satisfaction scores lends itself to built-in bias because the phrasing of questions greatly influences the replies. The wording of a questionnaire can easily elicit the desired responses. Furthermore, customers who defect to the competition never show up in the sample, even though the defectors are likely to have available more candid insights than the opinions of the current customers who still depend on the good will of their supplier.

Technical experts have no incentive to write adverse comments about their purchasing decision. It is likely to reflect poorly on their initial judgment to make the choice. Unless the collectors of satisfaction surveys can demonstrate that they have assembled a random and unbiased sample, one should treat all satisfaction survey results with skepticism.

Possessing survey results encourages some consultants to feed this information into statistical programs that deliver an appearance of rigorous analysis. For instance, an IBM consultant published findings that correlate the relationship between adaptive culture measures and process

---

225 Surveys are helpful if consistent findings are reported using different sampling methods from random sources.

effectiveness.[226] The evaluation of what an "adaptive culture" is came from responses to questions such as:

- What are the visions of the firm that positively affect behavior of the employees?
- What is the level of employee confidence in the organization's leadership?
- To what extent do firms encourage innovation and risk-taking?
- To what extent does management focus on the competition?

These questions are certainly interesting, even though I find it hard to believe that any consultant-vendor could get valid answers to the views of employees on such matters. My credibility is stretched when the weighted measure of adaptive culture is plotted on a scale ranging from "low" to "high" against a "low" to "high" index of effectiveness for twenty-two IT processes such as: migrating legacy systems, measuring the business value of projects, supporting business with IT plans, and developing architectures. Claiming a numerical correlation between esoterica such as corporate visions and coping with legacy systems is as close to hocus-pocus as I can find in computer magazines.

The IBM consultant's approach is not rare. The misuse of satisfaction surveys and the misapplication of statistics happens so frequently that it merits comment. Consultants are not the only ones who commit these transgressions. I referee over twenty-five papers each year as one of the editors of an international journal of information management. About eighty percent of these papers originate from professors in departments of information systems, systems engineering, systems management, or computer science.[227] Over half of these papers reflect survey results. The responses are expected to prove or disprove an author's hypothesis about the effectiveness of information technologies. The cited conclusions always reflect subjective opinions, usually on a scale of one to five. In the last fifteen years there have been only two papers that related IT to verifi-

226 Baxley, D.J., "The Cultural Formula for Success," *Enterprise Reengineering*, March 1996, p. 14. The cultural success was predictable with a coefficient of $R^2 = 0.53$. A critical discussion of the pitfalls of customer satisfaction surveys can be found in Reichheld, F.F., "Learning from Customer Defections," *Harvard Business Review*, March-April 1996.

227 In almost every case the surveyed population are the professor's students who fill out the forms as a classroom exercise or through voluntary response at the end of the course.

able data, such as profitability, revenue, or growth in market share. It seems that qualitative inquiries remain respectable methodologies until such time as information management may evolve into a better developed scientific discipline.

INFORMATION WEEK EXCELLENCE AWARDS

The widely read *Information Week* magazine annually recognizes the "... best users of IT, allowing them to improve customer service, cut costs, and improve products and services."[228] The magazine solicited opinions from experts regarding people to select for recognition.

One of the important criteria in considering such awards should be the judgment of the customers. Only paying customers can value quality, low costs, and improved products by paying good prices that yield superior profits. In a market economy it is the Economic Value-Added that is by far the most reliable indicator of what customers think. So what did customers think about the *Information Week* choices? Figure 44 is a summary of the top twenty-one 1994 winners.

Forty-three percent of the top winners were economical losers. The losers incurred greater losses than the winners. *Information Week*'s selections do not offer a good model for evaluating success, because opinion polls, even by experts, are likely to rate appearances or reputation and not substance. Much of what we know about the economics of computers remains exactly that. Appearance, publicity, promotion, and reputation take over too often in the absence of measurable productivity gains.

---

228 *Information Week*, October 17, 1994.

Amounts in $000	Equity	Net Profits	Economic Value
Deere & Co	2,085,400	(920,900)	(1,150,294)
RJR Nabisco Holdings	9,070,000	(145,000)	(1,142,700)
E I Du Pont De Nemours	11,230,000	555,000	(680,300)
Cigna Corp	6,575,000	234,000	(489,250)
Bethlehem Steel Corp	696,600	(266,300)	(342,926)
Corning Inc	1,711,500	(15,200)	(203,465)
Northrop, Grumman	2,158,053	154,807	(82,579)
Columbia Healthcare	1,656,000	139,000	(43,160)
Eli Lilly & Co	4,568,800	480,200	(22,368)
Subtotal, Losers			(4,157,042)
Southern Co	9,017,000	1,002,000	10,130
Sonoco Products	788,364	118,834	32,114
Gillette Co	1,479,000	288,300	125,610
Toys R US, Inc	3,148,282	482,953	136,642
Compaq Computer Corp	2,654,000	462,000	170,060
Gannett Co Inc	1,907,920	397,752	187,881
Mobil Corp	17,237,000	2,084,000	187,930
Texas Instruments Inc	2,315,000	472,000	217,350
United Parcel Service	3,944,509	809,635	375,739
Bell Atlantic Corp	8,224,400	1,403,400	498,716
Citicorp	13,980,000	2,219,000	681,200
Merrill Lynch & Co Inc	5,485,913	1,358,939	755,489
Subtotal, Winners			3,378,860

Figure 44   *InformationWeek* best users of information technologies for 1994

What to Do

- Validate all customer surveys against measurable gains.
- Survey opinions of customers who have defected to competition are some of the most reliable sources of useful information.

Part V
Outsourcing

- Outsourcing by losers
- Good and bad reasons for outsourcing
- Changes in industry structure and practices
- How to test the viability of outsourcing decisions
- Accountability outsourcing decisions

22 OUTSOURCING

A brain transplant is not feasible.

OUTSOURCING corporations are trying to return to profitability by cutting employment. Massive divestment of corporate IT resources appears to be more like downsizing rather than a miracle cure. Outsourcing of IT is often an excuse for getting rid of management accountability. Corporations that outsourced more than sixty percent of their IT budget tended to be economic losers. High performance companies do selective outsourcing but retain most of their information management capabilities as an essential ingredient of competency.

So far, there is only one good explanation that fits almost every case of outsourcing information technologies. The outsourcing corporations are trying to return to profitability by cutting employment. That is not, however, the rationale one finds in corporate press releases announcing the transfer of most corporate information processing assets to an outsourcer.[229] One hears assertions about computers no longer being a core competency. "Partnership for innovation" is another often quoted phrase. The plain fact is top corporate executives have become disenchanted with their capacity to digest information technologies. Massive divestment of a corporation's IT resources appears to be more like an emetic than a miracle cure.

THE PUZZLE

I did not start out thinking this way. What I read in trade magazines about letting professional firms manage the modernization of information technologies was entirely plausible. Nevertheless I was apprehensive about the benefits of outsourcing. I also knew a great deal about two huge outsourcing contracts that crippled their firms' information management for years and made them unable to respond to competitive encroachments.

---

229 For sake of clarity, the outsourcing corporations that contracts to someone else to handle all of a part of its information technology is the "outsourcee." The contractor performing the outsourcing services is the "outsourcer."

Announcements of the dismissal or transfer of computer personnel featured imaginative stories telling why a function with the reputation of being one of the corporation's critical success factors should now transfer safely into the hands of complete outsiders. Some corporations claimed that their information technologies were not an essential part of their business any more, but rather like the electric power or water supply. For others, the divestment of routine processing was expected to make it possible to concentrate on strategic systems. One also heard that outsourcing was preferable because the contractors offered technical expertise that the firm could not muster by other means.

It is impossible to list all of the reasons for outsourcing. It has become the fastest expanding segment of the computer business. The 1995 worldwide outsourcing revenue was $76 billion, with the US making up forty-eight percent of that total. Most of the outsourcing (sixty-four percent) was for processing standard transactions such as claims, billing, and credit cards. Only thirty-five percent was for IT services. Maintenance and support of centralized computing facilities accounted for about half of these services. So far, only a small fraction of that (less than ten percent) is for systems planning, integration, and implementation.[230]

Should top management view massive outsourcing of IT as a new and imaginative way of obtaining such services, or as an excuse for getting rid of responsibilities that they have not been able to manage all along?

The Search

One would expect outsourcing to be a widely spread occurrence throughout the *Fortune 1000* corporations if outsourcing does improve strategic fit, realizes lower costs, takes advantage of vendors' skills, and overcomes the dearth of technical expertise. Outsourcing should be an equally good solution for anyone. It would work well for all corporations, without regard to size, industry, assets, profitability, or growth, as each finds that one or more of the many claimed benefits satisfy their needs.

Applying such reasoning, outsourcing would show up as a random phenomenon, modestly biased in favor of growth corporations seeking added resources to enhance their capabilities. Statistical analysis would then reveal whether outsourcing is a random, evenly spread phenomenon or clustered around some causal connection.

230 International Data Corporation, *The Global Outsourcing Market*, 1996.

To examine the randomness hypothesis I asked a librarian to assemble a list of commercial companies that most frequently appeared in the trade press as corporations that have taken outsourcing actions. With this list I searched my productivity database, which includes data about operating performance of US corporations, as well as their IT budgets. With that I set out to determine if there were any discernible characteristics among corporations that chose to outsource more than a half of their IT resources.

THE DISCOVERY

I ran many statistical tests. They revealed that the occurrence of outsourcing was not random. The analysis showed a connection between outsourcing and a firm's Economic Value-Added. For each corporation that outsourced most of its IT resources I listed the Economic Value-Added for one, two, and three years prior to awarding their largest outsourcing contract:

Amounts in $000	Outsourcing Date	Prior Year	Prior Two Yrs.	Prior Three Yrs.
Halliburton	1994	($354)	($170)	($497)
Delta Airlines	1994	($1,147)	($1,239)	($1,075)
CSX	1994	($693)	($943)	($1,159)
USAir	1994	($621)	($954)	($1,011)
Unisys	1995	($472)	($818)	($1,636)
General Dynamics	1991	($952)	($229)	($98)
Polaroid	1995	$3	$44	($22)
Scott Paper	1994	($481)	($269)	($520)
Xerox	1994	($1,267)	($1,806)	($725)
McDonnell Douglas	1992	($308)	($315)	($351)
Southern Pacific	1993	($140)	($456)	($241)
Eastman Kodak	1990	($572)	$57	$27
General Motors	1985	($776)	($442)	$1,368
Total Economic Value-Added		($7,780)	($7,540)	($5,940)

Figure 45   Economic Value-Added of outsourcing firms

Those corporations that outsourced more than sixty percent of their IT budget were economic losers when they began outsourcing.[231] They were probably shedding IT resources along with other corporate functions, because they were in financial trouble. I could not find any corporation with a consistently large Economic Value-Added and rising employment which outsourced most of its information technologies, despite claims of synergy or the advantages of getting rid of commodity work. The losers were casting off IT because they were already shrinking their firm anyway, as shown below:

	1991	1992	1993	1994	% Change
Halliburton	73,400	69,200	64,700	57,200	(22.1%)
Delta Airlines	66,512	70,907	67,724	65,596	(1.4%)
CSX	49,883	47,597	47,063	46,747	(6.3%)
USAir	48,700	48,900	48,500	43,600	(10.5%)
Unisys	60,300	54,300	49,000	46,300	(23.2%)
General Dynamics	80,600	56,800	30,500	25,600	(68.2%)
Polaroid	12,003	12,359	12,048	11,115	(7.4%)
Scott Paper	29,100	26,500	25,900	15,900	(45.4%)
Xerox	100,900	99,300	97,000	87,600	(13.2%)
McDonnell Douglas	109,123	87,377	70,016	65,760	(39.7%)
Southern Pacific	23,396	22,793	18,982	18,010	(23.0%)
Eastman Kodak	133,200	132,600	110,400	96,300	(27.7%)
General Motors	756,300	750,000	710,800	692,800	(8.4%)
Total, Top Outsourcers	1,543,417	1,478,633	1,352,633	1,272,528	(17.6%)

Figure 46   Employment for companies outsourcing IT

If outsourcing truly had all of the advertised advantages, economically prosperous and growing companies would prefer it. Outsourcing would help in growth that cannot absorb a sufficient number of comput-

231 For instance, Xerox transferred 2,500 of its IS employees to EDS. Only 470 remained in the IS function, 200 took early retirement and 100 transferred to non-IS jobs. This represents 84% outsourcing. Nevertheless, Xerox still qualified in a magazine poll as one of the best places for pursuing an IS career. That must be a testimonial to the powers of superb press relations. See "The Best Places to Work," *Computerworld*, June 1996.

er people into an expanding business. For instance, the exploding needs of Microsoft made it expedient to outsource the labor-intensive network support for its sixteen thousand desktop computers. The three year contract for forty million dollars would be most likely less than fifteen percent of its total IT budget.[232] Financially successful corporations tend to secure ready-made technical expertise to manage commodity tasks but not more than that.

Best Companies Do Not Engage in Massive Outsourcing

Outsourcing may become a more credible solution to systems problems if prosperous and growing organizations start moving large numbers of their information systems staffs off their payrolls to outsourcer service firms. Although I may have shown that large outsourcing coincides with economic and personnel losses, I had yet to determine if high performance organizations engaged in massive outsourcing. Analysis that concentrates only on losers does not tell about the habits of winners.

It just happens that I have information that lends itself to testing the hypothesis of whether excellent companies develop a significant dependency on personnel from outsourcing vendors. The staff employed by the high performance firms shows a very high correspondence with their firm's IT spending levels. If any of these corporations would outsource an unusually large share of their IT costs, the graph of IT employment versus IT budget would fall substantially below the trend line. That is not the case for any of the best firms.

The high performance companies do selective outsourcing, ranging anywhere from three to eleven percent of their total budget, but retain most of their information management capabilities as an important ingredient of their overall managerial competency. Excellence flourishes through a steady accumulation of company-specific knowledge for which long-term career staffs are indispensable.

Anorexia

Outsourcing is, in reality, only one aspect of a currently popular downsizing trend among troubled corporations. It takes place under a more palatable label, just as reengineering is a euphemism for cutbacks in most cases.

232 "Microsoft Outsources PC Support," *Computerworld*, November 13, 1995, p. 8.

The information systems community has consistently ranked, in a wide range of surveys, as one of the least admired corporate functions and therefore becomes an attractive target when there is a decision that sets a quota how many bodies must leave.

Cutting staff, divesting businesses, and getting rid of hundreds of person-years of accumulated skill seems to be a prevailing compulsion among large firms that are seeking to improve profitability by shrinking their size. Although the number of papers that deal with outsourcing is considerable, only Brynjolfsson and Hitt have studied the relationship between outsourcing and profitability.[233]

They noted that "... companies that try to jump on the outsourcing bandwagon may be chasing a parked car. We found no association between outsourcing and success. If anything, companies that outsourced more of their information systems work tend to have lower productivity and profitability. The only performance measure heavy outsourcers did well on was stock market returns. In the short term, the market reacts favorably to outsourcing. Whether the market will continue to react favorably, especially if productivity doesn't improve, remains to be seen."

One could say that outsourcing has many of the attributes of a widely prevailing disorder known as anorexia nervosa, a psychological disturbance involving the refusal to eat to the point of starvation. People with anorexia have a distorted self-image which makes them feel fat even when emaciated. Preoccupation with food, low self-esteem, and emphatic denial of the problem characterize most anorexics. Similarly, executives in companies with poor financial performance seem to concentrate on downsizing as the preferred method for restoring competitiveness.

Unfortunately, shareholders and investors do not have a clue about the losses to the firm whenever knowledgeable workers leave in droves. There is no such a thing as a balance sheet write-off for human capital. When machinery or buildings become scrap, the auditors reflect that cost with a great deal of precision. The government even allows taking decisions to scrap as a tax deduction. Because outsourcing always takes computers off the list of financial assets, the accountants see that as a reduction in costs while neglecting the loss of the employees' know-how and commitment to serve the enterprise.

233 Brynjolfsson, E., and Hitt, L., "The Productive Keep Producing," *InformationWeek*, September 18, 1995

186

I am in favor of outsourcing for any of the good reasons that would take advantage of somebody else's capacity to accumulate knowledge faster than when it remains home-grown. It should not be a substitute for the corporate version of an emetic. I shall find encouragement about the prospects for outsourcing when I see a large list of prosperous and growing organizations that use this option to enhance their mastery of information management.

A DuPont Postscript

When the DuPont corporation announced its $4 billion outsourcing contracts a number of reporters called to find out if my anorexic diagnoses were still valid.[234] Increasing shareholder value by obtaining improved technology from the Computer Sciences Corporation and Andersen Consulting was the declared purpose of these contracts.

A check of the facts revealed an anorexic tendency. From 1994 to 1995 the shareholder equity of DuPont shrank from $12.6 billion to $8.2 billion and total capital assets declined from $19.4 billion to $14.3 billion. From 1993 to 1995 employment declined from 114,000 to 105,000.[235]

The 1995 information intensive sector of DuPont (SG&A) cost $4.1 billion. The 1995 net capital costs of DuPont were only $0.67 billion. Consequently information productivity rather than capital efficiency would be the keys to any attempts for increasing DuPont shareholder value.

The 1995 IT costs for DuPont were $690 million, or roughly 16.8% of their SG&A expense. This was not excessive for a company that employs over 65% of its workforce in information occupations. The key to value creation would then rest on enhancing the effectiveness of the $4.1 billion worth of information work. There is no evidence that outsourcing IT for cutting IT costs is effective in improving the productivity of the information workers. Therefore, reducing IT costs is likely to have only a negligible effect on increasing DuPont's sagging shareholder value.

With regard to technological modernization through outsourcing, the claims that contractors can do it better is questionable. With a $690 million IT budget DuPont has sufficient resources to obtain all of the economies of scale or technology advantages without needing outsourcing

---

234 Rifkin, G., "DuPont Acts to Farm Out Its Computing," *The New York Times*, December 12, 1996.
235 1996 financial results are not available at this time.

contractors to take over most of their systems. This leads me to conclude that DuPont is pursuing outsourcing as a downsizing tactic, by another name.

What to Do

- Make sure that outsourcing of IT is an imaginative way of obtaining improved services and not an excuse for getting rid of managerial responsibilities.
- Engage in selective outsourcing, but retain most of the information management capabilities as an essential organizational competency.
- Favor outsourcing to take advantage of somebody else's capacity to accumulate technological capabilities faster than when it remains home-grown.

23 Outsourcing Prospects

The destiny of technology is in specialization.

In THE GREAT majority of cases outsourcing led to problems and disappointments. To judge the success or failure of any outsourcing contract one needs information that is accessible only to trusted insiders. Keeping the IT budget level while employment declines and while the intrinsic technology costs available from vendors come down is not a praiseworthy accomplishment. When bills come in after outsourcing, they show figures that are comparable with the prior costs after adjusting for the volume and quality of services. There are good and sufficient reasons for selectively outsourcing. What we call outsourcing nowadays will evolve into a new form of international division of specialized labor as information transaction services become a commodity product. Policymaking executives will have to find new ways to obtain trusted advice about costs, economics, and technology choices that third parties will be making on their behalf.

Perhaps the most crucial contemporary issue of information management is whether to outsource all or some of the information technologies to specialized services firms. This issue is not a transient phenomenon; the shift from company-management computing to purchased services is accelerating. The decision when, how, and where to outsource is likely to be one of the few information management issues that will be coming for review at board level meetings in the future.

Is Outsourcing Effective?

Perhaps the most extensive assessment of the effectiveness of outsourcing is by Lacity, Willcocks, and Feeny.[236] They studied forty large US and European corporations and public sector organizations who went through

---

236 Lacity, M.C., Willcocks, L.P., and Feeny, D.F., "IT Outsourcing: Maximize Flexibility and Control," *Harvard Business Review*, May-June 1995, p. 84.

some form of major outsourcing. They concluded that in the great majority of cases outsourcing led to problems and disappointments.

Of the fourteen decisions to outsource the bulk of IT, three were outright failures and nine were likely to fail. Only two were successful and those involved limited outsourcing of only large data centers.

Of the fifteen decisions to keep most IT services but outsource some functions, five failed to produce anticipated cost reductions. The other decisions, which led to savings of up to fifty-four percent, were successful as seen by management but not according to the employees who thought that cost reductions took precedence over service quality.

Of the remaining outsourcing decisions only three were complete failures. It is too soon to tell the outcome of the remainder. Although the researchers could not demonstrate that outsourcing offers a good answer to corporate information problems, they offered useful recommendations that should improve the firms' chances. Their conclusions are sound and worth studying.

A number of executives disagreed with these findings. Particularly noteworthy are the objections from a senior officer of EDS, the world's largest outsourcing firm.[237] Accordingly "... the article ... exhibits little understanding of ... the vital connections between IT and business performance....Ultimately, success can be measured in only one way – not by manipulation of technology costs, but by the overall success of the client's business." I agree with this observation. One cannot possibly claim success in management of information technologies if a firm incurs large and consistent financial losses, especially after outsourcing takes place.

BUSINESS PERFORMANCE AFTER OUTSOURCING

It just happens that the General Motors Corporation's outsourcing of its information technologies represents the largest commercial sector contract ever. It also has the longest public track record. It would therefore be interesting to apply the critic's economical criteria. Here is the history:

---

237 Sullivan, B., "Letters to the Editor," *Harvard Business Review*, July-August 1995, p. 158.

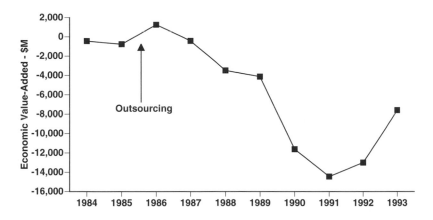

Figure 47   Economic Value-Added of GM for eight years after outsourcing

In the absence of a demonstrable correlation between IT spending and economic performance, one cannot provably demonstrate that outsourcing was somehow a contributor to GM's precipitous decline in economic fortunes.

To judge the success or failure of any outsourcing contract one needs information that is accessible only to trusted insiders. For instance, one would have to know if the turmoil resulting from the precipitous transfer to EDS incapacitated some of GM's critical competitive capabilities. One would have to understand whether there was a holdup in the capacity to speed up the introduction of new auto models while Toyota was gaining market share against GM because of accelerated responsiveness to shifting market demands. One would also need an understanding of the bottom-line consequences of any incremental costs for IT that appeared immediately after outsourcing took place. Most importantly, one would need insight if contractual and pricing disputes diverted the organization from responding to competitive challenges.

As much as I rely on financial metrics to make judgments about IT productivity, I also recognize the necessity to understand what the employees, customers, and suppliers have to say about the effects of outsourcing. Profitability before and after outsourcing in the GM case is only one of the many indicators one has to take into consideration before drawing any conclusions.

IT Costs after Outsourcing

Another perspective on the effectiveness of outsourcing by GM comes from an interview with the CEO and Chairman of EDS.[238] When asked what GM did get out the relationship with EDS, the CEO said "… we fixed their technology cost for almost ten years … that was unheard of in the industry, because when we first came into GM, they were growing [their IT] for a long time at fourteen, fifteen percent compounded expense rate."

I found the idea of EDS containing GM's IT costs curious and decided to look up the history of GM's employment since 1985. Public data is available only since 1987, when GM's employee count was 813,000. By 1994 that was down to 693,000. One should not compare rising IT expenditures during a decade of prosperity in the 1970s with a period of decline that began in the mid 1980s. Keeping the IT budget level while employment declines fifteen percent, while the intrinsic technology costs available from vendors come down by more than fifty percent is not a praiseworthy accomplishment.[239] There are executives who will gladly consent to outsourcing in return for the promise to cut their IT budgets by twenty to twenty-five percent.[240] Whether that is or is not a good deal would require a more thorough examination of the volume or complexity of the workload.

One can find only a few well-documented stories about gains from outsourcing. Even then, these claims need further scrutiny to make sure that they do not reflect a bias. Anecdotes about outsourcing problems are also hard to find. It is in everybody's interest to avoid unfavorable publicity. I found only one recent case study of a company that learned that outsourcing a major project, to save money, resulted in sixty-five percent greater costs.[241]

Savings from Outsourcing

There are many claims that outsourcing reduces costs. To my best knowledge none of the claims were substantiated by means of an independent

---

238 Nee, E., "One on One with Les Alberthal," *Upside*, October, 1996, p. 84.
239 The US Department of Defense has claimed good cost management by keeping its IT budget level while cutting its personnel by close to a million people.
240 For instance, Blue Shield of California in 1995 entered into a twenty-five year agreement with EDS. The contract calls for a twenty-five percent reduction of Blue Shield's total IT budget.
241 Gack, G., "A Cautionary Tale," *Computerworld*, September 12, 1994, p. 135.

audit. What exists are surveys in which CIOs reply to questions about outsourcing experiences. For instance, we have a 1995 Gartner Group survey in which forty-seven percent of 221 CIO respondents labeled their relationship with outsourcers, after two years, as a mixed bag. Twelve percent asserted outsourcing to be an outright failure.[242] That leaves forty-one percent who said that everything was proceeding according to plan.

Obtaining evidence about savings from outsourcing may not be feasible. All the reliable sources recognize that what corporations acknowledge as their IT budget may be a gross understatement. When bills come in after outsourcing, they show figures that are not comparable with the prior costs. This perhaps explains why some firms are disappointed when the expected cost reductions do not materialize.

The employment structure of a firm also affects its IT budget. Whenever IT outsourcing takes place, it does not happen in isolation from other corporate moves. Simultaneously, management is likely to pursue other structural changes, such as increased subcontracting of components, increasing dependence on distributors, or divesting labor-intensive operations.

For instance, when GM outsourced all of its information systems to EDS, the monthly bills for computer services, as seen by plant managers, showed substantial increases. EDS's response was that prior transfer charges from the internal systems organization did not properly reflect the full costs.[243] The plant managers argued that their work force and production output were declining while the contracting out for sub-assemblies was increasing. Therefore, they were paying more for less. The resulting impasse lead to much recrimination, which made reconciliation difficult. The fault was in the way that the original contract accounted for costs that would correspond to changes in the workload. GM outsourcing to EDS proceeded without prior agreement on the cost model that would

242 Pastore, R., "The Art of the Deal," CIO *Magazine*, May 15, 1996. The problem with such surveys is that one can never be sure whether it gives biased results, since outsourcing executives who promoted the idea are likely to defend their decisions. They suffer from the "My baby is not ugly" attitude. They surely would not wish to discuss their disappointments.

243 A 1987 executive level review showed that GM's IT costs were $3.3 billion, as compared with pre-outsourcing levels reported as $2.8 billion. In 1996 the IT budget grew to more than $4 billion, (Scheier, R.L., "GM's first IT chief seeks 300 CIOs," *Computerworld*, December 23, 1996), even though GM employment was below pre-outsourcing levels. GM expects to cut hundreds of millions of dollars from IT spending since outsourcing did not appear to contain IT spending, contrary to claims.

track of expenses as circumstances changed. Such a model, if tied to an agreement, could have saved everyone a great deal of discomfort.[244]

ESTABLISHING A BASELINE PRIOR TO OUTSOURCING

Recently, I had the chance to examine detailed accounting and employment data for two corporations that outsourced most of their IT budget to the same firm. In each case the outsourcer claimed the delivery of IT cost reductions of more than thirty percent per annum to the outsourcee. My task was to determine the credibility of these pronouncements.

As it happened, both of the outsourcing organizations simultaneously cut total employment by more than thirty percent, most of it coming from elimination of information-intensive corporate staffs. Therefore, the contractor's assertions about savings were not adjusted to correct for what actually took place. The lowering of corporate employment, especially if it reduces demand for computer services, warrants revisions in the baseline against which one may count any savings. Real savings are reductions in costs against an adjusted baseline, not against historic data.

The savings from outsourcing were also available to the firms that contracted out their information services. My only explanation for this situation was that it must have taken an outside force to eliminate surplus personnel and to carry out the consolidation of excessive data center capacity. Therefore, this outsourcing was not an act of business process redesign, but abdication by management to let an outsourcer perform the required amputations.[245] It was not cost-reduction through thoughtful subcontracting, but expense elimination through hired agents. The irony of the situation was that according to my adjusted baseline estimate, the firm's IT budget was now higher than before outsourcing took place.

---

244 The GM situation is unique in that EDS was an acquisition rather than a contract. I quote it because more information is public than for any other outsourcing case. The lessons apply to anyone considering outsourcing most of their IT assets.
245 In a number of recent cases involving banks I suspect that one of the motivations for outsourcing was to remove an exposure to liability suits in case of a major computer system failure, especially if this involves a breach in information security. Third party outsourcing firms are in a better position to insure against such a contingency.

A Perspective on Outsourcing

The medical profession has learned how to do heart transplants, to simulate the functions of kidneys, and implant synthetic knee, hip, elbow, and wrist joints. So far, it is inconceivable to do a brain transplant. The brain is individual-specific, whereas other parts of a body have only generic characteristics.[246] The brain stores a person's knowledge patterns and experiences, which make individuals what they are, whereas body parts are equivalent to interchangeable mechanical components.

The brain is also the center where a person retains a sense of individuality and privacy. Therefore, one of the critical issues in outsourcing is the safeguarding of uniquely confidential information. The outsourcing contract between the Swiss Bank and Perot Systems solved this problem admirably. The bank retained all of the input and output processing within the bank, while Perot Systems handled only encrypted data, without ever having access to the encryption keys.[247] The Swiss Bank gave up nothing of importance, because it had reserved to itself all options and privileges. It had not yielded any of its essential managerial functions.

My studies show that over eighty-five percent of corporations now spend more on information management than on financial capital. Therefore, I consider it unwise for management to let someone else manage all of their information systems processes. Information management and information systems (whether computerized or not) are indeed the core competence of almost every business in the information age. With the increasing embodiment of information management into software, the control over information systems remains one of the essential managerial functions that an organization should not fully abdicate.

Testing an Outsourcing Decision

The first test of whether a corporation did or did not abandon its essential information capabilities is simple. Does the firm retain the choice to repatriate, or move its systems to another vendor without excessive expense, no matter what has been outsourced? If the exit option from outsourcing has an executable plan, then the essential managerial competence of the firm remains intact.

246 There are instances of genetically or blood type incompatible transplants.
247 Goldman-Rohm, W., "Second Coming," *Upside,* June 1996, p. 38.

The second test of whether corporate management did or did not abandon its accountability concerns the price it pays for outsourcing services. If the prices are competitive and lower than internal costs, then the decision to outsource is a routine buy or build procurement decision. However, when an element of profit sharing with the outsourcer enters into the outsourcing relationship, it is as if the firm had issued preferred stock options that mature if computer projects succeed. How such options become cash is questionable, since the evaluation of the benefits from computer investments is notoriously difficult and always controversial. How such priority claims compete with gains due to other stock options holders or to shareholders interests is likely to be a source of much disagreement.

Outsourcing companies thrive on situations where top executives are eager to get rid of tiresome complaints about incompetent systems management. They are even willing to enter into contracts that specify the subsequent sharing of profits or productivity gains with the outsourcer.[248] One has to go back to the fifteenth or sixteenth centuries to find the widespread adoption of practices whereby contractors received entitlement to a share of the gains or losses from a venture. In feudal times, when profits were disrespectable, such rewards were called bounties or spoils.[249]

Firms invite irreconcilable conflicts of interest if the outsourcer contractor, with insider knowledge, can claim the amounts to be counted as the sharing of gains.[250] Only an arms-length deal, under competitive conditions, is consistent with the principles of free market economics.[251]

---

248 In a June, 1994 address to the World Computing Services Congress, Les Alberthal, CEO of EDS announced concept of CoSourcing, for the purpose of establishing long-lasting relationships with customers. He said: "Our compensation is directly tied to the success of the customer. As business objectives are achieved, we share in the rewards. Conversely, we share in the risks, and our compensation is affected accordingly should results fall short."

249 The rise of the English navy in the sixteenth century has its origins in the chartering of acts of piracy to royal bounties for the capture Spanish galleons.

250 This conflict, perhaps more than any other, made it desirable for EDS to split finally from GM.

251 Profit sharing by a contractor is not the same as profit sharing by employees. The contractor who controls a firm's information systems has bargaining power that is unmatched by individual employees. Long term employees acquire and apply company-specific knowledge capital, which makes them de facto investors. Outsourcing contractors usually get paid for their full costs, plus profit, at market prices.

GOOD REASONS FOR OUTSOURCING

There are good and sufficient reasons for selectively outsourcing. I call that out-tasking and it applies if any of the following conditions prevail:
- The organization is incapable of attracting or retaining talent for specialized technologies, especially for innovative uses. It is increasingly true in the public sector.
- The budgeting and capital investment process is spasmodic, short-term oriented, and subject to reversals in the goals, objectives, and preferences of top management. Increasingly, this characterizes much of the industry, as well as most of the public sector.
- The learning curve for a new or risky technology is especially steep. Therefore, it pays to have an experienced firm introduce the technology at a much lower cost. If the new service becomes attractive, one can always reconsider the outsourcing decision. I have used this strategy over the years with considerable success by negotiating favorable licensing and technology transfer agreements as a clause in the initial agreement. I call this approach knowledge capital transplanting without incurring the cost of capital.
- The organization is internally in turmoil and cannot manage IT because its managerial energies are concentrating on survival of the firm.
- The organization is very profitable but does not wish to devote scarce managerial resources to managing IT This calls for inventing new forms of relationships that may not be arms-length commercial contracts.

The outsourcing contract awarded by the Swiss Bank Corporation to Perot Systems Corporation may fit many of the categories. As part of the deal the Swiss Bank has acquired an option to purchase twenty-five percent of the privately held Perot. Meanwhile Perot has taken a forty percent stake in Systor, AG, the Swiss Bank's IT subsidiary. This allows both companies to share profits from their joint efforts through stock ownership.[252]

---

[252] Hildebrand, C., "The Odd Couple," *CIO Magazine*, May 15, 1996. It should be noted here that Perot Systems does not share profits of the Swiss Bank, only profits from the jointly owned data services company.

An innovative variant on the same theme is an arrangement for the outsourcer to share revenues.[253] Perot Systems will take over Citibank's processing of travel agency commissions. Instead of a contract fee, Perot will receive a fixed share of annual revenues. This will work well as long as the structure of the business remains the same. However, if the commission structure changes when airlines lower the allowable payments to travel agents, Perot stands to benefit more than Citibank.

- The systems organization does not have a costing mechanism for transaction or usage pricing. Therefore, it can function only as a bureaucratic monopoly that is always in conflict with its customers about resource allocation.[254] Out-tasking offers a neat solution to convert fixed (bureaucratized) overhead to a variable cost as reflected in the bills from a contractor.
- The organization is divesting itself of an entire business process, such as logistics, payroll processing, medical claims handling, or order fulfillment. The IT work associated with these processes must then accompany the divestiture. This is not IT outsourcing but dispossession.

A good example is the outsourcing of customer inquiry, order-taking, and sales support services from the Commodore Business Machines company to Federal Express. Federal Express offered twenty-four hour telephone staffing and a trained labor force that Commodore could not match. In addition, Federal Express offered tight integration of its shipping and delivery services with Commodore's customer support needs.[255]

WHERE OUTSOURCING WILL PREVAIL

The increased complexity of networks, the need for global interoperability and the demands for security will give rise to integrated computing and

253 Caldwell, B., "Perot's Pact," *InformationWeek*, October 28, 1996. In this case Perot Systems acts as an investor and shareholder.
254 Only thirty-five percent of companies fully charged MIS expenses back to end-user departments, according to the 1992 DP *Budget Yearbook* from Computer Economics, Inc., Carlsbad, CA. Thirty-three percent of companies did not charge back any costs for work performed.
255 This exemplary case is described in Quinn, J.B., *Intelligent Enterprise,* The Free Press, 1992, p. 91.

communication utilities. These organizations will deliver services that are, at present, hand-crafted by locally owned talent in each corporation. The current situation is comparable to that found in medieval towns. In that age, each municipality had its own guild of artisans producing goods of artistic quality, of limited choice, and at a substantial cost.

The transformation of computing from a local guild craft to an industrialized commodity will be analogous to what happened two hundred years ago when manufacturing migrated from small shops or cottage industries into factories. International service enterprises will supply much of the computing and networking power in the future. Only the largest organizations will be able to afford a self-sufficient information infrastructure.

During this transformation, numerous professional career opportunities will arise from the need to perform systems integration tasks on behalf of local organizations that buy a wide range of services from giant systems suppliers. Only the largest service organizations will be able to risk investing in and continued modernization of their infrastructure while offering predictable and low unit cost operations.

The handicraft approach to writing and maintaining software must also disappear. Information systems integrators will find it attractive to assemble customized systems out of low cost standard components. Computing cycles and bandwidth will surely become a commodity, readily available from any source that enjoys the advantages that occur with economies of scale and marketing presence. Computing tasks will have the capacity to seek, via real time auctioning for IT capacity, those sites that can offer the lowest costs for getting a job done.

What we call outsourcing nowadays will evolve into a new form of international division of specialized labor. These developments will be similar to the ways that the work products of local guilds were displaced by global suppliers offering high quality commodity products. The future of outsourcing is in the delivery of standard commodity offerings. This will ultimately lead to the abandonment of the uneconomical operations, currently sustained by most of the corporate and governmental information systems departments, in favor of market-driven services.

Outsourcing and Systems Integration

Short of outsourcing all information systems, every corporation will find it necessary to retain and directly manage a critically important share of its IT assets; the kernel that is vital to the functioning of the firm. Since almost every enterprise in advanced post-industrial societies is becoming primarily an information-intensive organization, total outsourcing will be a rare occurrence.

The steadily moving boundary between systems owners and systems contractors will surely generate conflicts, contractual disputes and technical incompatibilities. To overcome such problems, it will be necessary to place much greater emphasis on systems integration, which I define as the capacity of independent parts to cohabit as a coherent whole.

With the proliferation of equipment, systems software, applications, and communication offerings, achievement of seamless systems integration is already one of the most difficult challenges facing systems management. As long as heterogeneity prevails within an organization under the same management, the inherent conflicts are traded off, covered up or overcome by a tolerance of inefficiencies. When disagreements cross organizational boundaries, such as disputes with vendors or with internal suppliers about meeting performance standards or cost overruns, poor systems integration quickly turns into intra-organizational strife. When the responsibilities for systems performance split between the integrator and the owner, failures in systems integration will quickly propagate into disagreements, closely followed by rapid deterioration and eventual dissolution of the partnership.

IBM's integrated reporting system for the 1996 Atlanta Olympics is an example of what can happen with poorly conceived systems integration. The Olympics organizers hired IBM to design and operate an extensive network that would keep track of all events, logistics, and records. The primary customers for this information were the press and television networks that required reliable and instant information.

In past Olympics each news organization insisted precisely on what data formats they required, because each relied on different software to support their own reporting needs. For better systems integration IBM convinced everyone that standardized data feeds would be more efficient and reliable. This decision called for extensive testing. The Olympics organizers and the media agreed to perform such tests. However, the best plans do not always become a reality. Each media organization was responsible for conducting its own integration testing. It should not be surprising that on opening day the widely advertised network did not function. The press had to get their results through messengers. In the recriminations that followed, IBM received all of the blame.[256]

The lesson is the conditions that will favor outsourcing depend on making sure that proper systems integration takes place. There cannot be accountability for performance and costs in the absence of full responsibility for the results. Whenever obligations are not clear, dissent will creep in where nobody suspects it. Ultimately, it will be the skill to plan and manage systems integration that will determine the extent to which outsourcing may succeed.

CONSEQUENCES OF OUTSOURCING

Nowadays, most IT organizations still try to manage rapidly exploding technological complexity mainly by depending on their own resources to deliver what their internal customers need. They buy the equipment, select the operating systems, purchase the software, write the applications, and manage the telecommunications links. I do not believe that in the future even very large organizations will be able to sustain the required expertise to do all of this well. In the case of government, even giant agencies no longer have the capacity to keep the talent necessary to manage multi-billion dollar projects. The future belongs to specialists who can market and deliver network-based services whenever, wherever, and in any way a paying customer can articulate justifiable and implementable needs.

I see as many as half of the technical specialists migrating to the service providers. Meanwhile, the technical experts who also possess company specific know-how will merge into the mainstream of their respective organizations. Systems knowledge and a thorough understanding of computing and communications will become inseparable from the knowledge and maturity needed to be a manager. Every manager will have to become a systems manager with a sufficient expertise to make informed choice of when, where, and how to buy information services.

Not long ago, every village and every district of a large town had its own shoemaker. Shoemakers told their clients what to wear because they

---

256 For details see report by David Kirkpatrick in *Fortune*, September 9, 1996. The moral of this story is that you do not mess with the press; their story will always drown yours.

had access to only a limited set of patterns and not much choice of available materials. They are now all gone except for orthopedic specialists. Nowadays shoemaking experts are mostly employed in shoemaking factories, where they design footwear that shows enormous variety. The new footwear uses technologically advanced materials that require engineering expertise. The descendants of shoemakers are now managers of shoe factories. This change in the means and the form of production has now made it possible for consumers to learn just enough to know what to buy. The new products are now sufficiently inexpensive that it does not matter if the buyer does not make the perfect choice. There is always something else to try.

One cannot expect to find anything resembling the existing IT organization twenty-five years from now. The large glass-enclosed, raised floor computer shrines will be recycled for other uses. The computing craft, as we know it, will pass into history as a relic or a hobby. One must remember that shoemakers, ship chandlers, rope-makers, smiths, coopers, and candle makers are now mostly working in places frequented by tourists.

Top management should start planning now on developing the technical and managerial competence for the new era of information management. Employees hired for today's positions are likely to become an obsolete burden without investments in growth of their capabilities. If nobody cares about professional development, it will be only the outsourcers who will have the money and interest in retaining and renovating their employee's knowledge capital.

New Services

New institutions rise to fill the vacuum left when the old ones die. This is a regenerative process that constitutes what Schumpeter calls destructive creativity.[257] Most of the information lifelines for every enterprise will migrate to specialized suppliers and contractors. Policy-making executives will have to find new ways to obtain trusted advice about costs, economics, and technology choices that third parties will be making on their behalf. Only the largest firms will be able to afford the costs of maintaining a retinue of talent that matches the skills for negotiating with and monitoring the outsourcers. Even then, top executives will not ever be sure

257 Schumpeter, J.A., "Capitalism, Socialism and Democracy," *Harper*, 1963.

that they are getting unbiased opinions when their own staffs counsel insourcing as an alternative.

The existing reservoir of consulting advice, such as major accounting firms or computer vendors, cannot be impartial advisors. Most of them already engage in competing for outsourcing contracts. This creates a void into which an enterprise with a new mission and innovative offerings can enter.

Who will be able to assess the economic and technological soundness of a company's information capabilities? They are likely to follow the pattern that led to the creation of independent certification of financial accounts when large multi-divisional firms came into existence. The technology assessors will need exceptional technological know-how and an ability to come up with independent evaluations of costs and performance. They will have the authority to assert when and what a customer can reasonably expect to receive from its information service providers. Amid the confusion about the soundness of conflicting technological claims, corporate executives will surely find it comforting to obtain independent checks of the validity of the vendors' claims.[258]

The emergence of technical certification organizations is already taking place. The National Software Testing Laboratories (NSTL) have been certifying the performance of equipment and software since 1983.[259] Over sixty publications in thirty-five countries publish NSTL detailed test results and product comparisons. The influential Information Technology Association of America (ITAA), in cooperation with the Software Productivity Consortium (SPC), has a program for certifying vendor competency in dealing with year 2000 software problems. Certification of specific competencies will become available after a vendor satisfactorily answers a comprehensive questionnaire. The examiners charge a processing fee of $4,000.[260] The National Computer Security Association (NCSA) offers certification of web sites as meeting minimum security specifica-

---

258 With the rise in outsourcing one can expect an increase in litigation. The technology assessors may be spending much of their time explaining to juries how and why systems projects can get messed up so easily.

259 National Software Testing Laboratories, a unit of Datapro Information Services, a Division of McGraw-Hill Companies in Conshohocken, Pennsylvania.

260 Anthes, G.H., "Trade Groups Roll out Year 2000 Seal of Approval," *Computerworld*, October 7, 1996.

tions. A one year cost of such certification is $8,500, which includes submission to remote attacks and random site visits.[261]

Information services assessment enterprises will become the growth sector of the consulting business. Such groups may end up as the underwriters of technology risks for all firms which divest themselves of an independent capacity to make judgments about their computer investments.[262] The assessors may become an institution, somewhat similar to the existing Health Maintenance Organizations (HMOS). They now have the responsibility of watching out for the proper balance between the needs of the patients and the economic interests of the health providers on behalf of the employers, government, and insurance companies. The new assessors may therefore ultimately evolve and become the risk insurers against technological and economic disasters that nowadays are endemic to the practice of corporate information management.

What to Do

- Judge the efficiency of outsourcing on the basis of unit costs, not on total spending.
- Include in contract terms a financial and activity-based cost model for tracking of IT expenses prior and after outsourcing.
- Determine if a firm retains the choice to repatriate, or move its systems to another vendor, without excessive expense no matter what has been outsourced.
- Avoid outsourcing contracts that have an element of profit sharing with the provider of outsourcing services.
- Start planning now on developing and retaining the technical and managerial competence in an era of increased dependence on outsourcing contractors.

261 Fox, R., "Web Approval," *Communications of the ACM*, October 1996.
262 Over a hundred years ago, one of the most lucrative businesses was insurance of boilers and steam engines. The locally manufactured boilers had a tendency to explode. To increase profits, insurance firms with engineering know-how set up elaborate inspection and safety certification procedures. In due course only a small number of manufacturers could guarantee the safety of their products.

24 Managing Outsourcing

Contracting out need not be abdication.

IF OUTSOURCING occurs without fixing the fundamental flaws in information management practices, it is highly probable that the outsourcing arrangement will be no more successful than what it replaces. Flawed corporations should not rely on contractors to install disciplines that management would not put into effect. To safeguard a corporation's capacity to control its technological destiny, one of the CIO's principal roles must be the oversight over outsourcing policies and contracts. With outsourcing, a corporation may succeed in eliminating many of the contentious inter-departmental disputes only to become saddled with costly contract administration or even litigation expenses.

Corporations often engage consultants or auditors to identify flaws in their systems management and consider such fact-finding as a prelude to transferring IT functions to contractors. The resulting reports tend to refrain from asking why the corporations were incapable of managing their information systems economically and effectively. There is no incentive for the consultant or auditor to reveal that it is not the technologies but the management processes that have grown faulty. If outsourcing occurs without anyone fixing the original flaws beforehand, it is highly probable that the outsourcing arrangement will be no more successful than the arrangements it replaces.

Motivation for much current outsourcing is traceable to absence of attention to business process improvement methods. Firms get into trouble because of poor organizational design, neglect of benchmarking comparisons with competitors, and the absence of metrics that would highlight the gaps in the corporation's information processes. Outsourcing will surely happen if there is no history of encouraging a steady improvement in home-grown practices.

Corporations that are outsourcing find that they have neglected disciplines that would yield improved information systems designs. They do not posses a common information systems architecture, do not use integrated computer-aided systems engineering tools, neglect the necessity for common data elements, do not care about software portability, are reluctant to enforce standard communications protocols, and do not insist on systems interoperability internally or with customers or suppliers.

Such flawed corporations would now rely on contractors to install disciplines that past managers would not put into effect. There is a fault in this presumption. It does not recognize that the outsourcing contractor must impose its own standards on the newly acquired business to lower costs of operations in order to make a profit. The outsourcing contractor will have every incentive to wedge the newly acquired business into a mold that fits its own practices. As a result the outsourced business transforms itself into a supply controlled by a monopoly. It then becomes a classical case of customer lock-in. It will not be feasible to transfer to a competitor, or repatriate, except with disruptions and at an enormous expense.

A Repatriation Case

The 1996 decision by the General Motors Corporation to reassume its control over information technologies from EDS is a noteworthy example of such a situation. For starters, GM retained six recruiting firms to hire forty business unit CIOS, plus two-hundred sixty other information systems executives, plus associated support staffs, to perform business process redesign and to develop common systems.[263] These will hold titles such as sector information executives, business information officers, and process/knowledge management information officers.[264] That is in addition to hiring a new corporate CIO from a telephone company.

After eleven years of EDS guardianship GM finds its applications as piecemeal puzzles, serving the needs of individual operating units. The result is over seven thousand separate systems. Meanwhile, GM is struggling to standardize systems to achieve a higher level of global collaboration and greater interoperability across applications. One should not blame the existing conditions entirely on EDS. An outsourcing contractor cannot be accountable for the misalignment of IT with business objectives, even though that was the stated original objective of the CEO of GM.

A study of such disruption of the fundamental processes of how to align information technologies with business should be a required study

263 Caldwell, B., "IS Hiring Drive is On at GM," *InformationWeek*, December 23, 1996.
264 Scheier, R.L., "GM's first IT chief seeks 300 CIOS," *Computerworld*, December 23, 1996.

for all executives contemplating massive outsourcing of their information management functions. The lesson is that focusing entirely on reducing operating expenses and modernization of technology is a fallacy. What is most important is the preservation of organizational know-how how to manage.[265] If GM must now reconstitute its capacity to steer information technologies, that suggests that the outsourcing diaspora included a wholesale destruction of knowledge assets.[266] One must wonder why many of the eighteen-thousand information systems professionals who were hastily emigrated from GM to EDS in 1985 would not be readily available now to repopulate most of their former posts.

The CIO's Roles

To safeguard a corporation's capacity to control its technological destiny, one of the CIO's principal roles must be the oversight over all IT systems procurement, especially outsourcing policies and contracts. As corporations lose the capacity to retain qualified personnel, the outsourcing of information technologies will invariably emerge as the most attractive cost saving option in the short run. It must be the responsibility of the CIO to assure that the short term savings also remain a long term advantage.

The management of the outsourcing of information technologies raises a number of organizational dilemmas. How can a CIO's views be unbiased if his status, salary, and influence derive from the size of the organization managed? In all likelihood this will mandate shifting of the role of the CIO from operating responsibilities to policy, procurement, acquisition, and contracting. It will require the placement of the CIO job at a high corporate staff position that does not involve day-to-day management of information services. But, this will only work if operating management picks up the responsibility and accountability for information management, information productivity, and information effectiveness. I

265 It was Konrad Adenauer who said that with knowledgeable management one can make any country prosperous again after a totally destructive war. Without knowledgeable management, peace and rich natural resources will not make much of a difference.
266 It may be of parenthetical interest that the Egyptian, Babylonian, Persian, and Mongol empires practiced the annihilation of the priesthood of every conquered nation. This was to make sure that the enslaved population could never hope to recover their identity. It was the dissemination of knowledge capital by the rabbis (by writing the Bible) to all decision-makers, on the way to Babylonian captivity in about 560 BC, that has sustained the preservation of the foundation of our culture to this day.

believe that this is the only path for the CIO to attain a position that is comparable to that of the CFO, who also is a top corporate staff executive.

The Federal Government Case

According to a 1995 report by the Electronic Industry Association, seventy-five percent of the federal government's 1995 IT budget of $25.4 billion is already operated by commercial contractors.[267] Only twenty-five percent of the total IT budget remain as in-house government costs (*e.g.*, organic expenses, in fedspeak parlance). Consequently, federal CIOs must devote most of their attention to acquisition and contracting, not to managing systems or to process improvement. Congressional attention and elaborate procurement regulations accentuate this proclivity. As a result, the federal information management practices are particularly out of balance in comparison with successful commercial practices. A long history of failed federal megaprojects attests to this.

The federal information managers direct information systems design, installation, and operations only in rare instances. They are accountable for IT budgets, but know very little about a department's or agency's total information management costs. They have little say about the business processes that have levels of complexity piled on top of each other, yet persist under the zealous guard as local privileges of the resident bureaucracies.

The problem with this arrangement is that the operating bureaucracies have not been given any accountability for information management, for enhancement of information productivity, or for the assurance of information effectiveness. As previously pointed out, the federal budgeting system concentrates almost entirely on cost, with an almost total disregard for the measures of results. The almost complete severance of connections between the costs for IT and the costs for performing information management tasks is a guarantee of continued malfunctions that no amount of outsourcing can cure.

267 That accounts only for the costs of business data processing. It does not include comparable large sums for intelligence, surveillance, as well as for defense command and control.

A Commercial Outsourcing Case

The 1996 outsourcing award from the banking firm of J.P. Morgan highlights the importance of information technologies to this firm, as well as an apparent anxiety about realizing lower costs for computing while increasing quality. According to their 1995 annual report, J.P. Morgan spent $1,040 million for information technologies. This figure represents forty-two percent of their total expenses for employee compensation and benefits, or the unprecedented sum of $66,611 per capita per year. Despite these expenses, which rank among the highest recorded by any commercial firm, the information productivity of J.P. Morgan was only marginally positive.[268]

Outsourcing in-house computer operations to vendors may offer an easy way to solve the problem of managing information technologies. It presumes that such action will finally introduce a competitive market price as a way of balancing the practically unconstrained demands of customers against the need to realize value-added benefits from the computers. For competitively based outsourcing of real-time transactions to produce economically attractive results, the information services industry will have to charge real-time event-driven fees. In this way the value of each information transaction will be appropriate to its price and the value each customer attaches to it.

PRESERVATION OF CORE COMPETENCIES

One of the primary roles of the CIO as a policy-maker is to assure that the corporation will effectively manage, coordinate, and integrate information systems contracted out to vendors. This requires reaching an agreement at the executive committee level on the corporation's essential competencies, which must always remain under direct control. Such a policy should also specify how to acquire new systems and innovative technologies. It must articulate what to do with systems that are already in place and define how to transition to new technologies. It must describe the CIO roles in managing and integrating information resources that will reside in the hands of contractors.

---

268 Only US national intelligence agencies exceed such expenditures for information technologies.

Lest it be misunderstood, I do favor maximizing the amount of outsourcing of information services to commercial enterprises. However, outsourcing must offer a decisive cost advantage over its life cycle, preserve residual values, and include potential repatriation costs in all pricing estimates. Outsourcing makes sense as long as a corporation recognizes that contractors have good reasons to pursue their own technology choices, data definitions, systems design tools, and unique solutions. The role of the CIO is then to act as a safeguard against outsourcers' misuse of technologies for their own restrictive advantages.

Administration of Outsourcing

With outsourcing, a corporation may succeed in eliminating many of the contentious interdepartmental disputes only to become saddled with costly contract administration or even litigation expenses. Therefore, the CIO must put in place principles and guidelines for users of information services. This material must define who may deal with the service providers because improper or conflicting requests can produce costly mistakes. Moreover, the formulation of such a policy must be consistent with the original intent of the outsourcing relationship. An gradual drift from the initial discipline to opportunistic practices will invariably corrupt that relationship. CIOs must also provide oversight over local demands for information services to assure the corporation that it will end up owning portable, interoperable, and innovative outsourced systems. Such applications should deliver all benefits to the corporation and only allow incentive bonuses to the contractor for exceptional accomplishments. A corporation cannot abdicate its responsibility for reaping benefits from information technologies to an outsourcing contractor.

One of the major sources of conflict for a CIO operating largely with outsourced services is the management of inter-departmental, multinational, or multi-business systems that support shared processes across the entire organization. The CIO should be able to commission consortia that will deliver services for corporate-wide processes, such as those supporting finance, personnel, logistics, transportation, telecommunications, cash management, or banking functions. If this happens, the corporation may find it advisable to retain its own systems integration talent. Competition and conflict of interest among multiple contractors may leave the corporation defenseless in case of a breakdown of cooperation within a consortium.

Outsourcing and Managerial Accountability

In the information age the control of information is a critical attribute of power that every manager must possess. It is feasible and often economical to rent, contract out, sublet, license, and delegate the commodity supply of information technologies. I believe that the commercial sector should perform technology delivery functions to the fullest extent possible. However, I have great difficulty in accepting a policy that outsources the responsibility for integration of information systems away from well-functioning management processes. Systems integration is the function of the brain of the enterprise and should not completely passed over to a contractor.

What functions, safeguards, capabilities, and staff skills should then remain within the organization? This question can be answered only after a thorough review at the highest levels of management. It should be done before any outsourcing negotiations takes place. An explicit reservation of the retained responsibilities and functions must take place before employing contractors to do work. Guiding outsourcing policy must therefore be one of the principal obligations of any cio as the relative share of the budget under contract keeps growing.

Preservation of Talent and Outsourcing

An organization must be able to retain a cadre of skilled and dedicated professionals who see their careers attached to their employer and not to the outsourcing contractors. If this is not the case, the corporation or government agency will lose the capacity to manage its information resources. The cio must therefore articulate what expertise must remain before any part of the corporation may outsource elements that are operationally critical, or a likely avenue for future advancement. The cio must see to it that short-term cost reductions do not impede the ability of the organization to attract, retain, and motivate essential talent.

A policy of outsourcing critical applications to realize lower cost is not likely to deliver more effective information if it permanently demoralizes the most competent staff. Outsourcing without planning the careers of technical staffs will result in a massive exodus of the most talented people.[269] People who see no promotional prospects will leave. Individuals with the largest accumulation of company-specific experience will transfer to the outsourcing firms. The result is the corporation will have to pay substantially more for identical talent. The organization is also likely to lose the services of its best employees, who would otherwise remain essential for performing the work that outsiders cannot or should not do.[270]

Outsourcing Rationale

So far, I have managed to collect only a limited set of reliable data about the advantages or disadvantages of the outsourcing of computer-related services. Despite repeated assertions that firms contract out information technologies primarily for reasons of economic advantage, this does not appear to be the case. Figure 48 compares different levels of outsourcing to either overspending or underspending for IT in operating divisions of a large multinational firm.[271]

If outsourcing were to be economically attractive in these cases, more firms with a higher percentage of outside services would show up as underspending on IT. Such assumption receives no support from the data. About an equal number of firms are either under- or overspending, regardless of the extent of outsourcing. Two firms with the highest outsourcing ratio show that their actual IT costs are higher than can be reasonably expected.

Until proven otherwise, I shall maintain the hypothesis that outsourcing happens when management cannot or will not find a way to positively manage additional investments in information technologies. At that point it becomes expedient to turn to vendors to make the hard investment choices by proxy.

269 For instance, Xerox, after outsourcing, lost in short succession its chief technology officer, the VP of information management in charge of fixing the year 2000 problem, and the executive VP in charge of global systems solutions, as well as his principal deputy. Caldwell, B., "Exodus of IS Execs from Xerox Continues," *InformationWeek*, November 4, 1996.
270 It is not unusual for the same people to come back a day after outsourcing, charging a multiplier of two hundred fifty percent of their former salaries.
271 For a detailed discussion of the technique for coming up with an estimated IT budget see Chapter 37. The expected spending is calculated from the constants and coefficients of a regression equation that predicts IT spending for look-alike firms with a high level of confidence.

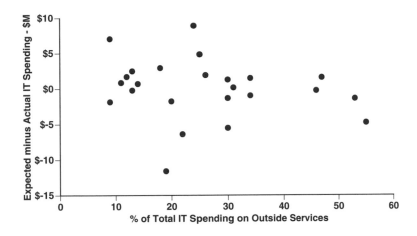

Figure 48   Greater outsourcing does not tend to lower overall IT costs

What to Do

- Fix intrinsic flaws in information management practices, such as insufficient definitions of accountability for information resource management, prior to outsourcing.
- Watch out for conditions that transform any outsourced business into a monopoly service or customer lock-in.
- Make sure that any outsourced business can transfer to a competitor or become repatriated, without major disruptions and excessive expenses.
- Specify what expertise must remain before any part of the organization may outsource elements that are operationally critical, or are the means for realizing competitive gains.

Part VI
Causes and Consequences

- Understanding the origins of computer practices
- Evolutionary phases in technological development
- Interactions between managerial and technological influences
- Destructive aspects of recent technological progress
- The emerging role of software as a critical asset

25 A Historical Perspective

Faster travel requires greater attention to the passage.

THE INTERACTIONS between socioeconomic forces in the workplace explain the character of past IT investment cycles. The conventional wisdom that views computers strictly as technical innovations does not offer useful insights. Identical computer technologies produce different consequences depending on the culture in which they function. Computing will become potentially useful to more than a billion people, as if it were a consumer appliance. The computer investment cycle will shift from that of a servant of commercial and government bureaucracies to electronic commerce, entertainment, and education. The next computer investment cycle will revolve around conflicts between the global promoters and national interests. Future events may dictate measures to defend our society against acts that corrupt information technologies so that they disrupt our society.

The pattern of capital spending for computers has not followed a smooth trend over the years. Since the advent of computerization, investments have followed a cyclical form roughly corresponding to the readiness of management to commit new funds to keep up with the competition. Periodic compulsions to follow the leader apparently attach to computers more so than any other invention except for military weapons. The motivation here is to stay ahead of what prolific publicity promotes as an inevitable historic trend. Such inexorable developments offer a good reason for futuristic magazine stories and celebration at industry get-togethers. One must invest to forestall somebody's takeover by using computers as a competitive weapon that would disrupt the customary ways of conducting business.

THE PERILS OF DISINTERMEDIATION

Since their inception, computers have always been a threat to the rising legions of information intermediaries. Their numbers have steadily grown as the share of national income from agriculture and industry declined. The information workers realized that in due course, they too could be stripped of their livelihood whenever machines became sufficiently smart to perform what they were doing. It is the interaction between the socio-economic forces in the workplace and progress in electronics that explains the character of the IT investment cycles. The conventional wisdom that views the development of computers strictly as technical innovations in electronic circuitry does not offer useful insights. Identical computer technologies produce different consequences depending on the culture in which they function.

The dating of the cycles that follow refer to the US. Although the underlying technologies are universal, with all countries buying essentially identical devices and identical systems software, the investment cycles vary depending on the levels achieved in national economical development. When the wages for the information workforce exceed one half of the total wage bill in an organization, computers become the preferred means by which the administrative functionaries will try to buttress their position.

It is not technology but the contention among information workers for preservation of their status that explains much of the dynamics of how computers evolved into their present forms.

1930-1957: THE MACHINE ACCOUNTING ERA

Much of this earliest cycle originated in increased government tax regulations that required the documentation of financial transactions. Centralization of control over logistics, the result of WWII controls, also required detailed accountability for physical goods. During this era even senior executives with a lifetime of experience in marketing punched card equipment were unable to understand the explosive demand for calculating devices.

Tabulating installations made possible the direct displacement of clerical labor since government and corporate bureaucracies were unable to hire sufficient staffs to perform boring, low-paid work with high reliability. Actual savings were subject to after-the-fact audits. However, there was a limit to how much of the routine low-grade clerical labor could be displaced by machine accounting methods. Costs rose as organizations hired more administrators, analysts, and accountants. At that time, the tabulating installations were typically under the supervision of a Tabulating Manager, who usually belonged to the Association of Machine Accountants.

1957-1963: THE MECHANIZATION CYCLE

The headquarters staffs of increasingly bureaucratized global corporations now expected to receive large amounts of detailed data from local operations. They also required a computing capacity to process the punched cards and the paper forms that flooded into their mail-rooms. The demand for data processing devices accelerated. Even the head of the world's largest tabulating equipment manufacturer underestimated the demand for stored-program computers by a wide margin. It was qualitative change in the relationships between central and decentralized operations that motivated corporations to create data centers at corporate headquarters.

This investment cycle took place almost exclusively under the auspices of financial executives who discovered that control over mechanization of financial records expanded their power enormously. Cost reduction was not the purpose of this cycle. It catered to the needs of the controllership function that used computers to enlarge their influence into every detail of production and marketing. Questions about the financial justification of IT investments did not arise because the financial executives were trusted to make the right decisions. Towards the end of this cycle large numbers of labor-intensive and inefficient local computers started to feed data to the central machines. This offered opportunities for new computing manufacturers, especially where national origin made it politically expedient to set up firms in protected markets.

The tabulating installations were then renamed, becoming the data processing departments. They fell under the supervision of a Data Processing Manager, who usually belonged to the Data Processing Management Association.

1963-1969: THE DATA CENTER CYCLE

In this stage the demand for computers expanded faster than the manufacturing capacity that produced them. Complex priority schemes assigned waiting list positions for equipment orders. Corporate IT budgets were rising at a rate of over thirty percent per annum. Consolidation of local marginal data centers and massive reprogramming of applications inherited from the tabulating cycle now took place. The primary objective was the extension of the influence and control of the financial executives over every routine business transaction. Mainframe technology fitted this approach perfectly and formed a symbiotic relationship between IBM and the financial executives. During this era IBM maintained a price protection umbrella over all equipment costs, which simplified the investment decisions. One negotiated delivery schedules and technical support, not costs or budgets.

From the standpoint of corporate financial planning, the expenses for information technologies did not require much justification as long as the data processing function remained under the tutelage of the chief financial officer. As reflected in national economic statistics, investments in computers became noticeable, but not significant, for the first time.

The rapidly rising group of information managers, now carrying the title of Director of Management Information Systems (MIS) or Assistant Controller, supported the ambitions of these subordinates to the chief financial executive. They achieved their control missions by means of a disciplined approach to standardized data and through the imposition of homogenized procedures for handling most routine paperwork.

1969-1975: The Time Sharing Cycle

The totalitarian-like reign of central mainframes and finance department dominance gave rise to intra-organizational conflict. The control of finance over all computers suffered erosion as other departments, such as production, engineering, and marketing discovered that the possession of information was synonymous with organizational power. The central information systems organization responded by instituting a new round of equipment acquisitions to preserve its hold on new technologies. They offered the non-financial organizations access to centralized computing through time-sharing of mainframe computers through slow telephone circuits. This was an attempt to preserve an untenable position by extending the reach of IT through inappropriate technologies.

Some scientific, engineering, and particularly production departments responded to these costly and nonresponsive services by taking their business to independent information service suppliers. The concept of outsourcing of information services took hold for the first time.

The defectors from the clutches of the centralized financial establishment also started purchasing small scale computers that offered online access to computing power through high-speed terminals over local cabling. This avoided dependency on expensive telephone circuits. The contest between centralized and decentralized computing stimulated the expansion of relatively sophisticated computing capacity at local levels.[272] It also generated budget growth where it escaped attention from corporate staffs. During this cycle the need for integration between computing and telecommunication became apparent.

Towards the end of this era questions about computer investments appeared on the agenda of executive committees. The usual reason was to settle disputes between competing groups, each claiming that they could save money by gaining computing independence. Business executives came to recognize that the life cycle support costs of information processing was much larger than the acquisition cost of computers as soon as each local site acquired their own staffs, consultants and suppliers.[273]

With rising budgets and increasing equipment acquisitions, a few corporations started to promote their Directors of Data Processing to Vice Presidents of Information Systems. In isolated instances, the shape of the future relationships became apparent when companies created captive Information Services Divisions to serve internal needs, as if the company's computer users were customers. This was the beginning of the breakdown of one-time monopolies into service-oriented units.

---

272 Throughout history all entrenched powers have resorted to preservation of their untenable positions by offering incremental enhancements or marginal compromises. That works as long as the subjects do not have other options. The status quo collapses when geography, politics, or technology offers a viable choice. Then the subjects will switch their allegiance. The mockery is that the entrenched powers are initially in a better position to offer genuine improvements than their opponents. For example, both IBM and DEC were initially in a better position to offer what Microsoft and Intel took away. Instead, they were too preoccupied defending what they could abandon gracefully. In the case of mainframe computing, the central systems staffs fought against the introduction of mini-computer clusters and lost not only the battles, but also their customers.

273 It took the US federal government until the summer of 1996 to recognize that one cannot control the costs of computing and information processing by relying exclusively on onerous regulations restricting the way that government acquires equipment.

1975-1981: THE MINICOMPUTER CYCLE

At this point the purchasing power of computing and information services started to migrate from being a central overhead, administered by the financial executives, to the realm of consumers of computing, where it disappeared into the cost of goods. This liberated enormous amounts of new discretionary spending. Operating executives now found it attractive to trade off expenditures for labor in favor of computerized automation. Local operations also acquired their own systems development staffs, or created relationships with consulting firms. This crystallization of enclaves of local competence acted as a catalyst for a chain reaction that then propelled the expanding demands for computing.

The minicomputer investment cycle inaugurated the proliferation of computing capacity. It initiated the shift from the relatively disciplined computing on mainframes to improvised computing whenever someone could afford to purchase their own equipment. Prices of computing dropped rapidly as competition became more intensive and the costs of information processing shifted from the central processing unit, where there was little competition, to computer peripherals and to software, where new and hungry entrants made prices drop precipitously. In this phase of development it became increasingly difficult to account for computer spending. Few directors of information systems could tell how much their firm spent on information technologies. Computing started to become embedded into a firm's goods-creation processes and therefore disappeared into accounts such as manufacturing machinery or research.

Toward the end of this cycle it is possible to observe the phenomenon that is to emerge in the future. Computer technologies would cease acting as the means for exercising control over individuals and their work.[274] The image of the omnipresent "big brother" watching employees would now be mitigated by the discovery that the possession of computing power

---

274 As is often the case, congressional hearings on a social problem may herald the end rather than the beginning of a political issue. In April 1983, I testified before the Committee on Science and Technology, US House of Representatives, Mr. Albert Gore presiding. A number of social activists presented a dismal view of the future for computing. I made the case that rising unemployment and increased totalitarian controls were not likely to result from computerization in the foreseeable future.

makes local management feel more empowered.[275] For the first time computer technologies became subservient to the capacity of local managers and professional employees to satisfy their rising information processing needs.

The emphasis on clever software ceased to be a priority concern. Increasingly wasteful uses of cheap computing offered affordable processing for even poorly designed applications. During this stage the traditional formality of systems development methodologies lost their importance as experimental and interactive improvisations offered faster completion schedules. As a testimony to the attractiveness of these approaches, a flood of new orders for computing capacity were placed with computer vendors. It set the conditions for the next investment cycle, as employees had acquired the taste for the instant availability and personal ownership of the coveted computing resources.

1981-1988: THE MICROCOMPUTER CYCLE

The overwhelming acceptance of the microcomputer by office workers is a phenomenon that hardly anyone foresaw. A business systems analyst, a financial controller, or a senior executive in the 1970s would find it inconceivable that, within fifteen years, approximately three quarters of us office workers would operate their own computers at their own desks. Hardly anybody in the computer industry could imagine that individuals would possess exclusive access to the calculating power of a 1972 mainframe computer and the storage capacity of a 1965 major data center.[276]

The driving force behind the microcomputer investment cycle was the anxiety of office workers that they may become obsolete. Another strong motivation was the desire to get rid of the burdensome dependen-

---

275 It is likely that this apprehension will come to haunt us again when computer networks become universally connected and the much needed disciplines of network control may be able to watch each keystroke at every terminal.

276 A small group at the Xerox's Palo Alto Research Center (PARC) clearly articulated and documented this point of view early in 1974 as a proposed business strategy for Xerox's future in the computing business. That contributed to the decision of Xerox to exit from the computer mainframe business acquired in 1969, at an enormous cost. However, exiting is always easier than sustaining a long-range commitment. Xerox never carried through its overwhelming initial advantages to become one of the dominant suppliers of desktop computing equipment. The author was a member of a four-man review board that recommended exiting from mainframe manufacturing and shifting Xerox's business strategy entirely to graphic-based, networked desktops.

cy on the monopolistic computer department. The microcomputer investment cycle reflects the shift from the dominance of computer experts to the defensive enthusiasm of the office workers. It was the office workers who wished to add computer skills to their resumes, as large corporations began downsizing. In many respects, it was the professional workers that led the charge to acquire total computing independence. This was also the beginning of a transition from people acquiring computer expertise to computer software acquiring a better match with the capabilities of people. At this stage, the introduction of microcomputers takes place without any pretense to attempt a financial justification. It provides no possibility for even the most elementary way for verifying the claimed benefits.[277]

The explosive nature of the microcomputer investment cycle introduced an element of discontinuity and surprise that is unprecedented in the history of technology. The firms that dominated the earlier investment cycles, such as IBM, National Cash Register, Digital Equipment Corporation, Burroughs, UNIVAC, and Honeywell-Bull towards the end of this stage showed enormous financial losses and dismissed a large share of their workforce. As an added insult these giants become increasingly dependent on industry start-up firms such as Compaq, Lotus, Microsoft, and Oracle.

The corporation that embodied the attributes of computing independence and local processing capacity better than others, the Digital Equipment Corporation, was unable to stretch its success from the mini-computer era into the microcomputer cycle. It was a reflection of a bias that could not conceive of the acquisition of a personal computer was more a matter of psychological effectiveness than of engineering efficiency. Students will study the DEC case for years as an example of engineering ideology overtaking socioeconomic comprehension, and how those misjudgments led an exceptionally successful organization to follow a path close to disastrous demise.

The personally operated computer offered an enormous expansion in accessibility to calculating power. From the standpoint of improving cooperation and coordination among office workers, however, the microcomputer became a means for inhibiting communication. Increasingly, it

---

277 A good case study of the rejection of the computer department by a personnel department is in Weston, R., "HR to IS: Resistance is Futile," *Computerworld*, December 9, 1996. Without any technological know-how, the personnel department of Blue Cross/Blue Shield set up its own data center, engaged consultants, and purchased a software package.

came to be recognized by management as a source of a spreading chaos.[278] Nobody could determine what the payoffs were from the microcomputer investments made during this cycle, since corporate overhead expenses rose faster than revenues and profits. The generous spending on personal computers did not produce convincing economic evidence, other than glowing anecdotes, that organizations became more productive.

Those who gained from the increasing confusion were the computer professionals, consultants, and sellers of prepackaged solutions. The revenues of the consulting firms rose four times faster than sales of computer equipment. The revenues of computer services firms grew twice as fast as those of the consultants. The sales of shrink-wrapped software topped the growth rates of everyone else in the computer industry while realizing gross margins exceeding those earned from luxury goods.

To cope with the proliferation of choice and the huge budget increases, corporate management now elevated their principal computer executive to the corporate rank with the title of Chief Information Officer. The newly minted CIOs flocked to gatherings that resembled the atmosphere of social or political clubs more than the gathering of professional associations, such as is customary in law, medicine, engineering or science where one listens to findings of carefully conducted research. In the short span of forty years the computer custodians graduated from an office next to the stock room to the executive corridor. They attained that status not as technologists, but as corporate politicians. The recognition of the critical role of computing in the power structure of organizations now manifested itself as an organizational reality.

1988-1995: THE CLIENT/SERVER INVESTMENT CYCLE

The client/server concept of organizing information services arrived as a reaction against the unmanageable proliferation of stand-alone computers.[279] It did not happen, as was claimed, as the need to replace expensive

---

278 By 1995 the corporate purchases of personal computers finally slowed down to an eleven percent per annum growth rate, down from the spectacular increases of one hundred percent per annum in the mid-1980s. Needle, D., "Corporate PC Buying Slows," *InformationWeek*, April 8, 1996.

279 By 1995 the annual shipments of personal computers reached fifty-eight million, forty-three percent of them in North America. The projected annual volume for year 2000 is 117 million, with thirty-eight percent in North America. See Martin, M.H., "When Info Worlds Collide," *Fortune*, October 28, 1996.

mainframe computing with a more distributed computing architecture.[280] The evidence is now overwhelming that mainframe computing is, in fact, more economical than the highly acclaimed server substitute.[281]

In terms of intra-corporate politics, it was not prudent to promote this investment cycle as a way of curbing microcomputer independence. Employees enjoyed their newly gained computing independence too much to sanction such an attack. However, something had to be done to restrain the mushrooming local initiatives. Excessive local autonomy inhibited attempts to interconnect individual microcomputers and did not remedy the burdens of incompatible, non-interoperable, insecure and costly local area networks. The client/server came into being because organizations could no longer afford to tolerate computing hobby-shop enclaves.

The generous funding for the client/server investment cycle, without much economic justification, was a form of counter-revolutionary response to the microcomputer uprisings against the central computer establishment. Unfortunately, instead of delivering lower costs of computing through consolidation of local networks under a network administrative discipline, the client/servers turned out to be more expensive and less reliable.

For example, the vendors of client/server architectures, who have claimed for the last five years to offer a low cost alternative to mainframe computing, will have to backtrack on their promises. In a recent survey fifty-three percent of respondents to a survey of two hundred twenty-five key IS managers reported that their client/server projects were over budget, late, and with fewer features than specified. The survey also found that thirty-one percent of all client/server projects suffer cancellation.[282] Nobody would ever fly an airline where thirty-one percent of flights

---

280 A client/server configuration for 5,000 end users would cost seventy percent more that a comparable mainframe/terminal setup. The five-year total cost of ownership of the client/server of $241 million exceeds substantially a comparable mainframe/terminal expense of $141 million. See Dec, K., "Client/Server: Fiscal Benefits and Justification," *Gartner Group Symposium/ITxpo '96*, Lake Buena Vista, Florida, October 1996.

281 This was put well in the following: "Remember the days when many executives thought client/servers were going to replace legacy systems and save a bundle? Everybody knew it was baloney, but not until big name market researchers like Gartner published numbers did the fallacy die." Baatz, E.B., "Digesting the ROI Paradox," *CIO Magazine*, October 1, 1996.

282 Caldwell, B., "Client-Server, Can It Be Saved?" *InformationWeek*, April 8, 1996.

crashed and where fifty-three percent of the flights did not arrive at their scheduled destination.

A major contributor to the rising expenses for client/servers arose from the propensity of supporters to specify the latest technologies for all new applications. This had and still has the unfortunate result that quick obsolescence sets in soon after the initial installation takes place. The proponents of the best and latest equipment choices rarely, if ever, included the costs of the upgrades in their project life-cycle projections. Yet the costs of upgrades keep rising steadily as the technological life of equipment and software shrinks. For instance, a reliable source of financial data estimates the cost of upgrading to a Windows 95 environment for a client/server configuration to be as much as eighteen thousand dollars per server. The estimated cost to the US economy to proceed with the Windows 95 upgrades would then be twenty billion dollars.[283] Such expense may more than double the costs per capita for computing in the year of the upgrade.[284]

The personnel support costs for loosely organized distributed computing far exceeds any conceivable reductions in the costs of processing equipment. However, favoring the client/server architecture is its capacity to improve response times to inquiries. The increased independence of the microcomputer operators from the disciplines of the central regime also allows the quick development of local adaptations, modifications and enhancement of standard applications, now readily available at a low cost from off-the shelf software packages. However, the greatest gain from the client/server environment is in its facility to permit a great deal of local experimentation that leads to innovative computer solutions. With the increased attainment of computer literacy, microcomputer customers now demand instant network feedback and application flexibility. They now demand superior network performance, rapid database access times, and instant response to the key-strokes that they became accustomed to when they had a stand-alone desk-top machine at their complete control.

To obtain these conveniences somebody must pay a higher price for technology, support services, and training. For instance, the estimated first year client/server training costs for a midsize network of two hundred clients is $150,000, for customer education $32,850, and for support staff

283 Garber, J.R., "The $20 Billion Upgrade," *Forbes*, September 26, 1994.
284 Gerber, C., "Client/Server Price Tag: 40% of is Dollars," *Computerworld*, November 6, 1995, p. 7.

training $87,000. That adds up to $1,350 per client per year, or at least fifty percent more than the first year depreciation of hardware and software.[285]

The dynamics of the client/server investment cycle arise from the perceptions of the increasingly demanding customers that they require better computing capabilities regardless of economics. This spending cycle slows down only when corporate management notices that instead of creating more efficient computing, the IT budget continues to grow faster than any other corporate expense category without demonstrable improvements in competitive results.

PROSPECTS

If history teaches anything, it is the lesson that there is much we can learn from the patterns of the past. Understanding history can prepare us for contending with difficulties when the unexpected appears. The faster we progress, the greater the importance of understanding the forces that have propelled us. The rapidly growing population of microcomputers creates the foundation upon which all future developments will materialize: [286]

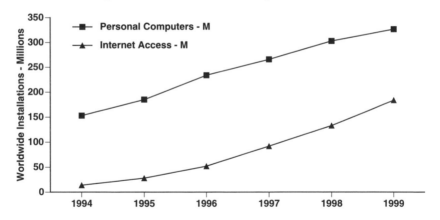

Figure 49   Installed base of personal computers

285 Caldwell, B. "The Five Percent Solution," *InformationWeek*, August 8, 1994, p. 59.
286 *Solutions Quarterly*, UNIVAC Corporation, Summer 1996.

The adoption rates of computing are uneven. They vary from country to country, with the US clearly leading in the acceptance of personal computers as an essential technology: [287]

	Computers per 100 People
United States	35
Australia	27
Canada	25
Britain	20
Netherlands	20
Singapore	18
Germany	17
France	16
Hong Kong	15
Japan	14
Italy	12
Taiwan	9
South Korea	7

Figure 50   Computers per one hundred people, 1995

The 1995 population of the US was 263 million, with a labor force of 123 million, of which 71 million were in information occupations. The ratio of 35 computers per 100 people suggests that a significant share of the installed base of computers must be in households. With 92 million computers installed, the US would have about half of the world's computers. This also suggests that most of the people in information occupations already have a computer for their business uses.

The current dominance of the US in computer ownership cannot continue. In 1995 the US share of shipments of personal computers declined to thirty-eight percent.[288] Considering the current state of com-

287 "The Hitchhiker's Guide to Cybernomics," *The Economist*, September 28, 1996.
288 "Worldwide PC Market Share by Region," *Washington Technology*, December 5, 1996. The share of Western Europe was twenty-five percent, Japan nine percent, the rest of the Asian/Pacific region eleven percent, and all others the last seventeen percent.

puterization, the new IT investment cycles will have to reach out to completely new opportunities. The blossoming of an information-based society is yet to unfold in the cycles to come. In the cycles so far, we have only organized the initial steps towards an uncertain journey ahead.

1995-2002: The Internet/Intranet Cycle

The spasmodic interactions between information technologies and changing customer attitudes will unfold more clearly as the Internet/intranet outburst becomes the dominant mode for most computing.

The Internet, in its present form, has existed for more than twenty years. It took the widespread acceptance of a few relatively simple software man-machine standards to achieve the totally unprecedented exponential growth that has gained new adherents at a rate that sometimes exceeds twenty percent per month.[289] This just proves that it is innovation that reduces customer use costs, and not just technology equipment expenses that becomes decisive in shaping future developments. Simple economics dictates that. The cost for the equipment, per hour, of a personal computer is 38 cents.[290] The average fully allocated hourly cost of an information worker is about forty dollars.[291] What matters from now on is not the purchase cost of computers, but their ease of use, since the costs of the user of a personal computer is now 99% of the visible expenses for the equipment.

The dominance of Internet-based activities have their origin in the adverse reactions to the excessive support costs, as well as the difficulties in dealing with the complexity of applications, whether delivered by mainframe programmers or coming from ready-made application packages residing on client/networks. Corporations will continue setting up Intranets without even the most perfunctory cost justification. Everyone perceives that this technology is simple and inexpensive without necessarily needing any proof that this is so.[292]

---

289 Nothing in the history of technology has shown a comparable adoption rate. Ten million customers signed up for the Internet in three years. It took thirty-eight years for the spread of the telephone, twenty-two for fax, and seven for the personal computer. See "Years to Reach 10 Million Customers," *Computerworld*, September 30, 1996.
290 Assumes the purchase price of $3,000, four year depreciation and 2,000 hours of connect time per year.
291 $80,000 per year, including benefits, pensions, overhead costs and an allocation of corporate administrative expenses working for an estimated 2,000 hours per year.
292 Nash, K.S., "Figuring Dollars, Sense of Intranets," *Computerworld*, May 27, 1996, p. 1.

The Internet/Intranet solutions deliver a devastating blow against whatever dominance remains in the hands of central computer staffs. Any department, group or even individual now has the capacity to develop fairly interesting and low cost applications with a minimum initial investment. During this cycle individuals discover dramatic improvement in their ability to learn how to take advantage of computer applications. With only a few minutes of experimentation, every application may seem to be intuitively similar. This presumes that an organization has adopted a standard software package (i.e., browser) to perform the essential applications and network management tasks.

The Internet/intranet solutions offer, for the first time the capacity for universal connectivity among organizations independent of hardware, software and communications solutions from particular vendors. The current business uses of the Internet illustrate how this technology's logical independence works in improving the flow of information. Seventy percent of the companies have reported using the Internet for information distribution internally, as well as to suppliers and customers. Seventy percent of companies use it to distribute marketing information internally. Forty-five percent have shifted to this means of communication for internal administrative purposes.[293]

All the prior IT cycles increased their served population only at a relatively slow rate dictated by the length of the training time. The almost intuitive grasp of Internet/intranet applications rapidly opens computing to mass markets on a global scale. New developments in language recognition and automatic language translation will make access to applications not only technologically but also somewhat culturally independent.[294]

---

293 From a survey of two hundred twenty-five IS managers, as reported in *Information Week*, April 8, 1996, p. 44.
294 One way of scaling the impact of the investment cycles is to count the number of individuals who actively participate in programming information logic, at each development stage (global estimates):

1930-1957:	The Machine Accounting Era	5,000
1957-1963:	The Mechanization Investment Cycle	25,000
1963-1969:	The Data Center Investment Cycle	50,000
1969-1975:	The Time Sharing Investment Cycle	150,000
1975-1981:	The Minicomputer Investment Cycle	250,000
1981-1988:	The Microcomputer Investment Cycle	5,000,000
1988-1995:	The Client/Server Investment Cycle	25,000,000
1995-2002:	The Internet/Intranet Investment Cycle	500,000,000

In many respects, the Internet/intranet revolution will provide many of the same liberation attributes as did the introduction of microcomputers. The difference will be that the cost of accessing Internet-based information will be extremely low when the cost of access to communications drops, as it will. As a result computing will become potentially useful to more than a billion people, as if it were a consumer appliance. At this stage of development the computer investment cycle begins to shift from its original mission as the servant of commercial and government bureaucracies. We will soon observe the first glimmers of developments that favor electronic commerce, entertainment, and displacement of conventional print or video media as we move towards a computer-based civilization.

2002 and Beyond

Computer cycles have occurred regularly every six to seven years because it takes at least that long to institute the necessary managerial reforms. Although the technology innovation cycles have become shorter, that has not made much of a difference in the computer cycles, which just reinforces the idea that it is the social and organizational contexts and not the technology potential that paces the achievable progress.

As before, the proponents of each next wave will claim that investment funds must become available to correct for problems and abuses created during the prior phase of development. Therefore, to predict the future one must first focus on what will be remedial needs, prior to guessing what technological progress one may expect.

The most likely problem that will need correction during for the next computing wave will be the need to find remedies for the opportunistic permissiveness of the client/server as well as Internet phases. Management will now hear about large amounts of the lost employee time "surfing" the Internet, about periodic systems failures that stop all work and about incidents of massive security collapses that idle information workers. The blame will be placed on systems management practices that tolerated undisciplined local improvisation. The flimsy and fragile applications will require a complete overhaul, with little salvage value. Requests for new funds will carry the justification that applications without adequate engineering or security need replacement to become fully network-compatible.[295] This will be particularly true of mission-critical applications built with easy-to-learn tools such as *PowerBuilder* and *VisualBasic.* Systems constructed with these makeshift tools from client/server vendors will not satisfy the rigorous demands for seamless network integration and certifiable network security. Everyone will regret the earlier haste into designs that placed excessive logic within the desktop computers. The resultant entanglements of application programs with specific hardware and operating systems produced impromptu solutions that were non-interoperable while making it extremely difficult to attempt any integration of network computing services. Consider the estimated $300-$600 billion costs of fixing a relatively minor violation in elementary systems management discipline, the missing two calendar year digits for year 2000. That negligence pales into insignificance of what it will cost to remedy the abandonment of any discipline that concerns data, applications and systems interoperability, which typify the client-server and Internet eras.

Another reason for launching a new wave of computer spending will be the need to lower transaction costs by means of electronic commerce. A glimmer of this future is noticeable in the rapidly expanding EDI (Electronic Data Interchange) commerce that automates what are, at present, paper-shuffling functions. The truly large gains will come from electronic telepresence that allows people at remote locations to see and use programs on any computer.[296] Such developments will result in enormous reduction in the number of costly intermediaries such as wholesalers, brokers, interpreters, agents, coordinators, administrators, examiners, and expediters. These occupations presently make a good living by intervening in the flow of information between the sources and destinations of goods and services. They offer cost reduction opportunities just waiting to happen, though the expenses for technologies will now tend to be so small as to become almost irrelevant. At this stage of development the social and organizational costs will surpass every other consideration.

Costs and Prices

295 In announcing the March 1997 conference "Client/Server Confronts the Internet," the Gartner Group enticed attendance by offering the following perspective: "Did you know that by 1998 sixty percent of an organization's existing client/server applications will be rewritten, competing for the resources that are needed to maintain fragile legacy systems?"

296 Upton, D.M., and McAfee, A., "The Real Virtual Factory," *Harvard Business Review*, July-August, 1996.

A sense of the cost of a typical commercial transaction comes from benchmarking studies. For instance, the low labor cost Tandem Computers RISC-based server, optimized for transaction processing, costs $1,530 to process 21,000 transactions per minute. Assuming a four year depreciation, this amounts to 1.8 cents per transaction.[297] Transaction costs on conventional PC local area network systems are much higher at forty-six cents per transaction (for $7,000 + annual cost per client). Traditional mainframe processing costs about three cents per transaction (for about $2,100 annual cost per client). These enormous ranges in unit costs are more a reflection of where the processing takes place than any differences in the intrinsic costs of electronics.

The way that the network architecture distributes the transaction workload determines the processing costs to a greater extent than the individual technology choices for computing. This gives rise to increased questioning of the politically expedient insistence on ownership of local computing power, regardless of its economics.[298] When this happens, a dynamically reconfigurable computing network will come into being. The new computer utilities will continually adjust and re-adjust their processing and storage capacities as dictated by market forces. The acquisition of equipment will not follow dictates of bureaucratic ownership, but what customers find of value.

Cybercash will be the currency of choice to pay for transaction services. This will activate a new wave of spending to redesign existing applications to meet more demanding standards for secure and economical processing. Supply of services will be wherever and whenever the demand takes place. The recent episodes of having to incur huge costs of redesign, because of the year 2000 problems, will become just a rehearsal for much larger costs to come. All the software that is currently in place, or in the ongoing re-design for the client/server cycle, reflects the bias of local quasi-feudal enclaves. For economically and security-driven networks to function, applications now locked into organization-specific architectures will require a complete overhaul.

Whereas the estimated cost of the year 2000 modifications is about three hundred billion dollars, the comparable expense for network re-

---

297 Bozman, J.S., "Popular Himalaya Gives Tandem New Options," *Computerworld*, September 12, 1994.
298 DePompa, B., "Rising from the Ashes," *InformationWeek*, May 27, 1996.

design may be an order of magnitude higher.[299] Such a number is clearly unaffordable, since it would mortgage the profits of every corporation on earth for several years. The next computer investment cycle must organize investments to create software that has a much greater residual value than is currently the case. That will invariably lead to software manufacture by a few large corporations. It will be the end of the production of software as a craft enclave within each corporation or organization. It will abolish the dominance of these monopolistic guilds that enjoy their position by virtue of having gained exclusive charters to serve only one customer.

At the consumer level the next cycle will see the initial steps leading to the eventual obliteration of banking organizations as we know them. Electronic commerce and electronic cash will dispense with much of the costly overhead labor now employed by the retail financial services. It will squeeze out the excessive processing capacity of institutions that employ too many physical and financial assets to perform tasks that are essentially information processing and not money handling.

The Coming Conflicts

The next computer investment cycle will revolve around conflicts between the global promoters and national interests. The globalization proponents will confront local interests that will try to preserve home-grown computing, software, information processing, native banking, insurance, travel, medical, and mail-order shopping services. Despite the opposition from agents who will try to preserve the status quo in high-cost national markets, the universality and substantially lower costs of the electronic medium will ultimately prevail.

When this happens the veterans of the mainframe, microcomputer, and Internet confrontations will be looking back with nostalgia on the era when these contests were obvious. They will forget that what may have retrospective clarity was not understandable at the time when it looked like a confusing challenge.

299 Recently the Gartner Group increased their estimated year 2000 correction up to six hundred billion.

The Most Likely Scenario for the Next Decade

We can expect the inauguration of a concerted effort to reduce the costs of computing. IT will not be able to claim that it is a cause of productivity. It will become just another cost for delivering support so that organizations may continue to function.

At the corporate level, the expenditures for computing will be sufficiently large, and the service levels sufficiently non-responsive, that a massive backlash is highly probable. This will give rise to demands for increased cost accountability, easily understandable cost controls, and services performing according to standards. The worship of IT for its own sake will disappear. Cost-minded mangers will take over the superintendence of computing as attention finally becomes refocused on what really matters, the capabilities of computer-assisted individuals and teams to create wealth or improve public sector effectiveness. There will be no computer paradox, but only a demand that information processing expenses be kept at a minimum.

A Long-Term View

It is the curse of those who do not study history that the present is an unsurpassable surprise, whereas the past receives praise for its transparency. Reluctance to take the trouble to understand history stems from a mistaken view that the past was simple and technologically backward and therefore is not worth the bother. Then, only the future is unfathomable, and therefore one ought to heed gurus, soothsayers, prophets, oracles, and seers. It is precisely this mistaken sentiment that has been the source of the faddish flimsiness that still characterizes much information systems work.

It was the purpose of these remarks to argue against the persistent bias that favors the technocrat's view that it is the information technologies that are the cause of organizational change. I adhere to the view that computers are nothing more than powerful agents that merely accelerate the forces of progress which are external to technology and that would eventually happen anyway. Organizations will continue to invest in IT to improve the business, cut costs, and take advantage of technical innovations. Yet it is not primarily economics and alignment with business that paces the acceptance of computerization. Much of the explanation for installing computers is a reflection of the struggles among factions for how to keep control over information. It is the conflict over control that unfolds as information becomes the principal means of production in a post-industrial society.

The assumption that all future computer cycles will lead to favorable social and economic advancement should remain a questionable prognosis. Lurking in the background is a threatening scenario that computer technology may find its ultimate perversion in surveillance and restrictive controls.[300] Central controls may reassert themselves in reaction to the incursions of information terrorism and the threats of information warfare to disrupt essential services. Historically, national security has often replaced economic, social, and cultural goals as the dominant political purpose. Future events may dictate measures to defend our society against acts that corrupt information technologies and disrupt our beliefs that cherish individual freedoms above all.

MISGUIDED UTOPIANS

One of the persistent themes of the admirers of information technologies is the claim that computer networks will aid in the spreading of American cultural and democratic values to everyone else. The American-bred concepts of a cyberculture freely traversing the global information pathways is seen as a way of extending the influence of Hollywood, Coca-Cola, and McDonald's in a world progressing along American lines. While adopting the English language for commercial and scientific communications and embracing our technologies, the rest of the world would be adopting much of the Western commercial culture, accepting democratic views of how to govern and ultimately blending into a peaceful and economically interlinked global community.

The idea of an emerging homogeneous and Westernized world through use of our technologies is misguided, arrogant, false and dangerous.[301] Adoption of consumption habits of another nation does not make them alike. Eating sushi or feasting on pizza does not make Americans more Japanese or Italian. However, the question is still open whether the Chinese, Ukrainians, Iraqis, or Iranians will end up changing their cus-

---

300 As suggested in the biblical prophecy, the book of Revelation, 13:17 "And that no man might buy or sell, save he that had ... the number of his name." According to such apocalyptic thinking, the Bible anticipated universal numbering of all transactions.

301 My comments reflect agreement with the views articulated by Huntington, S.P., "The West Unique, Not Universal," *Foreign Affairs*, November 1996.

tomary ways of governing, increasing their respect for civil liberties, and Westernizing their culture if they acquire Intel-based personal computers, Microsoft software, and Netscape browsers.

I do not think that one can expect nations to change their cultures because they use American information technologies. There is no indication that computers can shape a social culture of a nation, since it cannot accomplish that even for a corporation. It is the socio-economic context that will determine how information technologies will be applied, because it is the management of information that reflects how political power is deployed.

Western civilization is based on three thousand years of evolution along a unique path. Very little of that has been shared by four fifths of humanity.[302] Western institutions are based on the distribution of power among the governors. Other cultures concentrate power. In the West the rule of law is above that of any temporal authority, which is not the case in most of the world. The West cultivates social pluralism, hardly anybody else subscribes to that. Most importantly, Western culture is committed to protecting a strong sense of individualism, personal property rights, and unrestricted liberties, whereas much of the world rejects that point of view as encouraging decadence and corruption of a communal sense that binds a people, a religion, or a culture. The rest of the world also deeply resents the wealth, military power, and technological prowess of the West, especially when it is defenseless against Western acts.

The West is giving (or losing) its technologies to all in the hope that this will make everybody a peace-loving ally. I have no doubt that non-Western societies will do everything possible to acquire and master information technologies, especially for economic and military purposes. In the coming cultural backlash against everything that represents Western values we may find that information technologies will be applied not for empowering of individuals, and certainly not along lines visualized by the cyberspace liberals. There is every reason to believe that the social uses of computer technologies by most non-Western societies will be channeled primarily towards reinforcing the hegemony of the ruling regimes, and possibly as a means for countering the dominance of the West where it is most vulnerable.

---

302 Differences in the rate of growth of these two population groups is likely to reduce this ratio to one in ten within fifty years.

One should not trust American techno-utopians in making forecasts about the future uses of information technologies. Computers are a means by which organizations promote and defend their interests. When speculating about the effects of computer networks on international relations one should not assume that whatever applies and inspires individualistic "netizens" in Palo Alto, California will find a comparable reception in Tiensin, Kiev, Baghdad, or Qum. The chances are that what we see as a liberating force could easily become perverted for implementing an Orwellian scenario that others will find operationally and economically feasible to install and to operate.

The favorite recent slogan of the cyber-utopians is that "The Network is the Computer." We should consider the possibility that this may be perverted into the slogan "The Network is the Government" because information technologies make that not only possible, but also attractive to everyone who holds a totalitarian view of how to organize society.

What to Do

- Devote attention to socioeconomic forces in the workplace to better assess readiness for innovative information technologies.
- Diminish the emphasis on technological decisions and shift attention to the costs of employee training, the effects of organizational disruption, and the causes of workplace resistance.
- Get ready for enormous new investments in network redesigns that will favor open systems architectures.
- Consider scenarios and contingency actions if IT becomes a means for obstructing the functioning of our society.

26 Investment Politics

All visions degenerate into budgets.

CONTROL over computer capital has become the fulcrum of organizational influence. Information politics thus becomes the politics of legitimizing not only the consumption of additional capital, but also a reinforcement of the position of those whom it will serve. CIOs are in no position to deliver the operational savings which they discuss in magazine interviews. A systems architecture must show how it distributes the political control over information, because all economic benefits arise from use and not from design. One of the basic principles of information politics should be a strong bias to coping with external threats before focusing on internal information that concerns operating matters.

In the same way that taxation becomes the crux of all public politics, decision-making about making IT investments is the essence of all information politics.[303] The control of IT assets is what separates the power of management from that of workers. The capital that supports management is mostly IT, because furniture, office space, and general office equipment are relatively inexpensive as compared with wages and salaries. The capital that supports workers is invested in factories, process plants, transportation equipment, and inventory. Little of that is in computers, except where it is embedded in machines that support the means of production.[304]

FROM ECONOMICS TO POLITICS

Control over computer capital has become the fulcrum of organizational influence. It is no wonder that managers in vulnerable overhead positions see to it that their positions get reinforcement through ample computer

---

303 The term politics has an unnecessarily bad connotation. We have politics so that we can reach consensus by means of a due process without having to resort to force. The purpose of organizational politics is to prevent breakdowns in organizational cooperation.

304 The exception applies to firms whose business is based on information processing for others.

support. The insertion of value-added methods for justifying expenditure for more computers will surely give rise to unwelcome questions. Such methods will examine claims about the value-added of any function that requests an expensive means of raising productivity. A quandary arises when one realizes that hardly anyone knows how to measure the productivity of overhead personnel. Any thorough inquiry concerning further investments in computers could lead to an examination of the value of their operators. Information politics thus become the politics of legitimizing not only the consumption of additional capital, but also a reinforcement of the position of those whom it will serve.

The effect of the politicization of computer budgeting has been to corrode the presumed effectiveness that information systems were to bring to business processes. The flight from analysis to faith and visions shows up in sharp focus when one examines IT investment proposals, especially in government.[305] When that happens, it may be the misuse of information management, and not the technical complexity of information technologies, that forces the outsourcing of information management. Contracting out information services converts them from a coveted bureaucratic possession to a purchased commodity. Obviously, because of the threat of dislocation from their contracts, the contractors have every incentive to stay out of intramural politics. Playing one internal faction against another is never a good idea, since one cannot ever predict for sure who will award the next round of contracts.

Managing the Costs and Benefits

There is a long list of relatively safe ways for containing the costs of IT projects within a budget. One can:
- Omit promised system features.
- Meet the budget by completing undone work as follow-on maintenance.
- Shift the cost of startup and training to the customer.
- Pass overruns to other projects that have been funded more generously.

---

305 Tom Stewart put it well when he quoted "... there is a fine line between vision and hallucination" in Stewart, T.A., "A Refreshing Change: Vision Statements That Make Sense," *Fortune*, September 30, 1996, p. 195.

- Ask for budget adjustments whenever the client requests anything for which there was no prior explicit agreement.

This list is extensible almost indefinitely. Government contractors are experts in finding imaginative new ways of keeping within budget without liability for results. In some way they must compensate for the excessive costs of bidding and administering onerous contract terms.

The politically most perilous difficulties are not on the cost side. Costs are always confinable. Costs are measurable and visible and therefore will always receive concerted attention from project managers, clients, and auditors. The traps are all on the benefit side of the investment. The diffusion of accountability for the delivery of cross-functional business solutions often makes it necessary for CIOs to explain and re-explain the benefits.[306] That is very difficult to do. CIOs are in no position to deliver the operational savings about which they boast in magazine interviews. CIOs cannot account for savings stated by business executives who have long ago moved to different jobs. There is no way to demonstrate that operational savings show up as originally promised to the investment approval committee. There is no way they can predict with any assurance what benefits will result from projects currently underway. Whatever gains may eventually emerge will occur as changes in business operations over which CIOs have little influence and even less visibile results (Figure 51).

The greatest damage to computer projects happens when the implementation schedule slides. When this occurs, the divergence between expectations and delivery creeps up imperceptibly until it becomes sufficiently intolerable to wreck the entire venture. Much of this divergence is due to managerial turnover, both on the supplier as well as the customer side. For this reason, the planned elapsed time for any project should never be more than one quarter of the time during which both parties can work together and keep up their shared understanding.[307]

---

306 Almost all high-payoff systems solutions are cross-functional. It is in the information gaps between organizations where one can find most of the opportunities for systems-guided improvements.

307 This allows for one quarter of a manager's tenure to be devoted to learning the job, a quarter to make commitments, a quarter to get something accomplished and the final quarter to getting promoted or fired. This rule suggests that any projects for the US Air Force must be done in less than six months. At Xerox in the mid-1970s this made it necessary to complete projects even faster than that.

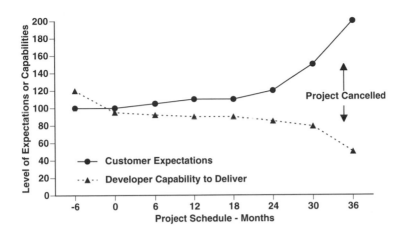

Figure 51   Gap between customer and developer widens with time

RESEARCH ON PAYOFFS

There is a need for research that clearly defines how computer investments affect organizational excellence or failure. The best example of how to do that is the research performed by pharmaceutical firms in assessing the curative power or potential damage from new drugs. Government regulation and legislation define the required procedures. Pharmaceutical companies must produce both convincing proofs of superiority, as well as the absence of damage, to public health. IT researchers need to work towards similar methods before they state that computers are an effective investment. The following example illustrates my point.

Drugs must meet the government standards of potency, safety, and cost-efficiency. Those who pay for most of the health care, such as employers, insurance companies, and health maintenance organizations, insist on cost-effectiveness as well. They demand positive proof that a new drug will reduce hospital stays or lessen employee absenteeism and will accomplish all those at a lower cost than any other cure. To prove that their products are worth the price, pharmaceutical companies such as Synergen have hired specialists in pharmaco-economics. These experts have qualifications both in economics and pharmacology to examine the cost effectiveness and quality of life issues. Their objective is to produce comparisons illustrated as follows: [308]

Standard Treatment with Antibiotic plus:	Survival Rate	Days in Hospital	Days in Intensive Care
No Antril (a placebo instead)	56%	31	20
17 mg of Antril per hour	68%	28	15
67 mg of Antril per hour	75%	28	14
133 mg of Antril per hour	83%	24	12

Figure 52   Drug dose, survival rate, and hospital stay

In the case of the antisepsis drug *Antril*, the pharmaceutical firm decided to conduct cost effectiveness tests alongside clinical trials of the medical effects. This is good marketing, as well as good politics, when extraordinary profits threaten the imposition of price regulation by the government.

Very soon, the overwhelming majority of organizations will realize that spending for information technologies exceeds their total Economic Value-Added. This will give rise to a renewed insistence on demonstrating the profitability of computer investments. It may be good information politics for vendors as well as CIOs to anticipate such pressures. Otherwise, executive management will surely resort to arbitrary measures, such as making decisions about technology policy by fiat.

ARCHITECTURAL AND POLITICAL SOLUTIONS MUST ALIGN

Corporate and government bookshelves overflow with dust-covered architectural plans conceived by task forces, consultants, and vendors. These are ideal technological concepts that usually do not link to the power structure that will depend on the use of such systems.

There can be no workable enterprise architecture without a direct link to the maintenance of the balance of power among various corporate interests. There can be no long-range reductions in IT spending without a coherent systems architecture that assures the longevity and low mainte-

308 Study by Synergen of *Antril*. Describes shortening of hospital stay for sepsis patients. [Sepsis is blood poisoning, a massive bacterial infection.] Quoted from Fischer, L., "New Standard for Drug Makers," *The New York Times*, January 18, 1993, p. D3.

nance costs of computer investments by reducing intra-organizational conflicts.

The authors of architectural documents that define only technologies confuse form with substance. The architecture that shows how to distribute information must always be subordinated to the decision of who can use it, because all economic benefits arise from use and not from design.

Characteristics of a Technical Architecture

A technical information systems architecture tells us how to build information systems. It sets in place the foundations that will determine much of the expense for supporting an organization through information processing power. In contrast, information politics tells us how an existing human organization can become successful and adapt to future changes. These are not separate but intertwined relationships. An information systems architecture should be the result of efforts to mediate the conflicting interactions between technology and economics. Information politics attempts to balance the interactions among people who may not always cooperate in the pursuit of a common purpose.

Corporations may impose a technical information systems architecture unilaterally. Enforcement of such an architecture is by technological means, network control, central purchasing, standardization of applications, and imposition of a uniform operating systems. The economic consequences of such acts come under scrutiny one budget cycle at a time. Therefore, the connections between architecture and the underlying cost structure will remain hidden unless the planning cycle matches the longevity of the architectural decisions.

A technical information systems architecture provides the framework for the capture, storage, and manipulation of data. If it is excessively redundant, failure-prone, or inefficient, this will show up as spending that will be greater than the competitors'.

Information Intelligence

Information politics, in the sense I am using the term, must reflect social consensus that is multilateral and negotiated. It is the means by which the implicit capabilities of information technologies realize conversion into recognizable benefits. The connections between information technologies and information politics become instantly visible in the seizure of control over information budgets and assets.

Only effective governance can suggest how to organize information so that it can be converted into knowledge that generates attractive economic payoffs. Implementation of a technical architecture should take place only after a firm has a clear understanding about political governance. Politics always comes ahead of technology. There is no point in pouring a technically sound concrete foundation for a skyscraper if the owner intends to live in a trailer home. There was no point in perfecting the civil engineering of steel reinforcement for the Maginot Line without ensuring that the enemy could not easily deploy troops around it.

Mainframe-dominated corporate information departments withered because they tried to impose a well-reasoned technical architecture on an environment that had different concepts of governance. Customers were demanding solutions that fit their social and organizational needs more closely, even if that need did not provide for the best economical value. This lesson should be on the mind of anyone who receives a commission to write yet another technical architecture document.

One of the basic principles of information politics should be a strong bias towards giving priority to coping with external threats before focusing on internal information that concerns operating expenses. Competitive forces are external and uncontrollable, whereas bureaucratic forces are internal and manageable if there is a will to do so. Both forces are dangerous, except that the external threats are swifter and without mercy. Perils from the outside threats must always receive priority attention.

The capacity to translate warnings about danger into responses that can counter it effectively determines how well an organization will cope with external challenge. Information intelligence is one of the few essential central information functions of an organization. It is essential not only for survival but also for the assurance of continued prosperity.

Information intelligence is only one of the means for achieving success but certainly not the only one. A sense of purpose and direction overrides everything. Even a building that wins the top architectural prize is just an empty shell if people do not find it useful to serve their needs.

Planning Information Architecture and Information Politics

There is no such thing as a off-the-shelf enterprise architecture or a standard information governance template. These must be as unique as fingerprints, because enterprises differ in how they function in the competitive arena. The adoption of enterprise designs that align with competitive objectives is one of the top priority tasks for all systems management.

Fundamentally, an information architecture is the technological manifestation of the organizational doctrine that defines who will have what types of information to make decisions, and how such information will be used to generate competitive advantage. Never delegate the completion of an information architecture plan to consultants or to computer experts. Never delegate to anyone the promulgation of an information doctrine. Outsiders can hardly judge what needs to be done, because they can only react to what the most vocal actors have to say, which may not be a reliable reflection of reality.

The underlying assumptions concerning information politics and information architecture are hardly ever articulated in documents or reports. Ultimately they are a reflection of the ways people cooperate toward shared purposes with a common understanding of what needs to be accomplished.

What to Do

- Do not get into the position of having to document operational benefits, such as revenue gains, market share improvement, inventory reductions, product quality gains, or enhancement of customer satisfaction. Leave all such explanations to line executives who are directly responsible for them.
- Commit only to schedule, systems capabilities and information services budgets. Everything else is beyond a CIO's capacity to explain or to prove.
- Manage benefits by thoroughly understanding the sensitivity of the proposed financial model to changes in the proposed business payoffs. On every project there are only a few capabilities

that deliver most of the benefit.[309] Sensitivity analyses showing which elements of the model cause the greatest possible benefit or damage are essential for deciding what to watch to ensure that the project does not get out of control.

- Realize benefits are primarily an outcome of good management and not necessarily the best technology. The generation of benefits does not originate with information project managers, unless they are improving the efficiency of what they already control. Benefits are realizable only by indirect means. The systems recipients can make or break any process because they remain in control and must live with the system after completion.
- Invest in the means for exercising preventive damage control to keep dormant risks from becoming catastrophes. This requires an early warning process based on gathering operational intelligence at the lowest levels of the organization.
- Anticipate risks, prepare contingency plans, and hold adequate funds in reserve.[310]
- Keep the planned elapsed time for any project to not more than one quarter of the time during which both parties can work together and keep up their shared understanding.
- Define a systems architecture not only in technical terms, but also how it will distribute political control over information, because all economic benefits arise from use and not from design.
- Assign high priority to coping with external threats before focusing on internal information that concerns only operating expenses.

---

309 The so called Pareto distribution, where eighty percent of the gain comes from twenty percent of the effort.

310 This assumes that project managers understand the risks. For instance, the us Department of Defense estimated that it may cost anywhere between $350 million and $3 billion to fix its computer code for date-keeping after year 2000. See Anthes, G.H., "Feds Garner Failing Grades for Year 2000," *Computerworld*, August 5, 1996, p. 15. A project estimate that could miss by a tenfold factor is not risk assessment, but blind gambling.

27 Build and Junk Solutions

All wealth is based on accumulation.

THIS RISK to computer projects does not arise from technical failure, but from a steady drift in intent which persistently widens the gap in expectations between the technologists and their customers. It is a short-term view of the value of systems that ultimately leaves an organization with hundreds or even thousands of inconsistent and non-interoperable solutions. Software must be readily adaptable to changes in workflows, and acquire independence from operating systems and hardware-specific solutions. Looking out into the future beyond five years carries an enormous advantage over short-term thinking, provided that interest rates are low and risks are manageable.

Short-term thinking about investments in software and people can produce disastrous consequences. The typical breakeven point for major innovations in information system is anywhere from four to six years or even longer for major restructuring of how an organization plans to operate. Long lead times from authorization to delivery increase the possibility of never reaping the planned benefits. This risk does not arise from technical failure, but from a steady drift in purpose and intent which persistently widens the gap in expectations between the technologists and their customers.

Because it is very hard to keep systems development to unswerving goals and limited objectives, project managers come under great pressure to get something done quickly. Projects that are only partially complete do not give much consideration to future maintenance costs, particularly if they are over budget or out of time. Project managers are under continuous pressure to pick solutions that fit an existing vendor's proprietary products. There is also and urgency to choose off-the shelf solutions, even if that forms a new enclave that is technologically unique. It is this short-term view of the value of systems that ultimately leaves an organization with hundreds or even thousands of inconsistent and non-interoperable solutions. With excessive proliferation of technology choices, the systems organization finds it increasingly difficult to afford the money to upgrade what is already in the IT inventory. What remains is costly, does not easily adapt to the changing needs, and is neither interoperable, maintainable, nor compatible.

SYSTEMS CONSTRUCTION PRACTICES

If the build-and-junk approach becomes the only acceptable method for supporting business operations, it is likely to cause grief in due course. Such practices explain the growing customer unhappiness with systems responsiveness and operating executives' displeasure with rising systems costs. When attempting to treat the symptoms without curing the underlying problems, firms hired consultants to redesign business processes. Simultaneously, new computer managers came aboard to redesign systems that were hurting the business the most. The new systems managers and the consultants had great difficulties in acquiring sufficiently detailed knowledge to figure out how the organization really functioned. Under budget and schedule pressures they had to commit to incredibly short implementation schedules, which tended to perpetuate the disease they were asked to cure.

After decades of piling up incremental automation investments on top of the already accumulated store of high-maintenance application programs, the collection of defective assets is simply too large for any affordable budget to absorb the costs of making improvements through a complete redesign. Even when a firm decides to dump everything and adopt a competitor's system they may find it extremely difficult to make the transition from what they have to what they would like to have. After an organization buys someone else's applications, they are likely to find that what they get is not much different from what they have tried to escape. This is because few companies have engineered their information assets for long term life. Those who have will not sell the knowledge because it is one of the sources of their competitive advantage.

THE CONSERVATION WAY

One must create conditions for top management to seek not only short term payoffs from continuous improvement but also long term residual values for the software investments. This is the only way to break the investment cycles that often destroy as much as they create.

Top management must insist on receiving alternative life cycle plans from computer executives. Such plans should show different technical solutions for managing a portfolio of applications that are essential to the success of the enterprise.[311] Instead of making presentations filled with qualitative indicators, it is the first obligation of every chief information officer to display the most likely long range budget forecasts for technology cash outlays. Each alternative budget projection should portray the proposed policies that will increase the cumulative value of software. This is critical, because in the long run it is software that has an overwhelming effect on the magnitude of operating costs.

If most of a firm's software is readily adaptable to changes in workflows, and is independent of operating systems and hardware-specific compilers, these investments could have a very long life.[312] If the applications are an assembly of reusable standard software components and are independent of the databases, then the future maintenance costs are likely to be low. In these cases, the budget projections will show a remarkable drop in IT expenses for operationally essential applications. This will open opportunities for spending more on innovative uses, such as work enlargement, expert systems, decision support, distance learning, and competitive intelligence.

I have completed many computations to examine the financial effects of residual values on the net present worth, risk-adjusted discounted cash flow value of typical projects. For open systems, the contribution of the residual value is to double the net present worth dollars as compared to the usual analytic practice which considers only the cash flow during the planning period.

As I write these lines interest rates are lower than they have been in over twenty-five years. The residual value of all software investments could be worth a large multiple of what project management customarily shows as the net benefit cash flow. Perhaps the best way of illustrating the powerful effect of interest rates is by showing how an investment with a life of

311   These are usually defined as the risk-adjusted discounted cash flow of benefits minus development, maintenance, and operating costs for the business plan period, plus the risk adjusted residual value of software. The uses of commercially available software packages as well as outsourcing options must be included as an alternative.

312   The exception would be a radical change such as changing what customers are served or what products are delivered.

over twenty-years (e.g., long-term investment) compares with one having a life of only five years (e.g., short-term investment): [313]

Interest Rate	With Residual Value	Without Residual Value	Long Term/Short Term
40%	$250	$204	123%
30%	$333	$244	137%
25%	$399	$269	149%
20%	$497	$299	166%
15%	$655	$335	195%
10%	$937	$379	247%
5%	$2,693	$433	622%

Figure 53   Comparison of the value of long-term and short-term investments

In the above figure, when the interest rates are as high as forty percent there is not much of a difference between short-term and long-term thinking. At that rate a long term proposal would have only a twenty-three percent advantage over a five-year life expectancy. As interest rates decline to five percent, long-term planning and commitment pay off enormously. Looking out into the future beyond five years carries a 522% advantage.[314]

If the cost of capital is low, then it is imperative to plan for the long run. It is worthwhile to expend every effort to extend the useful life of open systems applications. This is made feasible by accumulating a library of reusable software components for insertion as modular templates that describe typical business applications. This suggests not only reuse of software, but also re-use of systems requirements. A well thought out architecture makes it possible for software components to continue functioning even as the organization keeps changing. Open and reusable systems make it possible to merge, break up, centralize, and then again decentralize without having to discard software logic and associated employee training. If one has to reengineer workflows, that can come through reju-

313   I have also recalculated this table for a short-term planning horizon of only three years, which is typical of current thinking. Only an interest rate of over seventy percent would make the residual value worthless.
314   It is noteworthy that current business investment interest rates in Japan are below five percent, whereas us venture start-up capital costs are well above twenty-five percent.

venation or reincarnation instead of burying the body and then suffering again the pains of new birth followed by error-prone youth.

What to Do

- Deliver alternative life cycle plans that display a range of different technical solutions for managing applications that are essential to the success of the enterprise.
- Prepare budget projections that portray approaches that will increase the cumulative value of the installed software.
- Include in all project proposals a calculation of the residual value of project investments.

28 The Decay of Information Assets

Information expenses must grow into information assets.

Obsolescence is due to continuous rearrangement of the essentially identical logic elements that make up business processes. Much of a firm's IT budget already carries a mortgage for keeping up the operations, maintenance, feature enhancement, and technological updating of existing computer applications. Corporate management will trust CIOs as investors if they can also demonstrate the capacity to deliver measurable operating savings from which to fund further innovation. To realize operating savings one needs to exploit the thirty to forty percent annual cost reductions in equipment costs that industry will continue to deliver into the indefinite future. Executive management expects that their information management experts will produce results that will surpass all other available means for generating economic surpluses.

People in every enterprise are facing tough IT budget reviews. Where businesses are expanding, unproductive overhead expenses have to come down, so that more resources can be added and made available for new services. Since most of IT expenses support people whose salaries are in overhead accounts, computer budgets are always a prime prospect for cuts. Where businesses are contracting, computer budgets will always be high on the cutting list in order to conserve scarce cash.

The Decay of Applications Software

While cutting budgets, organizations are discovering that much of the software in place no longer meets real enterprise needs. Ways that business processes are operating and methods they use to integrate with one another are increasingly becoming obsolete. This is not primarily a result of changes in the necessary work functions, since reorganizations, outsourcing, acquisitions, divestment, reengineering, and restructuring rarely alter the elementary components of business processes.

Indeed, obsolescence is due to continuous rearrangement of the identical elementary ingredients that make up business processes in the hope that the changes will produce gains in overall effectiveness. Consequently, the fundamental challenge faced by IT executives is to find a balance between mutually opposing forces. On the one hand, one must steadily reduce ongoing operating costs. On the other hand, one must find the money for funding large new investments that adapt the old systems to meet the rapidly changing conditions. All of this must take place with only a modest increase in total expenditures, requiring much of the funding to be extracted from cuts in operating expenses. Such an act is only comparable to performing surgery while running a marathon.

Much of a firm's IT budget already carries a mortgage for keeping up the operations, maintenance, feature enhancement, and technological updating of existing computer applications. In most organizations this will consume well over eighty percent of the IT budget. Many systems executives prefer claiming a much smaller number for support of ongoing operations. In this way they can declare that some of the expenses used in patching up earlier neglect are really investments to keep costs from escalating or operations from deteriorating.

What carries the label of either maintenance or development depends very much on circumstances. To fix a large accumulation of negligent upkeep, a systems executive would request additional money for "mandatory investments." [315] This approach would avoid an inquiry about why a recent system turned into binary refuse so fast. Conversely, an incomplete project that has exceeded its budget by a wide margin now receives the classification of maintenance to get it ready for operational use. This avoids giving the overrun the visibility that may result in an unwelcome audit.

BALANCING OPERATING AGAINST INNOVATING NEEDS

Regardless of how the essential expenses show up on reports, the CIO will have to use large portions of whatever cash is available just to keep the existing business functioning. Only a well funded firm has discretionary cash in its IT budget for making investments in major innovations. Only

---

315 That is how the estimated $300 – $600 billion dollars for the year 2000 bug will be funded.

well-managed organizations can support the necessary talent for experimenting with ways to conduct business by radically different means.

If a firm wishes to make leading edge improvements such as using advanced technologies, the cash to fund such projects must come, to a significant extent, from reductions in ongoing costs. Balancing cash needs against cash drains becomes the essential skill of experienced information executives. It also tests the ability of every CIO to retain his job. Corporate management will trust more CIOS as investors if they can also demonstrate the capacity to deliver measurable operating savings from which to fund further innovation.

The primary skill necessary to accomplish innovation is knowing how to manage the speed with which one can introduce cost reductions. The ideal circumstances are those that occur when an organization can generate operational savings faster than the amounts required for modernization. That's like having a water turbine that generates enough surplus electricity so that it can afford to pump the water back upstream. Theoretically it should not be feasible, except that in the case of IT it is achievable. To realize that, one needs to exploit the thirty to forty percent annual cost reductions in equipment costs that the semiconductor industry will continue to deliver into the indefinite future. If new technology can migrate into an organization gracefully, without uprooting the software in place, every CIO could become a cost-reduction hero without much effort.

If an organization can come anywhere close to the intrinsic technology cost-reduction curves that the electronic industry keeps delivering, it should be possible to support much of the innovation while simultaneously generating net cash gains. Helping an enterprise to create surpluses for reinvestment should be perhaps the principal measure for judging the effectiveness and results of any chief information officer.

A CIO's Role in the Economy

Business is a societal invention in which output ought to exceed input if it is to live and thrive. In other words, the revenues from the business should always exceed the costs of conducting the business. This inequality violates the general laws of physics, because no machine can produce more energy than it consumes. Yet, output (i.e., revenue) must exceed inputs (i.e., costs) in order to provide a surplus (i.e., Economic Value-Added).

Without continued surpluses a business has no legitimacy in claiming its position as the primary source of economic power that delivers improved livelihood for a society.[316]

The fundamental predicament of information executives is that they are supposedly in charge of devices that have surpassed in growth of potency every other human invention in history. The CIOs are custodians of technologies that have the inherent capacity to shrivel the costs of almost all information inputs. Computers are the only engines that have shown dramatically decreasing unit costs for more than four decades, with unit costs coming down at least thirty percent per annum. All evidence points out that these shrinking costs will not only continue, but probably will accelerate.

For these reasons executive management expects that their information management experts will deliver results that will surpass other available means for generating economic surpluses.[317] Consequently, the executive in charge of information technologies should be able to command exceptional privileges, because no other member of the top executive team is likely to command comparable capabilities.

Unfortunately, the computer executives do not enjoy such esteem. So far, they have been unable to demonstrate that the resources under their guardianship deliver the results that are feasible or claimed by the computer advocates. The reason is that the rate of decay of information systems has always exceeded the rate at which innovation can take place. The CIOs appear to be in charge of a field where the pests consume at a rate that keeps up with how fast the crop grows.

---

316 Government can only distribute or detract, not create wealth. That distinction is frequently lost by the advocates of more government intervention in all matters.
317 Strassmann's Rules of Information Systems are based on Isaac Asimov's Laws of Robotics:
    1: IT shall do no harm to anyone, by action or inaction.
    2: IT shall deliver net added economic value for the benefit of an organization, without violating Rule 1.
    3: IT will serve the information needs of an organization without violating Rules 1 and 2.

What to Do

- Adopt a policy of funding a large share of the systems modernization costs from reductions in ongoing operating and maintenance expenses.
- Exploit the thirty to forty percent annual cost reductions in equipment costs that suppliers will continue delivering in order to extract operating savings of at least twenty percent per annum from baseline costs.

29 THE ECONOMIC PREDICAMENT

All progress arises from prior progress.

INFORMATION costs of most corporations, and especially of public sector institutions, are bloated with excess overheads. This means that improving the capacity for value creation can be self-funding. It is also possible to extend the economic life of software indefinitely with a minimum of upkeep. System immortality is approached when corporate reorganizations can be supported by simply reconfiguring software components. Corporate mergers and the frequent oscillations from centralization to decentralization and back generates huge outbursts of software destruction followed by eruptions of new software development. With each new round of technical transformation the worth of past accumulations keeps growing. To carry these assets across the threshold of yet another major conversion requires long-range planning and interchangeable software components.

The lack of recognition of the positive economic contributions of information technologies has its roots in the fact that CIOs are not providing acceptable financial measures that disclose their accomplishments. Computer executives would receive recognition as contributors to prosperity if they could start generating demonstrable cash inflows greater than the obvious cash outflows. To prove their accomplishments, CIOs would need a method of reporting and assessing the net gains from information technologies. In the absence of such metrics, systems departments appear like expensive but unavoidable additions to overhead burdens. Accordingly, the systems department is a cost sink, not a money-generator.

How it is possible for cash inflows to fund cash outflows in managing corporate information resources? That would call for a policy of "cash in" before asking for "cash out." This is not the way CIOs operate nowadays. Computer people prefer the policy of "cash now" and only then "cash tomorrow, maybe." The current practice promises hard to verify savings in the future to get large cash infusions immediately.

The pay now, expect later approach to funding information technologies is not necessary. The fact is the information costs of most corporations, especially of public sector institutions, are bloated with excess overheads. This means that overhead cost reductions, while generating an improved capacity for value creation, can be self-funding.[318] The only exception to this generalization is a small number of high-growth performers, who may have cash flow problems as they invest in market expansion.

It is noteworthy that most firms that have outsourced their information systems have contracts that call for up-front cash gains. In a typical outsourcing deal the plan calls for positive cash flow to the company that is getting rid of its IT operations.[319] Thus cash management is a skill that CIOS must acquire if they are to continue presiding over a viable computer establishment. Outsourcers understand this, and it makes their sales pitches so alluring.

CIOS who fall behind in cash or value generation will descend into a spiral of missed deadlines and a need to make continued excuses for missed opportunities. If their positive contributions escape measurable recognition, they will fall into a trap from which there is no escape. Good timing and trustworthy metrics are therefore essential.

There is an important element of timing that proponents often neglect when proposing new systems investments:

- How does one ensure that the new projects will generate quick economic returns as well as create software assets that have low maintenance expenses during a long life?
- How does one create software assets that do not continually depreciate?

---

318 Much of the current approach to the downsizing of organizations follows that course, even though an overemphasis on shrinkage may damage the viability of the enterprise forever.

319 The outsourcer buys the existing assets at book value; this is usually technologically obsolete, but operationally perfectly useful mainframe equipment. The market value of this equipment is always lower than the book value. Nevertheless, the outsourcer can manage this asset for better economic advantage because there is nothing wrong with the equipment if properly maintained. In return, the outsourcer offers an immediate cut (usually twenty percent) in operating expenses. The firm that does the outsourcing could have done the same but has been either unable or unwilling to make the unpopular decisions needed to realize the identical benefits.

- What designs assure that new features and functions do not require expensive reprogramming, enhancement and conversion?
- How does one create an asset such that its total expense keeps dropping as fast as the plunging costs of computer technologies?

IMMORTALITY OF SOFTWARE

Every CEO should demand answers to the above questions. Fortunately, the solutions are simple and increasingly available. The basic starting point is to replace the existing practice of custom glued-together special-purpose applications with solutions that are an assembly of components that individually have a long life. If one constructs systems from robust, well-tested, replaceable and upgradeable components, it should be possible to extend the economic life of software indefinitely with a minimum of upkeep.

The same reasoning also applies to data administration. The proliferation of data definition dialects is the cause of the greatest disarray in the preservation of software. Computer applications are not portable if the cost of data cleansing and data translation from one computing environment into another is unaffordable. Therefore, the standardization of data models and of data dictionaries is at least as important as the attention devoted to software logic.

System immortality is nearly possible when one can plug or unplug chunks of software logic irrespective of the hardware on which it runs, while continuing to support ongoing business functions without interruption. System immortality is approached when corporate reorganizations can be supported by simply reconfiguring software components. Such components have to be primarily a reflection of revenue generating and production support processes. How such software accommodates the prevailing arrangements among corporate bureaucracies can take place after the basic business functions are working.

When an organization reshuffles its internal relationships, most of its basic business functions remain without much alteration. As long as an organization remains in the same business, radical changes in how it serves customers are infrequent. The problem with computer programs is that they reflect more how management manages than what they deliver.

That is counterproductive. Whenever intra-corporate relationships get embedded into the control and decision logic within computer programs, this glued-together patchwork cannot change without tearing it apart. That's why corporate mergers and the frequent oscillations from centralization to decentralization and back generates huge outbursts of software destruction followed by eruptions of new software development.

When each cycle becomes temporarily stable, which is usually from exhaustion, nothing much has changed as seen from the customer's point of view. Most of the commotion and expense for software modifications would be unnecessary with a more robust design. All it takes is accommodating the changes in the managerial organization through reconfiguration of those components that continue doing whatever they have been doing all along.

Software components should represent basic business processes. The definitions should be at a sufficiently high level of abstraction so that they can be used as modular work elements independent of how an organization decides to assemble them to suit its needs. A suitable analogy would be of installing prefabricated kitchen cabinet modules and appliances to reflect particular tastes, available space, and the owner's budget.

I built up applications from individual computer instructions when I started programming forty years ago. This was the equivalent of sawing kitchen cabinets out of unfinished lumber and hammering nails out of iron ingots. In those days there was no prefabrication, no re-use, no portability. All logic and instructions had to be examined and tested whenever my boss wanted to make significant changes. My applications had a very short life.

With trillions of dollars worth of software now in place, nobody has the money to afford short-lived assets. Low cost of ownership of information systems now depends on the capacity to extend the useful life of all assets. Much greater longevity is now possible, though the ideal of pursuing the immortality of logical elements remains a most desirable goal. From a business management standpoint I find that, in the pursuit of systems immortality, adopting open systems solutions will get us closest to this goal.

Prospects

Corporate chief executives and the heads of government departments welcome outsourcing. It offers an easy way of passing on to others the technical and managerial mistakes that flourished during decades of insufficient top management attention to computerization.

After outsourcing, there is still a question to answer: Who will fund the modernization cycles that will surely follow the current client/server or Internet phases? One should expect that the systems taken over by contractors will not hold up as well as predicted, especially if the outsourcing contract emphasizes short-term operating savings. There are some interesting questions:

- Will the subsequent wave of innovation that arrives under the guise of network services relieve corporate and government executives of information management responsibilities altogether?[320]
- How will corporate management verify that the modernized applications delivered by outsourcing contractors will have residual values that are larger than the ones now scheduled for oblivion?
- What safeguards will assure that outsourcing contractors do not subordinate their technology choices to profit maximization?
- What talent will remain in the firm to manage, specify, and, if necessary, transfer work from the outsourcing contractor to another choice if that becomes desirable?
- Who will end up owning the information assets paid for by the firm that has outsourced its work? Even if ownership is clear, will the systems engineering choices of the outsourcing contractor inhibit, if not prohibit, making such transfers except at a prohibitive cost of conversion?

The answers will depend on the loyalties, technical skills, and managerial capabilities of those who will retain the ultimate responsibility for systems performance. This requires the retention within the corporation of the expertise capable of providing oversight. This also demands authen-

---

320 This is a likely scenario, especially for the public sector, which appears to be incapable of acquiring, motivating, nurturing, and retaining qualified technology talent.

tic assurances that a corporation continues to possess the capacity to retain the mastery of its information processes. It also will require a capacity to control the rate of technological advancement as the latest technology cycle finds its replacement by yet another and another.

The gradual demise of the client/server boom has already begun with the massive flight to Internet-based systems solutions. If the history of computer progress teaches us anything, it is the prediction that even the current Internet era will be only a passing phenomenon. It will be displaced by another wave within ten years and perhaps sooner. Middle aged executives should expect at least four major technological migration cycles within what remains of their career.[321]

With each new round of technical transformation the worth of past accumulations keeps growing. To carry these treasures across the threshold of yet another major conversion requires long-range planning. That becomes increasingly important, since the costs of an orderly exodus from one technological cycle to another will become prohibitive for those who do not prepare for it. Expectations that technological journeys into unexplored space will happen call for software designs now that make it feasible to port the greatest possible share of knowledge assets into technologically different environments. Corporate leaders who would enter into ten-year outsourcing contracts should ask whether they will be able to keep in their employment the talent and managerial skills necessary to remain in charge of such a journey. Preserving an option to change directions is a requirement if the need ever arises, if the current contracts expires, or if disagreements make it necessary to commission another set of actors.

I worry as I listen to the current crop of decision-makers talking about system outsourcing. Instead of concentrating on the preservation of a capacity to manage their knowledge assets, they focus on short term fixes. This could involve forced conversion to monolithic solutions as offered by some vendors, precooked and predigested applications, or buying solutions that lock out all other alternatives. In the information age the capacity to manage the quality of an organization's information resources becomes one of the supreme tests of whether an organization can function properly. Quality does not happen, it requires concerted attention and care. Abdicating information management, which surely is one of the

---

321 With the elimination of early morbidity from a wide spectrum of diseases, careers may now stretch beyond the customary retirement age.

essential attributes of all excellence, means relinquishing the capacity to operate effectively in the information economy. Such a prospect should give any executive something to think about before committing to a decision that could cripple the preservation of knowledge assets.

THE MOST LIKELY SCENARIO

There is no easy escape from the quandary that pits immediate needs which are always demonstrable against long range potentials which are hard to prove. It seems outsourcing is here to stay. The likely outcome will be that more than half of systems work now performed internally will emigrate to competent and low cost contractors in the next twenty to thirty years.[322] In the case of the public sector that migration may reach well over three quarters of all information systems expenditures.

Yet this projection still does not address the question of how corporations will manage their remaining core capabilities. It does not address how organizations will retain control over vital information work performed by others. Market economics will drive the outcome by steering the IT talents from corporate staff overhead to independent consultants. The contracts will flow to those firms that do not suffer from conflict by acting both as bidders and advisors on the performance of outsourcing services.

One should anticipate the growth of firms which will act as trusted counsel to corporate executives on matters related to their governance, oversight, and performance metrics. Such firms will find a place in the marketplace as credible judges. They will mediate the resolution of the conflicts that are inherent in the relationship between the outsourcing contractors and their clients.[323]

---

322 The Gartner Group estimates that by year 2000 thirty percent of ineffective MIS departments will become candidates for outsourcing. See Stewart, B., "The Second Age of IT: Increasing the Return on Technology," *InSide Gartner Group*, October 1995.

323 The acquisition of IT consulting firms by outsourcing firms will continue causing conflicts of interests between the consultants and the operators, now linked in the same firm.

What to Do

- Display the results of IT investments in terms of cash flows, not ratios or breakeven times.
- Place the standardization of data models and data dictionaries high in priority as a means of increasing the long-term service-ability of systems.
- Design software components to represent basic business processes. The definitions of the processes should be at a sufficiently high level of abstraction so that they can be used as modular work elements, independent of how an organization decides to assemble them to suit its needs.

30 PRICING

There is no zero cost for something of value.

THE FUNDAMENTAL flaw in current pricing models for computer services is that factory-like cost accounting works only for equipment-driven or transaction-paced activities. Support costs and software are an overhead multiplier. As the share of all other costs declines relative to overhead expenses, the relevance of traditional cost accounting disappears. Poor pricing and accounting practices, rather than technology, are frequently the reason why one technology replaces another. Collecting processing statistics from hundreds of outlying sites and keeping track of remote events that involve thousands of clients is an enormously complex and costly undertaking. The high fixed cost, fixed capacity structure of client/server networks dictates charging an all-inclusive monthly rental fee, regardless of the volume of work. Cost-based pricing supports unproductive management overhead which can survive only under the protection umbrella of exclusionary arrangements. The market for packaged software will largely disappear; instead, there will be a global network auction for services that deliver predictable results.

Traditional industry wisdom says that you either do not charge for computer services at all or you are forced by the complexity of computer tasks to set rates by an elaborate accounting scheme. The latter is generally costly to administer and irrelevant to those who do not have a budgetary accountability. Billing for services can easily result in detailed invoices for incomprehensible computer resource units, disk storage, tape mounts, tape storage, kilobits of data packets, pages of printouts, and disk accesses. Generating such details is feasible for large and homogeneous computing complexes that keep all cost elements and all people under central control. The fundamental flaw of this model is that factory-like cost accounting works only for equipment-driven or transaction-paced activities. Support costs and software become an overhead multiplier attached to physical events. As the share of equipment costs declines relative to the overhead expenses associated with computing, the relevance of traditional cost accounting disappears. What is on customer invoices is therefore unlikely to bear much resemblance to what are the full costs to serve them.

The disparity between prices and costs is tolerable if there is no competition. Vendors will allocate costs for affordability, thus cross-subsidizing inefficiency. Customers who use low cost services will foot the bill for a small number of customers who enjoy the luxury of expensive features penalties. This cozy arrangement shatters when a customer paying an excessive price can find an alternate source of service. This is exactly what happened with the increased uses of minicomputers and subsequently microcomputers. Local operators could show apparent local savings by removing overpriced transactions from the central organizations. Data centers that continued invoicing on the basis of equipment transactions lost their most profitable customers. Invariably, this forced prices up for the remaining customers who in turn found it even more advantageous to defect. Poor pricing and accounting practices, rather than technology, are frequently the reason why one technology replaces another.

PRICING CLIENT/SERVER NETWORKS

A large organization that decides to follow the current client/server model ends up with hundreds of small computing sites. Each of these locations employs people who manage the servers, keep track of local area networks, and generally give assistance to people who do not know what to do. The local site managers then buy technology whenever someone says they need it. Once a firm had a hundred people under the same roof, under the same management and in the same budget. Now it has several hundred part time helpers, contractors, consultants, and enthusiastic dabblers who have taken up computing as a hobby or an opportunity for occupational diversification by means of on-the-job training.

When a corporation adopts the distributed client/server model, the matter of charging for services does not come up, because nobody can figure out how to capture the needed information. While the distributed networks remain under local control, there is also little incentive to find out what the local enthusiasm and autonomy costs. It will be certainly more expensive than anybody ever promised. It is unlikely to deliver cost-reductions as asserted in the initial justifications.

Finally, when rising costs make the expenses for all information technologies a target for cost reduction, somebody brings all the loosely organized efforts under the control of a consistent network management discipline. At that point the corporation finally begins to discover its total information processing expenses. Somebody will then recommend instituting a scheme so that expenses somehow relate to usage.

Unfortunately the factory-like cost accounting methods used in central processing installations will not work in a fully distributed network environment. Factory cost accounting always assumes that variable costs are discrete and corresponded to discernible activities. Infrastructure expenses are relatively small in a factory setting, relative to the costs of labor and materials. Measurable activities and transactions then absorb overhead through simple allocations based on activity. None of these assumptions hold when every person has the equivalent of a mainframe computer on the desk and the key asset is not the computer but the network and the support infrastructure, which are costly fixed assets and not a variable expense.

Outsourcing Client/Server Networks

The matter of pricing client/server networks attracts attention when the controller finally suggests outsourcing the entire operation. This happens when the total administrative overhead rises, despite promises to the contrary. Outsourcing is the only way to arrest uncontrolled overhead if nobody can identify a way to contain the steady escalation of expenses. What the controller seeks is a bid that would take over all client/server management services and everything that's needed to support them. Furthermore, the controller wishes to accomplish it for at least twenty percent less than the existing budget.

The target cost reduction creates several problems. Nobody knows what "twenty percent less" means if the base costs are not determinable.[324] In data center operations computer service organizations charged customers for work using an activity-based pricing scheme to recover costs whenever a customer's volume of work changed. The difficulty occurs

324 In a survey of fourteen firms which have totally outsourced their operations, six were unable to determine the financial outcome of their actions. See Lacity, M.C., Wilcocks, L.P., and Feeny, D.F., "The Value of Selective IT Sourcing," *Sloan Management Review*, Spring 1996, p. 15.

because the client/server customer needs are even less predictable than the hard-to-forecast processing volume of data center operations.

The data service pricing model, based on hardware-driven events, is not applicable. Collecting processing statistics from hundreds of outlying sites and keeping track of remote events that involve thousands of clients is an enormously complex and costly undertaking. Even if someone could accomplish it, it would not matter anyway. Client/server costs are overwhelmed by hard to measure work activities. Their expenses depend on the costs of network utilization and the frequency of software usage. They must also cover the costs for helping customers deal with applications for which the users have not received adequate training. The most often quoted cost of client/server configurations is about $8,000 per client per year, on a fully allocated basis. Only about ten percent of that is for hardware and even that number is declining to a likely target of only five percent in the next ten years (Figure 54).[325]

A large share of the costs of servers and clients is independent of the number of measured transactions. What varies are the functions and availability that a client asks from the server and the network needed to deliver it. Those items are not volume sensitive. It is not how many transactions a customer makes, but how much support the customer requires that determines the standby cost necessary to maintain a high level of service. Thus the average costs per client that are so frequently quoted by various consultants can be grossly misleading.

As an example, a nurse's station that processes only two or three forms and runs on well depreciated equipment can easily cost only $2,000/year to operate. In contrast, a high-power UNIX workstation serving a currency trader can easily exceed $50,000/year in support expenses. Without metrics that identify the parameters of usage, much of the prevailing discussions about the relative merits of "lean clients" or "fat clients" is rhetorical, not analytical.

325 Caldwell, B., "Client-Server Report," *InformationWeek*, January 3, 1994, quoting the Meta Group. Buying a personal computer is like getting married. The costs of the marriage license and the wedding reception is never as much as what follows.

	Costs
Personal Computer	$3,522
Share of Server	$285
Share of Peripherals	$164
Network Equipment	$445
Personal Software	$1,309
Share, Server Software	$468
Host Interconnectivity	$1,355
Total Direct Costs	**$7,548**
Installation	$295
Administration	$5,600
Training	$1,350
Support Costs	$4,720
Maintenance	$622
Software Upgrade	$221
Total Indirect Costs	**$12,808**
End User Hidden Costs	$17,887
Informal Fussing	$2,175
Total five-year Costs	**$40,418**

Figure 54   Five year costs of office computing, per seat

The high fixed cost, fixed capacity structure of client/server networks therefore dictates charging an all-inclusive monthly rental fee, regardless of the volume of work. Everybody's rental does not have to be the same. There can be an equipment installation fee, an equipment lease charge, and a priority availability charge that depends on the features and attachments the customer wishes to use. There could also be special software feature charges, including fees for consulting services. The installation of applications such as electronic mail, inventory management, or executive

271

information systems may take place remotely.[326] The pricing of such basic services could include everything from training and support to software licenses and telecommunications. Only unusual demands such as high priority response time, special security protection, and transmissions to high-cost locations warrant adding pricing premiums. The viability of real-time charging for rentals of online software that costs only a few pennies offers innovative pricing options. This lowering of the administrative costs for doing business will surely happen as electronic money (or e-cash) becomes commonplace.

Pricing options based on electronic commerce place economically appropriate incentives on the provider of information services, whether that is an internal information processing operation or a commercial enterprise. The firm that provides the best support at the lowest cost will allow the customer to use more applications. Any new pricing schema should have as its primary purpose a means of encouraging customers to grow their repertoire of computer assisted capabilities. Successful providers of computer services will recognize that the personal productivity of their clients grows with work enlargement, not from working faster. The purpose of any services pricing model should be to make it easy and inexpensive to access the global store of accumulated knowledge assets. By means of such mechanisms, the knowledge assets that once were a privileged possession of a few become a globally traded low-cost commodity.

Adherence to industrial age pricing methods based on local cost recovery will continue to encourage the local acquisition of information technologies. Industrial age pricing prefers monopolistic pricing, territorial concessions, and imposition of regulatory restraints in support of the existing institutions.[327] Cost-based pricing cannot afford free market com-

326 Interesting statistics about the total administrative costs to support LAN-based email have been provided by InforCorp Consulting of Westborough, MA, in *Comparative Study of E-Mail Administrative Costs*. The annualized managerial support costs of ownership range from $87 to $579 per user. This large cost variance arises from major differences in the costs of training, in frequency of calls for assistance, in systems set-up costs, in downtime occurrences, in the difficulties with directory management, and in user account management practices for software packages such as Banyan, Microsoft Mail, Word Perfect, and Lotus cc:Mail.
327 Monopolistic pricing aims for recovery of costs plus a comfortable guaranteed profit margin. The pricing for services is not based on cost or value, but on the capacity to extract revenues from those who have no choice of another source of supply. Monopolistic pricing is usually sanctioned by government, or in organizations by whoever has the power to use computer charges as a taxing mechanism.

petition, especially not on a global scale. Cost-based pricing supports unproductive management overhead which can survive only under the protection umbrella of a government or by means of other exclusionary collusion.[328]

PRICING DIRECTIONS

Every chief information officer proclaims a goal of creating a computer aided work environment that will help every employee enhance his or her capabilities through new software. What used to carry the label of job enrichment now receives the more glorious tag of "computer-aided skill augmentation." Computer software should ideally appear to be thousands of servants readily available to run errands and get work done better and faster. From this perspective it makes sense to continue the anthropomorphic analogy and pay for software services the way one pays for hired staff or professional assistance.

People should be able to contract for an unlimited number of software assistants in any future information network. Networks should make it easy to bid competitively for services from a potentially large number of suppliers. The services should be as-needed rentals, happening much the same way as one rents an automobile. As people learn how to use these powers they should be willing to pay more for superior performers and guaranteed results. It is the value of the assistants' services that will determine how much the encapsulated software is really worth. The most likely outcome of such evolutionary development will be that the market for packaged software will largely disappear. Instead, there will be a global network auction for interactive functions that deliver predictable results. Right now, when one buys software, it is used to aid an input process that is hard for a non-computer person to understand and even harder to apply in producing the desired result. Customers do not want to buy inputs, they

---

328 A dismal example of such policy was the decision by the Brazilian military intelligence organization, in the early 1980s, to assert total control over all production and import of information technologies. It was also a means for levying high taxes. This slowed down progress of informatics in Brazil for about a decade until the restrictions lapsed. This author advised a commission convened by the Brazilian Senate of the likely consequences of the proposed restrictions. Placing extreme inhibitions on information technologies under the guise of national security and national industrial policy is often counterproductive.

wish to receive results. New network pricing methods will aid in deliver such transformations.[329]

Increased productivity in the information age requires real-time value pricing of services that deliver results. It calls for renting because this approach can enable global shopping for services wherever and whenever it is more economical. Value pricing allows greater reliance on the marketplace when making software choices in the form of assistants. It allows the substitution of competition for politically controlled monopolies.

CENTRAL VS LOCAL COMPUTING

In the last ten years no computing issue has stirred up as much discussion as disputes about the relative merits and costs of mainframes compared to PC/LAN installations. The commonly accepted wisdom was that MIPS (millions of instructions per second) were much less expensive on microcomputers than on mainframes. These arguments usually presented themselves as contrasts between centralization and decentralization, hierarchy versus autonomy, or control by specialists versus empowerment of users. Questions of the relative economic merit have not received adequate attention because the competing arguments have not been able to provide credible cost data. Instead, many of the debates turned into polemics about managerial philosophies. The resulting debates have therefore lost track of the simple insight that differences in the cost of ownership can be material and always favor some centralization of critical enterprise-wide functions, while preserving the capability for local innovation.[330]

329 As reported by Nash, K.S., and Picarille, L., "Vendors Deliver IS-Specific Apps Over the Net," *Computerworld*, May 6, 1996, p. 16. The electronic shipment of applications on demand, or just-in-time automatically is on its way. Stream International, Inc. – a $1.6 billion software distributor – has announced Internet delivery programs that will include a Java-based Internet Software Store, an online software application component re-seller licensing capability, and a technical support site staffed by thousands of support workers.
330 Economics is only one dimension of such dialogues. More important are matters of governance or, in corporate parlance, questions of information politics. See Strassmann, P.A., *The Politics of Information Management*, The Information Economics Press, 1993, for discussion of these issues.

What to Do

- Articulate a pricing policy for computer services that mimics the methods used by the most profitable outsourcing firms.
- Institute network pricing policies that charge a fixed monthly fee for all services that are not sensitive to increases in high cost activities.
- Operate networks that make it easy to bid for services from many suppliers.

Part VII
Residual Value

- The economics of software as an asset
- The economic significance of open systems
- Managing the residual value of information assets
- How to preserve information assets while outsourcing
- Planning and budgeting for conservation of information assets

31 Importance of Residual Value

Value is having a useful, long-lived, low-cost possession.

ONE SHOULD not construct software as a unique edifice, but as a collection of reusable assemblies. A wide variety of software applications can originate from relatively simple rearrangements of a limited set of standard elements. Yet, management continues to believe that information systems have preordained short technological lives. They keep accepting the prevailing build-and-junk view of how to manage systems. It will not be the accumulation of financial assets that will matter in the future, but the deliberate encouragement of growth in knowledge capital that will represent the means for creating new wealth.

How does one reconcile organizational flexibility and functional adaptability, all short term influences, with the economic advantages of long term life for software assets? How does one sustain the value of software investment and make it part of an architecture that is flexible yet long-lived?

SOFTWARE DOES NOT WEAR OUT

A typical software routine that computes calendar dates and the differences in elapsed time is not more than four hundred lines of procedural code. Once such a routine defines the logic in a computer language that is independent of a particular machine or operating system it could, in principle, function forever. This assumes that the software custodians own the tools and have the methods for translating such code to run in different computing environments. In this way a corporation could end up owning only one software routine for computing calendar dates on thousands of applications running at hundreds of locations. There would be no further maintenance expense associated with it, except when the computing environment changes and a suitable code needs regeneration from the original logic.

Contrast this with current practice, in which a corporation may end up owning hundreds of calendar date generation routines, each custom fitted to run in a particular computing environment. This scenario consumes maintenance and conversion labor to keep programs in synchronization so that they can pass information back and forth while management keeps changing where and how the applications will be used.

One should not construct software as a unique edifice but as a collection of reusable assemblies. The difference between building apartments and software is that the labor cost of taking an old house apart for reuse of materials requires too much labor. For software, reuse should take little effort provided one has the right tools and the software comes with standard connectors. The other difference between construction materials and software is that any reproduction of material objects incurs considerable expenses. Copies of software components cost practically nothing. The clones are as good as the original and will improve with time as they are used and tested in different applications.

SOFTWARE IS EASILY REPRODUCED

The incremental cost of reproducing software is approaching zero. A million copies of a piece of software logic can be cheaply available to anyone who wishes to have it. This suggests that it should be very profitable to make software out of general purpose standard components instead of spending the labor to define each logic element individually. Software components should be as purchasable as standard supply items, as hammers and saws are in any hardware store. They should not be unique artifacts, hand-crafted for exclusive use by only one customer.

If you have ever examined ancient furniture you will discover that the hinges, screws, and joints are all custom-made to fit the piece. The chairs around a table are not the same, because they come from whatever lumber pieces were available. When I visit old castles and admire the objects, it reminds me of the current programming methods: they are still like an ancient handicraft. The difference lies in costs. The feudal lords had the advantage of extremely cheap labor that produced durable artifacts. Current production methods yield software that is neither inexpensive nor durable.

REPLICATION OF SOFTWARE

One can assemble most commercial applications from a relatively small number of software elements that have similar logical structures. If you examine the code of business applications, most of it deals with data entry, retrieval of data, and display of data abstractions. Application-unique business calculations normally require very little software: the equations are trivial.

A wide variety of software applications can originate from relatively simple re-arrangements of standard elements. In this respect software has the potential of mimicking the behavior of biological organisms. All living matter, from plants to humans, exhibits an infinite variety of form even though the DNA blueprints consist of only eight basic components! It is conceivable that it will be possible to construct a repertoire of software components that will allow the assembly of a limitless recombination of business functions.

THE WASTEFUL POINT OF VIEW

Why is software so difficult to manage if it does not wear out, if its cost of replication is minimal, and it takes only a relatively small number of basic building blocks to construct most systems? Why do we have so much trouble adopting reuse of logic that would make software components more valuable?

The problem lies with how management views the value of software. Management constantly hears from reengineers, vendors, and consultants advising them to acquire or build brand new solutions, because whatever is old has little value. Of course, these are not unbiased sources of advice. Building something new is much more lucrative for the purveyors of building materials and for the building trades than renovating. Constructing a brand new system can obscure the original intent during a long delivery schedule. When late schedules force the curtailing of the deliverables, one can conveniently forget many of the original promises. The advantage of renovation is that you can immediately see what you are getting while you wait.

If management continues to behave as if information systems have preordained short technological lives, they will accept the current build-and-junk view of systems design. In financial terms this means that management will assign a low residual value and a high risk penalty to anything that has to do with computer-based innovation.

Without much thought executives can accept that computer equipment becomes obsolete every three years (or two, or one). They can then reason by analogy that if hardware ages so quickly, software cannot last much longer. This view justifies short payback or breakeven periods. It also explains why the assumption of premature worthlessness is implicit in the calculations of economic value of information systems.

This short-sighted view reflects the ways people are managed. Since the average tenure of a chief information officer is less than three years, management must not believe that CIOs gain much from company experience. Whenever one applies the build-and-junk view of systems to people, a hire-and-fire approach, the organization ends up losing its most valuable asset. Other than financial assets, which are of diminishing importance anyway, the only remaining equity of a firm is the capacity of its employees to learn. It will not be the accumulation of financial assets that will matter in the future, but the deliberate accumulation of knowledge capital that will represent real value-creating wealth. The accumulation of useful software assets will always represent a significant share of that wealth and therefore will need the fullest attention from top decision makers.

THE PREDICAMENTS

Management alone should not bear full responsibility for the shoddy state of software assets. Software obsolescence also comes from contention between technical experts and vendors caught by the rapid confluence of strong competitive forces.

Erosion in Compatibility

There is an increasing erosion of compatibility in microprocessor architectures. They are the foundation for all operating systems, on top of which all application software resides. The capacity to pack millions, and soon billions, of semiconductor elements on a silicon chip rapidly alters the foundation on which everything else rests. As hardware moves from an eight-bit processor to a limited instruction sixty-four bit processor, the software must adapt accordingly. Also, the concept of what one processes centrally and what one handles locally undergoes radical change as communication upgrades from teletype speed to super-high-bandwidth transmissions.[331] The layers upon layers of technology on which the useful applications rest are not bedrock but continually shifting thixotropic quicksand.[332] It is no wonder that the uppermost layer applications are not only shaky but prone to sudden collapse.

Creeping Features

It is easy to characterize the software business by its creeping features that are the consequence of software vendors competing through advertising claims. Firms wishing to survive must cater to the fickle whims and fads of the readers of computer magazines and computer catalogs. The software market is a race that gathers its fuel from generous advertising allowances, conventions, trade shows, magazines, and clever vendor tactics that support only the latest version of a software package.[333] For instance, the most prominent software vendor, Microsoft, makes sure that a new version of software creates files that are indecipherable to earlier versions of the identical software. Consequently, if a top computer executive upgrades to such software to take advantage of some new feature, this creates a forceful compulsion for subordinates to follow. Under such conditions one cannot expect programmers to have an incentive to create something that may have greater permanence than what is barely necessary to sell the latest version.

Unqualified Programmers

Even though the market will deliver, in due course, platforms that are more stable than current ones, it is unlikely that most programmers will take the time to write robust, stable, and well designed software. Software that is not fragile will appear only if management insists on it, pays the

331 A web page containing a short video of seventy million bits would take 1.4 hours to transmit using a standard 14.4 kbits/second modem. A standard cable modem with the capacity of four million bits/second would taken only 18 seconds. A wideband direct broadcasting satellite digital channel can do it in half a second.
332 Thixotropy is the property exhibited by some sands and clay soils. They are hard and can support considerable weight until disturbed by vibration. While working on the Maine Turnpike I saw a bulldozer totally swallowed into the earth in a matter of a few seconds.
333 With disfavor for liquor and tobacco advertising, magazines and newspapers now depend on information technologies for a major share of their advertising revenues.

price for it, and then verifies that it has been delivered. The majority of today's programmers are unqualified and are not subject to any tests to certify their competence. Plumbers, beauticians, and truck drivers must pass tough standards of certification. Programmers can get jobs on claims in resumes and interviews. A surprisingly large share of programmers are self-taught refugees from other careers ranging from accounting to zoo-keeping. They work on unreasonably short deadlines, with woefully mediocre tools, under ill-informed corporate bureaucrats.

The year 2000 defect is only one example of the myopia of what some claim to be a profession. A typical programmer can make hundreds of such myopic decisions in each project. The only reason that the year 2000 "insufficiency" has attracted so much attention is that it is ubiquitous and has a deadline when its effects will become visible. There are millions of other bugs just as negligent as this, but they pop up randomly, one location at a time, to be squashed with as little publicity as possible.

The significance of the year 2000 problem is its visibility. How computer professionals permitted such a enormous penalty to accumulate may lead to abolishing the protected status heretofore enjoyed by computer experts. As is often the case in the history, it takes a symbolic mishap to concentrate long-festering resentments into an explosion of corrective reactions.

Vendor Incentives

Vendors have a strong economic incentive to ship software that is tolerably failure-prone, because its earlier delivery preempts competition that may wish to ship a more reliable product that requires additional testing. Besides, a vendor with a large market share can then charge for maintenance, support, and upgrades that become more profitable than the original merchandise. It is a reflection on the present poor level of market expectations that customers accept frequent systems crashes from software through accidental incompatibilities. This is a matter of conditioning. Business people expect to get a dial tone from their phone 99.99 percent of the time, which is less than about one incident per year. However, most users of personal computers consider themselves lucky if their desired applications stay up for a week without a mishap.

Prospects

Erosion in compatibility, feature creep, inexperienced programmers, and vendor venality result in conditions that are wasteful and onerous. In due course a correction has to appear. Competent management will tolerate damage to their business only if the effects are either insignificant or a remedy is unavailable. The current deplorable state of the software business will not continue forever. The costs are too significant, and in many cases represent a large multiplier of the costs of the computer equipment. Eventually some vendor will start marketing computer technologies that recognize the total costs of the customer's ownership over the life of the enterprise rather than over the life of a technology. When that happens, the information industry will convert from peddling the latest technological marvel to delivering long lasting information assets that assist in the production of superior economical values.

What to Do

- Adopt computer-aided systems engineering tools that enforce the construction of software from a repository of standard reusable assemblies.
- Make the accumulation and preservation of useful software assets one of the principal technology objectives.
- Offer incentives to the systems staff to include the accumulation of reusable assets as one of their key objectives. Consider adopting a royalty-like reward scheme to encourage that.

32 Economic Value of Open Systems

Without legacy each generation would start in the stone age.

Open systems signify low-cost interoperability of non-homogeneous software and hardware. Conformity with standards does not guarantee interoperability, vendor independence, or software portability. The major economic problem nowadays is not how to build new systems to new standards, but how to make sure that whatever is new will also work with what already exists. There is a considerable risk in choosing only one vendor's solution for something as complex as the information system of a diversified corporation. Monolithic answers reduce the adaptability to changing conditions. Monopoly solutions can eliminate diversity and diminish the technical capacity of an organization to make thoughtful choices. The economics of software in embedded applications is inseparable from the product life cycle costs for the device it supports.

Open systems software has a residual value that exceeds ninety percent of its accumulated development costs. In that context the residual value is the discounted cash flow of investments that keep generating utility beyond the end of the planning period used to justify that investment.

What is Openness?

The specification of the requests for open systems proposals usually define the desired condition through standards with which the vendors must comply. That is necessary but certainly not sufficient. What comes as a great shock to many management committees is that conformity with standards does not guarantee interoperability, vendor independence, or software portability.

When I receive what is claimed as an open system solution, I first test where and in what ways the new application will cooperate with the old ones. The major economic problem nowadays is not how to build new systems to new standards, but how to make sure that whatever is new will also integrate smoothly with what already exists. Will the new system have the capacity to pass data back and forth from the current databases? Will the new application have the capacity to process results delivered from another application?

Most importantly, I will always evaluate open systems in terms of the financial costs and personnel disturbances they incur or avoid. I compare such solutions with proposals that call for reprogramming, retraining, upgrading, or conversions. Will the desired innovations in business processes require costly new hardware purchases and funding of new systems development projects? Will there be a delay in responding to competitive challenges? If the answers to all the above questions is that the costs and delays to innovations are negligible, then one can allege that an open systems strategy is indeed in place.

Open systems do not require that all information systems always be fully interoperable. There are many instances when such flexibility is unnecessary or uneconomical. Information managers must be selective and clear in what they are willing to pay to deliver integrated open systems. Just saying the words "open," "integrated," and "interoperable" in a request for quotation will not guarantee that the final result will match the original intentions.

I become exasperated whenever I hear that openness of software can occur through standardization on products available only from a single vendor. In other words, systems management takes the easy way out by granting an exclusive license to a vendor with monopolistic ambitions. None of the exclusive single vendor choices, whether they were IBM twenty years ago or Microsoft today, have offered the presumed universal solution. There is a considerable risk in choosing only one vendor's solution for something as complex as the information system of a diversified corporation. Monolithic answers reduce adaptability to changing conditions. Monopoly solutions can eliminate diversity and diminish the technical capacity of an organization to make thoughtful choices. Such dominance can creep in under the guise of cost reduction. For instance, there are network management features that make it possible to initiate system lockouts, restrict software choices, control all equipment configuration, and check on unauthorized local actions.[334]

Biology has taught us that the viability of a species depends directly on its ability to adapt to changing conditions. This underlies evolutionary advancement. It is this perspective that makes me skeptical of the claims

334 Trott, B., "NT 5.0 to Ease Management," *Infoworld*, November 11, 1996.

by anyone who says that he will deliver open, integrated, and interoperable systems through choices that favor only one vendor's products. Accepting the safety and uniformity assurances from a single vendor to the exclusion of others could well signal a decision that ends in permanent bondage or lock-in. It is also an option that could favor a supplier's economic interests over the customer's welfare.

What one means by vendor independence and by application portability also requires definition. Will it require that every new application must be able to run on every conceivable hardware produced by any vendor? Is it necessary for every application to run easily with any operating system, past, present, or future? That is not realistic. Open systems is a boundary fence within which a corporation's information systems can expect to function in the future. The bigger the fence, the more difficult it will be to find anything that will fit all of the requirements. The smaller the fence, the greater the long-term economic penalty when the limited choices become obsolete.

Defining what one means by open systems requires making economic tradeoffs which surely will be different for every organization. Coming up with such tradeoffs is a significant policy matter that has long-term financial consequences. One should not change such policies capriciously or frequently without first investigating the financial outcomes. You may have to live for a long time within the fences you erect today.

FEASIBILITY OF OPEN SYSTEMS

Open systems denote low-cost interoperability of software and hardware from different sources. Is that a realistic objective? It is and it must be. There is much that computer executives can do to achieve interoperability. This does not necessarily require having identical hardware and software. Such uniformity is not achievable because such homogeneity is neither enforceable nor manageable in a complex organization. Much is achievable though the elimination of redundant data definitions. One can require adherence to uniform messaging codes. A corporation should be able to place limits on the capricious variety of graphic formats. Corporate standards can mandate the detachment of graphic interfaces from application programs and the separation of data from applications. To reduce chaotic conditions the CIO can ordain a unified computer-aided software engineering environment.

288

Open systems are similar to the conditions that are necessary for peace in a civilized society. Everybody does not have to show identical habits. Variety and diversity should be welcome as a source of richness. However, civilization is only possible if norms of conduct exist. It is up to information systems management to promulgate, manage, and, if necessary, require compliance with such norms. If one calls that open systems, that's OK with me.

The Economics of Residual Value

Calculating the future value, or the residual value, of applications is the best way to evaluate the economic advantage of migrating to an open systems architecture.[335] The residual value is the discounted cash flow of an investment today that keeps generating utility beyond the end of the planning period of the investment. For the Department of Defense and most US corporations that is three to five years. In some electronics and consumer goods companies such planning periods are shrinking to less than two years.

Businesses do not disappear at the end of a planning period. The objective of planning is to make a business worth more at the end of the planning cycle than at the beginning. Similarly, the purpose of a sound investment plan should be increase the longevity of the information assets instead of accepting the assumption that they will be worth nothing after a breakeven period. To understand the economics of openness and residual value, here are some issues in managing software assets.

Embedded Applications

If one programs using a vendor specific language supported by a vendor-specific operating system which only works on a vendor specific computer architecture, then one will probably will have a very well integrated application. However, such a system is not transportable to any other hardware or software combinations, except with large conversion costs that may exceed the initial development investment. Sometimes there are

---

335 The residual value is a common term used in financial planning. It is an estimate of what an asset could be worth at some time in the future. For instance, if you buy a computer today, what will its resale worth be at the end of your planning period, such as five years hence.

good reasons in pursuing such solutions in producing software for high value durable goods, such as automobiles, missiles, or cameras. For such equipment the software is embedded into the physical artifact and is inseparable from the functions it has to perform. When the physical object has ceases to be of value, the software expires with it. The residual value of that software would then be zero.

Special purpose software running on special purpose microprocessors tends to become uneconomical as microprocessors become more powerful and memory less expensive. Complex mechanical equipment such as lathes or precision grinders now requires hundred of thousands of lines of code to function. A manufacturer soon finds it attractive to reuse as much of that software for a new or upgraded model, even though the initial version may suit only a single model. Under such circumstances the software for the embedded application may have to become more open within the limits of the microprocessor on which it resides. For instance, all Xerox copiers have similar commands and readout messages. Xerox found it advantageous to apply variations of identical software throughout the entire product line.

The economics of software in embedded applications is inseparable from the product life cycle costs for the device it supports. Part of the calculation of the life cycle costs of such software depends on the expected production volume of the physical devices. Production quantities are decisive, since the cost of development and testing of software now approaches or exceeds tooling costs for physical parts. Therefore, assembling device control software from standard and well-tested software components offers many advantages over special purpose solutions. Even if it means adding excessive processing power and an overabundance of memory, general purpose devices assembled out of standard modular components will always provide greater reliability and lower integration costs.

It is now clear that the information age will be typified by hundreds of tiny powerful computers serving each person's needs.[336] Their production economics will influence the speed with which the information society may advance technologically.

---

336 Just as the industrial era has been characterized by the presence of dozens and even hundreds of electrical motors in each household and workplace.

Dedicated Single Applications

Consumer applications such as VCRs, home heating equipment, tele-phones, and kitchen appliances depend on high residual values of software to support rapid product innovation. Only in this way is it possible to offer an increasing variety of product features to customers. The high residual values are possible because of the relatively narrow range of functions a device must support. Reuse is also desirable for standardization of the process a customer uses to command programmable devices.

As an example, a washing machine may now contain up to six micro-processors that communicate by means of an internal network about se-quences, timing, and malfunctions. All of this involves coordination of tasks that change only in minor details from one model to another. When upgrading to a product line with new features, the manufacturer will take the old code and convert it to whatever new microprocessors control the next version of washing machine. This requires a degree of standardiza-tion that we have seen only in telecommunication networks.

The residual value of the software, then, is the difference between the costs of writing a brand new application and the costs of upgrading. Typically, the residual value of microcode written for consumer appliances would have to be very high. This assumes that the devices will adopt industry standards for passing command signals from attachments made by other suppliers. Such software can be then carry the label as a ninety percent open system solution.

What to Do

- Test where and in what ways a new application will cooperate with the old ones.
- Judge open systems in terms of the financial costs and personnel disturbances they avoid.
- Reject the safety and uniformity assurances from any one vendor to the exclusion of others as a journey that ends in lock-in.
- Increase the longevity of the information assets instead of accepting the assumption that they will be worth nothing after a breakeven period.

33 Managing for Residual Value

To afford growth there must be surplus.

Much of the spurt in computer spending since 1990 is attributable to the replacement of mainframe code to make some of it transportable into the distributed computer environment. Despite these large investments little is showing up as discernible long-term assets that will make it easy for subsequent migrations taking place to Internet, Intranet or whatever comes next. In absence of a software application portfolio with a high residual value, the typical *FORTUNE* 500 firm will incur modernization costs of well over two times its total annual IT budget. The planning for the lowering of life cycle costs calls for lasting commitments to long-range technology directions. Local network and database installations that adopt some vendor's off-the-shelf instant solution should be particularly suspect from the standpoint of life cycle cost and longevity. A large share of personal computers in US corporations are still waiting to connect with a corporate and national information infrastructure that would lower local costs. Organizations must lower the exorbitant costs of network services through the use of automatic maintenance, fault diagnostics, interoperability, security, and crash-proof performance.

Managing information systems not as an expense, but as means for creating information assets, must become one of the principal measures of performance for every Chief Information Officer. To that end, all actions will need to focus on creating high residual values in equipment, software, networks, and employee training.

Conservation of Value During Conversions

Moving applications from centralized computing to local processing in order to improve response time invokes conversion costs. The average development budget for new systems consumes from twenty to forty percent of the total IT budget. Even if all innovation comes to a stop, it would still take between five and eight years to migrate the central systems to a distributed environment. This assumes that all the client/server software would be brand new. Unfortunately, the need for innovation and adaptation to change does not come to a halt in the meantime.

Much of the spurt in computer spending since 1990 is attributable to the replacement of mainframe code to make some of it transportable into the distributed computer environment. Despite these large investments little is showing up as discernible long-term assets that will make it easy for subsequent migrations taking place to internet, intranet, or whatever comes next. Firms simply rearranged logic from an old closed architecture to one that is new but even more restrictive. Therefore, when they finally finish this journey they will still not possess sufficient assets to settle down and start cultivating new grounds. With the rapid obsolescence of supporting technologies they will have to pick up and move out with yet another conversion. Such restless wandering about by the computer tribes explains the enormous increases in the revenues of consulting firms who thrive on packing up salvageable pieces of technology and reassembling them elsewhere.[337]

At present, individual applications and their unique supporting databases suffer from linkages that are too rigid. This makes it hard to distribute workload to multiple sites. The generation of proprietary displays also tends to be an integral part of every application. That limits the software changes that are possible without increasing training costs. Often the communication methods are hardware and network specific. Hence, one must first separate the applications from the embedded proprietary links that were put in place when designing the connections to and from the terminal devices to central computing. Under such conditions a corporation can consider itself lucky if there is any residual value remaining at all at the end of a computer cycle. There is little salvage value when the portfolio of systems lacks an architecture, exhibits too many erroneous transactions, suffers from extensive maintenance costs, and lacks compatibility across applications.[338]

Machine-aided or automatic translation of software code for transplanting existing business routines into new applications is, for all practi-

337 Somehow I cannot shake the image of business systems as a wandering tribe which moves the tents, sheep, goats, and camels whenever a pasture become exhausted. There is no permanence to build an irrigation system and settle down to agriculture.
338 The salvage value could be negative because it would cost money to extricate from the existing code before one could consider any modernization.

cal purposes, not suitable in cases where the software code is hopelessly jumbled after decades of patching up. Much of the present code needs discarding because its original design requires frequent interventions from operators, job schedulers, or special purpose devices. Without such assistance most of these systems do not work smoothly. The documentation of these systems is also nonexistent or impossible to trace. There are often only a few people who fully understand how an application functions from the operational standpoint so that its transformation can be adequately tested.[339]

Often the relationship between a business process and the ancient embedded software logic that supports it is incomprehensible in most of the currently running applications. Such software is not ready for re-use by either a maintenance programmer or an outsourcing contractor. Migrations or conversions call for enormous efforts to discover and document how the business functions and how it is related to other systems from which it feeds, or to which it supplies answers. Such understanding is essential before any software can make the transition from a central to a distributed environment. If such a transition coincides with outsourcing, the difficulties will be compounded. When a systems organization faces high conversion costs it has every incentive to throw away the old software and request hefty budget supplements to pay for modernization. In return management will receive a promise of future cost reductions and a few necessary new features.

Top management rarely finds out what assets, which cost millions or even billions, will be junked when they approve the funding for yet another round of computerization. They will never know because application software assets usually do not show up on the balance sheet. Something that is invisible requires no accountability for write-offs.[340] Top management will never know because their approval processes always concentrated on the acquisition of capital assets. The only capital asset remaining, mainframe computers, is of diminishing value and importance.

339 For two fearful years I was held hostage by a programmer who was the only one that understood how the Xerox payroll system was held together. The problem was not primarily the obsolete autocode for an IBM 7010, but how to move it to a replacement system. The old payroll systems suffered from too many complex manual interventions to cope with exceptions.
340 Comparable write-offs of physical assets would certainly warrant a footnote in the firm's audited annual report. Also there is often a scrap value attached to such write-offs, but only very rarely for software.

Top management will never know because it would require devoting a degree of attention to information management that is at least equivalent to that given to product research or market development. It would also call for expertise and understanding that is difficult to learn because the effects of information technologies are less obviously visible than whatever emerges from factories. Top management will therefore find it difficult to get at the facts. Neither the consultants, vendors, nor short-tenure CIOs will find it easy to uncover the causes of past neglect because their remedies may not be much different than what caused the disease.[341] Moreover, such discoveries may not be in their best interests anyway.

The Year 2000 Fix Demonstrates Poor Asset Custody

The enormous costs currently projected for fixing the incompatibilities across systems to reconcile year 2000 calendar dates are a telling illustration of the state of managerial laxity. There is absolutely no justification for allowing this condition to burst to executive attention at this late stage.

For instance, the Social Security Administration has some thirty million lines of software of which five to ten percent contain date records. Despite having started in 1989 on fixing its programs, it still faces the expenditure of thirty million dollars and the deployment of three hundred person-years of staff effort to prepare for the end of the century. Despite the relative early start of the Social Security Administration's efforts, the work that remains overwhelms their capacity to keep up with all other demands.[342]

Since 1964, and in the worst case since 1970, there has been no justifiable reason to keep the space allowed for calendar dates as only two digits. For more than thirty years computer installations operated with inexpensive magnetic tapes and cheap magnetic disks of enormous capacity. Punched card processing, perhaps the only legitimate rationale for keeping record formats to a barest minimum, expired in large organizations more than thirty years ago. The insistence on retaining for more than thirty years a calendar recording scheme that everyone knew would fail after December 31, 1999 is inexcusable management of corporate software assets. The year 2000 problem will remain a blemish on the credibility

---

341 The recent large increase in legal suits against outsourcing contractors offers a wealth of good information about common systems malpractice.
342 Anthes, G.H., "Year 2000 Problems Drag On," *Computerworld*, October 7, 1996.

record of all computer management, computer consultants, and computer vendors.[343]

FINANCING MODERNIZATION

The average age of the software portfolio of a *Fortune* 500 company is about six to eight years. That suggests the accumulated acquisition costs of its in place software is at least two to three times greater than its total annual budget for IT spending. Most of it is in COBOL and runs on large-scale central mainframe equipment.[344]

In absence of a software application portfolio with a high residual value, the typical *Fortune* 500 firm will incur modernization costs of well over two times its total annual IT budget. Without residual value such exposure could appear with at least every third investment cycle.[345] If the firm happens to be one of the largest four IT spenders in the US, with respective budgets ranging from $3.5 billion to $9.6 billion, the age of its applications will be above the average for the industry.[346] This means that it will have to pay anywhere from $600 million to over $10 billion in the next ten years for modernization.

Unless such projects include a large dose of business process redesign and workflow streamlining, that money will not buy new capabilities. After spending large sums the firms will find that the new software and hardware only perpetuate obsolete functions on technologically more modern networks. Such expensive conversions are not likely to show a favorable risk-adjusted payback, regardless of optimistic promises. The advantages of reducing only the operating costs will not offer sufficiently

343 A clever way of defusing the issue is by labeling the crisis as caused by the Y2000 bug. As everyone understands it, software bugs are the result of complexity and the inability of humans to fully comprehend the interactions among thousands – even millions – of logical statements. The year 2000 problem is not a bug. The calendar has been perfectly predictable for a long time.
344 Assuming that twenty-five percent of the budget is dedicated to developing and upgrading software and that the average cost per line of code is about fifteen dollars.
345 See Chapter 25 for descriptions of computer cycles.
346 A good measure of the obsolescence and age of an application portfolio is the estimated budget for fixing the year 2000 problem. The project manager of AT&T's year 2000 program has stated publicly that their expected cost is in the $300 million dollar range, to come out of a total annual IT budget of over three billion dollars. The official estimate for the US federal government, with an annual IT budget of twenty-eight billion, is that an expenditure of thirty billion dollars is needed to fix the year 2000 defect.

attractive financial returns to be worth the effort after allowing for the risks of managerial diversions and implementation delays.

Requesting twenty to twenty-five percent budget increases is one way of financing such modernization. Unless a firm has ample funds, the modernization money will not be available.[347] Every financial executive should question whether the frantic efforts by computer executives to build, junk, and then replace can continue indefinitely. Any astute budget analyst would recommend against budget increases unless the information systems executives can demonstrate how the proposed new investments will guarantee a longer asset life.

One justification for the "build and junk" approach would be that the systems innovation rate is accelerating. This makes the prospect of lower life cycle costs questionable unless the firm is ready to adopt a comprehensive systems architecture, uniform systems engineering methods, and enforce an open systems policy. Unfortunately, very few CIOs are in positions to offer such forward looking solutions. The planning for the lowering of life cycle costs calls for long term commitment to long range technology directions. If that is not feasible, CIOs will have to work hard to prove that business benefits outside the scope of their influence will somehow offset the costs and risks of modernization.

This is why most of the stories about large payoffs from information technologies are like sugar-coated medicine. The sweetness of business savings must compensate for the bitterness of spending for repeatedly redoing the same applications. The problem is that a CIO has no way of accounting for or capturing the business savings. The business managers will always keep those sweet profits as their own accomplishments.

SHORT-TERM FIXES

The immediate pressure for delivery of short-term solutions fosters the continuation of undisciplined systems engineering practices. The demand for rapid introduction of locally controlled client/server applications is notorious for fostering such precipitous actions. Local network and database installations that adopt some vendor's off-the-shelf instant solution should be particularly suspect from the standpoint of life cycle cost and

---

347 My research shows that in the 1993-94 prosperous period top-ranking firms in information productivity committed fourteen percent increases to their IT budgets, whereas the bottom-ranking firms managed only six percent increases in IT spending.

longevity. Their initial hardware acquisition costs will be uncommonly low, but that does not mean much if one considers that the visible capital investments will be perhaps as little as fifteen percent of the total bill.

The tolerance that large organizations show for locally constructed systems and databases has an analog in the land rush into the west one hundred fifty years ago. The eagerness to settle the new lands gave rise to isolated homesteads, each with its own well, latrine, and stove for cooking and heating. It took almost a century to overcome these problems by means of public water supply, sewers, and electric power.

A large share of personal computers in US corporations are still waiting to connect with a corporate and national information infrastructure that would lower local costs. Organizations must lower the exorbitant costs of network services through the use of automatic maintenance, fault diagnostics, interoperability, security, and crash-proof performance.[348] This is unquestionably the reason that the idea of corporate intranets has risen to such high prominence on everybody's agenda. The intranet could offer a unifying means for countering the prevailing tendencies that favor diverse and undisciplined computer networks.

Who will pay for and how can a firm justify investment in constructing a low-cost information infrastructure? This has become the topic of arguments between computer executives and their customers. CIOs understand that expenditures for building a corporate communication, systems engineering, and software infrastructure calls for the allocation of costs across a broad customer base. User executives wish to pay only for the variable costs that support their specific needs.[349] They expect others to carry all other costs because they do not trust the infrastructure builders to do anything that will ever lower their expenses. It is no wonder that the corporate allocations for infrastructure projects are an arena for intense battles between central and local powers. The only way out of such dam-

348 The fragility of widely distributed networks becomes obvious when they fail. A good example is the one day downtime of the widely used Internet hub operated by BBN, one of the most respected originators of many Internet technologies. A single rat shorted out the power source to BBN's computers. This short circuit made a backup switch fail, upon which the power company disconnected all circuits. For further details see Bruno, C. and Wexler, J., "Rats!," *Network World*, October 21, 1996. One can only imagine what could happen with a well planned terrorist attack on critical power supply installations.

349 John F. McLauglin put it well when he said "Much of what gets labeled as infrastructure is stuff that people want, but are unwilling to pay for," at hearings of the Committee on Commerce, Science, and Transportation, US Senate, 4 April 1990.

aging confrontations is for the infrastructure builders to commit to clearly identifiable operating cost reductions. Such promises are realistic only if the organization possesses a historically consistent method for reporting unit costs. Without that, infrastructure modernization investments will take place under the disguise of an essential project expense for someone who can afford it.

How to Get Support for Modernization

The preferred way of justifying large modernization investments is to prove that the next generation of software will offer lower support costs as well as a very large residual value. This suggests that the specifications for any major new IT investments should meet the following criteria:
- Ability to port over ninety percent of any new software without any additional expense to any future computer hardware architectures
- Installing application software that is independent of the choices of hardware vendor, operating system, or language compiler
- Maintenance logic changes that are independent of the way users are trained
- Capacity to accept functional upgrades from off-the-shelf computer modules available from competitive sources

Until most of the above criteria become an integral part of all systems requirements, I suspect that knowledgeable chief corporate executives may hold back on funding the next round of modernization investments.

What to Do

- Question all efforts to build, junk, and then replace software.
- Prove that the next generation of software will offer lower support costs as well as a very large residual value.
- Recommend against budget increases unless the information systems executives can demonstrate how the proposed new investments will guarantee a longer technology life.
- Put into effect detailed plans that lower life cycle costs through

commitment to long-range technology directions.
- Lower the exorbitant costs of network services through the use of automatic maintenance, fault diagnostics, interoperability, security, and crash-proof performance assurance.

34 Modernization through Outsourcing

Divorce impoverishes.

WRITING off the accumulated knowledge of prior years, whether it is in people or software, opens the door to outsourcing contractors. Upgrading is usually more cost effective than complete replacement. The burden of proof should lie always with those who advocate replacing rather than upgrading a computer system. The justification for any investment should include rigorous analyses of the costs, benefits, and risks of several alternatives. Well designed software has an inherent capacity for accepting continuous improvement. The drastic solutions offered by outsourcing contractors frequently offer a welcome relief from the incapacity of top executives to steer information systems functions. The advantage of outsourcing is that the contractor renders a monthly invoice so that a firm can finally find out its full costs instead of paying attention to the nominally watched IT budget.

Whenever corporate management discovers that they must write off a large portion of their existing systems assets and enter into another round of modernization, their first reaction is to replace their computer chiefs. To avoid a confrontation with the accumulation of neglectful practices, the new CIO then launches a program of modernization that calls for brand new applications. Old programs become useless junk. That software is branded by the euphemistic circumlocution of legacy software.[350]

The act of writing off the accumulated knowledge of prior years, whether it is in people or software, opens the door to outsourcing contractors. Unencumbered by maintenance and operating problems, there is a hope that these experienced mercenaries are more likely to get the job

350 This is in the good tradition of reclassifying all unpleasantness to escape notice. Dwarfs become vertically challenged persons, employment quotas are equal opportunity, and killing becomes termination with prejudice. The term legacy software is a way of shrugging off inquiries that ask why undocumented, improvised, and high-maintenance software turned into junk so fast.

accomplished. Meanwhile, the talent that previously guarded the information assets of the organization gets the unglamorous custodial task of keeping daily operations going while waiting for the newcomers to collect all the prizes. No wonder this creates conditions ripe for a disaster.

New research shows that junking old systems is not generally a good idea. Upgrading is usually more cost effective than complete replacement.[351] In a study of eighteen manufacturing organizations in North America, Europe, and Japan, the researcher concluded that renovation of old systems, while difficult, made more sense than a totally new system. The projects that called for total replacement have the characteristics of underestimating life cycle costs and overestimating their utility. Two wise conclusions emerged. First, the burden of proof always should lie with those who advocate replacing rather than upgrading a computer system. Second, the justification for any investment should include rigorous analyses of the costs, benefits, and risks of several alternatives. Finally, the researcher added, when project justification carries the label of being a mandatory strategic solution, it is a sure sign of trouble.

When computer people recommend modernization they usually concentrate on the desirability of replacing equipment and software. What they miss are the problems of organization, motivation, and conflict that take place when previously essential talent learn that they are about to become a dispensable rear guard.

SHIFTING POWER FROM THE CORPORATE INFORMATION STAFF

As a cure corporations appoint systems review boards that then reposition much of the decision making power from the untrustworthy computer executives into the hands of operating executives seeking immediate, reliable, and tangible improvements.

At this point it would be constructive for the newly appointed review boards to learn why systems that were less than five years old had suddenly became unserviceable and ready for the trash bin. Logical instructions are not subject to physical deterioration. Software should improve with use as that leads to the discovery and correction of errors. Well designed software has an inherent capacity to accept continuous improvement. Its adaptability is unmatched by any artifact ever constructed by humans. If software suffers from rapid obsolescence, it is more likely to have been a

---

351   Kiely, T., "Computer Legacy Systems," *Harvard Business Review*, July-August, 1996.

fault in the original design and poor management rather than any inherent limitation of the logic.

Unfortunately, action-seeking systems review boards exhibit little patience for probing into technical complexities and conflicting claims about competing systems engineering solutions.[352] Consequently, only technology modernization projects that emphasize rapid and low cost replacement of discarded applications receive adequate funding. It is always difficult to focus attention on an examination of the causes for short-lived systems. Review boards have little forbearance while searching for remedies. Top corporate executives do not have the motive or time to learn why the failed investments of the 1980s did not have a longer life. They would have to acknowledge their past abdication of decision making on critical policy matters to technical experts.

Political appointees, with average on-the-job-tenure of less than thirty-six months, do not mind blaming computer failures on previous government administrations. Given the extremely cumbersome procurement and project management practices that characterize all systems work in the public sector, there is never enough time to consider ways to provide a more viable solution. Politicians cannot afford to spend their limited time and pressured attention span on anything as far-reaching as changing the ways of managing computer projects.

Chief computer executives certainly have no incentive to explore the causes of technical mismanagement. The potential pitfalls are just too numerous. These include broken links between technology and business processes, poor documentation, unintegrated databases, disregard of elementary standards, and refusal to adopt systems engineering tools. Also covered is neglect in planning for an architecture that would provide consistent guidance for the construction of individual applications.

Any reforms that would correct for past omissions would require a long-term perspective. They would call for well thought out commitments at least five years ahead and a deferred bonus compensation plan. With CIO tenure expectancy, a prudent computer executive will trade lasting

---

352 Congressional investigations into failed multibillion dollar computer projects overlook the fact that it is the acquisition and management processes – which the legislature has ordained to begin with – that explain a large measure of the inability to adapt to changing conditions.

improvements in favor of dramatic rescues.[353] Besides, even if the promised long term gains ever came to pass, it would not be easy to identify them for easy recognition by top management. It is not yet possible to demonstrate the superiority of most long-term solutions without generally accepted metrics.

INDUCEMENTS FOR OUTSOURCING

The drastic solutions offered by outsourcing contractors offer a welcome relief from the incapacity of top executives to steer information systems functions. Having experienced outsiders take over the responsibility for most, if not all, of the information systems budget will relieve most of the accumulated managerial anxieties. Outsourcing lends itself to comfortable responses to troubling questions. For example, why did the corporation discard most of its investments in information technologies that only a short time before were the topics of much boisterous publicity?

Outsourcing is attractive because it legitimizes the removal of the mastery of information management from the qualifications to hold a senior management position. It makes it unnecessary to expend large amounts of energy in learning from mistakes.

Outsourcing is welcome as an act that follows the cardinal principle of all radical reengineering. It sanctions the idea that starting with a clean canvas and discarding everything that is already in place offers the best way out of inferior performance. Outsourcing advances the revolutionary view that it does not have to justify itself by any formal analysis, and certainly not by any formal financial payoff evaluation that would consider the full life cycle costs. Outsourcing the entire information services function to a contractor wipes out the relevance of history. One can unload accumulations of past grudges and misdeeds onto a third party.[354]

353 For analysis of CIO job tenure see Strassmann, P.A., "The Dangers of CIO Turnover," *Computerworld*, June 10, 1996. The CIO's on-the-job expectancy is not much worse than that of the Chief Financial Officer. According to McCorkindale, D., "Is Everybody Happy?" *CFO Magazine*, September 1996, fifty-one percent of the present CFOs have been on their jobs less than thirty-six months.
354 The psychoanalytic and theological aspects of such a relief are left to the interpretation of the readers.

MERITS OF OUTSOURCING

Outsourcing delivers something that is of great and long overdue merit. It renders a monthly invoice so that a firm can finally find out its full costs instead of paying attention to the nominally supervised IT budget.[355] It overlooks the circumstances that each company could have disciplined itself to obtain most of the identical results. Every long-term outsourcing arrangement carries some sort of front-loaded cost reductions as its inducement. In most cases such savings disappear into long overdue modernization projects to compensate for past mistakes. No wonder chief information executives continue to be attentive participants in seminars that offer instructions on negotiating outsourcing contract terms. In the short run, outsourcing will always show up as a source of new cash.

What to Do

- Place the burden of proof on those who advocate replacing rather than upgrading a computer system.
- Require that all investment justifications include rigorous analyses of the costs, benefits, and risks of several alternatives, including upgrading.
- Design software so that it has the capacity for accepting continuous improvement and upgrading.

---

355 In my detailed surveys of information management expenses I always include the question "What percent of your IT expenses are not included in your formal IT budget?" The answers from 182 questionnaires range anywhere from zero to 85 percent, with a median value of 21 percent.

35 Reaching out for Payoff

Conservation frees resources for modernization.

A THIRD of the costs for maintenance arise from the idiosyncrasies of the hardware, software, and telecommunications environment that a firm puts in place over several decades. Another third is attributable to the compromises each company makes to accommodate the constant shuffling of organizational charts and the peculiarities of personalities that insist on special reporting privileges. Delivering open systems solutions that allow customers to migrate from one technology to another with little pain may reduce the customers' costs, but will surely not increase the suppliers' profits. The bottleneck in achieving conversion to open systems is the training and retraining of the systems and programming staffs. Extending the useful life of software logic beyond twenty years offers one of the most attractive opportunities available to systems managers. There is no other way for coming up with comparable gains, not even by the most opportunistic procurement of computer hardware. The widespread acceptance of high discount rates on IT investments receives inspiration from the super-optimists. These include consultants, vendors, and journalists who have much to gain from promoting additional computer spending.

The economics of managing IT in a business enterprise improves considerably whenever the residual value of the software applications is high. Consider the case of a typical large company in our database. Officially it has an annual IT budget of $110 million. This does not count for all the stealth computing omitted from the nominal estimates. The hardware expense, including mainframes, minicomputers, microcomputers, and terminals, will be less than $18 million per year. Software maintenance, development, upgrades, and conversions will be more than $60 million. The rest is for communications and for administration. Clearly, maintenance and upgrades are the largest discretionary expense. Trouble-free and stable software could reduce much of that cost.

MAINTENANCE DEGRADES ALL PAYOFFS

A third of the costs for maintenance arise from idiosyncrasies of the hardware, software, and telecommunications environment that a firm has put in place over several decades. Another third is attributable to the compromises each company makes to accommodate the constant shuffling of organizational charts and the peculiarities of personalities that insist on special reporting privileges. For an excellent company whatever remains in the software maintenance budget will go for improvements that are essential for supporting profit-generating business needs.

Computer managers mortgage up to half of their IT budgets to keep disparate versions of software, hardware, and communications from collapsing. This happens as applications keep losing interoperability through each round of technical upgrades or technical improvements. Incidentally, when IBM was the sole supplier, the management of diversity was not easy. IBM never came up with workable standards for keeping their software in harmony with its diverse hardware. The variety in the IBM product line was always sufficiently large to give rise to a continuous stream of upgrades, revisions, and maintenance improvements to overcome IBM's growing incompatibilities. Although there were many customers who relied exclusively on equipment and software from IBM, there was no way of avoiding costly changes that delivered no value-added to the customer.

In the last decade the software portability problem has grown much worse. There has been an enormous proliferation of hardware, software, database, and communications suppliers. The rapidly growing number of participants in the computer industry are all trying to carve niche positions from which customers would find it difficult to extricate themselves. Delivering open systems solutions that allow customers to migrate from one technology to another with little pain may reduce the customers' costs, but will surely not increase the suppliers' profits.

Raising the residual value of software to eighty percent could save a typical firm in my data base up to twenty million dollars per year. Attaining such savings would require shifting to a policy that insists on vendor independence. It would call for compliance with industry standards, as followed by at least three major suppliers. The problem would be in migrating from applications that behave as if they were welded to the existing hardware and operating systems to solutions that can be easily reassembled as conditions change.

On the journey toward open systems the customer will discover that in the short run, which is the tenure of most systems chiefs, continuing with proprietary solutions is usually more attractive. Restructuring software for technology independence may take many years. For project with quick delivery deadlines, vendor specific solutions will appear less costly than software built to open standards, because compliance with standards makes it necessary to subject all software development and maintenance to a systems engineering discipline that uses standard tools. The bottleneck in achieving conversion to open systems will be the training and retraining of the systems and programming staffs.[356] Their productivity sinks every time they have to learn new ways.

DESIGN ARCHITECTURES

Organizations following the path to open systems are likely to underfeed and technically underpower such efforts. They find that the cost of upgrading existing talent is very high. Failures happen if ambitious project managers try to fund such migration from ventures they already control. Unless migration projects to open systems obtain stable funding for at least five years, the launching of yet another comprehensive architectural blueprint is likely to fail. The open systems path is rarely the easiest course to follow, despite noble intentions at inception.

What are the chances of introducing some semblance of discipline into a firm's technologic chaos? To assess this one should inquire about the results of the various architectural planning experiences over several decades. I do not know of a single IT organization that has not started comprehensive systems engineering or architectural projects. In each case, there have been hopes that the effort would lead to a unified approach and bring greater order to conflicting technological choices. Finding out the extent to which such endeavors have influenced the conduct of the IT staff may be one of the most telling indicators of the technological maturity of the organization.

Despite many obstacles, software designed to maintain a high residual value will, in due course, show economically attractive payoffs. Extend-

---

356 The estimated cost of completely retraining a computer professional is $50,000, or the equivalent of four years of college tuition costs for obtaining a Bachelor of Science degree at good public institution. See Moad, J., "Calculating the Real Benefit of Training," *Datamation*, April 15, 1995.

ing the useful life of software logic beyond twenty years offers one of the most attractive opportunities available to systems managers. There is no other way for coming up with comparable gains, not even using the most opportunistic procurement of computer hardware. What then does it take to achieve a high residual value from software and employee know-how?

You Get what You Plan For

Comptrollers often demand demonstrations of thirty to fifty percent returns on investment before agreeing to computerization projects. They insist on such usurious rates because they realize that nobody may be ever able to prove that the promised improvements actually happen. In all my years as CIO and consultant I have never come across a valid and totally independent post-implementation audit. Conditions always change, and therefore the original plan does not correspond to what is finally delivered. The observable results evade comparison with the approved proposal.

Appropriation committees know that project overruns and feature enhancement requests will show up in reports as operating costs to cover any shortcomings at the time of project authorization. The excessive discount factors applied to computer-related investments prove that non-computer executives recognize that systems projects are risky, erratic, and unpredictably short-lived.

The financial calculations, if done at all, usually offer months-to-breakeven as an indicator of investment attractiveness. I have seen financial investment guidelines from major corporations that mandated all computer projects pay off in less than two years. That implies ridiculously high risk discount factors of more than fifty percent per annum. It dictates short term thinking that is even more discouraging of good practices than excessive return on investment hurdle rates.

The widespread acceptance of high discount rates on IT investments also gets inspiration from corporate super-optimists and public policy utopians. That is in addition to consultants, vendors, and journalists who have much to gain from promoting additional computer spending. They often tout fantastic rates of return from investment in information technologies. Why should a controller not discount all benefits to weed out anything but the candidates that match the reported profits? This would surely make sense if one believes that profits from computers are astronomical. Boasting about thousand percent or better profit expectations offers every financial executive a justifiable rationale to expect more of computer investments than from any other cash outlay.

Along with a bias for proposals that tout high multiples of the cost of capital comes a risk that a firm may get what it asked for. Makeshift solutions fit short term payback projections quite nicely. Proposals will promise fantastic returns by requesting unrealistically low budgets. In these circumstances computer people will be reluctant to disclose full implementation costs. Management will subsequently hear about unachievable implementation schedules.[357] Worthy projects will receive authorization only when an imminent disaster is pending.

A noteworthy example of such a debacle is the case of FoxMeyer Drug Company. In 1994 Robert R. Brown, its CIO, was describing in *Computerworld* plans for a $65 million advanced information system. The president enthusiastically endorsed the project, saying that it will "enable us to accelerate sales growth without proportional increases in personnel and expense." Brown said: "We are betting our company on this." In retrospect it became obvious that the schedules were overambitious, the budgets inadequate and the results unachievable.

A year later FoxMeyer filed for bankruptcy.[358] The drug wholesaler was overwhelmed by huge expenditures for new computers, software, and consultants who were supposed to make the new system work. A major problem was their inability to make the powerful SAP software handle up to half a million items per day. When the systems failed to function according to plan, the firm collapsed.

In many cases where a company manages to complete a rapid payback project, the firm will probably get applications that are built to bare minimum levels of acceptability. The customers will obtain delivery of the equivalent of plywood-and-tarpaper shanties instead of worthy dwellings. High maintenance, retarded functionality, costly upgrade paths, and little residual value characterizes such misbegotten projects for the rest of their economic life, which will be short.

Designs that take a long term view by subjecting all development and maintenance to sound and open systems engineering practices are more likely to be in a sufficiently robust condition to be of longer lasting value.

---

357   This paragraph explains some of the dramatics that take place between Congressional Appropriation Committees and the computer project managers at the Social Security Administration, Federal Aviation Agency, and the Internal Revenue Service.

358   Bulkeley, W.M., "When Things go Wrong," *The Wall Street Journal*, November 18, 1996.

They must possess a capacity for adapting to changes, modifications, and upgrades gracefully. Such design must have a longevity that surpasses the frequency of reorganizations. They must possess a capacity that allows for rearrangements in workflow whenever business processes need to be improved.

What to Do

- Adopt a policy that insists on vendor independence.
- Insist on compliance with industry standards, as followed by at least three major suppliers.
- Extend the useful life of software logic beyond twenty years because it offers one of the most attractive cost reduction opportunities.
- Take a long term view by subjecting all development and maintenance to standard systems engineering practices.

36 Leadership in Value Creation

Progress requires mastery of complexity.

THE DISTRIBUTION and decentralization of computing power started with the introduction of minicomputers. Forecasting the future costs of the distributed computing hardware was relatively easy because of the declining costs of semiconductor memory. The increased capabilities of microcomputers were also predictable. The chaos of the 1990s is therefore the consequence of not only the myopia of IBM, but also of the institutional obstinacy of DEC. There is no reason to believe that the rapid rise and demise of new entrants into the computer industry will not repeat itself in the years to come. Thus independence from any one vendor must remain one of the most coveted goals of all systems management. Customers will continue to desire lower costs of ownership, an open architecture, application portability, and technological adaptability to meeting rapidly changing conditions.

The general acceptance of the obliterate-not-improve school of systems modernization has its origins in the wasteful practices of the 1970s. Enormous funds poured into the expansion of computer capacity presumably to provide firms with a lasting competitive advantage. Maybe as much as $500 billion found its way into new computer applications. This buildup took place without a unifying architecture. There was little regard for the portability of the software to technologically distributed environments because most of the corporate computer chiefs were following directions set by IBM.

FAILURES IN LEADERSHIP

IBM Corporation's SNA (Systems Network Architecture) solution initially hoped to fill the leadership vacuum for migrating from monolithic to distributed computing. SNA turned out to be technologically inadequate, though it is still not clear whether that was an intentional limitation to maximize profits from mainframe computers. SNA did not satisfy the demands for greater autonomy of people who were seeking independence from the heavy-handed monopolistic practices of the central computing hierarchies. This proved to be unfortunate for the US computer industry and costly for its customers. Previously, the corporate and public sector computer establishments followed IBM's view of systems organization at each turn of the investment cycle. With the faltering credibility of IBM everyone was affected. It was also a calamity, though predictable, because the objectives of SNA were ultimately to prop up IBM's tradition-bound marketing methods. SNA catered to the desires of the central computer staffs for greater control but not to the customers' wish for easily implemented simple solutions.[359]

There was no technological reason for such a failure. The greater flexibility and arguably lower costs of pursuing a distributed computing architecture were understandable, even in the mid-1970s. The networking successes of products from the Digital Equipment Corporation (DEC) certainly demonstrated how this could work.

The distribution and decentralization of computing power started with the introduction of minicomputers. Forecasting the future costs of the distributed computing hardware was relatively easy because of the declining costs of semiconductor memory. The increased capabilities of microcomputers were also predictable. The chaos of the 1990s is therefore the consequence of not only the myopia of IBM, but also of the institutional obstinacy of DEC. It was DEC that mastered minicomputer-based distributed computing early on, but it would not grasp how take advantage of its lead in networking systems.

One should not, however, place all the blame on vendors. The technologies placed in the 1970s and early 1980s now have a remarkably low residual value. Top management did not demand that information executives make commitments beyond immediate needs. Corporate systems review boards did not fund multiyear investments that would accelerate the acceptance of open systems. In my many years of making presentations to investment review boards, the agenda mostly covered the allocation of next year's development and maintenance money. The vendors have the excuse that they only did what their customers asked.

So who is to blame for the present sorry state of information assets? Why are the conditions in the public sector worse than for commercial

359 The insensitivity the IBM corporation showed during this period of its greatest prosperity is comparable only to the way King George III treated the American colonists.

firms? Why is the federal government incapable of sustaining modernization projects? Whose fault is it that the application software in the inventory of most organizations cannot survive from one technology cycle to another? Who will explain the current high expenses for elaborate networking schema whenever the Internet becomes the universal means by which organizations communicate internally, as well as with suppliers and customers?

Judgment day has already arrived for IBM and DEC, for Honeywell and Siemens, for Burroughs and NCR, for Bull and Xerox, for Amiga and Apple.[360] All these firms, or their successors, are recovering from a period of disastrous losses of cash, employees, and customer credibility. I still wonder when the day of reckoning and retribution will arrive in the offices of many surviving corporate CIOs. I suspect that the current onslaught of outsourcing contracts is rendering the verdict without taking time to deliberate about the chances for rehabilitation.

REMEDIES

The remedy for delivering low residual values will not come from process reengineering. It will not come from consultants, who are gladly party to delivering results with high short-term payoffs but little long-term worth. It will not arise from adopting generic best practices, as advocated by various maturity models.

The cure will come from innovations that originate with newcomers to corporate technology architecture. The traditional providers of enterprise computer services will increasingly have to compete by delivering systems that offer guarantees of longer life. But, if the past is any indication, none of the newcomers will end up with a firm hold on a position of leadership for a sustained period. A venture that is yet unidentified may ultimately become a dominant force. There is every reason to believe that the rapid rise and demise of stars of the computer industry will repeat itself in the years to come. This is just one more reason why independence

---

360 The decline of Apple Computer, with a distinctly superior technology, is a particularly sad litany. See Perelman, L.J., "Opportunity Cost," *Wired*, November, 1996. It describes how the obsession of management with the education market incapacitated the organization. The article reminds me of the self-inflicted sight-deprivation of Xerox top management while presiding over the best technologies available in the early 1980s.

from any single vendor should remain one of the most coveted goals of all systems management.

It is interesting that each of the new contenders for the position of industry leader promises what everyone has always wished to have. Customers want lower costs of ownership, an open architecture, application portability and technological adaptability to meeting rapidly changing conditions. Events have yet to unfold to show if the solutions from the new competitors will turn out to be more lasting than those that claimed primacy in the 1970s. Whoever delivers on this promise will unlock much of the potential business value of computers. Meanwhile, these values will remain elusive because of the inherent instability in the practice of information management.

What to Do

- Seek out suppliers of computer services who compete through delivery of systems that have a low life-cycle cost of ownership.
- Insist on independence from any one vendor as one of the objectives of systems management.

315

Part VIII
Evaluation Methods

- Determining the right amount of computer spending
  - How to benchmark computer expenditures
    - Calculating residual value
  - Methods for valuation of technology assets
    - Cost of ownership of computers

37 THE EXPECTED COMPUTER BUDGET

The patterns of computer spending are as unique as fingerprints.

THE ARMS race point of view maintains that computer budgets and the competitive capacity of a firm must be related. This has been one of the most persistent fallacies about computer spending. Statistical analysis revealed that for companies with common characteristics and a similar employment structure, a small number of selected variables could be used to estimate expected computer spending with exceptionally high levels of correlation. The presence of professionals such as accountants, financial analysts, market researchers, and engineers, explains about twenty percent of the total spending level for computers in a corporation. Therefore, the allocation of computer funds is at least as important as making sure that the total amount expended is not excessive. The decision to provide access to networked personal computers to all information workers is usually the single costliest IT investment act. Averaging all development and operating expenses against the number of personal computers that benefit from these expenditures could be a useful measure.

If provable profit is not the reason, firms may be employing computers to match spending by competitors for the latest technologies. Applying such rationale makes computerization comparable to an arms race. If an adversary has machine guns, one cannot survive by relying on flint lock rifles.[361] Affordability and payoff are not usually relevant under such circumstances.

---

361 In the early 1900s Basil Zaharoff obtained an exclusive marketing license from Maxim, a French gun-maker. Zaharoff took a few of Maxim's machine guns and gave them to the Turks. Zaharoff then traveled to Moscow, Berlin, Zagreb, London, and Vienna, informing each General Staff in succession how many of the new weapons were ordered by others. In five years Zaharoff started a massive arms race in Europe and became one of the richest men. This story explains some of the marketing methods for selling computers and the compulsion of the customers to buy what may not be of benefit.

Explaining IT Spending

The arms race point of view maintains that computer budgets and the competitive capacity of a firm must be related. This has been one of the most persistent fallacies about computer spending. Elaborate schema have been constructed to come up with indicators that would support this. The results show that, for a particular industry, there does not exist a required ratio for IT spending to remain competitive.

The cost drivers that determine computer spending are more diverse than is apparent from an examination of any one indicator. Influences such as the differences in employment patterns, the degree to which a business may be computation intensive and the extent to which some firms have distributed access to computing power to employees shape the IT budget. Companies with above average profits are also more likely to open their purses for computer investments than those who must economize on all discretionary spending.

For selected corporations I explored relationships that could correlate with thirty-four data elements that measured key financial and operational characteristics of firms. Statistical analysis showed that for companies with common characteristics and a similar employment structure, a small number of selected variables could be used to estimate expected computer spending with exceptionally high levels of correlation.[362] Data about the employment structure (for example professionals vs. clerical vs. factory operatives), the extent of automation (for example number of personal computers per employee), and affordability (for example profits of the firm) explained over ninety percent of IT spending.

The analysis that follows covers US firms that have distinguished themselves by scoring high information productivity values. This includes an assorted spectrum of industries with a broad range of computer budgets. Similar correlation studies for other groups found that one can generate the expected IT budget from just a handful of variables with better than ninety percent confidence.

362 My consulting engagements have provided a verified sample of 138 US industrial companies with look-alike characteristics. A multiple linear regression model of six variables generated a regression coefficient of 0.945 percent, with an F ratio of 471 and t-ratio values for each variables ranging from 4 to 15. The probability level for each variable was equal to or less than 0.001. A 0.945 regression coefficient indicates that nearly 95% of the total variance in the expenditure is statistically explained by the set of predictor variables.

This method of calculating the estimated IT budget uses simple linear equations that are applicable for assessing the levels of IT spending: [363]

$$IT\ Budget = K + (A \times SG\&A) + (B \times Profit\ After\ Tax)$$
$$+ (C \times Desktops) + (D \times Professionals) - (E \times Officials)$$

To apply this method the client picks the peer group against which the company will be compared. This may include firms with a similar capital structure or global firms in the same Standard Industrial Category (SIC). The equations that estimate the IT spending will vary, but in almost all instances the following relationships emerge:

- Computer spending rises with increases in Sales, General, & Administrative expenses (SG&A).
- Computer budgets are higher if a company is profitable and are cut if it is losing money (Profit after Taxes).
- Computer budgets expand if a company employs a large number of professional, administrative, and clerical workers.
- Computer budgets grow in direct proportion to the number of personal computers installed per information worker.
- Computer budgets decrease for each employee classified as an official, which means executives and managers. This decrease has its origin in officials receiving an already large allotment of IT funds because their high salaries represent a disproportionately large share of SG&A. Since the expenses for officials are always in SG&A accounts, this line item generates excess funding for supplying the officials' computing needs. The negative entry then corrects for such excess funding.
- Computer budgets decrease if a large proportion of the workforce is operatives and laborers.

363 In this equation K stands for a constant expense which represents the approximate expense for a firm's information infrastructure unrelated to any volume of work. This formula has been applied in numerous cases to make a reasonably reliable assessment whether a firm's IT budget was under- or overspending the patterns set by comparable firms. The values of A, B, *etc.* stand for the coefficient weights that indicate the relative importance of each variable.

Understanding the IT budget

Data that includes a wide range of variables lends itself to the discovery of relationships that have some influence on the IT budget. Prominent among these are profits, the extent to which information workers have access to personal computing, and hidden spending by customers in performing IT work without including it in any IT budget.

Effects of Profit

Regression equations can aid in assessing whether computer budgets are more or less than should be expected. The variables that shape the expected IT budget are plausible except when corporations with superior profit performance kick in extra money for computer spending because they can afford it. If one cannot find a direct relationship between computer expenses and profits, such generosity may not have much value. Any surplus funds should go into projects that can demonstrate the potential of increasing value for shareholders.

The opposite argument applies to budget cuts for companies in trouble. Corporations in a profit crunch place a reduction in computer expenditures high on their priority list. Computers are often successful in supporting the simplification of business processes. In such circumstances increasing the computer budget is a desirable investment priority. Management must then demonstrate that it knows how to deploy information technologies for supporting business process redesign. Information technologies can offer attractive opportunities under such conditions. They may offer a welcome relief from competitive problems that are not amenable to any other form of managerial intervention.

Effects of the Occupational Profile

The presence of professionals such as accountants, financial analysts, market researchers, and engineers explains about twenty percent of the variance in spending level for computers in a corporation. Of these, the controller's department is always one of the largest consumers of computing power. Some sections of the finance department spend more on computers than on employee compensation. A corporation may find that it is spending the expected amount for computers, but still misallocates these

resources on activities that do not generate profits. Therefore, the allocation of computer funds is at least as important as making sure that the
total amount expended is not excessive.

The depressing effect of the number of executives on the computer
budgets is amusing, but not surprising. It does not mean that executives
do not use computers. It only suggests their share of SG&A costs is greater
than what executives can consume in computer services. Most executives
have little need to use computer power that is commensurate to their
salaries. They spend little time on decision-support systems, executive
information systems, and sophisticated war-room displays. Each of these
expensive showplace systems are surrounded by a flock of professional
analysts who exercise the executive applications. The expense for executive
information systems is mostly in the labor costs of the acolytes and not in
the expense for the gadgetry.

The job of executives is primarily political. Their purpose is to keep
an organization from sinking because of chaos and conflicts. Officials do
not need much computer-based data for that because their organization
balancing activities depend mostly on ideas, experience, and personal relationships. What executives do and what they think about is not yet
amenable to processing by computers. It is likely to remain that way long
into the future.

The Effects of Personal Computers

The decision to provide access to networked personal computers for all
information workers is usually the single costliest IT investment act. The
average annual cost of ownership of a standalone personal computer, with
a minimum of network functionality, is over twenty percent of the average
compensation of information workers.364 Fifty-seven percent of this is for
activities that do not show up in the reported IT budget. What top management will get to see in the usual budgeting exercise is only the remaining forty-three percent of the total expense.

---

364 The Gartner Group, *Monthly Research Review*, July 1996. The estimate is for the total
cost of ownership of a Windows 3.x computer. The comparable total support cost of
ownership for a Macintosh computer is approximately $1,000 less per year. The user
training and learning costs for the Macintosh are at least a third less than the time
spent coping with a Windows 3.x machine. This proves that the price of computers is
not the only factor in making a computer acquisition decision.

Networked computers are particularly costly because they must carry an allocation of the expenses for network management and central processing. The annual cost of such installations may be as much as $13,000 per station, or approximately thirty to forty percent of the average salaries of clerical personnel.[365] Some network operators realize significant economies from the automation of help desk tasks, from electronic software distribution, from central equipment configuration management, from software licensing fees, and from remote access to user client workstations. Such organizations gain efficiency from the performance of tasks that would otherwise would be too expensive to handle locally. Operators who can enforce a high level of network standardization on large networks can expect to realize at least $3,000 to $4,000 savings per station per year.[366] But the biggest savings arise from network reliability that avoids work stoppage because the computer does not function. The cost of computer equipment on the desktop, per hour, is less that fifty cents. The fully burdened cost of information workers is about forty dollars per hour. Every minute that computer services are not available wastes more than the total expenses for computing equipment for a full hour! Therefore, one should concentrate on the effectiveness of people and not the costs of computing as the principal measure of performance.

Effects of Ownership Costs

There are times when a development program ends up supporting only a minuscule customer population. Under such abnormal circumstances no standard IT cost estimating equation will yield meaningful estimates. Often this is the result of a shortfall in delivering promised capabilities. If project schedules take years instead of months, customers improvise their own solutions. During the long wait for results they commit to a patchwork of systems that may not be elegant or efficient, but nevertheless deliver useable results.

One of the record-holders for improvised bypassing of strategic intent is the JCALS (Joint Computer-Aided Logistics Support) program of

---

365 Ubois, J., "Tending Computer Assets," CFO *Magazine*, June 1996.
366 One of my reviewers commented that this was not a "savings" but "cost avoidance." That is not a matter of semantics, but a question of cash. When a well managed organization avoids useless work, it must spend less. In the public sector computer advocates claim cost avoidance as the benefit of systems projects to avoid budget cuts. A benefit is not a benefit unless it reduces costs or increases value-added.

the us Department of Defense. According to the General Accounting Office, after ten years and an estimated commitment of $5.2 billion dollars "... defense has not made the basic decisions necessary to successfully implement CALS. Defense has expanded the CALS initiative several times since its inception in 1984, but has not clearly defined what the initiative should be, what it should encompass, and how it should be implemented."[367]

After an expenditure of more than $200 million over a five year period in just one part of this ambitious program, JCALS has finally delivered software. Unfortunately, it works only on 1,200 personal computers instead of the large multiple of that number projected in the original plans.[368] Thus the cost of software is $166,666 per user.[369]

Averaging all development and operating expenses against the number of personal computers that benefit from these expenditures could be a useful measure. It reveals places where employees are consuming IT services that cost a large multiple of their salaries. If employee compensation is an indicator of value, then the fully allocated per capita costs for IT services could be a good proxy for assessing the worth of the services.

Fully allocated per capita costs are metrics that can also reveal whether tight controls over personnel headcount have resulted in unnecessary mechanization of trivial administrative chores. Indeed, there are many situations where a task is computerized even though an additional clerk could do it better for a fraction of the cost.[370]

SATURATION OF COMPUTER USE

The average 1994 IT corporate spending in the us, per employee, was $4,970, though one must consider that well over half of the workforce still does not have much to do with computers in the workplace. Increasing the percentage of the workforce equipped with networked computers could double the size of total computer expenditures, even though this could still

---

367 US Government General Accounting Office, *Report on the CALS Project*, September 30, 1994.
368 Constance, P., "JCALS: The Teflon Initiative," *Government Computer News*, August 12, 1996, p. 63.
369 Based on the value of the contract with a software vendor. Added expenses by the Department of Defense for acquisition, administration, and installation are at least equal to that amount.
370 For a description of a project that tried to solve a problem with expensive technology where adding staff could have cost less, see the description of the us Patent Office case in my book *The Business Value of Computers*, p. 337 and p. 344.

understate the true costs.[371] The large cost element of end user operations can easily inflate administrative costs without ever showing up as a larger computer budget. Ultimately, the full effects of computerization will be discernible only as an increased ratio in overhead to direct expenses.

The extent of saturation of personal computer usage in a firm becomes apparent in displaying the relationship between the population of terminals – personal computers as well as workstations – in comparison to the number of information workers. Such graphics offer an indication of whether the proliferation of personal computers is above or below industry trends. A high or low deviation from the trend warrants asking questions.

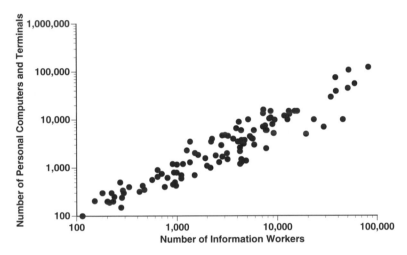

Figure 55   Information workers create terminal & microcomputer demand

For large organizations I find a remarkable consistency in the extent to which personal computers have captured the corporate desktops.[372] In 1994 the number of personal computers for close to the two hundred largest us corporations equals eighty-one percent of the number of employees classified as information workers.

371 Dec, K., "Client/Server Payoff", CIO Magazine, April 15, 1996, p. 72.
372 From Information Worker database. The regression coefficient equals 0.838 percent for 67 cases. In 1993 and 1994 over 75 percent of the information workers had a terminal or a personal computer. There are notable exceptions to this average, such an airline that reported 1.4 terminals per information worker.

How long such a simple relationship will remain a fairly reliable predictor of expenditures for information technologies remains an open question. As each individual acquires several low-cost computing devices for connecting to networks, the operating and training expenses will overwhelm our estimating equations. The most likely outcome of this trend will be that the cost of computing will become largely a characteristic of the workforce and the functions they perform rather than just the number of individuals.

What to Do

- Employ statistical analysis of selected variables to estimate expected computer spending.
- Allocate and track computer spending, by business function, to gain an understanding of over- or underfunding.
- Measure the effectiveness of people and not the costs of computing as a measure of IT performance.
- Use the fully allocated per capita costs for information technology services as a proxy for assessing the worth of the services.
- Analyze the relationship between the population of terminals, personal computers, and workstations, and the number of information workers.

38 Residual Value

Tangible outlays require tangible benefits.

THE APPROPRIATE planning horizon for computer systems varies depending on the quality of the initial project investment and the expenses for keeping up with change. The amazing thing about computer project investments is their longevity. Many computer executives can recall installing applications over twenty years ago that, with some technological reincarnation and reasonable maintenance expense, are still in place today. There are elements of all systems investments that inherently become very long-term commitments. There is no sound way one can establish data dictionaries and data models in an enterprise without taking a very long-term view of the undertaking. Strategic planning for IT projects must include scenarios that recognize cash flows that extend beyond the usual three- or five-year long-range plans. Rather than considering information systems as technologies that have value until they becomes outmoded, one should realize that most of the costs of systems obsolescence arise from the operators' difficulties in making good use of a system. The accumulation of data represents the facts about the enterprises' environment and how it copes with it. Everything in between, whether it is equipment or operating software, should be seen as a commodity that loses its worth at a prodigious rate. To be able to detach outdated technologies from the underlying business processes, organizations should adopt tools that keep the long-term knowledge assets and short-term technological assets separated.

In the children's tale of the three little pigs and the big bad wolf, the little pigs' project planning horizon determines the form of their construction projects. Similarly, we have project managers who deliver applications that crash easily and require heroic efforts for restoration of the data and its processing. Project managers with the put-the-twigs-together mentality are a widespread phenomenon. Their costs are low. They deliver on budget. But woe to anyone who takes up occupancy in what they produced.

Their successors take over a legacy of escalating maintenance expenses, customer complaints, and blame for poor management.

There are also project managers who build systems as if they were bomb-proof edifices. Their budgets are large but after installation, the maintenance expenses remain low. Their well-architected systems can withstand a great deal of alteration in occupancy and use.

When disaster strikes, the little pigs with flimsy legacy systems do not necessarily end up in the house erected by their long-range-planning brother. In my updated version of the old tale, the pigs end up in living quarters run by the wolves.

Why do project managers persist in delivering flimsy results? It is not because they are self-destructive or ignorant of the likely consequences. The primary reason for the delivery of shoddy projects is the myopic approach to planning and budgeting of information systems projects.

PLANNING HORIZONS AND RESIDUAL VALUE

The appropriate planning horizon for computer systems varies depending on the quality of the initial project investment and the expenses for keeping up with change. Any investment that has an annual maintenance expense of fifty percent of the initial cost, which is a common occurrence, implies a planning horizon of less than twenty-four months.

The controller may insist on project investments that have a payback of less than twenty-four months. Indirectly, he is saying that what remains of systems projects after two years is not worth anything. In financial terms a two-year payback requirement means that the corporate treasury considers systems development a sufficiently high credit risk that it will charge an interest rate of fifty percent per annum. If a bank were to give similar terms for a business loan it would be taken as illegitimate usury.

Computer project managers respond by delivering on demand. They can assume that the life of what they deliver will be short. The two-year payback will turn out to be a self-fulfilling outcome. Yet the amazing thing about computer project investments is their longevity. Many computer executives can recall installing applications over twenty years ago that, with some technological reincarnation and reasonable maintenance expense, are still in place today. I have clients that are running applications whose core has aged gracefully over thirty years.

There are elements of all systems investments that inherently become very long-term commitments. There is no sound way that one can establish data dictionaries and data models in an enterprise without taking a very long-term view of the undertaking. This will require a very costly and difficult initial effort, as evidenced by the great pain and costs of all firms currently installing integrated applications. However, once a data dictionary and data model process are in place, they are probably going to remain in place for more than twenty years, and perhaps longer.

Strategic planning for IT projects must therefore include scenarios that explicitly recognize cash flows that extend beyond the usual three- or five-year long-range plans. In other words, the residual value of a project must become an element in all project payoff calculations.

I do not find corporations using the idea of residual value in IT planning and budgeting. Yet nobody who does not apply this concept would ever consider buying a house instead of renting unless they intend to relocate soon. Without estimating the resale value of a house, one would always continue to rent.

The reason information project managers feel compelled to construct the flimsiest solution to systemic problems is their failure to consider residual value. In so doing they shortchange their corporations. Whatever management saves in initial investment expense will ultimately show up as higher ongoing overhead expenses and lower profits. Without paying attention to residual value, executive management will get exactly what it locked into in the payoff calculations when approving a project budget. The corporation will get what the little pig got when it made a shelter out of twigs to have more time for play and fun.

FINANCIAL ANALYSIS FOR RESIDUAL VALUE CALCULATION

The key financial cost parameters for project investment decisions are:
- The initial cost (investment), which receives everyone's attention. Sometimes this includes ridiculous details, such as voluminous schedules detailing electric cabling for projects costing hundreds of millions of dollars
- The installation costs beyond the project manager's control, such as training, support, and conflict resolution (which rarely shows up in project budgets)

- The ongoing maintenance costs over the life cycle, including costs of errors, effort needed to retrace undocumented logic, retraining, and enhancements to accommodate organizational change. These elements are usually left out of project planning and budgeting, lest management become discouraged
- The residual value (the value of the investment at the end of the planning period), which nobody calculates because nobody wishes to raise troublesome questions about the lost value of prior investment decisions

CALCULATING RESIDUAL VALUE

The residual value is the discounted cash flow today from the values that still generate net benefits to the corporation beyond the planning period. I have found that for well-conceived projects, approximately half of the discounted cash value comes from a cash flow beyond a six-year planning horizon. Figure 56 below shows how an investment would look without a residual value. This is the usual portrayal of such analysis. The number that is important is the cash benefit to cash expenditure ratio of thirty-one percent. This allows for the discounting of the risks of future gains at a high interest rate of twenty-five percent.[373]

$Millions		1986	1987	1988	1989	1990	1991
Benefits		$0.0	$0.0	$83.4	$72.3	$82.2	$91.4
Costs		$63.3	$31.5	$14.5	$15.0	$15.0	$17.2
Benefit/Cost Ratio	31%						

Figure 56   Calculating a project benefit/cost ratio

Figure 57 offers the identical example but includes a residual value. The payback has now gone up to eighty-one percent. What this demon-

---

373 For an elaboration of this case using different discount rates and methods for making the identical facts generate different payoff numbers, see Strassmann, P.A., *The Business Value of Computers*, The Information Economics Press, 1990, Chapters 9 and 10. The net present value of cash benefits at 25% is $123 M. The net present value of cash costs at 25% is $94 M. The benefit/cost ratio is equal to ($123-$94)/$94 = 31%.

strates is that if the useful life of the application extends beyond the corporate planning cycle, the return on the investment could be almost three times larger.[374]

$Millions		1986	1987	1988	1989	1990	1991	Residual Value
Benefits		$0.0	$0.0	$83.4	$72.3	$82.2	$91.4	$340.5
Costs		$63.3	$31.5	$14.5	$15.0	$15.0	$17.2	$64.1
Benefit/Cost Ratio	81%							

Figure 57   Project benefit/cost ratio with a twelve-year residual value

Any standard spreadsheet can calculate the present value of discounted cash flow.[375] It is in the interest of information managers to come up with a standard approach for determining the risk-adjusted discounted economic value of every project over its entire life cycle.

How to Create a Greater Residual Value

When one examines the benefits of information handling, the most valuable attributes are the capabilities of people to understand and apply the information available from computers. Rather than considering information systems as technologies that have value until they becomes outmoded, one should realize that most of the costs of systems obsolescence arise from the operators' difficulties in making good use of a system.

Learning costs are specially taxing when online systems enlarge the operators' scope of work activities. This holds true particularly when employees must learn how to use computers for rapid-response actions under stressful conditions. Dissimilar protocols, inconsistent graphic interfaces, and application-unique commands are not only costly but confusing and lead to errors. For these reasons the most valuable asset in calculating the life cycle costs of information systems will be employee competence, not technology investments.

374   The net present value of cash benefits with residual value at 25% is $195M. The net present value of cash costs with residual at 25% is $107M. The benefit/cost ratio is equal to ($195-$107)/$107 = 81%.
375   The risk-adjusted cash flow residual method of determining payback is now available as the *BizCase* software package. It is based on the calculations included in *The Business Value of Computers.*

Enhanced residual value of individual projects can arise from an imposition of familiar information manipulation methods across all applications. It is this capability that explains the amazing growth in the acceptance of the Internet Explorer and Netscape browsers. The unprecedented rate of adoption of network browsers is a testimonial to the recognition that instinctive simplicity carries enormous benefits.

The other crucial long-term information assets are data and software. Software increasingly represents the collective intelligence of how an enterprise works as a system of systems. The accumulation of data represents the facts about the enterprises' environment and how it copes with it. Everything in between, whether it is equipment or operating software, should be seen as a commodity that loses its worth at a prodigious rate.

Consequently, the goal of the residual value approach is to preserve the long-term assets. Residual value grows if the underlying intelligence of the enterprise is preserved while the hardware and operating system software is upgraded, modified, or migrated.

IMPORTANCE OF SYSTEMS ENGINEERING TOOLS

To be able to detach outdated technologies from the underlying business processes, organizations should adopt tools that keep long-term knowledge assets and short-term technological assets separated. This calls for the creation of a snap-in, snap-out, modular type of information infrastructure. This also calls for standardization of global and enterprise-level methods while leaving much autonomy in adapting to immediate user needs in local applications. To achieve this the firm must provide an integrated computer-aided system engineering environment. One way of looking at the value of systems tooling is to define them in terms of how much of the residual value they can deliver.

Open systems will not work without good tools. You must have a way of attaching large quantities of reusable code onto new hardware without incurring much loss during migration from old to new. The underlying principle is to have a development environment sufficiently long-lasting that some of the most important possessions, such as data structures, remain useful for twenty-five to thirty years.[376] Ideally, the systems engi-

---

376 Medical records should be kept throughout life, now averaging seventy years. With the advent of genetic medicine, multi-generation records may extend the required longevity of clinical tests even further.

neering tools should be independent of particular procedural code or hardware. They must preserve the logic of functional processes that define the operational rules and work flow patterns. They should employ machine-independent computer languages.

Nothing here is just wishful thinking. The overwhelming and rapid welcome extended to the Java language is good evidence that the time has come for organizations to seek solutions that have a more lasting residual value. The Java slogan "Write once, run anywhere" is perfectly appealing, except I would append to it the "... run anytime" phrase to emphasis longevity as well. It remains to be seen if the vendors will show a sufficient discipline to keep Java software implementation in compliance with standards. This is why the decision to brand and certify truly interoperable Java applications as "100% Pure Java" is a brilliant move by a consortium led by Sun Microsystems.[377] If such standardization works out it will bring us closer to a realization of open systems than the many abortive efforts to achieve the same objective through UNIX.

I cannot overemphasize the pivotal importance of systems engineering tools as the enablers for linking long-term software investments to transitory assets such as hardware and operating systems. Open systems toolsets are the means for creating greater economic value through the enhancement of the residual value of the technological investment.

Are standard software engineering tools sufficient to preserve the long-term residual values? In the same way that operating systems standards, interoperability architectures, and communications protocols are necessary but not sufficient, systems engineering tools are necessary but do not guarantee the retention of knowledge capital. We have to raise our sights to safeguard the safekeeping of organizational knowledge because it will inevitably suffer from the corrosive influence of opportunistic proposals. It is important that top management quizzes proponents of new systems projects about the longevity of their creations. During such an

---

377   Bank, D., "Sun Microsystems Brews Up a Logo," *The Wall Street Journal,* December 11, 1996. A surprisingly large number of companies signed up for testing by Sun's JavaSoft subsidiary of compliance with some 5,000 compatibility criteria. The only comparable instance of such a unity of purpose took place forty years ago with government and industry reaching agreement on COBOL standards. Without strong government support it is unlikely that the new coalition may hold together as each vendor will seek out a variant of Java to protect its proprietary interests. If that happens, Microsoft with the strongest market share position, will succeed in hijacking the Java language to serve its purposes.

inquiry management may find that what offers an immediate shelter may not be good enough to withstand the next major storm.

What to Do

- Set the planning horizon for computer systems depending on the quality of the initial project investment and the expenses for keeping up with change.
- Make long-term commitments when establishing data dictionaries and data models.
- Include the residual value of a project in all project payoff calculations.
- Adopt tools that keep the long-term knowledge assets and short-term technological assets separated.
- Follow the principle of "Write once, run anywhere, any time" as the fundamental strategic direction for managing IT assets.

39 Valuation of Technology Assets

Expenses that do not evaporate may become assets.

To MAKE valid judgments about IT yearly spending levels, one must check out what is happening to IT assets. The essence of good asset management is the capacity to reapply and reuse a valuable property for new needs. To do this one needs to know what property is reusable, which in turn defines what it is worth. An examination of the recent history of microprocessors shows that often it is not the technological obsolescence of the hardware, but its use, that dictates its depreciation rate. The accounting approach of calculating the worth of assets from a set amortization schedule of acquisition costs will give misleading estimates. An organization that can satisfy most its computing needs by means of low-cost, network-dependent computers will end up with short-lived, throwaway equipment assets of minimal value to the firm. Today's software can easily rate among the most poorly constructed, unreliable, and certainly least maintainable technological artifacts invented by man. If one projects the future costs of computers and modular software, these projections favor investments in training in preference to spending for technological innovations. The advantage of distance learning is not only in cost savings, but also because it forms a bond that allows long range upkeep and refreshing of knowledge. An examination of the total asset buildup, as a residual from the annual IT expenses, can offer business executives an improved understanding of how well they manage information resources.

To make the case for the preservation of technology assets, whether they are equipment, people, software, databases, or employee training, one must be able to explain how much they cost.[378] Anybody can cut operating costs instantaneously. Anybody can keep IT expenditures in line with

---

378 The need for a systematic approach to the valuation of information assets is in The Hawley Committee Report, *Information as an Asset – The Board Agenda*, KPMG IMPACT Programme, London, 1995. The report calls for action but does not suggest how to act.

any arbitrary budget that someone has allocated. There are many options for accomplishing this in the short run, mostly at the expense of the long-term viability of information services. To make valid judgments about IT yearly spending levels, one must check out what is happening to IT assets.

The essence of good asset management is the capacity to reapply and reuse a valuable property in the service of new needs. To do this one needs to know what property is reusable, which in turn helps to define what it is worth.

VALUATION METHOD

Except for purchased computer equipment, accounting records do not keep track of the asset value of systems development, software acquisition, or investments in employee training. The asset value of computer hardware, the amount that shows up on the balance sheet, is also declining as compared with all the other expenses for information technologies. If hardware leasing or outsourcing takes place, the financial records will not reveal what a firm owns as a result of its steady stream of automation investments. For all practical purposes the existing approach to valuing IT assets is useless except as a way of complying with regulatory and taxation purposes. To remedy this deficiency one must include in reviews of IT plans and strategies an assessment of a firm's IT assets as follows: [379]

Change in Information Technology Assets =
+ Equipment Acquisition - Equipment Depreciation
+ Development Acquisition - Development Depreciation
+ Software Acquisition - Software Depreciation
+ Training Acquisition - Training Depreciation

Making these calculations requires a thorough analysis of the elements that add and detract from a firm's IT assets. The tendency of cost accountants would be to apply a standard depreciation schedule to all cash outlays, as they do to machines, trucks, or furniture. Such treatment of IT expenses does not work.

The realistic depreciation of information assets cannot depend on tables that specify a predetermined life expectancy. Depending on where

---

[379] This analytical service is now available from Strassmann, Inc. as the *Information Technology Assets* valuation service.

and how the software functions, it may lose its value in a year, in ten years, or even longer. Learning how to use a computer-aided drafting application may be useful for a very short time or for an entire career. A poor systems design will have the longevity of only a few weeks before a replacement must take its place. A good systems architecture will retain its use-value for decades, because its utility remains workable regardless of changes in people or organization.

An examination of the recent history of microprocessors shows that often it is not the technological obsolescence of the hardware, but its use, that dictates its depreciation rate. For instance, the three year technology of the 80286 microprocessor (1982-1985) found its replacement in the four year technology of the 386 microprocessor (1985-1989), followed by the four year 486 (1989-1993) and now the two year Pentium (1993-1995).[380] Yet, for a large number of applications that perform only limited functions, such as in hospitals and warehouses, a 1985 vintage microprocessor could remain fully serviceable. Its useful life would continue even after eleven years and two generations of technology. The steady stream of hardware upgrades are more a reflection of the voracious appetite of new operating systems and applications for computer cycles and memory than a change in what people do.

Hardware can become obsolete with new applications or vice versa. Applications may depreciate rapidly if the software vendor discontinues support. Any perturbation in workplace relationships will degrade the employees' capacity to perform their jobs. The depreciation of training will also set in when applications change, equipment receives major upgrades, or workflow restructuring takes place. The value of training and accumulated experience will then dissipate.

Therefore, judgment about the depreciation of IT assets must originate in a top-down view of how the organization functions in its entirety. The accounting approach of calculating the worth of assets from a set amortization schedule of acquisition costs will give misleading estimates. In the examples that follow, I will be using budget ratios to illustrate how one should approach the valuation of IT assets.[381]

---

380 The estimated market value of a 200 MHz Pentium personal computer declines to less than twenty percent of its original purchase price after eighteen months. See Pucciarelli, J., "Desktop and Distributed Equipment Procurement," *Gartner Group Symposium*/ITxpo '96, Lake Buena Vista, Florida, October 7, 1996.

381 The ratios are actual results for a large and very successful firm.

VALUATION OF EQUIPMENT ASSETS

My preferred approach of calculating the value of hardware assets is to take historic data, add the acquisition costs, and subtract the depreciation in use value for major equipment categories as follows: [382]

	1985	1986	1987	1988	1989	1990	1991	1992	1993	1994
Total IT Budget- $M	116	142	174	213	260	284	303	309	324	356
Hardware Costs (% of IT):										
Data Center Acquisitions	26.0%	25.5%	25.0%	24.5%	24.0%	23.5%	18.8%	17.5%	16.5%	16.5%
Data Center Depreciation	6.0%	6.4%	6.7%	7.1%	7.3%	7.6%	3.6%	3.6%	3.6%	3.6%
Desktop Acquisition	3.0%	3.3%	3.6%	4.0%	4.4%	4.8%	5.3%	5.8%	6.4%	7.1%
Desktop Depreciation	2.0%	2.0%	3.0%	3.3%	3.6%	4.0%	4.4%	4.8%	5.3%	5.8%
Departmt. Server Acquisition							3.0%	3.9%	5.1%	6.6%
Departmt. Server Depreciation							0.0%	3.0%	3.9%	5.1%
IT Asset Impact - $M										
Hardware Acquisition - $M	34	41	50	61	74	81	82	84	91	107
Hardware Depreciation - $M	(9)	(12)	(17)	(22)	(29)	(33)	(24)	(35)	(42)	(52)
Cum. Net Asset Change - $M										429

Figure 58   Asset changes for computer equipment

In this computation the cumulative investment in computing assets, including the communications devices, exceeds the total 1994 annual budget for information technologies. After ten years of accumulated spending on equipment, the accumulated value of the assets remains sixty percent of cumulative spending. This suggests conservative equipment asset management.

It is also noteworthy that the spurt in equipment acquisition starting in 1992 involved a substantial increase in replacement of old computing capacity by new. This happened as longer-lived assets (i.e., mainframes) were replaced by shorter-lived assets (i.e., desktops and servers). The depreciation of communication gear was not dramatic. It remained serviceable, because it was the phone companies who continued to incur the cost

---

382   One calculates the depreciation in use value by watching the physical replacement activity. If an Intel 286 personal computer is replaced by an Intel 386 model in three years, it does not matter that the depreciation schedule is five years for tax purposes, the real cost must be depreciated in three.

for innovation at central sites. I find that the major asset value is still in the data centers, not at the desktops where the most visible growth took place.

If the depreciation rate catches up with the acquisition rate for new equipment, the asset values will be reduced as a ratio of the total IT budget. As the purchase costs of equipment decline and the rates of obsolescence increase, the inordinate attention that management has always devoted to equipment acquisition will cease to matter. An organization that can satisfy most of its computing needs by means of low-cost, network-dependent computers will end up with short-lived, throwaway equipment assets of minimal value to the firm. Like file cabinets, electrical motors, fuel pumps, toner cartridges, and batteries, they will become expendable replacement supplies instead of mainstays of capital investment.

VALUATION OF DEVELOPMENT ASSETS

With the benefit of good analytic techniques I believe that even technologically inexperienced executives can comprehend the differences between the acquisition and depreciation costs for equipment. Unfortunately, there is little that business executives can draw on from everyday experiences to understand why and how software degrades with time. Software fails because its engineering and fabrication methods are poor.

Nobody would tolerate a car that requires daily checkups from mechanics. Nobody would pay bills to a phone company that gives a dial tone only randomly and where the phone service crashes every other day. Nobody would buy a house where the annual taxes, upkeep, and commuting expenses are seven times the purchase price. Nobody would acquire a microwave oven that makes it necessary to rewire the entire house every time a homemaker plugs in a new toaster. Nobody would purchase a waffle maker that requires registration with the electric utility before one can bake waffles. Nobody would accept the idea of having to buy a shop full of tools to use a screwdriver. Nobody in their right mind would purchase a car which requires a new instrument panel every other year, with all the buttons relocated and relabeled. Absolutely nobody would accept the idea of having to spend a year's rent to replace all the doors in a building because somebody attached the hinges with only two screws instead of the required four. No sane cook would prepare duplicate meals because one of the pots is likely to self-destruct. Nobody would install a refrigerator for which spare parts are available only for the latest model. Nobody would send their child to a private school where teachers charge ninety dollars for answering a question after the first four inquiries.

Yet it is analogous situations such as these that executives come across when they wrestle with the explanations they receive from their systems developers. It is no wonder that they become exasperated and are prepared to pass on these aberrations to contractors who can make the software mess appear to be orderly. The mess often does not disappear, but only hides behind a screen of costly upkeep, upgrades, maintenance fixes, and reengineering.

Most people have no choice but to suffer along with the idiosyncrasies of software bugs, glitches, bombs, and crashes. Today's software can easily rate among the most poorly constructed, unreliable, and certainly least maintainable of technological artifacts ever invented by man, with the possible exception perhaps of Icarus' wings.[383]

Development spending for new applications always looks attractive because there is always a champion who demands a new computer solution for coping with operating problems. What is not visible is the steady erosion of the serviceability of applications as an unceasing stream of upgrades and maintenance replaces what came into existence at great expense.

Software does not physically wear out. Potentially, it ought to improve with use as customers discover and programmers correct errors. Yet software tends to degenerate much faster than any computer equipment, or any other consumer appliance, because of its inherently defective design. From a consumer's standpoint, the current state of software is scandalous and intolerable. For a corporate applications portfolio. one can illustrate the attrition of software values as follows:

---

383 According to the Greek legend, Icarus made himself wings by pasting feathers together with wax. As he flew toward the sun the wax melted, whereupon Icarus plunged into the sea and drowned.

	1985	1986	1987	1988	1989	1990	1991	1992	1993	1994
Total IT Budget - $M	116	142	174	213	260	284	303	309	324	356
Development Costs (% of IT):										
For New Systems	10.0%	10.5%	11.4%	12.0%	12.6%	13.2%	13.9%	12.6%	12.3%	12.1%
For Upgrades	3.4%	3.6%	3.7%	3.9%	3.6%	3.7%	3.9%	3.9%	3.9%	3.8%
For Maintenance	6.6%	6.9%	6.9%	7.2%	4.8%	5.1%	5.3%	6.4%	6.5%	6.5%
IT Asset Impact										
Development Acquisition - $M	12	15	20	26	33	38	42	39	40	43
Development Depreciation - $M	(12)	(15)	(18)	(24)	(22)	(25)	(28)	(32)	(34)	(37)
Cum. Net Asset Change - $M										61

Figure 59   Asset changes for applications development

It should not come as a surprise that after ten years of spending we find only twenty percent of the cost of new systems development remains as an asset. That loss rate is likely to persist unless systems management finds ways to change the cost ratios for upgrade and maintenance expenses. The situation is more favorable than what one generally finds. If the costs of maintenance steadily exceed the costs of new systems development, that signifies that the firm will not end up owning any worthwhile application assets.

VALUATION OF PURCHASED SOFTWARE ASSETS

One would expect that organizations buying ready-made software packages would have a better record in preserving their software assets than firms who develop their own. A supplier of software packages should be able to have superior maintenance economics, as errors are discovered faster and the costs of fixes benefit from amortization over the entire user population.

Although the argument that purchased software should be superior as compared to custom-made solutions, the evidence that this is so is still too scanty to make it conclusive. In my illustration the value of the purchased assets in place after ten years is forty-six percent, which is certainly superior to custom-made solutions.[384] However, it is hard to judge the reliability of this data. Many of the costs of adapting purchased software to fit company conditions show up as application development or software

384 Cumulative net assets/total software acquisition costs is equal to 41%.

maintenance. Selling ready-made software as adaptable components instead of as a monolithic solution will certainly make the preservation of software asset valuations easier.[385] The best technique to use in judging the merits of pre-packaged software is to consider all software costs combined, whether developed or purchased.

	1985	1986	1987	1988	1989	1990	1991	1992	1993	1994
Total IT Budget - $M	116	142	174	213	260	284	303	309	324	356
Purchased Software (% of IT):										
For New Software	3.3%	3.7%	4.3%	4.9%	5.7%	6.3%	7.3%	8.6%	9.8%	12.0%
For Upgrades	1.1%	1.2%	1.4%	1.6%	1.8%	2.0%	2.3%	2.8%	3.2%	3.9%
For Maintenance	0.7%	0.8%	0.9%	1.1%	1.2%	1.4%	1.6%	1.8%	2.1%	2.6%
IT Asset Impact - $M										
Software Acquisition - $M	4	5	7	11	15	18	22	26	32	43
Software Depreciation - $M	(2)	(3)	(4)	(6)	(8)	(10)	(12)	(14)	(17)	(23)
Cum. Net Asset Change- $M										84

Figure 60   Asset changes for purchased software

COMBINED DEVELOPMENT AND SOFTWARE SPENDING

If one adds up the software spending over a ten year period, it is sure to stun business executives. More often than not this number is likely to represent a hefty share of what shows up as shareholder equity on the balance sheet. What is devastating in most cases is the small share of the total that remains as a reusable corporate asset, as shown in the following:

385   It is an idea whose time has come. Bank of America has just formed a subsidiary to market reusable object templates to financial firms, as reported in Hoffman, T., "BankAmerica Branches Out," *Computerworld*, September 9, 1996, p. 9. Not to be outdone, in 1996 Netscape opened a web site for downloading free software modules that include finance, human resources, and marketing software.

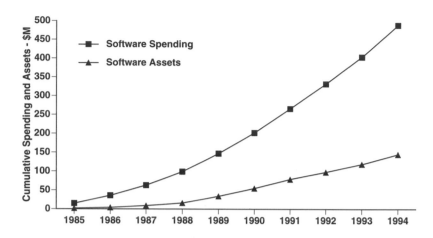

Figure 61   Cumulative software spending and cumulative software assets

As much as the gap between cumulative spending and cumulative assets may be disturbing from an executive standpoint, what really matters is the rate at which the spread between the two is either widening or narrowing. When the forces that drive software asset accumulation become understood, it will be possible to discuss their effects on systems engineering, software acquisition, and systems standardization policies. Perhaps the best way to focus such deliberations is to show changes in the ratios of software assets to software spending:

	1985	1986	1987	1988	1989	1990	1991	1992	1993	1994
Cumulative Software Spending - $M	15	36	63	99	147	202	266	332	404	489
Cumulative Software Assets - $M	2	4	9	16	34	55	79	98	119	145
Ratio of Assets to Spending	11%	12%	15%	16%	23%	27%	30%	30%	30%	30%

Figure 62   Ratio of software assets to software spending

In the above figure we see a gratifying growth in software assets in the first five years, followed by an almost stagnant rate of software asset accumulation. This is traceable to increased software obsolescence as decentralized information processing took off after 1991. However, making a judgment about the relative merits of network computing is not answerable solely by an examination of costs of equipment and software. Any juggling of technology has far-reaching effects on the time it takes to train people for competence in coping with change in operating methods.

VALUATION OF TRAINING ASSETS

Of all the uncertainties that involve the management of information technologies, the issue of training costs and performance readiness are perhaps the most troublesome and therefore that the most likely to escape executive attention.

The considerable training costs required to keep staff qualified in the uses of computers are never readily apparent. Excessive software and operating expenses will camouflage incompetence arising from the lack of proper education. The steady dose of systems training needed by the users remains hidden as expenses for assistance, idle time, errors, and poor customer service.[386] Nevertheless, it is possible to estimate the value of the capabilities residing within the workforce.

A model that includes only a few critical variables such as employee turnover, new applications introduction rate, and speed of modernization will offer strong indications of how a firm consumes its knowledge assets. Understanding employee attrition rates is particularly important in highly unstable sectors such as banking. The Bank Administration Institute reports annual turnover rates of fifty percent for consumer credit officers, thirty-five to forty percent for tellers, thirty-three percent for commercial loan officers, and ten to fifteen percent for branch managers.[387] However, this pales in comparison with Allied Signal, the record-holder for IS staff turnover. Allied reported an eighty percent attrition rate in one year due to a move to client/server. Such losses are comparable to what happened to the population when the Huns sacked Rome in AD 407.[388]

---

386 These surface only when the staff is producing revenue. This may explain why Andersen Consulting spends $300 million every year in training its 62,000 person staff. At $4,840 per person per year, this amount is at least three times higher than typical corporate systems department allocate for training. For further discussion see Moad, J., "Calculating the Real Benefit of Training," *Datamation*, April 15, 1995.

387 Keltner, B., and Finegold, D., "Human Resource Innovations for Service Firms," *Sloan Management Review*, Fall 1996.

388 Fryer, B., "Allied Signal Technical Services," *Computerworld Client/Server Journal*, August, 1996.

Constructing a training cost and a residual asset model is an elaborate matter that deserves separate treatment. An executive summary of that process would reveal the following:

	1985	1986	1987	1988	1989	1990	1991	1992	1993	1994
For Training ($ per capita):										
For Systems Staff	1,361	1,456	1,558	1,667	1,784	1,909	2,043	2,186	2,339	2,502
Less: Retraining	299	320	343	367	393	420	449	481	514	551
For Employees	379	406	434	464	497	532	569	609	651	697
Less: Retraining	152	162	174	186	199	213	228	244	261	279
ITAsset Impact										
Training Acquisition - $M	27	29	32	34	38	41	43	47	49	54
Training Depreciation - $M	(11)	(12)	(12)	(13)	(15)	(16)	(17)	(18)	(19)	(21)
Cum. Net Asset Change - $M										241

Figure 63   Spending for training and estimate of residual value

In this example, the annual training costs for the systems staffs are four percent of their pay.[389] The annual training costs for employees who operate fairly simple point-of-use terminals would be equivalent to about three days.

The asset buildup embodied in the skill of the workforce is considerable. The illustrative example shows a steady accumulation of training capital. Sixty-one percent of cumulative spending remains a corporate asset. If one projects the future costs of computers and modular software, these projections favor investments in training in preference to spending for technological innovations. One can therefore conclude that the value of training and employee retention are perhaps the best investments a firm can make.

389   This assumes full technological depreciation of a systems person every twelve years, which is probably too large. It assumes that half of the knowledge replacement cost would be incurred on the person's own time, since the individual would end up possessing all the newly gained knowledge. For a commercial software firm or a consultancy, this number would have to be much larger.

346

Distance Learning

Training is expensive and its benefits are hard to quantify. Sending an employee to attend a three-day training course will cost as much as $1,800 for tuition, plus travel expense and time away from work. A conservative estimate of the cost of such experience would be about $200 per hour of learning. For a consulting company that number would be close to $400 per hour because of loss of billable time.

The problem with typical classroom training is the absence of a verifiable means for establishing the gains made in a student's capabilities. The model for a typical classroom experience is that of factory mass production. It is synchronous, which means that all learning must take place at the same rate, without much allowance for individual capability. It is a process for taking uncontrolled raw materials (e.g., students) through a batch process for delivering higher quality products (i.e., competent employees). The resulting outcome only rarely passes through a verifiable performance checkout. Since newly acquired knowledge suffers from high forgetfulness rates, the absence of follow-on maintenance and support shows up as unreliable capabilities.[390] It is an obsolete, costly, and uncontrolled method for creating knowledge capital.

The advantage of distance learning is not only in cost savings, but also because it forms a bond that allows long range upkeep and refreshing of knowledge. Because of economies of telepresence the equivalent of a three-day course, or eighteen hours of tutoring, will cost only about $600. Only a small time element is attributable to the student's payroll cost since the asynchronous features of distance learning allow students to take lessons while waiting for other work, while in transit or after hours. Consequently, the per hour cost is in the $30 to $60 dollar range. Most importantly, one can capture and record the entire educational experience in a form that lends itself to testing and verification.

As compared with current classroom teaching, on-line, interactive, and asynchronous distance learning offers enormous gains. Instead of offering standard batch-processing experiences, distance learning provides training as just-in-time, point-of-use experience. I have no doubt that its

---

390 Post-testing of students after thirteen weeks following a typical educational slide presentation showed less than a seven percent recollection rate, unless the knowledge was put to use immediately. Such tests were conducted at the Xerox Leesburg Training Center in the early 1980s.

intrinsic effectiveness and economic attractiveness will greatly stimulate an expansion of distance learning expenditures while simultaneously increasing the productivity of information workers.

TOTAL ASSET VALUATION

An examination of the total asset buildup, as a residual from annual IT expenses, can offer business executives an improved understanding of how well they manage information resources. There will be a large share of the total annual IT spending such as communications charges, supplies, data center operations, and customer assistance that will always remain an operating expense. One should expense such costs as incurred. However, there are annual IT costs that can accumulate potential value over several years, such as equipment, software, and training. The question then is how much of the annual expense is convertible into an asset that reduces the need for having to incur the identical cost relatively soon.

In my illustrative example shown in this chapter, the ratio of information assets to IT budget has been declining from thirty-seven percent in 1985 to thirty-two percent in 1994. As the total IT budget keeps growing faster than the IT assets, the prospect of a steady deterioration in asset values looms in the future:

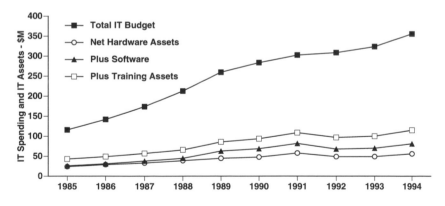

Figure 64   Comparison of total IT spending with accumulation of IT assets

It is the steady depreciation of software assets that explains why the rate of asset accumulation is not any better. The prospects of further decline in equipment costs means that software and training assets will become the foundation for effective information resource management in the years to come. The infatuation of the present generation of executives with computing equipment will ultimately find fulfillment only in antique shows. Computers will meld into appliances, servers, and communications switches. With control over training remaining in the hands of operating executives, the accomplishments of CIOS will have to rest on their capacity to nurture, preserve, and protect the accumulation of information capital.

IT INVESTMENT CYCLES

Valuation of information technologies shows that asset accumulation does not follow a consistent pattern. Rising IT budgets sometimes conceal cyclical swings in asset creation and asset destruction. This fluctuation can be illustrated as follows:

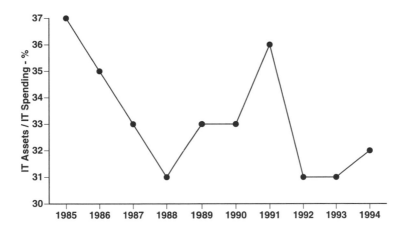

Figure 65   Changes in IT asset accumulation

Top management must become aware that one can not only create information assets but also destroy them. A review of technology modernization proposals should not only examine cash benefits and costs, but also how they will affect software and training assets. Modernization is desirable as long as new investments also account for the annihilation of what is already in place. Most importantly, every technology modernization proposal should also include a valid assessment of its life expectancy. How much of any new spending will remain and how much of it becomes scrap in short order are questions that need good answers. As the technology cycles become shorter it will be the steady accumulation of the intangible components of spending that will become the mainstays of sustainable competitive superiority.

What to Do

- Supplement IT spending plans with a schedule that shows the valuation of IT assets.
- Add the acquisition costs and subtract the depreciation in use value to arrive at the worth off IT assets.
- Value the merits of prepackaged software by considering all software costs jointly, including maintenance and upgrades.
- Develop model of training investments that includes employee turnover, new applications introduction rate, and the speed of technological modernization.
- Shift as much training as possible to just-in-time, point-of-use experiences.

40 The Mythical PC Cost

Inexpensive equipment does not yield low-cost computing.

THE SUDDEN interest in the real costs of personal computing originates from the prospects of Network Computers displacing
Personal Computers. Claims about delivering Zero Costs of
Administration further liven up these speculations. The problem is
that mythical savings based on mythical costs are an invitation for
a financial disaster. Only a verifiable model can explain what the
realistic opportunities are for reducing the exorbitant costs of PC
ownership. There are two major influences in determining the costs
of PC ownership: workload and management practices. In turn,
these are affected by the characteristics of customers, technology,
and applications.

The average costs of ownership of a personal computer have finally made
the headlines. In 1996 *Fortune* magazine quoted the annual cost of PC ownership as more than $9,000, *The Economist* at $6,400, *The New York Times*
at $13,000, *Business Week* at $8,000 and *Datamation* at $10,543. The most
frequent source of these numbers is the Gartner Group, who obliges with
estimates ranging from $7,138 to $13,000 depending on who asks the question and when.

I find these quotes remarkable. For the last fifteen years the PC was
touted as a low cost alternative to much of mainframe computing. Yet my
annual costs for supporting computer terminals from central computing
were always below $3,000 per year in the period from 1975 through 1995.

Talking about Large Sums

All of this sudden interest in the real costs of personal computing stems
from the prospects of a $500 Network Computer (NC) displacing a $2,500
Personal Computer (PC). Compounding this hyper-promotion are claims
that automation of PC management could lead to elimination of most PC

administration costs through Microsoft's Zero Administration Initiative.[391]

If you happen to be the CEO, CFO, or CIO of a large organization, such a proliferation of figures could cause confusion. A typical *Fortune* 1000 corporation, with an annual IT budget of $200 million, is likely to have about 10,000 personal computers. If your CFO takes the highest Gartner numbers and the lowball claims of $2,500 for the cost of ownership of an NC, that could lead to a hypothetical cost reduction of $105 million.[392] If you prefer *The Economist*, you could argue that there is only $34 million worth of savings available. However, to deliver Intranet-run NCs you will need $60 million worth of new development money to take you out of the latest client/server cycle that increased chaos under the slogan of local empowerment.

No wonder translating claims into bottom line cash becomes an arguable proposition. Mythical savings based on mythical costs are a sure-fire invitation for another CIO to come under the guillotine.

LEARNING ABOUT PC COSTS

My interests in the real costs of personal computing go back to 1991. I was searching for ways to find $35 billion in cost reductions over a seven year budget cycle in the Pentagon. With an estimated PC population of about 1.5 million, reducing the costs of ownership could make a material contribution to the "peace dividend." I commissioned a study of thirty-two PC local area networks. I wanted to pin down the labor cost of tending to these nets.

One net enjoyed the services of one highly paid support technician for six UNIX workstations masquerading as mainframes. After adding all of the related costs, that amounted to well over $14,000 per workstation per year. There was one net performing highly sophisticated functions where the costs were over $60,000 per seat. Another net managed to get by with only one part-time contractor. It consisted of sixty-eight Macintoshes run-

---

391 The Zero Administration Initiative, which imitates the phraseology of Washington-speak, makes these unrealizable claims. See Jacobs, A., and DiDio, L., "Microsoft Plans tools to Cut Cost of PC Ownership," *Computerworld*, November 11, 1996.

392 The Chevron Corporation expects to save $50 million in cost of ownership, or a ten percent reduction in its total IT budget by setting up a Common Operating Environment (COE) for managing an estimated thirty to forty thousand desktop computers. See Johnston, S.J., "Chevron Takes Control," *InformationWeek*, November 4, 1996.

ning three child-proof applications. That would cost barely $3,500 per seat. Clearly, there was no such thing as an average cost for personal computing. The Department of Defense never could demonstrate to Congress that it could save 1.5 million times $10,500 per year, or a neat $15.8 billion dollars.

THE FACTS

It just happens that I work closely with a network management firm that offers full PC support services for a fixed annual fee. The firm has every incentive to increase customer satisfaction while spending as little money as possible. Their price is below $3,000 per seat per year. How do they do this? They have a model that offers a structure for understanding of what creates the costs of PC ownership:

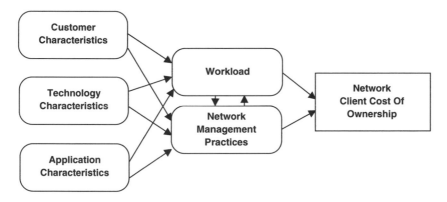

Figure 66   Cost of ownership model for a personal computer

This model suggests that there are two major influences that determine the cost of PC ownership: workload volumes and management practices. In turn, it is the characteristics of customers, technology, and applications that are the cost drivers of the volumes and the practices.

COMMON OPERATING ENVIRONMENT

To reduce the costs of ownership requires the creation of a Common Operating Environment (COE) to reduce the proliferation of options, standardize management practices, stabilize technology and simplify the support of applications. Some of the attributes of a COE are:

- Central distribution of applications, operating systems, and network administration software
- Central purchasing and administration of equipment and software licenses
- Central monitoring and problem alerts, including real-time diagnostics
- Network performance monitoring and capacity optimization
- Storage management, archiving, backup, and defragmenation [393]
- Configuration standards for equipment and software
- Real-time server resource and storage capacity monitoring
- Real-time LAN topology configuration monitoring
- Problem determination, with on line-diagnostic tools and preset warning trigger levels
- Operator error detection and recording
- Service dispatch for on-site support integrated with network administration, diagnostics, and spare parts management
- Hot-spares replacement in case of failure
- Central inventory management of all equipment, including peripherals
- Display of quality control limits vs. actual performance
- Pre-installation testing of applications, software upgrades, and network management capabilities
- Virus intrusion and unauthorized access controls
- Security access and password control methods and practices.

Each of these contributes to cost reduction. However, each requires sophisticated tools and the employment of highly motivated people, and that costs money. The highly promoted Microsoft campaign of offering a Zero Administration Cost Initiative as a way of easing the burden of PC

---

393 Simpson, D., "Cut Your Storage Management Costs," *Datamation*, November 1996. For every dollar per megabyte of disk storage purchase costs, the estimated costs for disk storage management is three to eight dollars per megabyte per year.

costs surely cannot promise superb administrative practices that cost nothing. The key elements of this solution offer some, but not all features of a Common Operating Environment:

- Automatic system updates
- Central application installation and control
- Central configuration management
- Capacity to initiate system, application, and customer lock-outs.

What we have here is a reincarnation of mainframe disciplines to deal with the problem aspects of distributed computing. That is desirable but certainly will not happen at zero expense. The issue is not one of technology choice but of economical gain. The question is: Who will collect what share of the savings from reductions in wasteful practices? Those who contributed to the current excess costs of PC ownership are the most likely to benefit from solutions that claim new savings. After all, those who spread the trash may be the best garbage collectors because they know where they dropped it.

Causal Characteristics

The occupational profiles of employees will drive computing demand. Professionals devour computing capacity whereas factory labor hardly uses any. Mobile workers require less computing than sedentary number crunchers. The uses of computing capacity will also vary. It is extremely high with engineers and accounting types, much less with technicians and sales people. Computer literacy also matters because novices generate greater demand for support than experts. Employee turnover places enormous burdens on support staffs for hand-holding, training, error correction, and equipment relocation. Any instability must surely increase the costs of all support.

Consistent technology architecture and adherence to standards will reduce costs. The use of identical versions of applications and operating systems across an entire enterprise greatly simplifies diagnostics and network maintenance. Liberal Internet access is a source of network congestion and places a burden on the capacity of the entire communication infrastructure. Without central configuration control over equipment and software, one can easily double the size of the staff at a help desk. Most importantly, there are enormous economies of scale in central network administration costs. The statistics of queuing theory will always favor large networks over small ones, if properly designed.

The failure of application software is perhaps the most severe cause of all user dissatisfaction. Some of it comes from poor design, insufficient testing of maintenance, and excessive permissiveness for local operators to futz around with features and options. Removable disk drives that allow insertion of private software increase cost and support workload for everyone. Strict enforcement of security procedures and controls may cost as much as a thousand dollars per PC per year.

COST MANAGEMENT

Though customer, technology, and application characteristics can easily account for thousands of dollars of additional expense for a PC, poor management explains most of the difference between low and high costs. I have no doubt that you do not need technological means to make up for the difference in hardware costs between a PC and an NC. All it takes is for the operators to become reasonably competent in what they are doing.

Increasingly sophisticated network management systems mean very little if nobody takes the time and sympathetic care to assist the few chronic incompetents. Tutoring and assistance must reach beyond technological fixes to reduce the costs of computing. Customer cost accountability and activity-based costing for services is essential to offer the right inducements for cost reduction and continuous quality improvement.

PC cost management is not doable by going after average costs. One must first understand the penalty of each of the causes of counterproductive choice or neglectful practice within a specific environment. That calls for value engineering, removing one source of expense after another. The techniques for accomplishing that resemble total quality management more than computer science. The fixes are managerial, not technological.

IMPLICATIONS FOR CIOs

Beware of averages. Average travel time does not tell much about traffic jams. Beware of promised lowering of acquisition costs. Expenses for the wedding do not predict the costs of a marriage. The amounts of the medical bills have little to do with life expectancy.

My cost of ownership model of personal computing now lists thirty possible PC expense drivers. Each of these drivers can increase the costs of ownership if managed poorly. Eliminating causes of counterproductive behavior will reduce PC costs if attention concentrates on their root causes. There is no such thing as an average cost benchmark for the cost of PC or NC ownership. The cost of PC or NC networks will differ for every firm, since personal computing reflects the unique characteristics of how each firm's management style.

CIGARETTES, STRONG COFFEE, AND MICROSOFT WINDOWS

There is an increasing chorus placing the blame for excessive costs of microcomputer ownership on those software developers who keep favoring Microsoft's expensive to support applications.[394] Accordingly, Microsoft likes standards only insofar as they promote the sale of Windows and thereby increase the dependency on Microsoft products and services. As result Microsoft's practices determine the residual value and support costs of any software.

Computing platform-independent systems and applications, unattached to operating systems, should reduce the costs of computer ownership. The platform-independent Java ideas embody these capabilities. Yet, Microsoft announced that they will provide developers with tools that create Java executable code that runs faster, but only on their proprietary Windows systems. Microsoft also announced a list of capabilities that will, *de facto*, make open systems Java a Microsoft captive.

The exhortations that developers should not conform to Microsoft's expropriation of Java goals miss the point. Developers will deliver whatever the marketplace will buy and not what minimizes the customers' life cycle PC ownership costs.

One must examine why Microsoft with its consistently lagging technologies has managed to win the battle for the minds and pocketbooks of PC customers. Regretting the latest move by Microsoft to co-opt Java for safeguarding its market dominance is not helpful. One must understand the customers' consistent preferences for Microsoft-specific solutions. It is important to comprehend why it is likely that they will do that again in the case of a Microsoft-mutant of Java.

394 Gilllin, P., "Standards Sham," *Computerworld*, December 2, 1996.

There is sufficient medical, physiological, and psychological evidence that a dependency on cigarettes and strong coffee is harmful. It lowers life expectancy. For instance, the life insurance premiums for smokers are significantly higher than for those who abstain. Nevertheless, people smoke and keep gulping down large dosages of caffeine. The reasons they do that are not scientific.

In the short run it makes them feel good in an easy way. Microsoft has earned its present position of dominance because they make it comfortable for people to feel good in an easy way. They have catered to the needs of the developers and microcomputer manufacturers better than their competitors. They have made hundred of thousands of amateurs feel as if they were professional programmers while delivering unmaintainable code. Microsoft has created an aura of omnipresent dominance that makes choosing them a safe bet. That is not much different from the 1960s when placing an order for more IBM equipment was always the right decision. Windows, like IBM solutions of yesteryear, also has the distinction of being habit forming, which makes the consumption of ever increasing Windows applications ever more satisfying.

The admonition about an increasingly monopolistic Microsoft is irrelevant. To do anything about it requires a grasp of why and how consumers make their impulsive choices. Appealing to the rationality of the tobacco farmers or coffee growers to stop producing will not make much of a difference in the consumption of nicotine and caffeine. Reproaching microcomputer manufacturers who bundle Windows with every PC is ineffective.

One can gain many worthy insights from medical studies about irresistible inclinations, whether they are for alkaloids or for software. Progress against harmful addiction have taken place when social workers could demonstrate that immediate gratification that follows from any habit-forming dependency is likely to produce undesirable long-term effects.

Unless organizations learn how to evaluate the long-term cost of ownership consequences of their technical choices, the continuation of current short-sighted decisions to disregard life cycle costs of PC ownership will persist. It is also probable that Microsoft will resort to strategies that will deliver demonstrably less costly ways of operating and maintaining personal computers, as long as this will generate additional revenues.

If that happens, the claims about the cost of ownership of computing will become the arena in which competitive battles will take place.

What to Do

- Develop and apply a total life cycle cost model of computer network ownership to determine the cost reduction potential of new technology offerings.
- Reduce the costs of network ownership by establishing a Common Operating Environment (COE) which manages the proliferation of options, standardizes management practices, stabilizes technology, and simplifies the support of applications.

Part IX
New Agendas

- The rising importance of information security
- Shifting focus of planning for computer spending
- A reappraisal of the roles of the Chief Information Officer
- Unresolved issues that inhibit evaluating computer expenditures
- Managing expectations

41 SAFEGUARDING VULNERABILITY

Anything of value invites thievery.

PROFESSIONALLY managed globalized information crime is a threat that neither the national police nor the national military can successfully challenge. The primary responsibility for protection and defense must reside within each organization. Those who do not protect themselves cannot expect others, and particularly the government, to do that for them. The ample funds available for executing a strategic attack that compromises national security make it possible to secure cooperation from insiders already cleared for network access. As the value of computerized knowledge assets increases and information criminals gain in capability, the relative importance of security in the total cost of ownership will certainly rise. Reducing the cost of ownership of personal computers though increased control will not only generate operating generate savings, but also increase information security as a byproduct. Increased systems integration and interoperability without increased emphasis on security are prescriptions for disaster. Isolation of personal computers from potential misuse, while preserving the privacy of personal computer files, is one of the most painful issues any information executive must address.

Information systems will sustain serious degradation, to the point of failure, from intrusions launched by technologically sophisticated attackers who use advanced software engineering methods for their subversions. When that happens, the Chief Information Officer becomes answerable for the fragility of the information system.

The purpose of the following guidelines is to discuss some of the issues that every CIO must address whenever the role of Chief Information Officer also includes that of the Chief Information Security Officer.

Dimensions of the Threat

UN officials estimate that globally managed crime now earns $750 billion a year, mostly from drug traffic.[395] In addition, floating through the computers of international financial institutions are corruption payoffs, tax-evasion transfers, and proceeds from the theft of government owned property that are always seeking a safe haven. These huge pools of money are injected into the world's enormous electronic funds transfer mechanism for transport to friendly places where the laundering of these funds converts electronic pulses into disposable wealth. Computer networks thus ease the criminal groups' problem of how to transport and then transform huge sums of hot cash into legitimate investments.

Professionally managed globalized information crime is a threat that neither the national police nor the national military can successfully challenge by themselves. That will require a degree of international cooperation which is unlikely to happen. A number of nations already have criminal elements in control of many of their vital banking and commercial institutions. As long as the criminal element concentrates on transnational targets and supports the local economy, the local government officials will keep cyberspace sufficiently porous so that criminal clients may continue their highly profitable business without much interference. That suggests that the primary responsibility for protection and defense will continue to reside within each organization. Those who do not protect themselves cannot expect others, and particularly the government, to do that for them.

The threat to national security arises from the availability and skill of a trained cadre of computer professionals to carry out information warfare attacks using techniques tested in the conduct of criminal acts. With states hostile to the Western world finding it profitable to offer a safe haven for cyber-criminals, using such experts to conduct strategic attacks on the information infrastructure of the US is certain. War games that have explored scenarios for such actions have already taken place. They show that a strategic attack on the information infrastructure of the US would occur when it reinforces terrorist extortion or as a diversion from a military coup.

The large sums of money that have become available to cyber-terrorists from services rendered to the criminal element will also assure that the

395 Mathews, J.T., "Power Shift," *Foreign Affairs,* January 1997.

technology they use surpasses anything available to the defenders. The ample funds available for executing a strategic attack that compromises national security will make it possible to secure cooperation from insiders already cleared for network access. Many of the prevailing ideas that favor easy access to computer networks will need to be tempered by the realization that the more we trust computers to manage some of the vital functions of our society, the more vulnerable we become to those who do not wish us well.

COUNTERING THREATS

The most severe threat comes from well organized, well funded, and highly sophisticated experts whose interests are either terrorist or criminal. The CIO must exercise aggressive leadership in all matters related to information security, because the attention of operating personnel remains largely occupied with everyday problems. This calls for the creation of central information security assurance, coordinating, and incident evaluation staffs that are independent from operating management. Most importantly, the CIO must see to it that funds earmarked for security do not suffer diversion for other purposes, such as making up for project overruns.

The problem with security funding is that its payback is not apparent until it is too late. Information security is expensive. A security-aware commercial organization with over 7,000 personal computers provided me with the details about costs of securing their distributed networks. It had a budget of $310 per person. That included the costs of secure ID "smart" cards, anti-virus software, an Internet firewall server, administration of secure ID numbers for employees in transit, encryption software, intrusion detection systems, central security administration, and a security testing staff.[396]

There must also be an allowance for the employees' inconvenience and delays caused by security practices. With inclusion of all costs, I estimate that the security expenses could approach $1,000 per person per year.

---

396 In military practice this is the "red team" or "tiger team." They are experts with no other job than to imitate the behavior of exceptionally competent attackers. Only complete outsiders can accomplish this. Whoever prepares the defenses always assumes what to protect and how to do it. A good "red team" will study the strengths of the defenses and demolish the defenders with unexpected assaults. "Red teams" are available for hire, but that must be done with enormous caution because a rogue hacker can easily turn against the employer.

This may account for as much as ten to fifteen percent of workstation expenses. As the value of computerized knowledge assets increases and information criminals gain in capability, the relative importance of security in the total cost of ownership will certainly rise.

FUNDING SECURITY THROUGH COST REDUCTION

There are ways for enhancing information security while saving money. The widely quoted estimates of the cost of ownership of a network connected personal computer are anywhere from $8,500 to $13,500 per year. A study of labor-consuming failures shows that at least a quarter of the cost of ownership is directly or indirectly traceable to incidents induced by means of removable media. When an individual inserts incompatible or faulty software they create conditions that will magnify the demand for support services. Furthermore, almost every breach in information security is traceable to network access by means of a removable disk.

If every house keeps a private door that leads to the countryside there is no point in building up expensive walls and defenses in a fortress that surrounds a town. If someone wishes to enter the town, they should come through a guarded gate. Removable disks should remain only where access is completely verifiable. Elimination of all other removable disks from the network will not only improve security but will also reduce computer support costs. If someone needs data or software they should get it only through controlled access. Therefore, reducing the cost of ownership of personal computers though increased control will not only generate operating savings, but also increase information security.

EXPOSURES TO RISK

There is a penalty for the current propensity of corporations to streamline, consolidate, standardize, and outsource their information systems because that allows concentration of attacks on a few homogeneous targets. There is an even greater price for the increased proliferation of locally managed information processing operations, because that exposes many poorly defended posts to raids. Global access from powerful desktop or laptop computers to databases, servers, and electronic archives magnifies the risks to all information processing of damage, corruption, and disruption.

Increased systems integration and interoperability without increased emphasis on security can be prescriptions for disaster. Just as efficiency and integration permit those with a legitimate need and authorization to access needed information, they provide a pathway for individuals without such authorization to obtain crucial and sensitive information.

Cyber-terrorists and hackers are not the only ones who pose a risk to a company's information systems. Information-intensive businesses that depend on proprietary technologies or marketing intelligence are now seeking an information advantage over competition through cyber-crime. They engage in what used to be industrial spying, and now is known by the euphemisms "electronic intelligence" or "data mining." Information warfare is already taking place on the economic front. Technology competitors, foreign governments, foreign intelligence services, and criminal elements are seeking every advantage by exploiting the security vulnerabilities of information systems because it is much easier and less risky than physically breaking in.

Managing Risks

Unless the increased vulnerability finds an offset in reliable and robust protective methods, many of the benefits of information technologies may vanish. Information security must be an inherent element of design of information systems from inception. Retrofitting security into a system designed on the presumption of innocence and honesty may be too expensive to be worth doing, or too late.

Responsibility for ensuring that information security design practices are in place calls for sign-off by an independent technical review organization, the CIO's security staff. They must have the charter to review all practices and procedures in order to attest that systems follow designs that protect the integrity and security of the organization's information assets. The fortunes of a corporation or the functioning of a government agency will increasingly depend on such certification.

Corporate executives sometimes find my observations about information security unduly alarming. I feel justified in asserting that there is a clear and present danger to the security of every corporation when their critical computer applications have a plausible probability of ceasing to function.

When a firm experiences the equivalent of an information Pearl Harbor, the board of directors will surely look for accountability from whomever was in charge of information systems security.[397] In the case of such a disaster involving public safety or national security, Congress will surely start an investigation to identify and penalize those who were not adequately prepared to counter the likely dangers. The central theme of such post-attack assessments would be the question if those in charge exercised due diligence by instituting adequate protective measures when they became aware of the potential threats.[398]

However, note that I did not say *if* a devastating event will happen. I said *when* because it is only a matter of time before a crippling failure of a critically important computer installation will surely take place.

PRIVACY

You cannot manage information systems without recognizing that human passions infuse everything that has become accepted generally acceptable behavior. Around the world a large share of the information workforce has a deep emotional attachment to its personal computer. If you try to tamper with this bond you will witness reactions similar to the fury of homeowners defending their property. Some of this infatuation is not selfless.

The personal computer allows office workers increased freedom of expression and choice. Perhaps the most attractive of these activities are the composition of resumes, correspondence to enhance one's public image, retention of corporate data for private agendas, private mail with questionable content, and self-education to acquire marketable skills.

Next in importance are actions to protect one's job. These include memoranda to prove and explain arguments, lists of contacts that may someday be useful, and files that make others dependent on the worker. A personal computer can assure an individual of perfect memory, including the ability to prove the source and time of pertinent communication exchanges.

397 The reluctance to obtain a realistic assessment of potential threats from a qualified professional source may be partially motivated by fear of negligence suits. An executive who commissions a study of potential security exposures and then does not follow up with protective precautions could be liable for any damages.

398 This raises the interesting question whether senior executives wish to attend briefings about information security threats. In the absence of awareness there can be no case that can show negligence.

Perhaps the greatest value in having a computer on the desk is the opportunity to play around with software without much interference from anyone else. Information workers are eager to use company time to compensate for the generally woeful inadequacies in the training provided to them to cope with computerization. Playing games and exploring the Internet when work becomes boring also offers much relief from workplace frustration.

It is important to note that neither resumes nor protective memos nor self-serving communications were easy to have under the old style regime in which the central computer recorded every keystroke. With personal computers an individual can acquire practically infinite memory as well complete privacy by means of easily available encryption software. In unfriendly hands a personal computer with unrestricted network access inside a firm is equivalent to having a CIA agent working as a Kremlin switchboard operator.

Isolation of personal computers from potential misuse while preserving the privacy of personal computer files is one of the most painful issues any information executive must address. It will not go away, even if you decide to overlook it. If you neglect it, it will come back someday to bite the CIO with potentially enormous costs for changing network access privileges and screening all personal computers for unauthorized contents. The expense may not be as damaging as the rising antagonism from the workforce that has come to accept unlimited use of personal computers as an implied right.

Currently the only practical way to offer personal privacy while protecting a firm's interests dictates the imposition of tight technical rules on how and when to enter, retrieve, and store information. After eliminating all personal removable media, except for those designated for personal use, a partition of memory dedicated to an individual on a server should be the only place where they could store private data. The individual could then initiate the copying of private data, but under network control. Access to a person's private storage would be password protected and possibly encrypted. An individual must erase all such information whenever leaving employment. The checkout of information assets during the exit interview should become more important than handing in the keys, badge and access cards.

Property Rights

If a firm permits private use of company property, it cannot control every detail of what people do with it. Such uses should be a matter of corporate explicit or implied policy rather than an asserted right by employees. Private computer files or personal computer applications should be able to receive exemption from conformity to corporate standards. Whether such exemptions also apply to liberal Internet access privileges is a matter that needs early resolution. Private uses of Internet can divert employee attention to non-productive activities and contribute to network congestion.

There must be a clear policy delineation of the boundaries within which individuals should be able to use computers for non-business purposes. It would be hard to prevent access anyway, unless it is in direct conflict with the requirement to achieve higher levels of security, such as through complete isolation of the network from any sources of corruption. Such a corruption is possible, because employees have, on their desktop, the power of what was once a supercomputer and the memory capacity of a early data center. With freedom of personal use there should come accountability of not abusing such a privilege. In such cases individuals should purchase their own software licenses if an application is dedicated to strictly personal uses, and be held financially accountable for misuses that result in company liability.

Most of the software for personal use, such as games, mailing lists, and checkbook management, are copies passed around among casual friends. Copyright infringement liability for such uses should clearly be the individual's and not the corporation's.

If employees receive the privilege of using some corporate computing assets for private use, they must be required in writing to consent to the organization's security and property protection standards. When a person identifies himself to gain access to a network, the screen should display text explaining the conditions of use that becomes a legally binding agreement.

Copying corporate information into personal files and then treating that information as a possession that could leave when the employee leaves warrants especially strict attention. Without explicit rules, attempts to seek damages for theft of information may not stand up in court.

Until legal doctrine catches up with the reality of personal computing, I favor prohibition of private uses of personal computers for organizations where clear security risk exposures exist. Microcomputers are now sufficiently inexpensive and compact that individuals can buy their own equipment or receive it on loan. Such arrangements would establish an unambiguous separation between corporate and private information. It also offers a clear-cut compartment for an individual's aspirations for privacy while giving the organization unconstrained capabilities for protecting information assets in a secure environment.[399]

AN ADMONITION ABOUT INFORMATION SECURITY

Paranoia is a state of anxiety in which you believe somebody wants to do you harm. It is not always imaginary; there may be real and mortal enemies. In such cases heightened worrying and precautionary prudence can be essential for survival. The time has come for information executives to turn fearful. Professional infoassassins, not amateurs or pranksters, routinely traverse the global networks seeking opportunities to steal money, obtain information for blackmail, launder illegal funds, or extort political concessions. This criminal element has now acquired an exceptionally high level of technological sophistication. It has the skills and the global organization to commit crimes that leave no fingerprints, while absconding with high value booty.

IT has made it possible to expand global financial transactions such as currency swaps, portfolio purchases, and exchange rate hedging. Private currency traders now trade $1.3 trillion a day, one hundred times the volume of world trade or an amount that equals the currency reserves of all governments in the world.[400] Commerce and check-clearing transactions are in addition to that staggering volume. That adds up to over one hundred billion dollars per hour, or twenty-eight billion dollars per second.

What has changed in the last decade is the extent to which this money flow has become fully automated, electronically conveyed, and concentrated in a few institutions. Meanwhile, there has been an increase in the number of people with powerful workstations who can acquire the expertise of how to dip into this cash stream without leaving much of a trace.

---

399 Allowing employees to access confidential records remotely while on travel or when working from home offers especially difficult obstacles to information security. Remote access can be secure. It is a technical topic beyond the scope of this chapter.
400 Mathews, J.T., "Power Shift," *Foreign Affairs*, January 1997.

One can find the identical vulnerability as it applies to financial systems in almost every enterprise that depends on information processing for the conduct of its business. The costs incurred in the accumulation of information assets are now embodied in engineering drawing, process flow-charts, experimental data, software, patent applications, testing results, financial data, customer prospect lists, business proposals, and litigation documents now exceed the book value of the financial assets. Consequently, it is likely that the implementations of secure systems architectures will begin taking precedence over the acquisition of low-cost systems solutions and in dictating systems designs.

The Chief Information Officer of a firm is accountable for ensuring the continuity, integrity, and conservation of information assets. The time is now: we must place the safeguarding of information security at the top of every CIO's agenda.

What to Do

- Exercise aggressive leadership in all matters related to information security, because operating personnel remains largely occupied with everyday problems.
- Reduce the cost of ownership of personal computers though increased control to generate operating savings while simultaneously increasing information security.
- Make information security an inherent element of the initial design of information systems.
- Favor prohibition of private uses of personal computers for organizations where clear security risk exposures prevail.

42 Planning Directions

Preparing the itinerary is easy. It's the journey that's difficult.

THE CRITERIA for making IT investments must be specific. They must propose actions that are explicit and verifiable. During and after completion of a project an independent checkup must be able to show if the accomplishments matched the promises. The visionaries, who placed the CIO into the role as the CEO's chief innovation agent, are now finding it difficult to make the reality fit their prophecies. The title "CIO" is an exaggerated misnomer. The overwhelming share of a firm's information resources, the pay of information workers, does not show up in any financial reports and is not anything the CIO must explain to anyone. The CIO must have in place the means for maintaining and monitoring compliance with information assurance policies. The board of directors, and specifically the audit committee of the board, should be looking to the CIO to certify that information security exposures do not exceed specified expectations.

EVALUATION BEFORE VISIONEERING

Conventional advice on information systems planning suggests the construction of a vision statement as the first step in developing a blueprint for the future. That is either irresponsible or an excuse to substitute fiction for hard analysis. If you do not know where you are, no map can help you much. A vision is not a strategy because it does not say what actions are necessary.

How can one construct a realistic idea with which to unify everyone in an organization, if the strategy does not reflect a realistic sense of the present position of the business? How can one tell the difference between a visionary goal and hallucinations if one does not understand where the journey begins before committing to its destination? [401]

Consultants and new CIOs find visioneering especially attractive. It is easy to concoct visionary declarations from scraps of publicity releases, the latest articles from magazines and a handy list of the latest buzzwords. The proposed vision promises to deliver high-quality, reengineered, workflow streamlined, customer-oriented, knowledge-based, and integrated information systems. Ambitious visions may include a much longer list of trendy remedies for curing corporate ills, such as: support of customers, suppliers, and employees with work-enlargement, functional enrichment, shareholder value-creation, superb leadership, world-class quality, and teamwork. It is easy to generate impressive presentation slides from combinations of this verbiage. Nobody can possibly object to it unless they have to commit to delivering something that will be later subject to measurement and evaluation by independent means.

Meanwhile, shareholder-pressed CEOs do not seem to care much about visions. According to a survey of one hundred CIOs' bosses, the top three critical success factors for a CIO should be 1: Responsiveness to business needs; 2: Controlling the costs of technology; and 3: Delivering quality solutions on schedule. Though successful project management was on the top of the CEOs' list, it did not even show up as a priority for CIOs.[402] Delivering on project promises is measurable. Delivering on visions can remain ephemeral.

FLAWED ASSUMPTIONS

Alignment efforts become crippled by flawed ideas of how to assess technology investments and practices. This covers assumptions one should avoid:

> • The more you use or spend IT, the better off your company will be. Spend more and profitability will increase. Or revenues will go up. Or headcount will come down. None of this is demonstrable. Many companies budget as the more you put into IT, while acad-

---

401 Taking drugs is one way of getting connected with inspirational visions. More practical executives may try culling phrases from half a year's worth of *Business Week*, *Wired*, and CIO *Magazine* for maximum buzzword-compliant appeal.
402 Bresnahan, J., "Mixed Messages," CIO *Magazine*, May 15, 1996, p. 74.

emics still try to show disprove the "computer paradox." In fact, the only correlation there is with IT
spending goes against the argument: companies that
spend more have more overhead costs and more information workers.
- There are best practices that fit all companies, such as
the prescriptive best practices offered by consultants,
or the Baldrige Award criteria. Stick to them, and you
will be successful and aligned. That does not hold up
by any independent measure of performance such as
profits or economic value.
- In addition, the information systems world is full of
techniques for assessing IT effectiveness and what IT
investments to make. Their origin is in subjective ratings or opinion polling. None of these techniques
relate explicitly to verifiable metrics or to a capacity for
post-implementation audit.

Before one can start on the path towards demonstrable business
alignment of information technologies, one must first clear away these
flawed views and methods. That calls for a renewed emphasis on integration of IT planning into business planning.

PLANNING GUIDELINES

The criteria for making IT investments must be specific. They must propose actions that are explicit and verifiable. During and after completion
of a project an independent checkup must be able to show if the accomplishments matched the promises.

Executives should not complain about poor results from IT if they do
not state what they expect. The following guidelines offer a prescription
for sound planning practices:
- Investments focus on the missions of the organization,
not on the ancillary functions.
- The plans align with the strategic directions of the
enterprise.
- The plans reveal the migration path from the status
quo to the desired end state for at least five years.

- The plans demonstrate that alternative solutions are not feasible.
- The proposal avoids customized software solutions and chooses only offerings available from multiple vendors who comply with open systems standards.
- Risk-adjusted discounted cash flow with residual value reveals the financial viability of every investment.
- The cost and benefit projections reflect the training, organizational, and performance impacts on the organization before and after the introduction of the new technologies.
- Simplification and cost reduction always precedes automation.
- Implementation proceeds in small evolutionary increments against measurable accomplishments at each successive stage of completion.

RESPONSIBILITIES FOR THE CHIEF INFORMATION OFFICER

In the unceasing competition for privilege, ambitious groups will seek legitimacy by declaring themselves the elite that deserve an exclusive franchise. The most ancient authorities for such claims were religious or by decree from a ruling family. When the number of aspiring claimants to special status grew, national, racial, tribal, or political reasons became substitutes for the divine origin of any legitimacy. For example, the leadership of totalitarian parties needed a rationale to justify their dictatorship. They did that by declaring themselves to be the vanguard of the working class. The computer czars of yesteryear claimed legitimacy on the basis of their custodianship of the data center which held all customer and employee records.[403]

The rise of democracy made special entitlements increasingly hard to explain. This is how we now get claims to special privilege based on professional qualifications. Lawyers, physicians, psychiatrists, auditors, and judges have successfully secured for themselves an elevated status. It was

403 The term "computer czar" for the position of the CIO was in widespread use during the 1960s and 1970s. Why pick the title of czar and not emperor, king, shah, or duke remains a mystery, except for the wishful thinking by the computer users that the whoever held absolute power over computers ought to suffer the fate of the holders of that title.

only a matter of time before senior computer executives, who aspire to the leadership of the information based society, came forth to ask for greater power. That is when the Chief Information Officer (CIO) title came into use in the late 1970s.

The original proponents of the CIO role argued that the position ought to be equivalent to the executive they envied most, the Chief Financial Officer (CFO). The CFO was perhaps the most powerful counselor to the supreme corporate being, the Chief Executive Officer (CEO). Partially displacing the CFO would overcome the ambitious computer executive's sense of inferiority, after laboring under the yoke of the comptroller for many decades.

It took less than five years for establishments to come into being to cater to the self-enhancement of the image of the CIO. Magazines, glossy journals, symposia, consultant surveys, and exclusive clubs came into existence to convey to the self-chosen few a sense that they were indeed the chosen elite. CIOs paid large fees to attend evangelical meetings where they discuss their own election to sublime status.

Loss of Status

The visionaries who placed the CIO into the role of the CEO's chief innovation agent are now finding it difficult to make the reality fit their prophecies. Recent surveys show that CIO turnover is closer to that of the captains of mercenary troops than the longevity enjoyed by a trusted chancellor.[404] Without an expectation of stability, CIOs cannot look forward to long-range planning or to reaping rewards from an accumulation of sound practice. However, I do not find the decapitation rate of CIOs as sufficient evidence that they may not enjoy positions of importance. One has to consider that the present survival rate of CEOs is not what it used to be, either.

It just happens that the 1993 *Computerworld* survey of the *Premier 100* companies included questions about the reporting relationships of CIOs. The extent to which CIOs were indeed the chosen elite would become evident if they were reporting directly to the CEO, which would signify their membership in the inner circle of confidants.

---

404 According to a survey by the Computer Sciences Corporation 38.5% of 365 corporations replaced CIOs within two years. 56% of these replacements were recruited from outside the company and 20% from another business function. See Computer Sciences Corporation, *Critical Issues of Information Systems Management*, CSC, 1996.

Only eight of the fifty-three *Premier* 100 companies with superior economic performance had the CIO report to the CEO. I also isolated the characteristics of seventeen companies that enjoyed exceptionally high information productivity. Only one of those had the CIO report to the CEO. The average CIO presides over a substantial operation, which is likely to be one of the top five cost centers in the firm.

It is worth noting at this point that the title CIO is an exaggerated misnomer. The overwhelming share of a firm's information resources, the pay of information workers, does not show up in any financial reports and is not anything the CIO must explain to anyone. At best, the CIO may be the CCO, Chief Computer Officer. Even the scope of that function is becoming questionable as oversight over computers migrates out of the CIO's reach. Sixty percent of corporate Internet webs, where much of the innovation and growth is taking place, are out of reach of the information systems departments.[405]

These observations certainly indicate that CIOs have top-ranking jobs. However, the reporting relationships of the CIO suggest that the responsibility for guiding IT does not yet earn a seat within the inner circle of the top corporate executive.

ORGANIZING FOR SECURITY

Ensuring the security, integrity, and availability of computing power, the firm's information assets, must become an added responsibility of the Chief Information Officer before we can witness the elevation in his rank and status.

The Chief Information Officer must be the proactive advocate to commit a significant share of corporate resources to improving the security of its information infrastructure. This calls for adopting realistic risk management practices throughout the organization, because interdependence, resource sharing, and consolidation increases vulnerability. This responsibility must remain with the CIO regardless of the extent of outsourcing. A corporation cannot ever abdicate to an information service provider its accountability for keeping its business operating without interference or interruption.

The office of the CIO must have the charter to collect, analyze, and understand incidents whenever there is any detection of an information

405 Maddox, K., "Masters of the Web," *InformationWeek*, April 29, 1996, p. 48.

security infraction, regardless of its location. The CIO must have in place the means for maintaining and monitoring compliance with information assurance policies. The board of directors, and specifically the audit committee of the board, should look to the CIO to certify that information security exposures do not exceed specified limits.

The top management of any large organization must have at its disposal knowledgeable experts who are able to identify threats to its business. Such organizations must have a trusted staff that can install countermeasures against information attacks that may receive assistance from insiders such as employees and contractors.

Presently, efforts that foster information quality assurance and security receive diversions that arise from organizational indifference, competing interests, and disincentives to cooperate. Usually the primary reason for a distinct aversion to all matters related to information security is risks to the careers of information workers. If they do not follow information security rules, they may be blamed for security failures. Without rules, there is no blame and no responsibility. Therefore, whatever security practices may prevail tend to be imprecise to avoid rigorous accountability, just in case there is a serious security incident.

Loose security practices will dissipate the energies and talent that could otherwise be applied to a coherent and decisive security effort. Therefore, statements that define the CIO's and the operating manager's roles must elaborate on the accountability and authority for making sure that information security works properly.

INFORMATION SECURITY RESPONSIBILITIES

These information security responsibilities should belong to every CIO:.
- Policy, leadership, goal-setting, and advocacy for information assurance and protection, including advocacy of information systems assurance to the board of directors or the executive committee
- Coordinating information security policies and activities of security auditors with local information security personnel, physical security staffs, independent security testing organizations, and law enforcement agencies

- Working with operating management to increase threat awareness and vulnerability assessment of what information may jeopardize operations if compromised, destroyed, or corrupted
- Performing independent assessments in case the processing of information is performed by contractors, suppliers, or service providers
- Oversight of planning, budgeting, and programming guidance over all matters related to information systems security
- Control over procedures, directives, processes, and standards that would apply to the support of information systems needs. Specifically, this would include central authority over encryption, authentication, and electronic signature verification.
- Facilitating joint industry and government coordination that deals with threats to national or industry-wide interests from potential compromises of the information infrastructure, such as telecommunications, electronic mail, electronic commerce, and electronic cash
- Ensuring that everyone responsible for managing and using the company's information systems receives adequate information security training and education. This would include unscheduled mandatory testing by an independent third party of compliance with security standards and procedures.
- Issuing guidelines that define the accountability of operating managers for making the tradeoffs between the risks and the costs of safeguards. The objective here would be to make information security a responsibility of general management and not of computer specialists. It would also prohibit unrestricted delegation of security matters to information technologists, contractors or suppliers.
- Defining the principles to guide an information systems security architecture, especially as it applies to network protection

- Validation, verification, and reporting of protective or countermeasure solutions, whether technical or administrative
- Setting information policies for security related practices and standards, such as pre-employment screening of employees, testing failure recovery, maintaining physical redundancy of processing capabilities, endorsement of configuration control tools, and selection of technical means for assuring compliance with information security policies

Such policies may become one of the principal sources of the legitimacy and high level status for the corporate Chief Information Officer. Just like the Chief Financial Officer, with fiduciary responsibility for financial assets, the CIO must assume board level accountability for the preservation of a firm's information assets.

What to Do

- Make IT investment plans specific by proposing actions that are explicit and verifiable.
- Include the ensuring of the security, integrity and availability of the firm's information assets as an added responsibility of the Chief Information Officer.
- Collect, analyze, and understand incidents whenever there is any detection of an information security infraction, regardless of its location.
- Monitor compliance with information assurance policies by independent means.
- Provide the board of directors, and specifically the audit committee of the board, with certification that information security exposures do not exceed specified expectations.

43 Follow-up

Progress starts with unfinished business.

Waiting for Agreement

This book dealt with many questions concerned with the evaluation of computer expenditures. Nevertheless, there is ample evidence that there is no generally accepted method for making such assessments. The following issues are still unresolved:

- Economists continue to use national statistics to analyze the effects of computerization. I believe that the US national productivity numbers are not reliable to make such judgments. The validation of government statistics is inadequate.
- Computer consultants and journals use metrics such as computer spending as a percentage of revenue in making recommendations, granting awards, and publishing ranking comparisons. This book has outlined the irrelevance of such ratios. Further work is necessary to develop better metrics.
- Financial executives and leading economists persist in evaluating computer spending in terms of capital productivity. It will take time before the realization seeps in that capital efficiency cannot be the principal measure for judging information performance. After all, firms now operate in an economy in which over sixty-five percent of wages are for information processing.
- Accounting statements devote most attention to tracking what happens to financial assets. Major revisions in generally accepted accounting standards are necessary. They should reflect the value of the information assets that do not show up on any accounting reports.

IMPLEMENTING EVALUATION METRICS

Computer executives often argue that even though computerization may not show measurable results, business would have been much worse without it. Since it is impossible to prove the consequences of events that never happened, the best one can do is to stick to facts as they are. That is the primary reason for my critical examination of theories about computer spending practices.

Despite corporate fascination with IT spending and its payoffs, the capacity to measure and assess the value of computers remains immature in most organizations. Five types of evaluations are necessary to allow top management to gain a better understanding of how to invest in information systems:

Evaluations Using Verifiable Benchmarks.

These are measures of IT cost efficiency. They include traditional ratios such as cost/million instructions, cost per function point, cost per workstation, cost per page, cost per kilopacket of transmission, or cost per gigabyte of storage capacity.

Many consulting firms already offer such assessment services. This involves applying well-tested industrial engineering methods to meticulously measured observations. This work will decrease in importance as fully automated operations and low-cost technologies make the operation of equipment and software object management a utility service.

The metering of information technologies becomes a byproduct of network measurements. The assessment of unit cost efficiencies becomes inseparable from the operating environment itself. When that happens, reaching for ever increasing efficiencies will produce diminishing returns because only highly efficient services will survive. The survival of the fittest rather then consulting assistance with metrics will ensure that all computer networks will deliver results at the lowest cost.

Evaluations Comparing with Expected Costs.

Statistically valid budget models become the basis for making evaluations. They offer measures of IT expense advantage. Such benchmarks analyze actual spending against expected spending for look-alike firms. These metrics are difficult to obtain because they require a steady accumulation of reliable data about the characteristics of computer usage. As the share of outsourcing services increases, such assessments will be essential for making judgments about the fairness of contractor prices. This book has shown some potential uses of such methods.

Evaluations of the Effectiveness.

Information management includes the costs of information technologies. Measuring information productivity allows comparisons with results realized by competitors. These would be measures of information management effectiveness. Foremost among such metrics are productivity indicators, such as *Return-on-Management®* and *Information Productivity®*.[406] Just about every major consulting firm and certainly all outsourcing contractors will be coming up with a proprietary schema that proposes some sort of effectiveness metrics. These will be necessary to assure increasingly apprehensive executives about what they are getting out of IT.

Once effectiveness metrics become acceptable, efficiency and cost-advantage measures will be acceptable only within the context of what enterprise-level measures may indicate. The forthcoming sequel to this volume, on *Information Productivity,* will describe the applicability of these ideas in planning of IT investments.

Assessments of Investment Projects

The planning, funding, implementation, and progress monitoring of information systems projects are the arena where technology either wins or fails. The principles for managing IS projects appeared in a prior book, *The Business Value of Computers.* The specific techniques for assessing payoffs and for aligning computer projects with a firm's purposes appeared in Chapters 9 and 10. These chapters became a well defined administrative process in the Department of Defense as well as a software program in 1991.[407] A comprehensive commercial version of these tools for securing

---

406 Return-on-Management® and R-O-M® are US registered trademarks of Strassmann, Inc.
407 Director of Defense Information, *Functional Economic Analysis Guidebook*, Department of Defense, July 1991, and *BPR Support Tool*, Institute for Defense Analysis, September 1991.

the alignment of projects with business objectives is now available as *BizCase* software.

Assessments of Long-term Payoffs.

Excessive concentration on efficiency and effectiveness metrics may result in flawed outcomes if they lead to short-term gains that jeopardize the future. To cope with such distortions, I developed the *Knowledge Capital®* metric. This tracks the capacity of a firm to keep increasing economic value-added at a rate that exceeds the growth in financial capital assets.

The forthcoming sequel to this volume, on *Knowledge Capital,* in the series on *Business Alignment of Information Technologies,* will describe the applications of these ideas to the accumulation of information assets.

VALIDATION OF IT INVESTMENTS

Investments in computerization projects should stand out as one of the principal means for attaining competitive superiority. Firms should set goals to reflect the ways that customers differentiate organizations with or without comparable computer-aided services.

How can a corporation establish such goals? It must be done by conducting in-depth customer surveys and by paying particular attention to the reasons why some customers switch to the competition. The validity of a firm's computerization goals is easy to check. Customer reactions should include praise about prompt and reliable responses to their inquiries. Customers ought to notice rapid turnaround in the handling of routine orders and non-routine problems. Customers should note some unique information-handling feature. IT should figure prominently in customers' comparisons with the competition's offering. If frequent reactions from customers reveal information-related deficiencies, there should be a major revision in information systems goals and method of operation. Therefore, metrics derived from experience in social and behavioral sciences will rise in importance in the IT portfolio of required measurements.

SETTING PROFIT EXPECTATIONS

The information systems delivery organization must be demonstrably a low life cycle cost producer of services. Competitive benchmarking, such as measuring unit costs compared with superior operators, is the best way of verifying this is so.

The information systems delivery organization must also demonstrate steady reduction in unit costs on a continuous basis. With hardware prices falling anywhere from forty-five percent per year for mainframes to six percent per month for personal computers, top management should expect savings in unit transaction costs of at least twenty-five percent per year. Long range plans should also target new systems projects, assuming at least twenty percent annual cost reductions per unit measure of software development and maintenance. Software reuse and an increased utilization of off-the-shelf packages will be the keys to realizing such results.

An organization must be able to show continued improvement in financial returns to shareholders. An information systems delivery organization should not boast about its profit contributions if the company is not making an economic profit or is losing customers in droves. IT cannot be a success if the firm's investment returns are below the cost of capital. The chief information officer of a firm cannot claim excellence if the organization suffers from consistently inferior profitability compared with industry leaders.

Computer technology will merit the distinction of endowing the enterprise with information superiority if the organization prospers. The emphasis in this book on economic success, or service quality in the public sector, presents the point of view that IT is nothing more than the conduct of successful management by other means.

SUMMING UP

Very soon the decades-long infatuation with spending money freely on information technologies will come to an end. It will become acceptable to admit that organizations were spending too much money because operating executives were afraid, unwilling, or untrained to manage it, while abdicating that role to technical experts.[408]

There will be a search for the reasons why IT kept escaping scrutiny that applied to everyone. There will be an inquiry into who approved sig-

---

408 Battles, B.E., Mark, D., and Ryan, C., "How Otherwise Good Managers Spend Too Much on Information Technology," *The McKinsey Quarterly*, 1996, Number 3. This excellent article by McKinsey consultants signals what's coming as the next trendy managerial idea.

nificant and risky funding that did not deliver on its promises. There will be reorganizations that will remove IT from its protected status to making it every manager's personal responsibility.

The knowledge of how and when to employ IT will be added to the list of required managerial skills, just as some understanding of finance and personnel matters is now an essential proficiency for guiding any business function.[409] After much analysis, ample consulting assistance, employment of additional auditors, and getting rid of yet another generation of CIOs, businesses will revert to placing accountability to where it belongs, a practice that should have been in place all along.

IT will remain an indispensable business function, but not exempt from tough examinations of its measurable contribution. It will have to abide by accepted management processes that proceed from strategic planning, though budgeting and implementation to periodic performance monitoring, just like manufacturing, sales, engineering, research, and marketing.

IT will have to demonstrate where it produces economic value added, or how it delivers improved performance in the public sector. It is then when the business alignment of information technologies will finally take place in a discernible reality and not as a wishful anticipation.

The reader will have to have the patience to wait for the completion of the sequel to this volume to receive additional prescriptions of what to do for achieving the fullest possible alignment of information technologies with business objectives. This book discussed only expenditures for computers, which should be a good start in an era of increasing pressures to cut IT spending. Knowing how to manage IT costs is necessary, but certainly not sufficient. Managing expenses is important but not the prime ingredient for success. Increasing the productivity of information workers and enhancing the effectiveness of knowledge capital are the generators of all value and all payoffs. Alignment of information technologies and business happens only after the productivity gains and asset enhancements exceed the costs in ways that are clearly demonstrable.

"Squandering" is descriptive of a waste of a worthy inheritance. When the history of the twentieth century is written, computers will cer-

---

409 None of this diminishes the importance of retaining the expertise that provides the leadership for the all systems activities, assessments of systems performance, checks on local initiatives, accountability for the integrity of computer systems, and a cadre of technology specialists.

tainly represent the most valuable gift that my generation has passed on to posterity. Therefore, this book was conceived in the hope that a few well-aimed admonitions may steer the prodigal beneficiaries of the computer legacy to mend their profligate ways. I trust that the readers will recognize this sentiment as the essence of this book. It is one of profound admiration for what computers can do in assisting people with what they can accomplish. It is this spirit that encourages critics to speak out about matters that they cherish with so much fervor.

Recommendations

Chapter 1

Show the discounted cash flow of a proposed business improvement that depends on information technologies.

Reveal the high and low expected financial returns for all computer proposals.

Display the business case for a computer investment as an add-on to a financial plan and as a gain in approved performance metrics.

Keep all investment proposals updated to reflect changing conditions as computer projects progress.

Chapter 2

Identify the sources of all misalignment.

Begin reviews of IT spending by an examination of all computing that is unrelated to revenue from external customers.

Remove from benefit estimates all savings that could have accrued anyway, without computer intervention.

Authorize pilot tests and small scale experiments that demonstrate how an organization performs with or without computer-enhanced assistance.

Institute competitive comparisons of the full costs of delivering computer services.

Chapter 3

Avoid quoting isolated anecdotal cases to substantiate economic gains.

Obtain reliable estimates of IT spending, including expenses that do not show up as the IT budget.

Track IT expenditures as a ratio of profits, economic value-added, and operating costs.

Collect consistent sets of data and performance indicators if organization consists of multiple operating units.

Benchmark total IT spending as compared with look-alike firms or government organizations.

Insist that only operating personnel are asked to justify their IT spending.

CHAPTER 4

Adopt Economic Value-Added metrics for assessing the contributions of information technologies.

Collect data about the Economic Value-Added of competitors for making comparisons of all spending.

CHAPTER 5

Do not compare IT spending levels using percentage of revenue ratios.

Trust only IT budget estimates from reliable sources, not from magazine surveys.

Collect indicators of IT spending that relate to the sources of demand for computing services, such as demographics of the workforce, customer transactions, or business characteristics.

Relate IT spending to activity-driven events and key business processes, especially in support of customer care, goods production, post-sale support, and product innovation.

CHAPTER 6

Separate the costs of the organization between information-generating and goods-producing segments for the purpose of analysis of IT costs.

Segregate external purchases for goods and services from all other expenses in order to obtain an index of demand for intra-organizational information services.

Collect administrative cost ratios for separate segments of the organization for the purpose of assessing the extent of computerization for each business function.

CHAPTER 7

Examine opportunities for budgeting and charging for IT services based on per capita assessments.

Keep track of per capita spending for IT, by employee function, as one of the indicators of lowered unit costs and IT efficiency.

Develop indexes of IT expense concentration ratios to identify unusually high usage patterns without corresponding value-added contributions.

Use the correlation between IS staffs and IT budgets as a measure of outsourcing intensity.

CHAPTER 8

Avoid using Return on Investment (ROI) methods for justifying computer projects.

Use only current cash values for making IT investment comparisons. Inflation-adjusted comparisons are unreliable and misleading.

Do not apply technical performance ratios, such as dollars per MIPS or costs for functions point, for predicting the performance of IT investments.

Prepare for dramatic cost reductions as outsourcing companies start competing for market share on a massive scale.

CHAPTER 9

Avoid using computer asset valuations as an indicator of IT spending because this information is irrelevant.

Rely primarily on verifiable corporate information instead of highly unreliable government data about information technologies & productivity.

Keep track of long-term growth rates of employment, overhead, purchases, economic value-added, and workforce composition to collect useful indexes of demand for information services.

CHAPTER 10

Prepare for an era where corporate management will start applying tough financial criteria to all its spending proposals, including an examination of ongoing operating and maintenance expenses.

Install comprehensive metrics that not only concentrate on technological efficiency but also convey convincing evidence of managerial effectiveness.

CHAPTER 11

Do not rely on government or economic reports for setting standards for what to expect from IT investments.

Set the threshold for investments in IT projects on the basis of risk-adjusted net cash flows, not on academic studies.

View with skepticism all survey data about IT spending gathered by means of mail-in questionnaires or telephone surveys.

Rely on prescribed financial methods for justifying investments, not on econometric equations that are accepted for academic purposes only.

CHAPTER 12

Adopt best practices of others only after verifying that this would solve, in a demonstrable way, existing problems.

Do not pay attention to average cost ratios for an industry or a set of applications. What matters is competitive performance and superior profitability, and that should be gained by applying unique solutions.

Obtain reliable data about information handling expenditures outside of the usual scope of a computer department, such as voice telecommunications, facsimile, copying, printing, microfilm, videoconferencing, and courier services.

CHAPTER 13

Do not depend on virtual savings that reduce invisible (stealth) costs. Real costs warrant real savings.

Use statistical sampling of a random group of customers to identify the probable stealth costs associated with computing.

Institute full configuration controls over computer equipment and software, which should include the tracking of the location and use of all information technology assets.

Encourage the spread of computer literacy through local computer experts.

CHAPTER 14

Do not expect to produce increased profits from computerization if work for the government increases the number of inspectors, clerks, administrators, and auditors disproportionately.

Highlight the costs of the impacts of government paperwork burdens during budget reviews of IT spending.

CHAPTER 15

Begin all remedial efforts by a thorough and uncompromising diagnosis of the current situation as it is, not what fits a preconceived idea of what the solution is.

Search for proven and workable best practices answers only after a thorough understanding of the prevailing conditions.

CHAPTER 16

Rely on consistent and superior profit performance in a competitive marketplace as the ultimate measure of corporate performance.

Encourage excellence, but not by adding to an unmanageable volume of practices and methods.

Insist on better ways of specifying the desired results and how to measure and track accomplishments.

CHAPTER 17

Evaluate full life cycle costs of IT projects.

Include impacts beyond the short-term, three to four year, corporate planning horizon.

Measure the economic utility of software in terms of life cycle discounted cash flows which include maintenance, upgrading, and migration expenses as well as retraining costs for the developers, maintainers, operators, and users.

CHAPTER 18

Adopt risk-adjusted discounted cash flow models for analysis of IT projects.

Apply consistent criteria to all available IT implementation choices. This should include quantification of "intangibles" in cash terms.

Pay disproportionate attention to the conception, definition, goals, and measures of performance when a project is initiated.

Beware of vendor IT investment justification methodologies. They will always reflect a bias favoring preferred choices.

CHAPTER 19

Use only cost justification techniques that translate dollar costs into dollar benefits.

Discount the expected benefits of computer using explicit risk assessments.

Include computer investments as an element in the firms' strategic long-range plans.

CHAPTER 20

Calculate the returns on computer investments as the difference between the costs of automation and the next least expensive solution.

Do not attribute to computerization gains that are attainable by other means.

Chapter 21
Validate all customer surveys against measurable gains.
Survey opinions of customers who have defected to competition are some of the most reliable sources of useful information.

Chapter 22
Make sure that outsourcing of IT is an imaginative way of obtaining improved services and not an excuse for getting rid of managerial responsibilities.
Engage in selective outsourcing, but retain most of the information management capabilities as an essential organizational competency.
Favor outsourcing to take advantage of somebody else's capacity to accumulate technological capabilities faster than when it remains home-grown.

Chapter 23
Judge the efficiency of outsourcing on the basis of unit costs, not on total spending.
Include in contract terms a financial and activity-based cost model for tracking of IT expenses prior and after outsourcing.
Determine if a firm retains the choice to repatriate, or move its systems to another vendor, without excessive expense no matter what has been outsourced.
Avoid outsourcing contracts that have an element of profit sharing with the provider of outsourcing services.
Start planning now on developing and retaining the technical and managerial competence in an era of increased dependence on outsourcing contractors.

Chapter 24
Fix intrinsic flaws in information management practices, such as insufficient definitions of accountability for information resource management, prior to outsourcing.
Watch out for conditions that transform any outsourced business into a monopoly service or customer lock-in.

Make sure that any outsourced business can transfer to a competitor or become repatriated, without major disruptions and excessive expenses.

Specify what expertise must remain before any part of the organization may outsource elements that are operationally critical, or are the means for realizing competitive gains.

CHAPTER 25

Devote attention to socioeconomic forces in the workplace to better assess readiness for innovative information technologies.

Diminish the emphasis on technological decisions and shift attention to the costs of employee training, the effects of organizational disruption, and the causes of workplace resistance.

Get ready for enormous new investments in network redesigns that will favor open systems architectures.

Consider scenarios and contingency actions if IT becomes a means for obstructing the functioning of our society.

CHAPTER 26

Do not get into the position of having to document operational benefits, such as revenue gains, market share improvement, inventory reductions, product quality gains, or enhancement of customer satisfaction. Leave all such explanations to line executives who are directly responsible for them.

Commit only to schedule, systems capabilities and information services budgets. Everything else is beyond a CIO's capacity to explain or to prove.

Manage benefits by thoroughly understanding the sensitivity of the proposed financial model to changes in the proposed business payoffs. On every project there are only a few capabilities that deliver most of the benefit. Sensitivity analyses showing which elements of the model cause the greatest possible benefit or damage are essential for deciding what to watch to ensure that the project does not get out of control.

Realize benefits are primarily an outcome of good management and not necessarily the best technology. The generation of benefits does not originate with information project managers, unless they are improving the efficiency of what they already control. Benefits are realizable only by indirect means. The systems recipients can make or break any process because they remain in control and must live with the system after completion.

Invest in the means for exercising preventive damage control to keep dormant risks from becoming catastrophes. This requires an early warning process based on gathering operational intelligence at the lowest levels of the organization.

Anticipate risks, prepare contingency plans, and hold adequate funds in reserve.

Keep the planned elapsed time for any project to not more than one quarter of the time during which both parties can work together and keep up their shared understanding.

Define a systems architecture not only in technical terms, but also how it will distribute political control over information, because all economic benefits arise from use and not from design.

Assign high priority to coping with external threats before focusing on internal information that concerns only operating expenses.

CHAPTER 27

Deliver alternative life cycle plans that display a range of different technical solutions for managing applications that are essential to the success of the enterprise.

Prepare budget projections that portray approaches that will increase the cumulative value of the installed software.

Include in all project proposals a calculation of the residual value of project investments.

CHAPTER 28

Adopt a policy of funding a large share of the systems modernization costs from reductions in ongoing operating and maintenance expenses.

Exploit the thirty to forty percent annual cost reductions in equipment costs that suppliers will continue delivering in order to extract operating savings of at least twenty percent per annum from baseline costs.

CHAPTER 29

Display the results of IT investments in terms of cash flows, not ratios or breakeven times.

Place the standardization of data models and data dictionaries high in priority as a means of increasing the long-term serviceability of systems.

Design software components to represent basic business processes. The definitions of the processes should be at a sufficiently high level of abstraction so that they can be used as modular work elements, independent of how an organization decides to assemble them to suit its needs.

CHAPTER 30

Articulate a pricing policy for computer services that mimics the methods used by the most profitable outsourcing firms.

Institute network pricing policies that charge a fixed monthly fee for all services that are not sensitive to increases in high cost activities.

Operate networks that make it easy to bid for services from many suppliers.

CHAPTER 31

Adopt computer-aided systems engineering tools that enforce the construction of software from a repository of standard reusable assemblies.

Make the accumulation and preservation of useful software assets one of the principal technology objectives.

Offer incentives to the systems staff to include the accumulation of reusable assets as one of their key objectives. Consider adopting a royalty-like reward scheme to encourage that.

CHAPTER 32

Test where and in what ways a new application will cooperate with the old ones.

Judge open systems in terms of the financial costs and personnel disturbances they avoid.

Reject the safety and uniformity assurances from any one vendor to the exclusion of others as a journey that ends in lock-in.

Increase the longevity of the information assets instead of accepting the assumption that they will be worth nothing after a breakeven period.

CHAPTER 33

Question all efforts to build, junk, and then replace software.

Prove that the next generation of software will offer lower support costs as well as a very large residual value.

Recommend against budget increases unless the information systems executives can demonstrate how the proposed new investments will guarantee a longer technology life.

Put into effect detailed plans that lower life cycle costs through commitment to long-range technology directions.

Lower the exorbitant costs of network services through the use of automatic maintenance, fault diagnostics, interoperability, security, and crash-proof performance assurance.

CHAPTER 34

Place the burden of proof on those who advocate replacing rather than upgrading a computer system.

Require that all investment justifications include rigorous analyses of the costs, benefits, and risks of several alternatives, including upgrading.

Design software so that it has the capacity for accepting continuous improvement and upgrading.

CHAPTER 35

Adopt a policy that insists on vendor independence.

Insist on compliance with industry standards, as followed by at least three major suppliers.

Extend the useful life of software logic beyond twenty years because it offers one of the most attractive cost reduction opportunities.

Take a long term view by subjecting all development and maintenance to standard systems engineering practices.

CHAPTER 36

Seek out suppliers of computer services who compete through delivery of systems that have a low life-cycle cost of ownership.

Insist on independence from any one vendor as one of the objectives of systems management.

CHAPTER 37

Employ statistical analysis of selected variables to estimate expected computer spending.

Allocate and track computer spending, by business function, to gain an understanding of over- or underfunding.

Measure the effectiveness of people and not the costs of computing as a measure of IT performance.

Use the fully allocated per capita costs for information technology services as a proxy for assessing the worth of the services.

Analyze the relationship between the population of terminals, personal computers, and workstations, and the number of information workers.

CHAPTER 38

Set the planning horizon for computer systems depending on the quality of the initial project investment and the expenses for keeping up with change.

Make long-term commitments when establishing data dictionaries and data models.

Include the residual value of a project in all project payoff calculations.

Adopt tools that keep the long-term knowledge assets and short-term technological assets separated.

Follow the principle of "Write once, run anywhere, any time" as the fundamental strategic direction for managing IT assets.

CHAPTER 39

Supplement IT spending plans with a schedule that shows the valuation of IT assets.

Add the acquisition costs and subtract the depreciation in use value to arrive at the worth off IT assets.

Value the merits of prepackaged software by considering all software costs jointly, including maintenance and upgrades.

Develop model of training investments that includes employee turnover, new applications introduction rate, and the speed of technological modernization.

Shift as much training as possible to just-in-time, point-of-use experiences.

CHAPTER 40

Develop and apply a total life cycle cost model of computer network ownership to determine the cost reduction potential of new technology offerings.

Reduce the costs of network ownership by establishing a Common Operating Environment (COE) which manages the proliferation of options, standardizes management practices, stabilizes technology, and simplifies the support of applications.

CHAPTER 41

Exercise aggressive leadership in all matters related to information security, because operating personnel remains largely occupied with everyday problems.

Reduce the cost of ownership of personal computers though increased control to generate operating savings while simultaneously increasing information security.

Make information security an inherent element of the initial design of information systems.

Favor prohibition of private uses of personal computers for organizations where clear security risk exposures prevail.

CHAPTER 42

Make IT investment plans specific by proposing actions that are explicit and verifiable.

Include the ensuring of the security, integrity and availability of the firm's information assets as an added responsibility of the Chief Information Officer.

Collect, analyze, and understand incidents whenever there is any detection of an information security infraction, regardless of its location.

Monitor compliance with information assurance policies by independent means.

Provide the board of directors, and specifically the audit committee of the board, with certification that information security exposures do not exceed specified expectations.

EPIGRAPHS

BIBLIOGRAPHY

Anthes, G.H., "Feds Garner Failing Grades for Year 2000," *Computerworld,*
    August 5, 1996. 248
————., "IRS Project Failures Cost Taxpayers $50B Annually,"
    Computerworld, October 14, 1996. 6
————., "Trade Groups Roll out Year 2000 Seal of Approval,"
    Computerworld, October 7, 1996. 203
————., "Year 2000 Problems Drag on," *Computerworld,* October 7,
    1996. 295
Baatz, E.B., "Digesting the ROI Paradox," CIO *Magazine,* October 1, 1996.
    23, 170
Baker, R., "The Corporate Politics of CMM Ratings," *Communications of the*
    ACM, September 1996. 141
Bank, D., "Sun Microsystems Brews Up a Logo," *The Wall Street Journal,* ,
    1996. 334
Barua, A., Kriebel, C., and Mukhopadhyay, T., "Information Technology
    and Business Value: An Analytic and Empirical Investigation,"
    University of Texas at Austin Working Paper (May 1991). 85
Battles, B.E., and Mark, D., "Companies That Just Don't Get IT," *The Wall*
    Street Journal, December 9, 1996. xv
Battles, B.E., Mark, D., and Ryan, C., "How Otherwise Good Managers
    Spend too Much on Information Technology," *The McKinsey Quartely,*
    1996, Number 3. 386
Baxley D.J., "The Cultural Formula for Success," *Enterprise Reengineering,*
    March 1996. 175
Bowen, W., "The Puny Payoff from Office Computers," *Fortune,* May 1986.
    24
Bozman, J.S., "Popular Himalaya Gives Tandem New Options,"
    Computerworld, September 12, 1994. 234
Bresnahan, J., "Mixed Messages," CIO *Magazine,* May 15, 1996. 374
Bruno, C., and Wexler, J., "Rats!," *Network World,* October 21, 1996. 298
Brynjolfsson, E., "Technology's True Payoff," *InformationWeek,* October 10,
    1994. 94
————., "Paradox Lost?" CIO *Magazine,* May 1, 1994. 98
————., "The Productivity Paradox of Information Technology,"
    Communications of the ACM, 35 (December): 66-77, (1993). 25

Brynjolfsson, E., and Hitt, L., "New Evidence on the Return of Information Systems," Revised MIT, Sloan School of Management, CCS WP #162, January 1994.   102

————., "Paradox Lost? Firm-level Evidence on the Returns to Information Systems Spending," MIT, Center for Coordination Science, October 1993.   99

————., "The Productive Keep Producing," *InformationWeek,* September 18, 1995.   170

————., "Creating Value and Destroying Profits? Three Measures of Information Technology's Contributions," *Proceedings of the Fifteenth International Conference on Information Systems,* 1994.   105

————., "Information Technology as a Factor of Production: The Role of Differences Among Firms," Working Paper #3715, Alfred P. Sloan School of Management, MIT, August 1994.   99

Bulkeley, W.M., "Data Trap: How Using Your PC Can Be a Waste of Time, Money," *The Wall Street Journal,* January 4, 1993.   122

————., "When Things go Wrong," *The Wall Street Journal,* November 18, 1996.   310

Caldwell, B. "The Five Percent Solution," *InformationWeek,* August 8, 1994.   228

————., "Client-Server Report," *InformationWeek,* January 3, 1994.   270

————., "Client-Server, Can It be Saved?" *InformationWeek,* April 8, 1996.   226

————., "Exodus of IS Execs from Xerox Continues," *InformationWeek,* November 4, 1996.   212

————., "GE Businesses Offer IT Services," *InformationWeek,* November 11, 1996.   126

————., "Perot's Pact," *InformationWeek,* October 28, 1996.   198

Caldwell, B., and McGee, M.K., "Kmart's IS In Turmoil," *InformationWeek,* March 13, 1995.   170

Christinat, D., "All about EVA," *CFO Magazine,* November 1996.   42

Computer Sciences Corporation, "Critical Issues of Information Systems Management," CSC, 1996.   377

"Computers Capture Capital Spending," *Business Week,* June 3, 1996.   73

"Computers Put the Zip in the GDP," *Business Week,* November 4, 1996.   78

Constance, P., "JCALS: The Teflon Initiative," Government Computer News, August 12, 1996.   325

Dec, K., "Client/Server Payoff," CIO Magazine, April 15, 1996.   33, 326

————, "Client/Server: Fiscal Benefits" "and Justification," Gartner Group Symposium/ITxpo '96, Lake Buena Vista, Florida, October 1996. 226

DePompa, B., "Rising from the Ashes," InformationWeek, May 27, 1996. 234

Digital Equipment Corporation, "Measuring Management Productivity," The Consultant, Merrimack, N.H., No.1, 1986.   30

Director of Defense Information, "Functional Economic Analysis Guidebook," Department of Defense, July 1991.   384

Disclosure Incorporated, Corporate Information on the World's Leading Companies, November 1996.   25

Encyclopedia of Computer Science and Engineering, 2nd edition, Van Nostrand Reinhold Company, 1983.   32

Fischer, L., "New Standard for Drug Makers," The New York Times, January 18, 1993.   244

Forbes, S., "Fact and Comment," Forbes, November 4, 1996.   129

Fox, R., "Web Approval," Communications of the ACM, October 1996.   204

Fryer, B., "Allied Signal Technical Services," Computerworld Client/Server Journal, August, 1996.   345

Gack, G., "A Cautionary Tale," Computerworld, September 12, 1994.   192

Garber, J.R., "The $20 Billion Upgrade," Forbes, September 26, 1994.   227

Gartner Group, "Asking the Right Questions about IT Spending," The Gartner Group Monthly Research Review, July 10, 1996 and Report TV-190-112 (6/27/96).   54

Gerber, C., "Client/Server Price Tag: 40% of IS Dollars," Computerworld, November 6, 1995.   227

Gilllin, P., "Standards Sham," Computerworld, December 2, 1996.   357

Goldman-Rohm, W., "Perot's Second Coming," Upside, June 1996.   195

Goren, S., Siong, N., Yin, W., "IT Payoff in Singapore," Proceedings of the 27th International Conference, IEEE, 1994.   115

Greising, D., "Quality, How to Make it Pay," Business Week, August 8, 1994. 140

Harp, C., "Winging It," Computerworld, October 21, 1996.   124

Hasek, K., The Good Soldier Svejk, Penguin Books, 1953.   138

405

Hawley Committee Report, "Information as an Asset – The Board Agenda," KPMG IMPACT Programme, London, 1995.   336

Hildebrand, C., "The Odd Couple," *CIO Magazine,* May 15, 1996.   197

Hill, C.G., "The Battle for Control," *The Wall Street Journal,* November 18, 1996.   25

Hopkins, T.D., "Profiles of Regulatory Costs," Report to the US Small Business Administration, November 1995.   129

Huntington, S.P., "The West Unique, Not Universal," *Foreign Affairs,* November 1996.   237

InforCorp Consulting, "Comparative Study of E-Mail Administrative Costs," Wextborogh, MA, 01581.   272

International Data Corporation, "The Global Outsourcing Market," 1996.   182

Jacobs, A., and DiDio, L., "Microsoft Plans Tools to Cut Cost of PC Ownership," *Computerworld,* November 11, 1996.   352

Johnston, S.J., "Chevron Takes Control," *InformationWeek,* November 4, 1996.   352

Jones, C., "Justifying Computer Integrated Manufacturing," *Gartner Group Research Notes,* December 1995.   165

Kaplan, R.S., and Norton, D.P., *The Balanced Scorecard,* Harvard Business School Press, 1996.   137

Karon, P., "Confronting ISO 9000," *Infoworld,* July 29, 1996.   147

Keen, P.G.W., "Putting the Payoff before Process," *Computerworld,* November 18, 1996.   141

Keltner, B., and Finegold, D., "Human Resource Innovations for Service Firms," *Sloan Management Review,* Fall 1996.   345

Kiely, T., "Computer Legacy Systems," *Harvard Business Review,* July-August, 1996.   302

Kivijarvi, H., and Saarinen, T., "Investment in Information Systems and the Financial Performance of the Firm," *Information & Management,* 28 (1985).   34

Koretz, G., "How to Raise US Productivity," *Business Week,* December 9, 1996.   89

————., "The Revolution in US Productivity May be Overstated," *Business Week,* August 29, 1994.   74

Krohe, J. Jr., "The Productivity Pit," *Across the Board,* October 1993.   33

Lacity, M.C., Wilcocks, L.P., and Feeny, D.F., "The Value of Selective IT Sourcing," *Sloan Management Review,* Spring 1996.   269

————., "IT Outsourcing: Maximize Flexibility and Control," Harvard Business Review, May-June 1995.   189

Landauer, T. K., *The Trouble with Computers*, The MIT Press, 1995.   25

LaPlante, A., "Rethinking the Numbers," *Computerworld*, June 24, 1996.   151

Loveman, G.W., "An Assessment of the Productivity Impact of Information Technologies," in *Information Technology and Corporation of the 1990s: Research Studies*, Allen, T.J. and Scott Morton, M.S., (ed.), MIT Press, Cambridge, MA, 1994.   84

Lucretius, *On the Nature of Things.*   135

Maddox, K., "Masters of the Web," *InformationWeek*, April 29, 1996.   378

Magnet, M., The "Productivity Payoff Arrives," *Fortune*, June 27, 1994.   97

Maibach, M.C., "Government Must Get Up to Speed," *Upside*, October 1996.   76

Manes, S., "A Bogus but Useful Measure," *InformationWeek*, January 15, 1996.   33

Martin, M.H., "When Info Worlds Collide," *Fortune*, October 28, 1996.   225

Matthews, J.T., "Power Shift," *Foreign Affairs*, January 1977.   364

McAteer, J.F., "Measuring the Return on Information Technology," SRI International Business Intelligence Program, Report D95-1964, November/December 1995.   40

McCorkindale, D., "Is Everybody Happy"? CFO *Magazine*, September 1996.   304

McInerney, T.G., and Weiss, S.A., "Re-engineering the Pentagon," *The Washington Times*, December 24, 1996.   18

Microsoft Corporation, *AnswerPoint Service Price List*, September 1996.   125

"Microsoft Outsources PC Support," *Computerworld*, November 13, 1995.   185

Millet, I., "Who's on First," CIO *Magazine*, February 15, 1994.   161

Moad, J., "Calculating the Real Benefit of Training," *Datamation*, April 15, 1995.   308

————., "Time for a Fresh Approach to ROI," *Datamation*, February 15, 1995.   159

————., "Calculating the Real Benefit of Training," *Datamation*, April 15, 1995.   345

Morgan Stanley, US *Investment Research Newsletter*, July 15, 1994.   73

————., "US Investment Research Newsletter," May 17, 1996. 92

Nash, K.S., "Figuring Dollars, Sense of Intranets," *Computerworld*, May 27, 1996. 230

Nash, K.S., and Picarille, L., "Vendors Deliver IS-Specific Apps Over the Net," *Computerworld*, May 6, 1996. 274

National Computer Board, "IT 2000, A Vision of an Intelligent Island," National Information Infrastructure Division, Singapore, 1993. 29

National Research Council, *Ada and Beyond: Software Policies for the Department of Defense*, 1996. 148

————., *Information Technology in the Service Society*, National Academy Press, Washington, DC, 1994. 96

Nee, E., "One on One with Les Alberthal," *Upside*, October, 1996. 192

Needle, D., "Corporate PC Buying Slows," *InformationWeek*, April 8, 1996. 225

Nolan, R.L., "Managing the Computer Resource: A Stage Hypothesis," *Communications of the ACM*, 16, No. 7 (July 1973). 46

Palvia, P., Means, D.B., Jackson, W.M., "Determinants of Computing in Very Small Businesses," Information & Management, 27 (1994). 34

Parker, M.M., Benson, R.J. with Trainor, H.E., *Information Economics: Linking Business Performance to Information Technology*, Prentice Hall, 1988. 153

Parker, M.M., Trainor, H.E. and Benson, R.J., *Information Strategy and Economics*, Prentice Hall, 1989. 153

Pastore, R., "The Art of the Deal," *CIO Magazine*, May 15, 1996. 193

Perelman, L.J., "Opportunity cost," *Wired*, November, 1996. 314

Pucciarelli, J., "Desktop and Distributed Equipment Procurement," *Gartner Group Symposium/ITxpo '96*, Lake Buena Vista, Florida, October 7, 1996. 338

Quinn, J.B., *Intelligent Enterprise*, The Free Press, 1992. 198

Reichheld, F.F., "Learning from Customer Defections," *Harvard Business Review*, March-April 1996. 175

Rifkin, G., "DuPont Acts to Farm Out Its Computing," *The New York Times*, December 12, 1996. 187

Roach, S.S., "The Economics of Competitive Advantage," Morgan Stanley International Investment Research, November 14, 1996. 26

Robinson, B., "GAO Study May Set Benchmark for IT Management," *Federal Computer Week*, March 21, 1994. 142

Santosus, M., "A Seasoned Performer," *CIO Magazine*, January 15, 1995. 170

—————., "Birds on a Wire – The *CIO* Enterprise Value Awards," *CIO Magazine*, February 1, 1996.   171

Savoia, R., "Custom Tailoring," *CIO Magazine*, June 15, 1996.   3

SBT Accounting Systems, "The PC Futz Factor," October 1992.   123

Scheier, R.L., "GM's First IT Chief Seeks 300 CIOs," *Computerworld*, December 23, 1996.   193, 206

Schumpeter, J.A., "Capitalism, Socialism and Democracy," *Harper*, 1963. 202

Semich, J.W., "Here's How to Quantify IT Investment Benefits," *Datamation*, January 7, 1994.   153

Simpson, D., "Cut Your Storage Management Costs," *Datamation*, November 1996.   354

Slater, D., "Rocket Science," *CIO Magazine*, September 1, 1996.   45

Sloan School of Management, "Management in the 1990s," Massachusetts Institute of Technology.   24

Standish Group, "Chaos," *Charting The Seas of Information Technology*, 1994.   7

Stern Stewart Management Services, *The Stern Stewart Performance 1000 Database*, New York, NY, 1994.   98

Stewart, B., "Enterprise Performance Through IT: Linking Financial Management to Contribution," *Gartner Group, Symposium/ITxpo '96*, Lake Buena Vista, Florida.   25

—————., "The Second Age of IT: Increasing the Return on Technology," *InSide Gartner Group*, October 1995.   39, 265

Stewart, G.B. III, "EVA Works, But Not If You Make These Common Mistakes," *Fortune*, May 1, 1995.   42

—————., "The Quest for Value," *Harper Business*, 1991.   42

Stewart, T.A., "A Refreshing Change: Vision Statements That Make Sense," *Fortune*, September 30, 1996.   241

—————., "The Invisible Key to Success," *Fortune*, August 5, 1996.   121

Strassmann, P.A., *Information Payoff – The Transformation of Work in the Electronic Age*, The Free Press, 1985.   84

—————., "Spending Without Results?" *Computerworld*, April 15, 1996. 93

—————., *The Business Value of Computers*, The Information Economics Press, 1990.   30, 154

————., "The Dangers of CIO Turnover," *Computerworld*, June 10, 1996. 304

————., *The Politics of Information Management*, The Information Economics Press, 1993.   274

Sullivan, B., "Letters to the Editor," *Harvard Business Review*, July-August 1995.   190

Terborgh, G.W., *Dynamic Equipment Policy*, McGraw Hill, 1949.   24

"The Growth of Computing Power," *Fortune*, December 13, 1993.   26, 28

"The Hitchhiker's Guide to Cybernomics," *The Economist*, September 28, 1996.   83

Tingey, M.O., *Comparing ISO 9000, Malcolm Baldrige and SEI CMM for Software*, Prentice Hall, 1997.   141

Trott, B., "NT 5.0 to Ease Management," *Infoworld*, November 11, 1996. 287

US Bureau of the Census, *Statistical Abstract of the United States*, 1995.   27

US Department of Commerce News, "Quality Management Proves to be a Sound Investment," National Institute of Standards and Technology, NIST 95-05, February 3, 1995.   140

US Government General Accounting Office, *Report on the CALS Project*, September 30, 1994.   325

Ubois, J., "Tending Computer Assets," CFO *Magazine*, June 1996.   324

Upton, D.M., and McAfee, A., "The Real Virtual Factory," *Harvard Business Review*, July-August, 1996.   233

Violino, B., "The Billion $ Club," *InformationWeek*, November 25, 1996. 35

Weston, R., "HR to IS: Resistance is Futile," *Computerworld*, December 9, 1996.   224

Wind, J., "Creating a 21st Century Enterprise," 2nd International Workshop on Economics and Management, Santiago, Chile, October, 1996. 141

Winter, S.J., Chudoba, K.M., and Gutek, B.A., "Misplaced Resources? Factors Associated with Computer Literacy Among End-Users," Proceedings of the International Conference on Information Systems, 1992.   121

Woolhandler, S., Himmelstein, D.U., and Lewontin, J.P., "Administrative Costs in US Hospitals," *The New England Journal of Medicine*, August 5, 1993.   61

Yosri, A., "The Relationship between Information Technology Expenditures and Revenue Contributing Factors in Large Corporations," Ph.D. Dissertation, Walden University, 1992.   36

Zarrow, C., "People Power," *cio Magazine*, May 1, 1996.   172

Zuckerman, L., "Do Computers Lift Productivity?," *The New York Times*, January 2, 1997.   27

INDEX

Billing for services 267
binary refuse 255
biological organisms 152, 281
BizCase™ 8, 332, 385
Blue Shield of California 192
Board of Directors 368, 373, 379
bondage 288
Bowen, William 24
Brazil 100, 273
breakeven point 249
Brown, Robert R., 310
browser 231, 333
Brynjolfsson, Eric *xix,* 25, 94, 97, 98,
    99, 100, 101, 102, 103, 104, 105, 106,
    186
budget models 383
build, junk, and replace 297
build-and-junk view 279, 281, 282
build-and-tear down 77
Bureau of Labor Statistics 65
bureaucracies 77, 89, 125, 171, 208,
    217, 218, 232, 261
bureaucratic possession 241
Burroughs 224, 314
business functions 71, 261
business performance 19, 41, 85, 105,
    106, 190, 256
business process 294
business process redesign 296, 322
business processes 5, 45, 52, 57, 58,
    78, 154, 208, 220, 241, 250, 254, 262,
    287, 303, 311, 322, 328, 333
buzzwords 109, 287, 374

C compiler 148
Cadillac 136, 140
caffeine 358
calendar dates 295
CALS 324, 325
capital investments 55, 78, 85, 104,
    162, 298

capital leasing 100
capture of configuration information
    287
Carlson, David M., 170
Carlson, Walter, xix
Carnegie-Mellon University 85
cash flow 3, 5, 75, 99, 150, 156, 251,
    260, 286, 289, 328, 330, 331, 332
cash inflows 157, 259
cash management 210, 260
casual learning 121
CB-90 154, 155
central computing 293
centralization 37, 116, 259, 262, 274,
    292, 312, 313
certification of financial accounts
    203
chain reaction 222
chaos 225, 308, 312, 313, 323
charitable organizations 61
Chase-Manhattan 38
checklists 137, 143, 144
Chevron Corporation 352
Chief Computer Officer 378
Chief Financial Officer 52, 115, 304,
    377, 381
Chief Information Executive 40
Chief Information Officer 225, 376,
    377, 378
Chrysler 100
CIO 30, 45, 54, 55, 103, 108, 115, 120,
    129, 131, 137, 151, 154, 155, 164, 165,
    168, 170, 171, 193, 207, 208, 209, 210,
    211, 225, 242, 244, 255, 256, 260, 288,
    295, 297, 298, 301, 303, 304, 309, 314,
    349, 374, 377, 378
CIO Enterprise Value 168
Citibank 198
Citicorp 38
civilization 76, 217, 232, 289
Clausewitz 151

maintenance costs 78, 245, 249, 251, 331

maintenance expenses 132, 260, 329, 342

Malaysia 68, 100

managers and clerks 62

mandatory strategic solution 302

marketing intelligence 367

mathematical modeling 159

maturity of firms 41

McDonnell Douglas Helicopter Systems 171

McLauglin, John F., 298

measures of performance 8, 37, 89

medical records 333

Medicare health insurance 61

megabyte transmissions 283

megaprojects 208

messaging codes 288

metering of the information 383

Mexico 100

microcode 291

microcomputers 75, 117, 226, 228, 232, 268, 274, 306, 312, 313, 326

microprocessor architectures 282

microprocessor life 76

microprocessors 27, 78, 290, 291, 336, 338

Microsoft 33, 76, 125, 126, 185, 224, 272, 283, 287, 354, 358

Microsoft Office Suite 125

mind-share 149

minicomputers 268, 306, 312, 313

Minnesota Mining & Manufacturing Co., 122

MIPS 75, 274

misalignment 11

misuses of technologies 210

MIT 25, 31, 83, 84, 86, 97, 103, 104, 106

modernization 294, 296

modernization investments 299

modular templates 252

monitoring compliance 373, 379

monopolies 72, 77, 221, 274

monopolistic pricing 272

monopoly 198, 235, 286, 287

monopoly guilds 235

monthly invoice 301, 305

Moore's Law 76

Morgan Stanley 24, 88, 91

Morgan, J.P. 209

Morgan-Stanley 27

Mortimer, Charles 162

Mosaic 333

Motorola 56, 140

MPIT 84

MPIT Project 41

must do 93

Mutual Benefit Life 141

myopic decisions 284

National Cash Register 224

National Computer Security Association, 203

National Defense University xviii, 39

national income 218

national interests 217, 235

National Performance Review 52, 128

National Research Council 95

national security 237, 273

National Software Testing Laboratories, 203

NationsBank Services 37

negligence and incompetence 143

Net Present Worth 150

Netscape 333, 343

network access privileges 369

Network Computers 118

network computing 344

network integration 233

network management 99, 231, 269, 324

This book was edited by Allan Alter, Peter Dolan,
B. Diane Martin, and Edgar H. Sibley.
The graphics were created by Paul A. Strassmann.

It was designed and set into type by David G. Shaw
at Belm Design in Somerville, Massachusetts,
and printed and bound by Braun-Brumfield in Ann Arbor, Michigan.

The cover was designed by David G. Shaw.

The text face is Minion, designed by Robert Slimbach,
issued in digital form by Adobe Systems,
Mountain View, California, in 1989.

The paper is Glatfelter natural smooth acid-free.

All text, graphics, and page design were created on Apple Power
Macintosh computers, using Quark XPress, Adobe Photoshop,
DeltaGraph Professional, and Microsoft Word software.